Imperial Isr[...]
Palestinians
The Politics of E[...]

Nur Masalha

Pluto Press

LONDON • STERLING, VIRGINIA

First published 2000 by Pluto Press
345 Archway Road, London N6 5AA
and 22883 Quicksilver Drive,
Sterling, VA 20166–2012, USA

www.plutobooks.com

British Library Cataloguing in Publication Data
A catalogue record for this book is available from
the British Library

ISBN 0 7453 1620 4 hbk
ISBN 0 7453 1615 8 pbk

Library of Congress Cataloging in Publication Data
Masalha, Nur, 1957–
    Imperial Israel and the Palestinians : the politics of expansion,
1967–2000 / Nur Masalha.
        p. cm.
    Includes bibliographical references (p.).
    ISBN 0–7453–1620–4 (hbk.)
        1. Arab–Israeli conflict—1973–1993. 2. Arab–Israeli conflict—1993–
3. Zionism—Israel. 4. Israel—Politics and government. 5. Israel–Arab War,
1967—Occupied territories. 6. Israel—Boundaries. I. Title.

DS119.7 .M31395 2000
956.04–dc21
                                                                00–027698

10   9   8   7   6   5   4   3   2

Designed and produced for Pluto Press by Chase Publishing Services
Typeset from disk by Stanford DTP Services, Towcester
Printed in the European Union by
Antony Rowe, Chippenham and Eastbourne, England

Imperial Israel and the Palestinians

Contents

Acknowledgements

The support of the Palestine Studies Trust, UK, and the Institute for Palestine Studies (IPS), Washington, DC, is gratefully acknowledged. At IPS, I am particularly grateful to Walid Khalidi, Philip Mattar and Mahmud Swaid, all of whom encouraged me to undertake the project of Zionism and the Palestinians. Among the institutions that made this work possible by helping with source material were the Israel State Archives, the Central Zionist Archives in Jerusalem, the Jabotinsky Institute in Tel Aviv, the Hebrew University of Jerusalem Library and the School of Oriental and African Studies Library in London. Many friends and colleagues have helped me greatly with logistics, ideas, criticism, material and discussions. Among them I would like to thank Elias 'Edey, Edward Said, Sa'id Khouri, Ahmad Khalidi, Ahmad Khalifa, Roger van Zwanenberg, Zein Mayasi, David McDowall, Hasib Sabbagh, Peter Colvin, 'Abbas Shiblak, Israel Shahak, Ghada Karmi, Tim Niblock, Uri Davis, Leila Mantura, Michael Adams, Michael Prior, Sharif Kana'ane, Anis al-Kassim, As'ad Ghanem, Ilan Pappe, Naseer Aruri, Farouq Mardam-Bey and the late Saliba Khamis. Needless to say that I alone am responsible for the book and its shortcomings, as well as translations from Hebrew. Finally, I owe an invaluable debt to my wife, Stephanie, for her insightful comments while this work was being written.

Introduction

Land and territory have always been at the heart of the struggle between the Zionist immigrants/settlers and the native Palestinians. To a large extent, the political history of Zionism and the Israeli state has been a description of an ongoing debate over territorial aspirations and concepts of frontiers. The territorial/boundaries issue has also been the most concrete expression of Israeli expansionism. Since its establishment, Israel has been defining and redefining its territorial ambitions. What are the final boundaries of the Israeli state? In May 1999, Israel's pragmatic expansionists, led by Ehud Barak, returned to power in Israel, with a pledge to maintain, further consolidate and ultimately annex to Israel the Jewish settlements on the West Bank together with large parts of the occupied territories. Barak's commitments to a united Jerusalem under exclusive Israeli sovereignty and the expansion of Jewish settlements in 'Greater Jerusalem' were affirmed in his election victory speech in Rabin Square, Tel Aviv.[1] Israel's physical border, he stated during the 1999 election campaign, will always be the Jordan River. It was the Labour government which had taken the lead after 1967 with the creation of a string of military kibbutzim and civilian settlements along the Jordan River.

However, although territorially expansionist ambitions are deeply rooted in mainstream Labour Zionism, the primary focus of this book is on Israel's territorial maximalists and their concepts of state frontiers. The work mainly deals with the supporters of Greater Israel who believe that mandatory Palestine (in Zionist terminology: 'the western Land of Israel'), or the area between the Mediterranean and the Jordan River, is the irreducible minimum for fulfilling the purpose of Zionism. These include Labour Zionism's 'activists', Zionist Revisionists and other supporters of Greater Israel (both secular and religious fundamentalists). Concentrating on the period from June 1967 to the present, the book covers a whole range of territorially maximalist parties and right-wing groupings, while comparing them with both pragmatic and radical expansionists of Labour Zionism. The focus on Israel's territorial maximalists should not underestimate the current threat posed by Israel's pragmatic

1

expansionists to the Palestinians. However, it does make perfect sense to explore the theme of territorial expansionism, especially in connection with the rise of Neo-Zionism and the supporters of the 'whole Land of Israel' in the post-1967 period and the implications of their demand for the whole Middle East for maximum territorial expansion. It is the fundamental premise of this work that 'Greater Israel' is both a territorial concept and an ideology aimed at achieving maximum territorial expansionism and imperial domination in the region.

Land 'redemption', settler colonisation and statehood have been the permanent themes of modern Zionism. Jewish nation-building, ever-expanding settlement, territorial ambitions and the effective use of myths/legends/epics of the Bible went hand in hand. The Zionists claim that events described in the Old Testament establish the right of twentieth-century Jews to establish an ethnic Jewish state in Palestine. For the Zionists, although the term Eretz-Yisrael (the Hebrew for the 'Land of Israel') was always vague as far as the exact boundaries of the territory were concerned, it clearly defined 'ownership'. The narratives of Genesis and Exodus present the origins of the traditions that connect the Hebrew and Israelite tribes with the land of Canaan (modern Palestine); however, the enormous efforts of several generations of scholars have not been able to uncover any historical or archaeological evidence for the existence of the events and personages referred to in these texts. There is no concurrence between biblical stories and demonstrable historical facts before about the eighth century BC.[2] The archaeological findings blatantly contradict the biblical picture. Zeev Hertzog, professor of archaeology and ancient studies at Tel Aviv University, has reported recently that, following decades of intensive excavations in Palestine/Israel, archaeologists have found that the patriarch's acts are legendary; that the Israelites did not sojourn in Egypt or wander in the desert; they did not conquer the land of Canaan in a military campaign, and did not pass it on to the twelve tribes. Neither is there any evidence of the empire of David and Solomon. The united monarchy under David and Solomon, which the Bible describes as a regional power, was at most a small tribal kingdom (*Haaretz*, 29 October 1999).

However, contrary to the actual evidence, the view that the Old Testament Scriptures provide for the Jews' title-deed to expand throughout the 'Land of Israel', for the alleged moral legitimacy of the establishment of the state of Israel and for its policies towards the native Palestinians since 1948, is still pervasive not only in Jewish Zionist circles but even within mainstream Christian theology and university biblical studies.[3] The link between Israeli territorial conquests and the Old Testament is also reflected in the propagandistic claim of David Ben-Gurion, Israel's first and secular prime minister: that the Bible is the 'Jews' sacrosanct title-deed to Palestine ... with a genealogy of 3,500 years'.[4] In fact, the term Eretz-Yisrael is used only once in the Old Testament Scriptures (1 Samuel 13:19); there is no exact historical or even religious map of the scope and boundaries of the 'Land of Israel', and no precise Jewish religious definition of the borders. However, as we shall see below, in modern times the 'Land of Israel' and other related biblical terminology have been invested with far-reaching historical, geo-political and ideological connotations in both Israeli rhetoric and Western scholarship.[5] The reconstruction of the past by Zionist authors has often reflected their own political and religious ideologies. Both Zionist authors and biblical scholars have based the historical claims of modern Zionism to Eretz-Yisrael on the biblical (mythical) narrative of the twelve tribes that conquered and lived on the land during the Israelites' premonarchical era; other Zionist claims have been based on the Davidic or Solomonic kingdoms, the subsequent southern and northern kingdoms of Judea and Israel, the early Second Temple period, the Hasmonean era, or the Kingdom of Herod.[6] Following in the footsteps of nineteenth- and twentieth-century biblical scholarship, Israeli scholarship has employed an array of terms for the region of Palestine and its surroundings: 'Eretz-Yisrael', 'the biblical Land of Israel', 'Greater Israel', 'the whole Land of Israel', 'Judea and Samaria are as the heart of the Israelite nation', 'the land in which the Israelite tribes had their settlements', 'the promised land', 'the land of the Bible', 'the Holy Land'.

To the casual reader of many standard works on historical geography or studies of the history of the region, these terms may appear interchangeable or even neutral. But these concepts and imaginary maps are also about power relations. Benedict Anderson, in *Imagined Communities*, has shown how the seemingly neutral map played a crucial role in conceptualization and control of European colonial territories.[7] More recently, in his seminal work, *The Invention of Ancient Israel: The Silencing of Palestinian History* (1996), Keith Whitelam has examined the political implications of the terminology of biblical scholarship chosen to represent this area and has shown how the naming of the land implied control and possession of the land; how the terms Eretz-Yisrael, 'the land of Israel' and Palestine have been invested with, or divested of, meaning in both Western and Israeli scholarship. Despite the fact that Western biblical scholarship has continually employed the term 'Palestine', Whitelam argues, the term has been divested of any real meaning in the face of the search for the ancient 'Land of Israel'. Palestine has no intrinsic meaning of its own, no history of its own, but instead provides a background for the history of Israel. Commensurate with the lack of history is also the absence of the inhabitants of the land. The history of Palestine and its inhabitants in general is subsumed and silenced by the concern with, and in the search for, ancient Israel.[8]

Many biblical scholars in Israel and the West assume (erroneously) that biblical narratives which purport to describe the past are in fact accurate records and that both the ancient and modern history of Israel have been conditioned by the geographical setting of the 'Land of Israel' to such an extent that knowledge of the geography of the region is one of the preconditions for a proper understanding of its history. When discussing the history of Israel, many biblical scholars and Israeli publicists begin with a section entitled the 'Land of Israel'. The land, until the arrival of European Jewish settlers, is virtually barren, desolate and empty, waiting to be made fertile and populated by Israel; it is the rightful property of Jews (a divinely 'chosen people'), and their superiority is defined in military power. In October 1991, Prime Minister Yitzhak Shamir, in his address to the Madrid Peace Conference, resorted to quoting from *Innocents Abroad* by Mark Twain. (Twain visited Palestine in 1867 and his description of its natives was either marked by invective or was humorously pejorative.) The aim of Shamir (who regarded the Madrid Conference as purely ceremonial and treated it as a propaganda platform) was to prove that Palestine was an empty territory, a kind of civilisational barrenness that (in Shamir's words) 'no one wanted': 'A desolate country which sits in sackcloth and ashes – a silent, mournful expanse which not even imagination can grace with the pomp of life'.[9] The same myth of a 'ruined'/'desolate'/'empty' country was used by Shamir and his successor, Likud Prime Minister Binyamin Netanyahu, to justify Zionist colonisation of Palestine and indifference to the fate of its native inhabitants.[10] Moreover, this (mythical) continuum between the ancient and the modern means that this is a difficult land, resisting agriculture, which can only be 'redeemed' and made to yield up its produce by the extraordinary effort of Jewish immigrants, Zionist pioneers and Israel's genius. It mattered little that in reality most of Palestine, other than the Negev, was no desert but an intensely and successfully cultivated fertile land. The Zionist propaganda – that only under Jewish cultivation did Palestine become a productive country with the help of Jewish labour and capital, that only Israel can make the land (and desert) bloom, that most Palestinians arrived in the area only within the past century – have long been part of the Zionist justification for Jewish immigration to Palestine, the founding of the state of Israel, its territorial expansion and the dispossession of the Palestinians.[11]

With regard to the territorial scope of the 'whole Land of Israel', the entire spectrum of Zionist opinion believed, and still believes, that Eretz-Yisrael extends to the east of the River Jordan; in Zionist terminology, Eretz-Yisrael is basically separated by the Jordan River into two major parts: 'the western Land of Israel' (Eretz-Yisrael Hama'ravit), which includes Israel proper and the 1967 occupied territories, and 'the eastern Land of Israel' (Eretz-Yisrael Hamizrahit), situated mainly in the modern state of Jordan. The founder of political Zionism, Theodor Herzl – an intensely secular and assimilated Jew – was in fact less concerned with the location of the Jewish state and the scope of its boundaries than with the fact that sovereign control over territory would provide Jews with guarantees against discrimination. However, the Zionist movement subsequently laid claim to Palestine and Transjordan at the Paris Peace Conference – which opened in January 1919 to dispose of the territories captured from the defeated Germany, Austria-Hungary and Ottoman Empire during the First World War – and at Zionist Congresses in the 1920s. Although certain sections of the Zionist movement (particularly right-wing Revisionists) insisted that the modern Jewish state should be established in 'the whole of Eretz-Yisrael', the majority came to terms with the parameters of the Palestine Mandate and focused its territorial aspirations on these boundaries. Yet, while the majority believed that the state of Israel could realistically be established only in part of Eretz-Yisrael, it remained committed to the ultimate vision of 'the whole Land of Israel'. Furthermore, the concept of Jewish 'historic rights in the whole land of Israel' was never only confined to the territorial maximalists of Zionist Revisionism or Israel's radical right. At the Paris Peace Conference, Chaim Weizmann, then leading the Zionist Commission that was to put forward Zionist political and territorial claims, called for the imposition of a British Mandate over an enlarged Palestine extending north to the Litani River in what is now Lebanon and east to the Hijaz railway line, which is well east of the Jordan River. It was at that conference, too, that Weizmann called for a Palestine 'as Jewish as England is English'.[12] For Weizmann, the projected Jewish state and the scope of its boundaries were indelibly tied to the British Empire and the British Mandate, which existed like some protective umbrella overhead.[13]

During the British Mandate, the Zionists insisted on Palestine also officially being referred to as 'the Land of Israel', but the most mandatory authorities were willing to concede was the use of the Hebrew acronym for Eretz-Yisrael after the name 'Palestine' on all official documents, the currency, stamps, etc.[14] Throughout the period of the Mandate, the Zionist pragmatic and gradualist state-builders, led by David Ben-Gurion, and his Mapai party (Mifleget Po'alei Eretz-Yisrael, or the Land of Israel Workers Party), dominated the Yishuv's politics; right-wing territorial maximalists of Zionist Revisionism (who sought Jewish sovereignty over all of mandatory Palestine and Transjordan and whose traditional slogan, still officially valid, was 'Both banks of the Jordan – this is ours and that one is also') won only a minority of Jewish votes. For Ben-Gurion, an eminent realist, the boundaries of the Jewish state should be flexible, never finally fixed, but dependent on the nature and need of the historical moment and regional and international conditions.[15] In 1937, Ben-Gurion, an archetypal pragmatic expansionist who had concentrated on many objectives at the same time, was willing to accept the British Royal (Peel) Commission partition proposal and the establishment of a Jewish state in part of the country, although throughout he remained strongly committed to a vision of Jewish sovereignty over all of Palestine as the ultimate goal of Zionism.[16]

The use of force to ensure state-building, the recovery of 'unredeemed national territories' and steady Jewish territorial expansion into the 'whole Land of Israel' had, too, a deep basis in the Ben-Gurion's thinking. For instance, at an important meeting of the Jewish Agency Executive in June 1938, which was held against the background of the British Peel Commission recommendation of partitioning Palestine, Ben-Gurion (then Chairman of the Jewish Agency which effectively was the government of the Yishuv) made clear his support for the establishment of the Jewish state in part of Palestine only as an intermediary stage. He was not 'satisfied with part of the country, but on the basis of the assumption that after we build up a strong force following the establishment of the state – we will abolish the partition of the country [between Jews and Arabs] and we will expand to the whole Land of Israel.' When asked by Moshe Shapira, a Jewish Agency executive member and director of the JA's Immigration Department, whether he considered that such expansion should be carried out by 'force', Ben-Gurion replied that the Arabs would come to terms with Zionism only when faced with a *fait accompli*:

> This is only a stage in the realization of Zionism and it should prepare the ground for our expansion throughout the whole country through Jewish-Arab agreement ... the state, however, must enforce order and security and it will do this not by moralizing and preaching 'sermons on the mount' but by machine-guns, which we will need.[17]

Ben-Gurion's objective of a Jewish state expanding into the whole of Palestine were also echoed in his memorandum to the Zionist Actions Committee meeting of 17 December 1938, a meeting held after Britain's formal abandonment of the Peel Commission's partition plan. There he argued that since the Arabs had already been given Iraq, Syria and Saudi Arabia, which he pronounced to be 'more than enough', the Zionists should demand all of Palestine.[18]

Ben-Gurion publicly excoriated right-wing Revisionist groupings and in 1948 he opposed their participation in the newly formed government. From 1935 to 1967, the Labour Party sought to maintain its political paramountcy within Zionism and the State of Israel by ostracising the Revisionist movement and its post-Second World War leader, Menahem Begin. In 1948, the military arm of Revisionism, the Irgun (National Military Organisation), was forcibly disbanded. When Begin organised the Herut Party and entered parliamentary politics, Ben-Gurion denounced him as a fascist and dangerous demagogue. But where the Palestinians were concerned, Ben-Gurion espoused some of the irredentist principles of Revisionist Zionism: the expansion of Israel's borders, the conquest of Arab areas, and the evacuation of the Palestinian population; since the Palestinians could never agree to a partition plan that would satisfy the Zionists, he argued, the borders of the Israeli state would have to be determined by military confrontation.[19]

In 1948, Israel – like many nineteenth and early twentieth-century European states – was born as an irredentist ethnic Jewish state committed to the recovery of the 'unredeemed' national territories.

During 1948–49, the borders of the newly established Jewish state were expanded by conquest from the 55.5 per cent of mandatory Palestine allotted to the Jews under the November 1947 UN Partition plan to 77 per cent. More evidence of its elitist expansionist instincts is found in Ben-Gurion's 1949 proposal to his Cabinet to conquer the West Bank, then under Jordanian control, assuming then that the Palestinian population would flee or be driven out.[20] Two decades later, in June 1967, the entire area of mandatory Palestine (including the West Bank and Gaza) came under Israeli control. Historians often argue that, as far as Israel was concerned, the 1967 war was of a pre-emptive character. The historiography of recent years, however, has shown that pre-emption was only one element in Israeli Third Round thinking – the Second Round being the 1956 war. Both Israeli Second and Third Round thinking also had a deep ideological strand anchored in the irredentist vision of Greater Israel; this vision was also based on the post-1948 conviction, widely held among the Israeli leadership, that the territorial character of the state was not final. In *Israel's Border Wars 1949–1956* (1993), Israeli historian Benny Morris argues that in the 1950s Zionist territorial maximalism and expansionism had been espoused for both ideological and strategic reasons:

> Zionist mainstream thought had always regarded a Jewish state from the Mediterranean to the Jordan River as its ultimate goal. The vision of 'Greater Israel' as Zionism's ultimate objective did not end with the 1948 war. The politicians of the Right, primarily from the Revisionist Herut Party, led by Menachem [sic] Begin, continued throughout 1949 and the early and mid-1950s to clamour publicly for conquest of the West Bank.
>
> More mutedly, politicians of the socialist Tnu'ah LeAhdud Ha'Avoda, who, like those in Herut, believed in Greater Israel (or the 'Whole Land of Israel') as the necessary fulfilment of the Zionist vision, also continued to speak of an 'opportunity' that might yet enable Israel to conquer the West Bank. Ahdut Ha'Avoda's leaders, including Israel Galili and Yisrael Ben-Yehuda, made no bones about their desire to see Israel expand eastwards to the River Jordan, through peaceful means or by war (they usually spoke of such conquest as resulting from an Arab-initiated war).
>
> These ideological expansionists were joined by those who espoused expansion for (mainly) strategic reasons. Officer in Command (OC) Southern Command Yigal Allon, an Ahdut

'Avoda [sic] general, in March 1949 (long after the effective termination of Israeli-Jordanian hostility...) formally proposed to Ben-Gurion the conquest of the West Bank.[21]

The 1950s presented Israel with a major new challenge. Following the 1948 *nakbah* (Palestinian catastrophe) and humiliating Arab military defeat in Palestine, old Arab regimes in the region started to disappear one by one, as the shock wave of radical decolonisation began changing the face of the Arab world. King 'Abdullah of Jordan was assassinated in East Jerusalem in 1950. Egypt, the most important Arab state, was experiencing a revolution, starting in 1952. Syria was radicalised and then Iraq in 1958. This changing Arab world presented Israel with new challenges which required new strategies. The new Arab world, following the lead of Nasser's Egypt, began divorcing itself from the traditional European colonial powers and began to form new alliances within the Third World as well as with the Soviet bloc. For Ben-Gurion, however, who could not imagine the Middle East without European colonialism, an alliance with one European power was 'more valuable than the views of all the people of Asia'.[22] A similar characteristic attitude of Israel's leaders in the 1950s was presented by Moshe Dayan, Ben-Gurion's favourite general, who was later to exert extraordinary influence in pushing Israel into the Suez War. Dayan apparently believed that 'in this part of the world Israel has a mission; it has to be a rock, an extension of the West, against which the waves of Nasser's Arab nationalism will be broken' (noted by Israeli journalist A. Schweitzer in *Haartez* in 1958).[23]

Israel's 'activist' political and military strategies in the 1950s were derived from the conviction that Israel could only realise its territorial and political objectives by means of the successful application of force in its relations with the Arab world.[24] Between the establishment of the state in 1948 and the Suez War of 1956 – which resulted in Israel's conquest of the Gaza Strip and the Sinai peninsula – within the Israeli politico-military establishment there was a great deal of preoccupation with the territorial issue; many leading figures believed that a chance to capture the West Bank, in particular, should not be missed. In the early 1950s, Dayan was open about his 'strategic inclination' for territorial expansion into the 'whole Land of Israel', mainly through war and conquest. As noted in the 'Meeting of the Ministers of Israel', 7–23 July 1950:

[He] does not give great weight to formal peace with the Arab states ... Dayan believes that the first battle in the process of the establishment of Israel as an independent state has not yet been completed because we have not yet determined whether the special character of today's state is final. The state must decide if our existing borders satisfy us and will remain as they are in the future ... During the [1948] war, a view prevailed that if we moved eastwards towards the Jordan [River] we would have to face the British. General Dayan is not sure that this view was well founded and he believes that our time is still open to changes.[25]

A year earlier, in 1949, Dayan talked more explicitly about Israel absorbing the West Bank: 'Boundaries-Frontiers of Israel should be on [the] Jordan [River] ... Present boundaries [are] ridiculous from all points of view.' He added that Israel was willing to absorb the West Bank 'with its Arab population, including refugees'; this 'expansion' would be 'by evolution and not ... fighting'. But in September 1952 Dayan told an American diplomat that the 'boundaries [with Jordan] will be changed by war', unless some form of political settlement, involving Israeli–Arab confederation, was reached.[26] According to Benny Morris, although the ruling Mapai Party never adopted an open platform advocating the conquest of the West Bank, Prime Minister Ben-Gurion in private occasionally proposed conquests of parts of the West Bank as 'an anti-infiltration measure'.[27]

Such attitudes were characteristic of Israel's leaders in the 1950s. In October 1956, Israel attacked Egypt in collusion with Britain and France, while Jordan remained outside the Suez War. Israel invaded the Gaza Strip and the Sinai Peninsula, holding both areas for four months before strong international, and especially American, pressure eventually compelled it to evacuate both areas. Originally, the Israelis had every intention of staying in what their government considered to be an integral part of the Land of Israel. Foreign Minister Golda Meir told a Mapai Party rally on 10 November 1956 that 'the Gaza Strip was an integral part of Israel'.[28] Menahem Begin, the leader of Herut (the second largest party in Israel) in an interview on 27 November, went even further, saying that 'he could not countenance withdrawal from the Gaza Strip under any terms because the area belonged to Israel by right'.[29] Israel went to war in 1956 against Nasser's Egypt for several reasons which are beyond the scope of this discussion. In his recent book *Israel in Search of a War*, Israeli scholar Motti Golani has shown how Israel was seeking a war long before the onset of the Suez Crisis and without any connection to it. Its motives for embarking on this military venture included the consolidation of its alliance (and nuclear cooperation) with France, territorial expansion, the overthrow of the Egyptian President Gamal 'Abdel Nasser and the destruction of his radical regime; and the establishment of a new political order in the Middle East.[30] In addition to its contribution to the efforts to try to stop the decolonisation of the Middle East, Israel's Sinai Campaign gave rise to a wave of yearnings for imperial status, for example, Ben-Gurion spoke of 'The Third Kingdom of Israel'.[31] He conceived the attack on Egypt as part of a wider plan for the political and territorial reorganisation of the whole region. Ben-Gurion had always seen the Jewish state as part of the West, not as part of the region: a Middle East without Western colonialism would be too dangerous for Israel; Israel should and could be turned into an American strategic asset in the region.[32]

On 22 October 1956, at a meeting at the secret Sevres Conference, held on the eve of the tripartite attack on Egypt, Ben-Gurion presented to the French Prime Minister Guy Mollet a far-reaching plan for creating a 'new order' in the Middle East. The plan included, apart from the occupation and annexation of the Gaza Strip and the Sinai Peninsula which gave Israel strategic depth, the overthrow of the Egyptian President Nasser, the dismantling of Lebanon and the annexation of southern Lebanon up to the Litani River to Israel and the creation of a Christian state in other parts of the country, and the partitioning of Jordan between Israel and monarchical Iraq: Israel would annex the West Bank and Iraq the East Bank, on condition that Iraq signed a peace accord with Israel and absorbed the Palestinian refugees in the camps on both banks of the Jordan River. According to Ben-Gurion's secret plan, the Suez Canal would be internationalised and Israel would control access to the Gulf of Aqaba. In his autobiography *Milestones*, Dayan, who attended the Sevres conference, wrote that, at Sevres, Ben-Gurion argued:

Jordan has no right to exist and should be divided: Transjordan – to be annexed to Iraq which would have to be committed to absorbing and settling the Arab refugees in it; the territories west of the Jordan [River] will be annexed to Israel, as an autonomous region. Lebanon will have to get rid of some of its Muslim regions to assure stability based on the Christian part. Britain will hold sway over Iraq (including Transjordan) and over the southern Arabian Peninsula. France – over Lebanon, perhaps even Syria, with close ties with Israel. The Suez Canal will have international status, and the [Red Sea] straits of Elat – under Israeli control.[33]

Ben-Gurion simply could not imagine a Middle East without Western colonialism. He believed that his Sevres plan suited the colonial interests of the French and British and would consolidate their crumbling positions in North Africa and the Middle East.[34]

Although Israel's decisive military victory of 1956 put the country on the map as a major military power, the main realistic lesson that Ben-Gurion drew from the Suez War, according to Avi Shlaim, was that 'Israel could not acquire strategic depth by expanding its territory at the expense of its neighbours because the Great Powers would not allow it to keep the spoils of war.'[35] Accordingly, Ben-Gurion scaled down his objectives of territorial expansion and emphasised a hegemonic political and military strategy of equipping the Israeli Army with the most advanced Western weapons – coupled with the secret development of nuclear weapons – and thus maintaining its qualitative superiority over the Arab armies. Other developments in Israel's policy towards the Arab world in the post-Suez period emphasised the 'alliance of the periphery' and alliances with non-Arab or non-Muslim minorities. When it became clear to Ben-Gurion that direct territorial expansion into 'the whole Land of Israel' without the support of the Great Powers was not possible under current conditions, Israel sought the forging of unofficial alliances with the non-Arab states of the outer ring of region, that is, Iran, Turkey and Ethiopia. These alliances were mainly designed to counter Nasser's brand of pan-Arab radicalism and to reduce Israel's isolation. The informal alliance with religious and ethnic minorities (particularly the Christian Maronites of Lebanon and the Kurds) was in part designed to keep the Arab East divided.[36]

Ben-Gurion had been an enthusiastic advocate of a Christian state in Lebanon in the early and mid-1950s, but he was strongly opposed on this by the more pragmatic Moshe Sharett. In his *Personal Diary*, Sharett recorded Israeli plans to destabilise and dismember Lebanon and to install a Maronite Christian puppet regime pliable to Israeli diktat. The entry of his diary of 27 February 1954 deals with the then recently retired Prime Minister Ben-Gurion, Defence Minister Pinhas Lavon, and Chief of Staff Moshe Dayan, all of whom wanted to take advantage of a *coup d'état* in Syria to order to dismember Lebanon. Ben-Gurion insisted that if Iraq invaded Syria, 'this is the hour to arouse Lebanon – that is to say its Maronites – to declare a Christian state'. Sharett demurred:

> I said this is an empty dream. The Maronites are split ... Ben-Gurion retorted furiously. He began putting forth historical justification for a reduced Christian Lebanon. If a fact is created [if a new power structure is to be created in Lebanon] the Christian powers will not dare to oppose it. I argued there is not a factor prepared to create such a fact and that if we begin to agitate and encourage we will get entangled in an adventure that will bring us only disgrace. Here there erupted a torrent of abuse regarding [my] lack of daring and shortsightedness. We should send emissaries and spend money. I said there is no money. The considered reply was that is nonsense, the money must be found, if not from the Treasury then from the [Jewish] Agency (!) – for such a goal it would be permissible to find 100,000 [IL – Israeli Lira] from the Tzvi fund, half a million, a million, anything to get the thing established, and then would come a crucial reshuffling in the Middle East system and a new era would begin.[37]

However, after 1957, following Israel's return to the 1949 armistice lines, those lines appeared to have been consolidated into semi-permanent borders (the 'Green Line') and the Zionist dream of 'Greater Israel' appeared to be receding into the background. None the less, in the post-Suez period, irredentist tendencies still existed within the ruling circles, tendencies which primarily focused on the idea of expanding into the West Bank. One deeply rooted tendency centred on the territorial maximalists of the Ahdut Ha'avodah ministers in Ben-Gurion's cabinet, who believed (in the late 1950s) that the Jordanian monarchy was doomed and they did not want Israel to miss a chance to conquer the West Bank.[38] In 1958, against the background of the rising tide of Nasserism and pan-Arab unity schemes, various contingency plans were prepared by the Israeli army to capture the entire West Bank or parts of it in the event of a pro-Nasserist coup against King Hussein in Amman. On the evening of 14 July 1958, Haim Laskov, the new army Chief of Staff, proposed the capture of Hebron, of the area around Jerusalem, and of the high ground all the way to Nablus. But Ben-Gurion, although he himself could not see that Jordan had any long-term future, was reluctant to endorse Laskov's proposals. One consideration was the strong opposition that Israeli expansion into the West Bank was likely to encounter from both the Western powers and the international community. Another consideration centred on the 'demographic problem': there were nearly one million Palestinians on the West Bank compared with only 1,750,000 Jews in Israel; 'This time the Arabs will not run away!', Ben-Gurion wrote in his diary entry of 14 July 1958.[39]

During the same period, other tendencies to expand into the Jordanian-controlled West Bank resulted in contingency operational objectives to rectify the 1949 armistice lines, such as those relating to the Latrun salient situated on the border of the West Bank, half-way between Jerusalem and Tel Aviv, which was of particular strategic importance for Israel. Latrun had also been the gateway to Jerusalem in 1948 and the Israeli Army had failed repeatedly to capture it. Apparently, for many years before 1967, the Israeli Army had contingency and operational plans for taking over the Latrun enclave and straightening the West Bank border with Israel. According to Israeli military historian Meir Pa'il, there had been a 'minimum plan' which included the occupation of the enclave and the destruction of its three large Arab villages ('Imwas, Yalu and Bayt Nuba), but without moving on beyond this part of the West Bank.[40] The June 1967 war created the opportunity to realise these plans. On order from the Commanding General of the Central Command, 'Uzi Narkiss, the Israeli Army bulldozers immediately moved in and wiped out the three Arab villages.[41]

Israeli historiography often divides Israeli wars into two categories: 'milhamot ein breira' ('wars of no choice': 1948, 1967, 1969–70 and 1973), and 'milhamot breira' ('wars of choice': 1956 and 1982). In fact, most of Israel's wars were 'wars of choice', motivated (in part) either by expansionist territorial ambitions or by the desire to maintain control of territories taken from the Arabs. In 1956, Egypt defended itself against the Israeli, French and British tripartite invasion. Israeli motives for embarking on this war included territorial expansion, the consolidation of an alliance with a Western power (France), the overthrow of the Egyptian President Nasser, and the establishment of a new political order in the Middle East. Egyptian–Syrian rivalry and attempts by each to outbid the other's radicalism, although neither had the intention of waging war, paved the way for the Israeli surprise attack of June 1967. The War of Attrition along the Suez Canal in 1969–70 was an attempt by Nasser to prevent Israel's occupation of Sinai from becoming a *fait accompli*. In 1971, the new Egyptian President Anwar Sadat offered to negotiate with Israel on the basis of the now-famous formula: 'Land for Peace', his *démarche* was dismissed by the then Labour government of Golda Meir. The October 1973 War was initiated by Egypt and Syria for the limited purpose of altering the context for diplomacy aimed at regaining the occupied territories of Sinai and the Golan Heights and possibly the West Bank and the Gaza Strip. In June 1982, the Israelis invaded Lebanon with the aim of destroying the PLO in order to facilitate the absorption of the West Bank and Gaza into Israel and to rearrange the Middle East map to suit their interests.

The June 1967 war produced a territorial earthquake in the Middle East, overnight transforming Israel from an ethnic Jewish state in control of a small amount of territory into, literally, a 'mini-empire'. Israel was suddenly in control of 90,000 square kilometres instead of the 20,000 it held before the war; its armies were entrenched on the east bank of the Suez Canal; they were forty-five kilometres from Amman, fifty from Damascus and a hundred from Cairo; the seizure of Egypt's oil fields in Sinai even opened possibilities for making Israel an oil-exporting country.[42] In Israeli popular imagination, the hero of the 'Six Day War' was General Moshe Dayan, who, perhaps more than any other Israeli official, typified Labour pragmatic expansionism and the reopening of the territorial issue of Zionism in the post-1967 era, a development which would also instantly be exploited to the full by both Zionist Revisionists and Labour's supporters of Greater Israel. Dayan, who between 1967 and 1974 was known in Israel as the 'emperor of the territories', had brought the splinter radical Labour Zionist party of Rafi (Reshimat Po'alei Eretz-Yisrael, or the Land of Israel Workers List, founded in 1965 by David Ben-Gurion) from isolation to the centre of national politics in Israel. In the wake of the 1967 conquests, leading Rafi figures were, too, the main founders of the Whole Land of Israel Movement (WLIM), an influential movement of territorial maximalism.

Dayan himself had done more than any other establishment figure to popularise the concept of Greater Israel and to begin the actual integration of the newly occupied West Bank and Gaza Strip into Israel proper. It was also Dayan who, upon arriving at the Wailing Wall in the Old City of Jerusalem, on the fourth day of the war, uttered the widely publicised words: 'We have returned to all that is holy in our land. We have returned never to be parted again.'[43] On another occasion that followed the 1967 war, during an emotional ceremony of the burial of Jewish casualties of 1948 on East Jerusalem's Mount of Olives, Dayan repeated the same vision of Greater Israel – an imperial vision which was also symbolically illustrated by the title of his 1969 book, *A New Map, Other Relationships*:

> We have not abandoned your dream and we have not forgotten your lesson. We have returned to the mountain, to the cradle of our people, to the inheritance of the Patriarchs, the land of the Judges and the fortress of the Kingdom of the House of David. We have returned to Hebron and Schem [Nablus], to Bethlehem and Anatot, to Jericho and the fords of the Jordan at Adam Ha'ir.[44]

The 1967 war not only reopened the question of Israel's border, but also rekindled mass interest and excitement in the so-called 'biblical whole Land of Israel'. The influence of the Hebrew biblical narrative in the secular intentions of Labour Zionism, particularly biblical conquests as narrated in the Book of Joshua, had always been evident. Ben-Gurion, Dayan and Yigael Yadin – another former army chief of staff – had all developed a keen interest in biblical archaeology and biblical warfare techniques and instruments. Dayan himself, who wrote *Living with the Bible*, became a notorious collector of 'biblical archaeological artefacts'. In the wake of the 1967 conquests, Amos Elon writes, the daily Hebrew press was filled with 'maps of Joshua's, Solomon's and Herod's conquests on both sides of the Jordan [River], and with argumentative articles proclaiming Israel's right to the whole of Palestine', irrespective of the wishes of its Palestinian inhabitants.[45] *Lamerhav*, the organ of Labour Minister Yigal Allon, and of course the right-wing party Herut's *Hayom*, became patrons of the Whole Land of Israel Movement.[46] According to Allon, Jewish 'biblical borders' included Sinai and the Syrian Golan Heights. Apparently, he was very upset by the Dayan declaration that Israel's 'historical borders' included only the West Bank.[47] On the other hand, however, it was Dayan who – before the October 1973 war – said: 'Better Sharm al-Shaykh [in Sinai] without peace than peace without Sharm al-Shaykh.' Zionist Israelis advanced their claims of Jewish rights to the whole land based on security or economic or demographic or religious considerations. And so the contest over the so-called Israelites' 'biblical borders' continued.

There were many reasons why the expansionist instincts of Greater Israel were sharply reawakened in the post-1967 period. First, the claims of 'Jewish historical rights in the whole Land of Israel' had a deep basis in mainstream secular Labour Zionism. Second, the spectacular and manifold consequences of the 1967 military successes emphasised the triumph of Zionism and the creation of a confident, dynamic, semi-militarised and expansionist settler society with distinct Prussian militarist characteristics; in *Between Battles and Ballots*, Israeli political scientist Yoram Peri has shown that political life in his country has been profoundly affected by militarisation and that the institutions of the military have actually encroached on every aspect of civilian life.[48] Third, there was the highly effective mobilisation of Neo-Zionist, Jewish fundamentalist political and social forces in Israel. Fourth, according to Amos Elon, the territory of Israel prior to the 1967 conquests, though rich in Roman, Byzantine, Nabatean, Crusader and Muslim historical sites, actually had almost no historical monuments testifying to an ancient Jewish past. According to the biblical narratives, the pre-1967 territory never embraced the ancient territory of the Hebrews – who were peoples of the hills – but rather that of their plainsland enemies, the Philistines, as well as the Edomites' Negev and 'Galilee of the Gentiles'.[49] The 1967 conquests suddenly brought the vast mythic repertoire of the Old Testament and its biblical sites of 'Judea', Hebron and Jericho under Israeli control. Fifth, it would also be illuminating to compare the irredentist drive for Greater Israel with some of its central European equivalent nations, which were born in the nineteenth or early twentieth centuries, committed to the recovery of their 'unredeemed national territories' which are populated by still more national groups.

More recently, several observers have pointed at certain parallels between the post-1967 vision of Greater Israel and the more recent expansionist nationalism of Slobodan Milosevic aimed at creating Greater Serbia. In his recent book *The Founding Myths of Israel* (1998), Zeev Sternhell, of the Hebrew University of Jerusalem, attempts to examine such parallels by focusing on the 'nationalist socialist' ideology of Labour Zionism, which dominated the Jewish community in Palestine and then the State of Israel from the 1930s into the 1970s, and illustrates ideological parallels between it and early twentieth-century 'radical, tribal and volkisch' organic nationalisms of central and eastern Europe that rejected both Marxism and liberal forms of universalism, along with individual rights and class struggle. Instead, Labour Zionists gave precedence to the realisation of their nationalist project: the establishment in

Palestine of a sovereign Jewish state. In this project, socialism was deployed merely as a useful 'mobilising myth'. Sternhell finds a similar style of tribal nationalism emphasising religion and ethnicity, promoting the cult and myths of ancient history, the revival of seemingly dead languages, a desperate drive for cultural renewal and a bitter struggle for political independence and territorial expansionism.

The analogy between eastern and central European populist nationalisms and Labour Zionism goes further: Zionist nationalist socialists repudiated liberal individualism and were suspicious of bourgeois liberal democracy. In this illiberal legacy of Labour Zionism, Sternhell finds the seeds of current Israeli problems – the lack of a constitution, an inadequate concept of universal human rights, the failure to separate religion and state, etc. Deflating the socialist pretensions of Labour Zionism, Sternhell implies that socialist Zionists and right-wing Revisionists, from Zeev Jabotinsky through Menahem Begin and Yitzhak Shamir to Binyamin Netanyahu, were all integral nationalists. He argues that Labour Zionism ran its course with the founding of the state and there were no social perspectives or ideological directions, beyond a nationalism based on 'historical rights to the whole land of Israel'. The mould set in the pre-state period did not change, and the Labour leadership was unable to cope with the consequences of the 1967 war. It continued with new settlements and territorial expansion and tried to test the Zionist method of creating 'facts on the ground'. Unable before the Oslo accords of 1993 to come to terms with Palestinian nationalism, Labour Zionism inevitably sank into the morass of the problem of the occupied territories.[50]

However, within the context of Israeli debates about Greater Israel, Labour Zionism has always been distinguishable from right-wing Zionist Revisionism and the Neo-Zionism of Gush Emunim in more than one respect. Until its ousting from power in May 1977, the Labour party did invest substantial resources in settling the Golan Heights, the Jordan Valley, the greater East Jerusalem area and the Gush Etzion area (south Bethlehem); however, following the pragmatic tradition of Ben-Gurion, Labour Zionism frequently adopted arguments, explanations and ideological justifications for the political situation which they had created. Revisionist Likud Zionism, on the other hand, demanded that reality be shaped to correspond to their 'monistic' ideology of Greater Israel.[51] Moreover, the Neo-Zionism of Gush Emunim, unlike Labour Zionism that tried in vain to reconcile settler colonialism with socialist norms, makes no pretence of being democratic; it covets the Arab land without the people and its vision is not remote from Jabotinsky's maximalist legacy, which remained the Likud government's inspirational guide until May 1999.

The establishment of Jewish political sovereignty over Greater Israel constitutes the vital focus of action for Israel's territorial maximalists. The Likud and other right-wing parties reject Israeli withdrawal from any territories of the so-called western Eretz-Yisrael – west of the Jordan River, or the West Bank. Moreover, since the Sinai Peninsula was not considered by the Zionist Revisionists/Likud as part of Eretz-Yisrael, the Israeli withdrawal in the early 1980s (endorsed by Prime Minister Menahem Begin) was not resisted as strongly as might be a possible future withdrawal from the West Bank. Although at present the Likud Party's support for settlement and territorial expansionism is largely confined to the post-1967 occupied territories (the West Bank, Gaza and the Golan Heights), this support is in large measure the result of adherence to Vladimir Jabotinsky's 'monistic' ideology: concern for the territorial integrity of the so-called 'Eretz-Yisrael in its biblical parameters'. For the Likud, 'Judea and Samaria' are situated at the 'heart of the historic Israelite nation' in the 'western Land of Israel'. Other, more radical, supporters of Neo-Zionism, such as the highly influential settlement movement of Gush Emunim, dream of territorial expansionism far beyond 'Judea and Samaria'. As Professor Ehud Sprinzak of the Hebrew University, a prominent expert on Gush Emunim and Israel's radical right, writes:

> When Gush [Emunim] ideologues speak about the complete [whole] Land of Israel they have in mind not only the post-1967 territory, but the land promised in the Covenant (Genesis 15) as well. This includes the occupied territories – especially Judea and Samaria, the very heart of the historic Israeli nation, and vast territories that belong now to Jordan, Syria and Iraq.[52]

With regard to the territorial issue, there are significantly different interpretations among the advocates of Greater Israel as to the territorial scope of 'the whole Land of Israel' and the realistic possibilities for maximum territorial expansionism given regional and international constraints. While the most extremist positions with respect to the destined borders of the State of Israel envisage a Jewish state stretching across the entire Fertile Crescent or even from the Nile to the Euphrates, others scale down their objectives to focus on the irreducible mimimum of controlling the West Bank, the Gaza Strip and the Golan Heights. In between, there are also political groupings advocating the reconquest of Sinai. For instance, the ultra-nationalist Tehiya, a small parliamentary party existing from 1979 to 1992, and leading figures in Gush Emunin, who formed 'Shvut Sinai' (Return to Sinai) in 1982, demanded the reconquest of Sinai after the territory was returned to Egyptian sovereignty in the early 1980s – a territory which had been returned to Egypt partly because Menahem Begin did not regard it as part of Eretz-Yisrael. Moreover, in 1990, during the Gulf crisis which was sparked off by the Iraqi invasion of Kuwait, Tehiya leader and Deputy Minister Geula Cohen threatened to invade the Kingdom of Jordan (the so-called 'eastern Land of Israel') and annex it to Israel[53] – a scenario which most Likud leaders viewed then as unrealistic.

The pages that follow deal with the ideas of the advocates of maximalist territorial expansionism and the supporters of Greater Israel, who are united in their position that the Palestinians have no legitimate claim to nationhood or to any other part of the country. The expansive conceptions of the territorial extent of Jewish sovereignty draw on three distinct ideological strands of Zionism, whose devotion to the 'whole Land of Israel' as the highest operational imperative also helps to explain the close and symbiotic relationship that developed among them in the post-1967 period:

1. The more militant and expansionist trend of Labour Zionism, as reflected in the Labour movement's 'activist' tradition, the Ahdut Ha'avodah movement and Hakibbutz Hameuhad, the Labour Zionist faction of Rafi and the Whole Land of Israel Movement.
2. Right-wing Zionist Revisionism with its heritage of territorial maximalism from Vladimir Jabotinsky to present-day Likud.
3. Nationalist-religious Neo-Zionism and the Kookist ideology: the teaching of Rabbi Tzvi Yehuda Kook; Kook's teachings have integrated the traditional religious longing for the land with the modern, secular activist settler Zionism, giving birth to a comprehensive fundamentalist nationalist-religious ideology.

The parties and movements of the far right are also discussed, and the final chapter examines the Israeli Jewish population's evolving attitudes to Greater Israel and the Palestinians.

In this volume, the theme of Israeli territorial maximalism is situated within the wider context of the conflict between Zionist immigrants/settlers and the native Palestinians – a conflict at the heart of which has always been land, territory, demography and water. The quest for land, territory and territorial expansion also underpinned the Zionist settlement drive in the pre-1948 period. In a sense, Zionism's long-lasting battle against the native Palestinians was a battle for 'more land, more territory and less Arabs'. This battle was dictated essentially by Zionism's premises and fundamentals: the 'ingathering' of the world's Jews in Palestine, the acquisition and conquest of land ('kibbush haadamah'), and the establishment of an ethnic state for the Jews – who mostly had yet to arrive in Palestine – at the expense of the native Palestinians.

The 1967 conquests altered only marginally Zionism's premises and objectives with regard to the Palestinians of the occupied territories. Indeed, the principal objectives of the Israeli state, as defined in terms of its Zionist ideology, are the fulfilment of the Jewish majority's aspirations, and those of would-be Jewish immigrants, frequently at the expense of the aspirations of the Palestinians.

At the same time, however, the June War of 1967 did mark a decisive turning-point in the history of Zionism, the State of Israel and the Palestinians, particularly those living in the occupied West Bank and Gaza Strip. The overwhelming Israeli victory, the seizure of the remainder of Palestine with its sizeable Arab population, the resultant outburst, and later upsurge, of messianic Zionism and growing Israeli confidence all contributed to the prompt and inevitable revival of the project of territorial expansionism. As has already been shown, in the wake of the 1967 conquests, the perception of Eretz-Yisrael as a whole was found not only in the maximalist Revisionist camp of Herut (later the Likud), but increasingly gained ground in all mainstream Zionist parties. Given the fact that ideological/historical and security claims to the occupied areas were to be put forward, action had to be taken to 'redeem the land' through the establishment of Jewish settlement without which the 'redemption' process was impossible. At the same time official and public concern at being faced with what it called 'the demographic problem', that is, the problem of absorbing too many non-Jews within the Jewish state, became manifestly stronger. Although nearly 300,000 Palestinians fled or were expelled in the course of the 1967 hostilities or shortly after, the Palestinian inhabitants of the territories largely remained *in situ*. The number of Palestinians living within the new cease-fire lines – including those who were citizens of Israel – was over 1.3 million in 1967, and given the high Arab birthrate, the prospect of the Palestinians becoming at least 50 per cent of the population – a Zionist/Israeli nightmare – was perceived as a feasible reality. The old Zionist dilemma of non-Jews in a Jewish state had to be resolved. Against this background of Zionist expansionism, ultra-nationalism and religious messianism, 'transfer/ethnic cleansing' ideas were revived in public debates, in popular songs, in articles in the Hebrew press and most importantly by political movements and parties of the radical right.

In some respects, however, the 1967 war did change Israel's geopolitical paradigm and cultural ecology. The war produced a spectacular territorial expansion. This territorial expansion made messianic religious and ultra-nationalist thinking seem highly credible. The 1967 conquests also made the historical Revisionist maximalist vision highly relevant. All the ingredients of Israel's new right radicalism – militarism, ultra-nationalism, territorial expansionism and neo-religiosity – produced political movements, including the new territorial maximalism of the Whole Land of Israel Movement and the fundamentalist settlement movement of Gush Emunim.

At the heart of this volume is the attempt to explore two interrelated themes: Zionist territorial maximalism (including the concept of 'Jewish historical rights in the whole Land of Israel') and the 'demographic debate' in Israel within the wider context of post-1967 Greater Israel. In my two previous books, *Expulsion of the Palestinians: The Concept of 'Transfer' in Zionist Political Thought 1882–1948* (1992) and *A Land Without a People: Israel, Transfer and the Palestinians, 1949–1996* (1997), I have dealt with the evolution of the theme of 'population transfer', a euphemism denoting the organised removal of the Arab population of Palestine to neighbouring or distant countries, which was a concept widely held in Israel after 1967. I have also shown that this concept – delicately described by its proponents as 'population exchange', 'Arab return to Arabia', emigration, resettlement and 'rehabilitation' of the Palestinians in Arab countries, etc. – was deeply rooted in Zionism and was embedded in the Zionist perception that the 'Land of Israel is a Jewish birthright' and belongs exclusively to the Jewish people as a whole. Consequently, Palestinian Arabs are 'strangers' who either should accept Jewish sovereignty over the land or depart.

Expulsion of the Palestinians also shows that the concept of 'transfer' ('voluntary', 'agreed' or 'compulsory') had a deep basis in mainstream Zionist thinking and the Yishuv (the Jewish community in Palestine until 1948) as a solution to the Zionist territorial/land, 'Arab demographic' and political problems, in the period between 1936 and 1948. Although the desire among the Zionist leaders to 'solve' the 'Arab question' through transfer remained constant until 1948, the envisaged modalities of transfer changed over the years according to the circumstances. From the mid-1930s onwards, a series of specific plans, generally involving Transjordan, Syria and Iraq, were produced by the Yishuv's transfer committees and senior officials.[54] *Expulsion of the Palestinians* also shows that the idea was advocated by the most important Zionist leaders, including David Ben-Gurion, Avraham Granovsky, Theodor Herzl, Zeev Jabotinsky, Berl Katznelson, Leo Motzkin, Arthur Ruppin, Moshe Sharett, Nahman Syrkin, Menahem Ussishkin, Yosef Weitz, Chaim Weizmann and Israel Zangwill.

The justifications used in defence of the transfer plans in the 1930s and 1940s formed the cornerstone of the subsequent argument for transfer, particularly in the proposals and plans put forward after 1948 and in the wake of the 1967 conquest of the West Bank and Gaza. After 1967, Zionist territorial maximalists and proponents of transfer continued to assert, often publicly, that there was nothing 'immoral' about these proposals; that the earlier twentieth-century transfers of Greeks and Turks, Indians and Pakistanis, Germans and other Europeans provided a 'precedent' for similar measures *vis-à-vis* the Palestinian Arabs; that the uprooting and transfer of the Palestinians to Arab countries would constitute a mere relocation from one district to another; that the Palestinians would have no difficulties in accepting Jordan, Syria, or Iraq as their homeland; that the Palestinian Arabs had little emotional attachment and few real ties to the particular soil in Palestine and would be just as content outside the 'Land of Israel'; that the Palestinian Arabs were marginal to the Arab nation and their problems might be facilitated by a 'benevolent' and 'humanitarian' policy of 'helping people to leave'. Such assertions were crucial to legitimise Zionism's denial of the Palestinian Arabs' right to self-determination in Palestine before 1948 or even in part of Palestine (the West Bank and Gaza) after 1967. Proponents of transfer asserted that the Palestinians were not a distinct people but merely 'Arabs', an Arab population, or 'Arab community' that happened to reside in the land of Israel.

Closely linked to this idea of the non-existence of the Palestinians as a nation and their non-attachment to the particular soil of Palestine was the idea of their belonging to an Arab nation with vast territories and many countries. After all, if the Palestinians did not constitute a distinct separate nation and were not an integral part of the country and were without historical ties to it, then they could be transferred to other Arab countries without undue prejudice. Similarly, if the Palestinians were merely a marginal local part of a larger population of Arabs, then they were not a major party to the conflicts with Israel; therefore, Israeli efforts to deal over their heads were justified. It is thus that Israeli territorial maximalists' pronouncements were full of references to the vast Arab territories and to the notion that the Palestinians were bound to other centres in Syria, Iraq and the Arabian Peninsula, the homeland of the Arab people.

After June 1967, the Israeli state had to deal with a territory entirely populated by non-Jews and a perceived major 'demographic problem'. Hence, the modalities of transfer changed after 1967 and the revival of the transfer concept since then points to the parallels that exist between the Zionist transfer schemes in the pre-1948 era and in the era since June 1967.

The use of force and coercion formed an important element in Israel's policy toward the Palestinians of the occupied territories in the post-1967 period. The institution of the military government, together with the imposition of the Defence Emergency Regulations promulgated by the British mandatory authorities in 1945, empowered the military governors to close off the Arab localities and to restrict entry or exit only to those who had been issued permits by the military authorities. These regulations also enabled the Israeli authorities to evict and deport people from their villages and towns, to place individuals under administrative detention for indefinite periods without trial, and to impose fines and penalties without due process.[55]

Among the parliamentary parties, the open proponents of territorial maximalism and the 'transfer' solution are the far right-wing parties, that is, those further to the right of the Likud, and are religious and secular alike, including the Zeevi-led Moledet Party, the Tehiya Party (led by Yuval Neeman and Geula Cohen until its collapse in the early 1990s), the Tzomet Party of General Raphael Eitan, who until May 1999 was Agriculture Minister in the Binyamin Netanyahu cabinet. In *The Ascendance of Israel's Radical Right* (1991),

Professor Ehud Sprinzak (a nephew of Professor Yair Sprinzak, a Moledet Knesset Member (1988–92) and the son of a former secretary-general of the Histadrut and Israel's first Speaker of parliament) shows that all the territorially maximalist far-right parties and movements advocated 'transfer' in one form or another; the difference lies between the 'manifest' and 'total' transfer of Moledet and the 'latent' and 'partial' transfer of the Tehiya and Tzomet.[56] The same three parliamentary parties, according to Professor Sammy Smooha of Haifa University, called on Israeli Arab citizens to do military/civil service or to 'demote their citizenship status to permanent residence; that is, to give up the right to vote in the Knesset elections'.[57]

In addition to the Israeli right's parliamentary parties, this volume deals with extra-parliamentary movements of territorial maximalism, including the influential settlement movement of Gush Emunim, the Kach movement, founded by Rabbi Meir Kahane, and the National Circle, led by Ora Shem-Ur. With the exception of the discredited Kach movement, which was disqualified from nomination to the Knesset election in 1988 and banned in the wake of the Hebron massacre in 1994, the Israeli radical right was represented both in the Knesset and the coalition cabinet of Yitzhak Shamir between 1990 and 1992. In comparison with the stridency of these far right-wing parties and movements, the territorial policies of the Labour coalition governments between 1967 and 1977 and between 1992 and 1996 look like the epitome of pragmatism.

Together, Moledet and Tzomet won four parliamentary seats in the 1988 general elections, while the Tehiya was represented by three seats and the National Religious Party had five seats; together these four parties received twelve seats and 10.5 per cent of the vote. The Western media coverage focused on the Labour Party victory in the 1992 general election, but tended to downplay the increasing support for the far right, which collectively gained 17 Knesset seats (out of 120) against 12 in 1988. In June 1992, Tzomet increased its parliamentary representation from two to eight seats, while Moledet gained one more seat, raising its total to three. The Tehiya lost its three seats, largely to Tzomet and the National Religious Party, which gained six seats. Together Tzomet, Moledet and the National Religious Party attained 17 parliamentary seats. However, if the extreme-right section within the Likud is added, then the extreme right would command 15 to 20 per cent of the Israeli vote. Moreover, taking into account the fact that the far right were represented by a number of ministers in the Israeli cabinet until 1992 (Neeman, Zeevi, Eitan, Shapira and others), its influence was much greater than its vote percentage would suggest.

The far-right parties and movements call for: 1) maximum territorial expansionism; 2) outright legal annexation of the territories occupied in 1967; 3) the suppression of the intifada and any form of Palestinian resistance by all means and necessary force; 4) the establishment of massive Jewish settlements; 5) the 'transfer' of the Palestinians. The terminology and style used by each party and movement to describe territorial expansion and 'transfer' varies according to organisational background and preoccupation. For instance, while the Gush Emunim settlers talked about 'persuading' the Arabs to emigrate, the Kach movement demanded outright expulsion and the Moledet Party crystallised since 1988 around the single-minded platform of 'agreed transfer'. Yet for some religious extremists, expulsion is not the final solution; they call for the total 'annihilation of the modern Amalek'. Moreover, the fact that both secular Generals Raphael Eitan and Rehava'am Zeevi come from the Palmah, the elite strike force of Labour Zionism in the 1940s, and the fact that the Moledet Party received the highest rate of its electoral support in 1988 – 45 per cent from Kibbutz Beit Guvrin in the south[58] – affiliated with the Hakibbutz Hameuhad movement – may point to the origin of the aspirations of territorial maximalism found in the 'activist' current of Labour Zionism of the pre-state period. Unlike the religious messianics of Gush Emunim, secular Generals Eitan and Zeevi justify their territorial expansionism not by religious messianic perceptions and Jewish theocratic notions, but as pragmatic answers to practical necessities; this echoes the argument often found in the 'activist' Labour Zionist tradition of the 1930s and 1940s.

Of course, Israeli public views on Greater Israel have been considerably affected by the Oslo process and the various interim agreements signed between Israel and the Palestinian Authority. Nevertheless, one still can observe a deep division between those who support territorial maximalism and annexation and those who prefer territorial compromise and complete or partial withdrawal from the occupied territories. Yet even those figures of Labour Zionism regarded as pragmatists also have reiterated their views in favour of various concepts of frontiers which retain maximum land and minimum Arabs in the West Bank and Gaza, views that demonstrate how deep-rooted in Israel are the instincts of territorial expansion.

It is hardly necessary to mention that the various ideas of territorial maximalism combined with 'transfer' discussed in this study do not carry the same weight. Certainly those put forward or supported by Likud, Labour or Tzomet figures are far more important that those advocated by Gush Emunim or the Moledet Party. This book will cover the whole of spectrum ideas, proposals and plans put forwards by the Israeli right from 1967 to the present. Methodologically this work will apply a historical approach. It is divided into five chapters: the first concentrates on the Whole Land of Israel Movement, the second on Zionist Revisionism and the Likud, the third on Gush Emunim and the religious fundamentalists, the fourth on the parties and movements of the far right, and the fifth on the evolution of Israeli Jewish public attitudes since 1967.

This work is based in part on archival material in the Israeli State Archives, the Central Zionist Archives in Jerusalem and the Jabotinsky Archives in Tel Aviv, as well as private papers in the Institute for Settlement Studies in Rehovot. The Israeli Hebrew press also has been a very important source for the period since 1967. These primary sources were supplemented by secondary works in Hebrew, English, French and Arabic.

1
Labour Zionism's 'Activists': New Territorial Maximalism and the Whole Land of Israel Movement, 1967-77

In the wake of Israel's 1967 conquests, the deep-rooted perception of *Eretz-Yisrael* as a whole was not only found in the traditional Zionist maximalism of the Revisionist Herut (later Likud) camp, but increasingly gained ground in all the main political parties, including the traditionally pragmatic Labour Party. This maximalist concept of state frontiers was based on a Zionist political and military strategy (backed by a very powerful army equipped with nuclear weapons) which served as a means to essentially imperialist ends: the creation of a Middle East more favourable to a greatly enlarged and regionally dominant Jewish state. This territorially expansionist and imperialist approach found its first manifestation in the Whole Land of Israel Movement (Hatnu'ah Lema'an Eretz-Yisrael Hashlemah) (WLIM), a secular elite organisation and an influential ideological movement of territorial maximalism which was founded promptly after the war with the aim of annexing and settling with Jews the newly 'liberated' territories.[1] In addition to Begin's Herut, the WLIM was one of the most significant organised efforts to push Israel towards the permanent incorporation of the occupied territories. Devoted to the 'whole Land of Israel' as the highest operational imperative, the highly publicised, founding Manifesto of the WLIM of 1967 was almost entirely supported by prominent members of the Labour establishment.[2] Full of historical imagery, the Manifesto laid the foundations of the project of imperial Israel in straightforward terms:

> Zahal's [the Israeli Defence Force] victory in the Six-Day War placed the people and the state within a new and fateful period. The whole of Eretz Israel is now in the hand of the Jewish people,

and just as we are not allowed to give up the State of Israel, so we are ordered to keep what we received there from Eretz Yisrael ... We are bound to be loyal to the entirety of the country ... and no government in Israel is entitled to give up this entirety, which represents the inherent and inalienable right to our people from the beginning of its history.[3]

The occupation of Sinai, the Golan Heights, the West Bank and Gaza – their combined territories four times bigger than Israel proper – and the destruction of the combined armies of Egypt, Syria and Jordan thrilled most Israelis and encouraged many of them to develop an imperial outlook and to embrace an imperialist project based on a conviction that their state was the strongest military force in the Middle East. The same expansionist instincts helped to sanctify the Zionist principle that 'never again should Eretz-Yisrael be divided.' As Professor Ehud Sprinzak explains, since 1967 this principle has become 'a most energetic and influential tenet in modern Zionism'.[4] Against the intoxicating backdrop of the new Israeli empire, the official founding conference of the WLIM was held on 31 October 1967.

The new movement of territorial expansion and imperial domination cut across all party lines in Israel and brought together diverse Zionist schools of thought, from Labour activists to Jabotinsky's Revisionists to smaller groups and individuals. By and large, however, the movement was set up and dominated by Labour intellectuals, poets, politicians, generals and kibbutz leaders, and other personalities prominent in the pre-1948 Zionist struggle.[5] It drew its inspiration from the pre-state 'activist' and militant tradition of Labour Zionism, which attempted to reconcile romantic Jewish socialism with colonial expansionism, and focused on the 'whole Land of Israel'. Within Labour Zionism, the activist approach was characterised by militant commitment to territorial expansion, tough policies towards the Arabs, and maximum extension of Jewish settlement and sovereignty. Its advocates were committed to the idea of creating settlements as a means of determining future political borders. The speeches and writings of one of its most influential ideologues, Yitzhak Tabenkin (1887–1971), were imbued with imagery of East European romantic and organic nationalism. Although explicitly secular, his message and that of other activist leaders, often featured references to the Bible and biblical Israelites. The militant ethos of the activist movement of Labour Zionism also contained mystical overtones of communion between Jewish workers and fighters, and the 'soil of the Land of Israel'. These ideas were most prominent within the Ahdut Ha'avodah political party (and its affiliated settlement movement, Hakibbutz Hameuhad[6]), whose concepts of state frontiers and Jewish territorial space also included parts of the Sinai Desert.

Another significant group within the WLIM was made up of people who had followed former Prime Minister David Ben-Gurion when he left Mapai in 1965 to form the Labour parliamentary faction of Rafi.[7] The list of the WLIM signatories included leading Labour figures such as Rahel Yanait, a prominent Mapai leader and the widow of Israel's second President Yitzhak Ben-Tzvi, Yitzhak Tabenkin, a prominent ideologue of the Hakibbutz Hameuhad movement, who had supported the 'transfer' solution in the early 1940s,[8] Haim Yahiel, former director-general of the Foreign Ministry, Isser Harel, Israel's first head of the Mossad, 'Uzi Feinerman, the secretary-general of the Moshav movement, Beni Marshak, Eli'ezer Livneh, the nation poet Natan Alterman, the novelist Yehuda Burla and Tzvi Shiloah, a writer and an old-timer of the Mapai party. These representatives of Israel's political elite were joined by a gallery of reserve generals: Major General Ya'acov Dori, the army Chief of Staff during the 1948 war, and the Generals Dan Talkovsky, Eliyahu Ben-Hur, Avraham Yoffe and Meir Zore'a. The writer Shmuel 'Agnon, recipient of the 1966 Nobel Prize for Literature was also present at the founding conference as were many other authors, poets and university professors. Members of the new movement were neither an opposition group nor an extremist protest movement; many of them were very close to the Israeli Labour government and taken together, Ehud Sprinzak writes, the 72 signatories of the manifesto of the movement were 'probably the most distinguished group of names ever to have joined a public cause in Israel'.[9]

Despite the presence of two rabbis among the scores of its manifesto's signatories, the WLIM was a manifestation of secular ultra-nationalist (mainly) Labour Zionism. It aspired to be neither a mass movement nor a political party, but a respected pressure group whose main objective was to influence government policy through newspaper articles, books and personal contacts with Labour government ministers.[10] A glance at the political background and public career of five co-founders and leading members of the WLIM, Eli'ezer Livneh, Yehuda Burla, Rahel Yanait, Dr Haim Yahiel, Tzvi Shiloah and Natan Alterman, is most instructive: they were all veterans and prominent members of Mapai, Israel's ruling party (later to become the Labour Party).

Eli'ezer Livneh (1902–75) was a typical elder statesman of the new movement, with an impressive Labour Zionist record. After emigrating to Palestine in 1920 and joining Kibbutz 'Ein Harod, Livneh rose from day labourer to Labour leader. He held many public offices, including a political job for the Zionist movement in pre-war Nazi Germany. Between 1940 and 1942, he headed the political section of the Haganah (Defence), the para-military organisation of the Yishuv's leadership, and edited the magazine *Ma'arakhot*, which subsequently became the main organ of the Israeli Army. From 1942 to 1947, he was editor of *Eshnav*, the Haganah's underground weekly. Meanwhile in 1942, he also became editor of *Beterem*, a political fortnightly, which opened its pages in the 1950s to Avraham Schwadron (Sharon) and his campaign for the total 'transfer' of the Arab citizens of Israel (see below). A prominent member of Mapai, Livneh was a Knesset member from 1949 to 1955 and served on the influential Knesset Foreign Affairs and Defence Committee between 1951 and 1955. He was also an editor of *Hador*, an influential Mapai newspaper. In the 1960s and early 1970s, Livneh was a distinguished columnist for Israel's most influential newspapers and magazines.[11] In the summer of 1967 Livneh put forward a plan for the transfer of 600,000 Palestinians from the occupied territories (see below).[12]

Yehuda Burla (1886–1969) was a director of the Department for Arab Affairs of the Histadrut before 1948. After the establishment of the State of Israel, he served as a director of the Department for Culture, Press and Information in the Ministry of Minorities. He received the Bialik and Ussishkin Prizes for literature in 1942 and 1949 respectively.

Rahel Yanait (1866–1979), the widow of Yitzhak Ben-Tzvi, the second President of Israel, was a founder of the Po'alei Tzion labour movement together with David Ben-Gurion and Yitzhak Tabenkin. In 1908, she emigrated to Palestine and later was a founder of the Hashomer Zionist defence organisation. After the First World War, she helped found the Ahdut Ha'avodah movement, from which the Mapai Party originated and the Histadrut. She served as a delegate to Zionist Congresses and as a member of Asefat Hanivharim, the pre-1948 Yishuv Assembly. After the establishment of Israel, she was one of the editors of the Labour weekly *Haahdut*. And in late 1956, after the Israeli Army overran the Gaza Strip and Sinai, she appealed to Ben-Gurion to 'transfer' the Gaza refugee camps' residents to Sinai.[13]

Haim Yahiel (1905–74) first arrived in Palestine in 1929 and there he joined Kibbutz Giva'at Hayim for a short time before returning to Europe. Returning to Palestine in 1939, he became a Histadrut official, serving first (1939–42) as director of its Education Department in Haifa and then (1942–45) as a member of the Executive Committee. From 1945 to 1948, Yahiel served as representative of the Jewish Agency in Munich, Germany, and was then (1948–49) Israeli Consul in the same city. Between 1949 and 1951, he was director of the Jewish Agency's Department of Absorption in Jerusalem. From 1951 to 1953, he served as head of the Information Department of the Ministry of Foreign Affairs, and from 1956 to 1959, he was appointed first as Minister to the Scandinavian countries and later became Ambassador to Sweden and Minister to Norway and Iceland. From 1960 to 1964 he served as director general of the Ministry of Foreign Affairs, and from 1965 to 1972 he served as chairman of the Israel Broadcasting Authority. Yahiel was a delegate to numerous Zionist congresses and for several years also served as head of the Centre for the Diaspora of the Jewish Agency. Even after becoming a leader of the Whole Land of Israel Movement and until his death in 1974, Yahiel still served the Ministry of Foreign Affairs in various capacities, including as Chairman of the Editorial Board of its major publication, *Israel's Foreign Relations, Selected Documents*. The first two volumes of these official documents, published in 1976, were dedicated to the memory of Haim Yahiel.

Natan Alterman (1910–70), the central figure of the Whole Land of Israel Movement, served on the editorial board of the daily newspaper *Haaretz* from 1934 to 1943, when he joined the Histadrut daily *Davar*, virtually the mouthpiece of the Mapai Party. In an article in the mass-circulation *Ma'ariv* shortly after the 1967 conquests, Alterman wrote that the transfer solution 'is only possible in an ideal peace situation between us and Arab states, which will agree to cooperate with us in a great project of population transfer'.[14]

It is also worth noting that in justification of his views on Arab 'transfer', Alterman cited the statements made by Berl Katznelson (1887–1944), the hero of Labour Zionism, and one of the most important leaders of the Yishuv period and the founder and editor of *Davar* (the Histadrut newspaper). In 1943 (the year Alterman joined *Davar*) he wrote:

Our contemporary history has known a number of transfers ... [for instance] the USSR arranged the transfer of one million Germans living in the Volga region and transferred them to very distant places ... one could assume that this transfer was done against the will of the transferees ... there could be possible situations that would make [Arab] population transfer desirable for both sides ... who is the socialist who is interested in rejecting the very idea before hand and stigmatising it as something unfair? Has Merhavyah not been built on transfer? Were it not for many of these transfers Hashomer Hatza'ir [which later in 1948 founded the Mapam Party] would not be residing today in Merhavyah, or Mishmar Ha'emek or other places ... and if what has been done for a settlement of Hashomer Hatza'ir is a fair deed, why would it not be fair when it would be done on a much larger and greater scale, not just for Hashomer Hatza'ir but for the whole of Israel?[15]

These leading Labour figures and representatives of Israel's political elite were joined by Menahem Begin and other personalities from the traditional camp of territorial maximalism, the Revisionist camp (or the Gahal as the Herut Party was now known), furnishing the campaign for territorial expansion and annexation with its organised political backbone. Signatories of the WLIM also included Professor 'Ari Jabotinsky, Vladimir Jabotinsky's son; Dr Reuven Hecht and Shmuel Katz, two veteran Revisionist figures; Uri Tzvi Greenberg, the poet laureate of the Zionist right since the 1930s, who is considered by Jewish ultra-nationalists as the greatest Hebrew poet of the contemporary era; several leaders of the National Religious Party, and Dr Yisrael (Scheib) Eldad, the former commander of Lohamei Herut Yisrael (Lehi or the Stern Gang), who was later to become one of the most articulate publicists of the settlement movement of Gush Emunim. In time, the WLIM was to give birth to Gush Emunim and a number of extreme right-wing and 'transfer' parties such as the Moledet Party – which will be discussed below.

Inevitably, one of the central questions for the new territorial maximalists of the WLIM was what should be done with the Palestinians of the West Bank and Gaza, who remained, by and large, *in situ*. According to Ehud Sprinzak, most members of the movement were open, democratic and tolerant in relations to the Palestinians of the occupied territories: 'The individual Palestinians of the West Bank were honestly invited to take part in building the new Israeli empire. Most of the members of the [Whole] Land of Israel

Movement agreed with Eli'ezer Livneh that the Arabs should get full political rights in the Jewish states.'[16] However, as we shall see below, the available evidence indicates the opposite; Livneh as well as many other leading members supported the 'transfer' concept. Moreover, the movement's spokesmen and sympathisers did not, on the whole, put forward new ideas in this regard but rather resurrected phrases derived from the classical Zionist arsenal of terminology and conceptions, such as 'only Israel's genius and the extraordinary efforts of Jewish settlers can make the untended and barren landscape productive', the Arab 'demographic problem' and 'demographic threat', the 'transfer solution', all of which had been so familiar in Zionist debates before 1948 and indeed in use since the beginning of political Zionism. Suddenly the deep-seated 'transfer' formula came out into the open.

The first set of proposals appeared in a book in 1967, immediately after the war, under the revealing Hebrew title *Hakol* [Everything].[17] It was a collection of articles from the Hebrew press edited by Dr Aharon Ben-'Ami, who had been brought up in the 'activist' tradition of Labour Zionism. In the 1940s, Ben-'Ami had served in the Palmah, the strike force of Labour Zionism. In the mid-1960s, he had been a member of the Labour Zionist faction of Rafi, headed by Ben-Gurion and Dayan, while teaching sociology at Tel Aviv University and Haifa Universities. After June 1967 he had helped organize the WLIM and wrote articles for its organ, *Zot Haaretz*. He later became one of the first residents of Ariel, a large Jewish settlement in the West Bank and since 1986 he has served as the editor of *Hayarden* ('Jordan'), an organ of the territorial maximalists of Greater Israel.[18] In *Everything*, the supporters of the new movement outlined their attitude towards the Palestinian inhabitants as well as the refugees residing in 'Judea', 'Samaria' and Gaza. Once again the theme of 'untended land', that the land can only be made to bloom and yield up its produce by the extraordinary efforts of Israel, was invoked in justification of Jewish colonisation of the West Bank and Gaza and Palestinian removal: the Palestinians – 'like the Crusaders' – forfeited their right to the country because 'they neglected it,' wrote Rahel Saborai.[19] Saborai proposed to resettle the refugees in northern Sinai between the Gaza Strip and El Arish: 'from the early period of Zionism they intended to develop these large tracts of land as part of the Zionist settlement. This [old, Herzl's] plan[20] should be reactivated by Israel as a giant water project for the settlement of the [Palestinian] refugees.'[21] The 'transfer' of the refugees to, and their settlement in, Sinai was also raised by Dr Yehuda Don, who believed that about 'one million refugees and their children', residing in the West Bank and Gaza, should be relocated to Sinai: 'The Israeli technology and experience in settling [Jewish] refugees and making the desert bloom have acquired fame in the whole world ... This proposal could also be a very important political weapon, since we are proposing a solution in one of the desolate provinces of a defeated country [i.e., Egypt] ... No doubt such a measure would require great capital.'[22]

Another recurring theme in this collection – which was reflected in the policies of the Labour government of the day – was that a large Palestinian minority could not be integrated into the Zionist/Jewish state. Consequently, old Zionist remedies were resurrected, namely a 'population transfer/emigration' of Arabs to neighbouring Arab countries as well as countries overseas. These transfer/emigration proposals came from old-timers and supporters of Labour Zionism, such as Eli'ezer Livneh, Professor Yuval Neeman (who was then still associated with the Labour establishment) and Tzvi Shiloah, who cited in justification the so-called 'examples' and 'precedents' of population transfer (repeatedly invoked in official Zionist schemes of the 1930s and 1940s), such as the Greco-Turkish, the German-Polish and the Indo-Pakistani cases.[23] Most contributors to this collection adhered to the orthodox, almost doctrinaire, Zionist conception that the Palestinians did not constitute a nation and therefore their real, historical, homeland was not in the Land of Israel, but in Arabia, Syria and Iraq to which centres they were bound and to which they should be encouraged to emigrate. Livneh, Shiloah and Moshe Tabenkin, the son of Yitzhak Tabenkin, also shared the view that the bridges on the Jordan River should be open only in one (exit) direction.[24]

The supporters and publicists of Greater Israel – contributors to the above collection as well as to other publications – proposed time and again the use of financial and economic incentives to encourage mass Arab emigration.[25] Some suggested the imposition of additional taxes as a means of engineering Arab emigration.[26] Another proposal put forward by the movement's sympathisers – which has found its way into the policies of all Israeli governments since then – was to exclude the inhabitants of the occupied territories from Israeli citizenship. These residents should be encouraged to take the citizenship of neighbouring Arab states and this would enable them to feel free to depart whenever they wished, or whenever other Arab regimes encouraged them to do so. The promotion of large Arab emigration combined with Jewish mass immigration – for example, great hopes were placed upon Jewish 'aliyah' from the Soviet Union – to be settled in the newly acquired territories would help to transform the 'demographic balance' and political reality in the 'whole Land of Israel'.

A decade later, in 1977, a large volume of the maximalist movement appeared under the title *The Book of the Whole Land of Israel*.[27] The many contributors to this book discussed various social, political, economic, demographic and regional considerations in the context of the advocacy of Greater Israel and the need to annex the West Bank and Gaza. Among the contributors to the book and propagators of the 'transfer' solution was Haim Hazaz, a prominent author who was awarded the top literary prizes, the Bialik and Israel Prizes. In fact, Hazaz's contribution to this volume was a reprint of the speech he made at the foundation conference of the movement held on 31 October 1967, and the speech had already been published in its entirety in *Davar* on 10 November 1967. Echoing the Zionist apologia of the pre-1948 era, Hazaz had this to say:

> There is the question of Judea and Ephraim [the West Bank], with a large Arab population which must be evacuated to neighbouring Arab states. This is not an exile like the exile of Jews among the Gentiles ... They will be coming to their brothers to large and wide and little-populated countries. One culture, one language and one religion. This is 'transfer' such as that which took place between Turkey and Greece, between India and Pakistan ... putting the world aright in one place through exchanging [the Arab population] to its designated place. We will assume responsibility for this task and assist in planning, organising and financing.[28]

Hazaz – who was willing to allow an Arab minority to remain in Greater Israel provided it 'would not disrupt or change the Jewish character of the Land of Israel'[29] – repeated his 'transfer' proposal in a simplistic way in an interview in 1968: 'the [1967] war cost us 3 billion [Israeli] pounds – let's take three billion more pounds and give them to the Arabs and tell them to get out.'[30]

Once again the leaders of the movement as well as its 'experts' on demographic affairs argued that transfer of the Palestinians of the territories is the best solution. Eli'ezer Livneh, a former prominent Mapai member, explained that in 1948 the Israeli leadership 'rejected the demographic-ethnic reality' of the country as a criterion for establishing the boundaries of the state by conquering predominantly Arab-populated areas and simultaneously transforming them by establishing Jewish settlements.[31] Yosef Shaked added that 'the right to change the existing demographic situation in the Land of Israel is the meaning of Zionism and the content of its war'.[32]

Two self-styled demographic 'experts' of the movement, Haim Yahiel and Dr Dov Yosefi, contributed two articles under the titles 'Demography and Israel's Uniqueness' and 'A Humane Solution to the Demographic Problem' respectively. Yahiel saw 'in principle ... in population exchange or in the transfer of minorities an efficient, just and in the final consideration the most humane solution to conflicts between nations'. He realised, however, that a large-scale outright transfer, which 'few are talking about but not a few are contemplating', could only be carried out under circumstances of war, and therefore, officially the Whole Land of Israel Movement should refrain from including such a proposal in its political programme 'not because of moral reasons but for political considerations'; 'such a plan would be received by [Arab, Western?] public opinion as a conspiracy for expulsion and would increase the enmity' towards Israel. According to Yahiel, mass transfer 'would only be possible as an agreed solution in the framework of peace agreement, ... or in the opposite case, that is a solution implemented in the midst of war'.[33] The second demographic 'expert' Yosefi came up with yet more strident conclusions – first:

If we want to prevent mutual and continuous bloodshed, there is only one solution – the transfer of the Arab population of the Land of Israel to Arab states ... True, this is a little painful (who knows this like us the Jews), but it is inevitable and preferable than cumulative poisoning which undermines the whole body. There is no doubt that this solution will come sooner or later. The question is only whether it will be by peaceful ways through regional planning and international assistance, or, God forbid, as a result of bloody events ...

second:

The State of Israel has to show political courage at an opportune moment ... and to announce that according to experiences in other places and similar situations there is no other solution but

population transfer ... The problem of the Arab minority in the
Land of Israel remains without a solution because this [minority]
has not been transferred to Arab states ...

third:

> We should also not be deterred from repeating time and again in
> the ears of the world nations that Jordan (or the combination of
> Jordan and Syria) actually constitutes a Palestinian homeland and
> only in it will the Arabs of the Land of Israel have self-determina-
> tion ... This should be the central Israeli demand in any
> negotiation with Arab countries. The author does not overlook
> the fact that this solution is not easy to implement in no-war
> situations. Because most cases of population transfer in the world
> were in time of battle or shortly after. In any case, this is a humane
> solution ...[34]

Yosefi's position appears to have further hardened since the mid-
1970s, as demonstrated in the more extremist version of his article
'A Humane Solution to the Demographic Problem', published in the
periodical *Haumah* in the autumn of 1987.[35] In this version, Yosefi
asserts that the 'Arab minority [including the Arab citizens] is already
endangering, and will endanger with greater vigour in the future,
the sovereignty and even the existence of the state of Israel' (p. 21).
'The main objective', he elaborates, 'so long as Judea and Samaria
are in our hands, there exists the hope that in a political or military-
political-regional, or international constellation, the ideal solution of
population transfer will be made possible. And in the region in
which we are living such a constellation is a permanent possibility.'
While Yosefi explicitly raises the 'military' solution for Arab removal
he proposes that in the interest of the two parties

> ... not to wait for painful and even tragic opportunities ... but to
> plan in good time the transfer of the Arab population from the
> West Bank to Arab countries – with the understanding and
> assistance of the world nations, if possible. Yet for that purpose
> the government of Israel must set up, as early as possible, a special
> information department, which would conduct a worthy
> information/propaganda [campaign] – with the assistance of
> experts on the mentality of the Arab leaders and the interests of
> Arab states, on the one hand, and the political, strategic and

economic interests of European states, and especially of the two superpowers, on the other. In question is an adequate information campaign which clearly proves that the solution proposed here is the only humane solution for the two parties.[36]

Yosefi, like several leaders of WLIM, was a senior Israeli government official and a member of the Labour Party and it is worth describing his public career in mainstream Labour Zionism and in various official posts. Yosefi was a Zionist publicist and journalist and Israeli diplomat. Born in Chile, Yosefi first joined the Hashomer Hatza'ir 'socialist' movement – the Mapam party youth movement after 1948 – and became a member of its Chilean executive. He immigrated to Israel shortly after its establishment at the age of 43 and was among the founders of the Mapam Kibbutz Ga'ash. He also held central positions in the Mapam Party: he was the secretary of the Mapam international movement and the editor of its Yiddish-language organ *Yisrael Stema'a*. After leaving Mapam in the early 1960s, Yosefi joined the Mapai Party and later the diplomatic service in Latin America where he stayed until 1970. And in the late 1960s, while he was still a serving diplomat, he showed an interest in the activities of WLIM. In the late 1980s, Yosefi joined the far-right Moledet Party of General Rehava'am Zeevi.[37]

Many leaders of WLIM believed that Zionism's mission of territorial expansion had not been completed and that military campaigns and 'wars of liberation' were still needed to recover other parts of the Land of Israel. A founder of WLIM, General Avraham Yoffe – a former member of the Mapam Party[38] and a longtime head of Israel's Nature Reserve Authority – stressed the necessity of war between Israel and Arabs for the sake of further expansion into the 'whole Land of Israel', an expansion which flows from the incompleteness of Zionism's mission: 'The State of Israel, as presently constituted, does not represent the fulfilment of Zionism. This is a state on the way ... Our duty is not completed ... The state must provide a refuge for the Jewish people as a whole. The Arab world will never accept this idea.'[39] Yoffe also believed that the extension of Israeli sovereignty over 'Judea', 'Samaria' and Gaza would cause at least 'part [of the Arabs] to emigrate from here and the other part to remain as loyal citizens of the State of Israel'.[40]

A deeply rooted strand in Israeli imperial thinking regarding the Middle East was the 'alliance of minorities'. Israelis preferred to portray the Middle East not as predominantly Arab or Islamic but as a multiethnic, multireligious, and multicultural area. David Ben-Gurion had often argued that the majority of the inhabitants of the Middle East were not Arab. He was referring not only to the Persians and the Turks but also to non-Arab minorities such as the Kurds, the Jews and the (allegedly non-Arab) Christian Maronites of Lebanon. By pursuing an imperialist political and military strategy which consisted of interfering in the domestic affairs of its Arab neighbours and forging an alliance with ethnic and religious minorities, the Israelis aimed at countering the forces of pan-Arabism and keeping the Arab world fragmented.[41] The Zionist movement had close clandestine links, going back to the 1920s, with many leaders of the Maronites of Lebanon.[42] Israeli–Maronite relations were maintained largely through clandestine contacts until the late 1970s. Under the Likud government from 1977 to 1984, they became more open with Israeli direct support and military intervention.[43] Leading WLIM figures not only did not accept the existence of the Arab nation, but also envisaged a complete political reorganisation and a cultural transformation of the region in which the predominantly Arab cultural character of the area would disappear. Professor 'Ari Jabotinsky suggested that the non-Arab peoples of the Middle East, with Israeli assistance, would ultimately break the cultural domination of the area by the Arabs.[44] Professor 'Ezra Zohar suggested pursuing an activist Israeli foreign policy designed to encourage the break-up of the Arab states and their replacement by ethnic and sectarian entities.[45] In November 1976, at the height of the Lebanese civil war, Tzvi Shiloah suggested the occupation of southern Lebanon and the establishment of territorial continuity between Israel and a pro-Israeli 'independent' Christian Maronite entity in Lebanon.[46] In the same year, relations with Christians along Israel's northern border were established under the interventionist 'Good Fence' policy of the Rabin government.[47]

Some spokesmen of the movement made little distinction between the inhabitants of the occupied territories and the Palestinian citizens of Israel and questioned the possibility of any Arab–Jewish co-existence. As Yosefi put it: even in the case of 'our withdrawal from Judea and Samaria, the demographic problem as well as the problem of Arab-Jewish coexistence in one state will not be solved. Because all the arguments regarding an Arab minority of one million and a half hold true for an Arab minority of one million and even half a million.'[48]

From the above discussion it appears that many protagonists of Greater Israel within WLIM sought maximum territorial expansion and the expulsion, (or 'transfer', as it was euphemistically put), of at least the bulk of the Palestinians from the West Bank and Gaza. The perusal of numerous publications by other leaders and sympathisers of the movement gives further substantiation to this argument. The following will discuss in detail the proposals put forward by three prominent WLIM campaigners: Eli'ezer Livneh, Yisrael Eldad and Tzvi Shiloah. The three publicists have contributed much to the revival of the 'transfer/ethnic cleansing' theme and its spreading in public debate in Israel in the post-1967 period. Although these figures rehash many of the classical Zionist arguments in justification of territorial expansion, they do however emphasise different facets of the territorial 'demographic' debates in Israel. The three figures come from diverse political backgrounds (Livneh and Shiloah from Labour Zionism, Eldad from Revisionist Zionism) and had different political weight and influence – as we shall see – but they all subscribe to the goal of Greater Israel, with as few Palestinian inhabitants as possible.

ELI'EZER LIVNEH'S PROPOSALS (JUNE–AUGUST 1967)

The new Israeli empire of 11 June 1967 thrilled Eli'ezer Livneh who, like other leaders of WLIM, represented a Zionist school of territorial maximalism, for which security was not the primary reason for holding on to the newly occupied territories. Livneh's mystical ideas on the territorial issue show a great affinity with the messianic ideas of the incipient settlement movement of Gush Emunim.[49]

Livneh's proposal to remove over half a million Palestinian refugees from the Gaza Strip and the West Bank was first put forward in the mass-circulation daily *Ma'ariv* on 22 June 1967. 'They will choose, willingly, resettlement in whatever Arab country, or emigration to countries overseas. The Prime Minister of Australia has already suggested cooperation,' he wrote. A few weeks later Livneh reiterated his proposal: 'The refugees are now within our boundaries. We could rehabilitate some of them in our country [in Sinai], and transfer others for productive life overseas or resettle them in neighbouring countries with which we will come to an arrangement ... Jordan ... is likely to be the chief beneficiary [to be able] to populate its wide territories.'[50] Livneh developed his proposal further into a plan in an article in the liberal daily *Haaretz* on 28 August 1967. In the last 19 years, Livneh wrote:

> ... tens of thousands of refugees have crossed ... to Saudi Arabia, Kuwait, Bahrain, Qatar, Abu Dhabi, Dubai and the [other] oil principalities. Tens of thousands of their families, who have remained in the camps have lived off money remitted by their distant relatives ... Just as half a million Jews immigrated to the Land of Israel from Arab countries ... hundreds of thousands of 'Palestinian' Arabs were crossing to Arab countries. The parallel is amazing ... What is happening in the refugee camps in a sporadic and limited way without the support of a governmental body [in Arab states] should be widened and developed by us from the side of dimensions and means. This means: 1) constructive emigration should be directed to all the countries in need of a workforce including the United States, Canada, Australia and Latin America; b) the emigrants would be entitled to financial support from Israel ...; c) the implementation must be planned for a prolonged time, let us say 18 years; d) the number of countries designated for migration and resettlement should be as large as possible.

'If these Arabs [would-be transferees] would want to maintain their Arabness in the United States, Canada, Brazil and Australia', it is up to them, Livneh wrote. Livneh made another little 'concession': 'To the extent that there might be a number of refugees who want, in spite of everything, to experience striking agricultural roots in a landscape close to their spirit and tradition, it is worth offering them settlement in northern Sinai ... in the opinion of cautious experts there are there water, land and other conditions for the settlement of tens of thousands of families (approximately 60,000 persons).'

Livneh argued that the 'carrying out of the [transfer] task' depended mainly on Israel and on the conditions it could create:

> ... a) 'the allocation of large sums; b) patience. If we spend 5,000 dollars on the emigration of a family of 6–7 persons on average (1500 dollars on the journey, and the rest for the exclusive control of the emigrating family) we would be able to finance every year the emigration of tens of thousands of families, or 60–70,000 persons by 50 million dollars (or 150 million Israeli Lira, 3 per cent of our state budget). There would be no lack of candidates and they would increase when encouraging information from abroad

on the settlement of the first ones arrived ... if we placed such encouragement sums ... within 8–9 years about 600,000 persons would be likely to emigrate at this pace, meaning all the refugees from the [Gaza] Strip, the Hebron mountain, the mountains of Ephraim [in the West Bank] and the Jordan valley.

While in his earlier proposal Livneh had suggested that the world powers should finance the transfer and resettlement, in the August plan he proposed that Israel should shoulder 'financing the project':

... there is no need to explain its importance from the national, security and propaganda point of view. It should be placed at the top of our national priorities. In so far as we need for it [financial] means greater than the estimate given here, we are entitled to appeal to world Jewry. This is more justified and blessed than the use of fund-raising to raise the standard of living [of Israelis] ... The Jews of the Diaspora will respond to this in understanding, and even in enthusiasm.

For Livneh, the success of the 'project' would depend on its

planning in the long term. In the beginning there will certainly be various difficulties of running it ... Our reckoning should not be for one month or one season. We will develop the project on our responsibility, without making it conditional upon the participation of other elements. To the extent that we carry it out we will gain the cooperation of others. The United Nations action in the refugee camps (UNRWA) would then assume constructive and purposeful meaning ... the training in the schools of UNRWA would be adjusted to the needs of emigration and resettlement.

From other references it is obvious that Livneh was not content with the removal of 600,000 Arab refugees from Palestine, as he put forward in his euphemistically-termed 'emigration project', but sought to transform the demographic and political reality of the occupied territories by clearing out other residents as well.[51] What is also noticeable is the absence of any discussion in his plan of the resistance the Palestinians would be likely to put up to foil such a mass removal. Such a deliberate attempt to ignore Palestinian resistance to transfer is common to several transfer proposals and plans put forward publicly in the euphoric period following the conquests of the 1967 war.

YISRAEL ELDAD (1910–96): A JEWISH STATE STRETCHING FROM THE NILE TO THE EUPHRATES

Dr Yisrael Eldad and the poet Uri Tzvi Greenberg were the most extremist right-wing founding members of WLIM. Eldad, in particular, espoused one of the most extreme positions with respect to the destined borders of the State of Israel. Echoing Avraham Stern's vision of the establishment of a Jewish empire across the Middle East, Eldad was well-known for his advocacy, throughout the 1950s and 1960s, of a Jewish state stretching from the Nile to the Euphrates. In the early 1970s, he still argued for territorial expansion that would at least include the modern state of Jordan and Sinai under Jewish sovereignty. [52] Judging that 'the map of the Middle East is still very much in a state of flux', Eldad believed that Israel 'will yet help many an oppressed minority to attain its independence and in turn redraw the map' of the region.[53] Although subsequently Eldad scaled down his objectives to focus on Israel's 'judaisation' of the West Bank and Gaza, in 1985 he still argued that Israel's northern border should be the Litani River in south Lebanon.[54]

A founding member of the Revisionist Betar movement, Eldad immigrated to Palestine in 1941, joining Lehi, the most militant of the Jewish underground groups, and editing its publications *Hazit* and *Hama'as*. He was soon considered the ideologue of the movement, whose political programme called for the 'transfer' of the Palestinian Arabs to neighbouring states. After Avraham Stern's death, Eldad was one of the triumvirate that ran the group, along with Yitzhak Shamir (later to become Prime Minister) and Natan Yellin-Mor. In April 1948, Lehi took part in a premeditated, murderous assault on the Arab village of Dayr Yasin, in western Jerusalem, in which 250 residents, mostly women, elderly people and children, were slaughtered. Most historians consider the Dayr Yasin massacre as one of the major single factors precipitating Arab exodus in 1948. In September of the same year, Lehi assassinated the United Nations Mediator for Palestine Count Folke Bernadotte in Jerusalem. According to Israeli historian Amitzur Ilan, the decision to murder Bernadotte was taken by the Centre of Lehi, which consisted of the trio: Yellin-Mor, Shamir and Eldad.[55]

After the establishment of the State of Israel, Eldad's political agitation for maximum territorial expansionism remained confined to the fringe of Israeli politics. Only after Israel's spectacular conquests of 1967 were his views accepted as 'relevant and legitimate'[56] and he became a regular columnist for the daily *Haaretz* and *Yedi'ot Aharonot*. In the 1950s he was appointed lecturer in humanities at the Technion and he also launched the monthly *Sulam* ('Ladder') in which he espoused a Zionist philosophy advocating the eventual establishment of the Kingdom of Israel ('Malkhut Yisrael'), or Jewish rule over all the 'biblical land' from the Nile to the Euphrates and strongly attacked the then Mapai-led government for not adopting territorial maximalism as an official policy.[57] Eldad used to print in *Sulam* a map of the 'Land of Israel' which included Transjordan and the Syrian capital Damascus. The main theme of Eldad's writings was that Israel had to conquer the 'entire land of Israel' by force, in a process that would inevitably involve blood, glory and honour.[58] For Eldad the 1967 conquests were a step in that direction. In conjunction with this territorial maximalism, Eldad called shortly after the 1967 conquests for 'total Arab emigration' from all the territories under Israeli control.[59] In 1990, 23 years later, Eldad was still calling for 'the ['organised'] transfer of the vast majority of the Arabs of the Land of Israel [presumably including the Arab citizens] to one of the countries which is their real historical homeland'; 'the Arab countries must receive one million Arabs and settle them'; 'there are those who are shocked by the term "transfer". So let them say "population exchange", "resettlement", "return to their ancient homeland in the Arabian peninsula".' For Eldad, while the euphemism changes according to the circumstances, the goal of wholesale Arab removal must not be a hidden agenda but rather placed at the top of the official agenda as a declared objective.[60]

The question of what to do with the Palestinian population in the 'liberated' territories was an obsessional topic in Eldad's writings. In an article entitled 'The Realpolitik of Our Sages', published by the Gush Emunim's Department of Information, Eldad maintained that the Palestinians faced the same problem as the Canaanites of old. He explained that the choice which he would like them to make was by no means new to political Zionism: 'the transfer as a Zionist solution',[61] was put forward by mainstream Zionist leaders such as Nahman Syrkin, Israel Zangwill, Yitzhak Tabenkin, David Ben-Gurion, Avraham Stern[62] and Avraham Schwadron. According to

Eldad, while 'Jewish morality' disallowed outright mass expulsion except in time of war, the best course of action would be to bring about mass emigration through the deliberate creation of economic hardship in the territories. Earlier, shortly after the 1967 war, he put it more bluntly:

> Had it not been for Deir Yasin [sic], half a million Arabs would be living in the state of Israel. The state of Israel would not have existed. We must not disregard this, with full awareness of the responsibility involved. All wars are cruel. There is no way out of that. This country will either be Eretz-Israel with an absolute Jewish majority and a small Arab minority, or Eretz-Ishmael, and Jewish emigration will begin again, if we do not expel the Arabs one way or another, and men of the spirit should tell how to do that.[63]

Eldad's 'transfer/ethnic cleansing' advocacy rested on the implicit racist assumption that the indigenous inhabitants of Palestine did not have the human and political rights that are naturally accorded to Jews. However, like other protagonists of maximalist Zionism and annexationist policies, his self-justification is couched in 'rational' argumentation and stems from his awareness that the annexation of the territories with their Arab population could end up in the creation of a bi-national state or even an 'Ishmael State'. He implies that unless the Arab population is expelled – made to flee by means of terrorism as in Dayr Yasin, and by the deliberate creation of economic distress – Greater Israel could in reality be transformed into a bi-national state. Hence, terrorism and massacres (such as Dayr Yasin) are neither a punishment nor a deterrent; they are a political instrument designed to precipitate 'transfer' which is the logical and 'rational' conclusion of the policy that aims at annexation.

Eldad's views do not appear to have been moderated since the early 1970s nor has his agitation for mass expulsion abated.[64] After the founding of the 'Transfer Party' of Rehava'am Zeevi in 1988, Eldad became a regular contributor to its magazine *Moledet* on this issue.[65] On 26 March 1989, Eldad gave an interview to the IDF (Israeli Defence Force) radio station, concentrating largely on the 'transfer' theme in Zionism. To a question from the interviewer Dan Patir on whether Eldad was the first to propose after the 1967 war 'a solution of the Palestinian problem' through means of transferring the Arabs, Eldad replied:

This is a great honour that I do not deserve. The idea is of greater men before me. If someone was telling me that the idea/solution was my brainchild, I would have wanted to receive for that the Nobel Prize or at least the Israel Prize, because this idea is a great idea! ... This is the most humane and acceptable solution. And also the most efficient one ... this idea was put forward by Berl Katznelson and Arthur Ruppin, respectable, liberal and democratic Zionists. Here we are not talking about their expulsion to some other state, but their transfer to a state of their brothers, to Arabs, to 22 Arab states ... We must help [carrying out] this thing. Otherwise there will be a catastrophe here, a terrible war for all sides.[66]

To a question about whether there is a Palestinian nation, Eldad replied: 'I very much loved the statement of Golda Meir regarding the Palestinians: There is no such a people.' Eldad was referring to the views expressed by the late Prime Minister Golda Meir of the Labour Party in her famous aphorism that 'It was not as though there was a Palestinian people in Palestine considering itself as a Palestinian people and we came and threw them out and took their country away from them. They did not exist.'[67] Eldad further asserted that the transfer must begin with the Arab refugees:

Anyway the refugees are displaced. If the refugee resides in Balata or Dehayshe [two refugee camps on the West Bank[68]] or any other camp, let us suppose that there are not many among us who would agree to his return to Jaffa or Acre. Kibbutz Ma'abarot would not return, God forbid, the lands to the Arabs who had lived there before and now are in Sabra and Chatila. And our notables at the University in Ramat Aviv [Tel Aviv University] which is situated on the site of Shaykh Muannis village would not, in their goodness, and much humanitarianism, give up the university and return it to the refugees in Sabra and Chatila.[69]

Eldad added that although he did not suggest the implementation of 'transfer' by force, such forcible methods would be sanctioned 'during wartime as in 1948'.[70]

In the 1980s, Eldad was also a founding member of the ultra-nationalist Tehiya Party but did not accept a place on its Knesset list. More recently and towards the end of his life, his uncompromising Greater Israel ideology led him vehemently to oppose the Oslo accords in numerous articles published in many respected Israeli newspapers. Eldad was also a recipient of the Bialik and Tcherni-chowsky Prizes and became a 'Distinguished Citizen of Jerusalem'.

TZVI SHILOAH'S PROPOSALS

Tzvi Shiloah, a veteran of the Mapai Party and former deputy mayor of the town of Herzliyah, was Chairman of WLIM. He was appointed by David Ben-Gurion as acting editor of the Mapai daily *Hador*, serving in this post from 1949 to 1954. He was also a member of the Central Committee of the ruling Mapai Party between 1949 and 1965. Between 1965 and 1968, he joined the Rafi List – which was headed by David Ben-Gurion and Moshe Dayan – and, together with Haim Hertzog, President of Israel between 1982 and 1993, was a member of its country-wide secretariat. From 1968 to 1973, he rejoined the Labour Party. Between 1973 and 1977 he became a member of the Likud–La'am List and remained a member of the Likud executive until his resignation in November 1977. Later, he became a founding member of the far-right Tehiya Party and its Knesset member (the Tenth Knesset) before ending up as a co-founder and ideologue of the extreme right-wing party Moledet. He also edited *Zot Haaretz* ('This is the Land'), WLIM's periodical, first published in April 1968, on the establishment of the Jewish settlement in Hebron[71] and wrote a weekly column in the mass-circulation Hebrew daily *Yedi'ot Aharonot*.

Shortly after the 1967 conquests, while he was still a member of the Labour Rafi faction, Shiloah wrote an article in the Histadrut daily *Davar* arguing for mass Arab expulsion:

> ... hundreds of thousands of Arabs are residing in the liberated territory ... the inclusion of this hostile population within the boundaries of the State of Israel is considered as a time-bomb in the heart of the state .... Leaving them in these territories endangers the state and its national Jewish character ... the only solution is to organize their emigration and settlement in Arab countries abundant in land and water such as Syria and Iraq.

Shiloah reminded the readers that the 'transfer' of Palestinian Arabs as a Zionist solution had already been advocated by Zionist leaders in the mandatory period, citing the 'transfer' proposal to Iraq and the al-Jazirah province in Syria put forward by 'Akiva Ettinger who headed the Land Settlement Department of the Zionist Executive (1918–25) and the Land Acquisition Department of the Jewish National Fund (1926–36).[72] Moreover, in private conversation with his colleagues (including former mayor of Kfar Saba and MK Mordechai Sorkis), also shortly after the June 1967 war, Shiloah expressed the view that Israel had lost the war 'because we didn't follow the Rambam [Maimonides'] advice regarding an enemy city under siege, and we did not leave one exit open for population exodus from the besieged city, and first of all from the capital Jerusalem ... it was clear to me ... that we were receiving a hostile Arab population that we wouldn't be able to digest in our state, and especially in our capital.'[73] For Shiloah, Israel failed to exploit the 1967 war to drive most of the Arabs out in the way Ben-Gurion had done in the 1948 war.[74]

Shiloah says that his advocacy of 'transfer' dates back to the mandatory period. During those days he was inspired by the ideology of, and worked together with, another strident public campaigner for Arab 'transfer', Avraham Schwadron.[75] Schwadron, who immigrated to Palestine in 1926, was a Zionist journalist, publicist and founder of the collection of Jewish autographs and portraits now in the Jewish National and University Library in Jerusalem, in which he worked for many years. Schwadron formulated and defined his outlook as the 'Theory of Cruel Zionism' and spelt it out in a series of articles published in *Davar*, the semi-official daily of the Histadrut and the dominant Mapai Party of the Yishuv. Schwadron's Zionist thinking included the view that no one who did not immigrate to Palestine could call himself a Zionist and that the projected Jewish state should be set up in the 'whole Land of Israel', including both sides of the Jordan River.[76] He also engaged in fierce polemics with a group of intellectuals from the Hebrew University with connections to Brit Shalom who advocated Jewish–Arab *rapprochement* based on minimal Zionism. In Schwadron's view, a solution to the Arab question can only be through mass 'transfer'.[77] Until his death in 1957, he continued to propagate single-mindedly his views on territorial maximalism and the 'transfer' of the Arab citizens of Israel. After the establishment of the Israeli state, he sent his articles to Tzvi Shiloah, the acting editor of the Mapai daily *Hador*, for publication. Apparently one article which was published caused an uproar and Shiloah was forced to halt the publication of these articles. 'Unfortunately', Shiloah writes, 'I was unable to print [these articles] in the Mapai daily, although I myself agreed with everything he wrote. I explained to him my reasoning: publishing an article written in such a spirit ... is likely to be interpreted as indirect consent on the part of the party and the state's leadership to the transfer solution.'[78]

Shiloah's imperial Israel also found its title-deed in the Bible. He envisioned the parameters of Greater Israel stretching broadly across the whole region. In his book, *A Great Land for a Great People*, published in 1970, Shiloah, while still a member of the Labour Party, restates his adherence to the Zionist doctrine of Schwadron and to the claim of a future Jewish state in the 'whole Land of Israel' on both sides of the Jordan River, encompassing the modern state of Jordan. He also calls for the occupation and annexation of southern Lebanon up to the Litani River. Shiloah, however, disagrees with Yisrael Eldad on the need to occupy the Syrian capital Damascus and incorporate it together with other parts of Syria into Greater Israel. Although he agrees with Eldad that the boundaries of the 'historic Land of Israel encompass parts of Syria including the city of Damascus', because Damascus occupies an important place in Arab history, if it were to be occupied by the Israeli Army, it should only be held temporarily as a means of pressure on the Arabs.[79]

On the basis of this imperial vision, Shiloah envisioned a military, political and economic reorganisation of the whole Arab East based on two federations, built out of 'ethnic mini-states' into which Syria, Iraq and Lebanon would eventually dissolve. The northern federation would include most of what is now the central and northern parts of Lebanon and Syria plus northern and eastern Iraq. The southern federation, dominated and led by Israel, would include what is now Israel and Jordan together with southern Lebanon and Syria, western and eastern Iraq, and Kuwait. This Israeli-led federation would become the 'United States of the Middle East', and emerge as an industrial, technological and military power of major international importance. Together with Turkey and Iran, this federation would form the 'geo-strategic axis of the entire area'.[80]

Shiloah also discusses the application of the 'transfer' solution to the Palestinian-Israeli conflict, while reviewing, and drawing inspiration and legitimacy from, those earlier proposals and plans put forward by mainstream and 'socialist' Zionist leaders, such as Dr Arthur Ruppin, David Ben-Gurion, Berl Katznelson, Dr Max Nordau and 'Akiva Ettinger. He castigates the left-wing Mapam Party for making 'demography' an argument for returning the territories 'liberated' in the 1967 war:[81] 'the entire history of Zionism is a continuous struggle to change the face of demography in this country. To this all trends in Zionism agreed, including Brit Shalom.'[82] He also cites Berl Katznelson's polemics with the Hashomer Hatza'ir movement – which later constituted the main component of the Mapam Party – in the pre-1948 period as the standard Labour Zionism apologia in justification of Arab removal:

> There could be possible situations that would make [Arab] population transfer from here desirable for both sides, and who is the socialist who is interested in rejecting the very idea beforehand and stigmatising it as something unfair? Has Merhavyah[83] not been built on transfer? Were the [Arab] inhabitants of Fuleh[84] not transferred from one place to another? ... Were it not for many of these transfers Hashomer Hatza'ir would not be residing in Merhavyah or in Mishmar Ha'emek[85] and other places. And if what has been done for a settlement of Mishmar Ha'emek is a fair deed, why would it not be fair when done on a much larger and greater scale, not only for Hashomer Hatza'ir but for the whole of Israel?[86]

In spite of the Arab states' opposition to 'transfer', Shiloah writes, 'in the end the transfer idea will materialise, either within a peace settlement or as a result of a war.'[87] He interpreted the announcement of the late Prime Minister Levi Eshkol immediately after the 1967 war that the refugee problem could only be solved through regional cooperation as leading naturally to transfer: 'The only meaning of these things is that when peace comes [with the Arab states] ... the refugees of the Land of Israel will be settled, for the benefit of all sides, in a sparsely populated Arab state abundant in land, water and oil, such as Iraq. And what is good for the refugees, is desirable – under the conditions of peace! – also for most of the Arab population of the Land of Israel.'[88] In fact, Shiloah makes no distinction between the Arab citizens of Israel and those of the occupied territories: 'The demographic demon is also threatening us in the State of Israel within the Green Line borders ... the demographic problem is threatening us in all situations. And it will not be weakened but will be stronger, whether because of the natural growth of the Arabs or because of the rise in their economic level in Israel.'[89]

Like many ultra-nationalist Zionists who have been traditionally in favour of conquering Jordan, Shiloah believes that there will never be any coexistence and peace between Arabs and Israeli Jews[90] in a Jewish state which would have to expand eastwards across the Jordan River into the 'whole Land of Israel' over which Jews have 'exclusive' rights. Even the native population of the Jordanian state is earmarked for dispossession and 'transfer' to Iraq and other distant Arab countries:

> Certainly, there would be many who would oppose giving up Transjordan when the Israeli Defence Forces occupy the Gila'ad, Rabat Amon [Amman], Moav and Edom[91] as a result of a war which will be forced on us ... there will be no escape from uniting the Land of Israel ... and the solutions which will be good for the Arabs of the western Land of Israel [Palestine] will be good for the Arabs on both sides of the [River] Jordan. In both cases Jewish 'aliya' [immigration] to the Land of Israel and Arab emigration from the Land of Israel – all the more so an organised transfer – will solve the [demographic] problem.[92]

The implication of Shiloah's views is that the next step for like-minded territorial maximalists would be to plan to conquer the eastern side of the River Jordan valley and the mountains of northern Jordan, and then to rush in with their biblical, strategic and demographic arguments in defence of Jewish settlement and Arab removal.

The advocacy of 'transferring' the Palestinians, the Jordanians, the Lebanese from southern Lebanon up to the Litani River and some Syrians by an old-timer of Labour Zionism, who in 1970 was still a member of the Labour Party and described himself as a 'socialist' Zionist, is one of the most extreme attitudes towards the Arabs ever adopted in Zionist history, resembling the views espoused by Avraham Stern. Moreover, all the evidence indicates that Shiloah has anything but moderated his views. In 1988, he was still arguing that expulsion of the Palestinians would be a humane and practical solution.[93] A year later he wrote 'the transfer idea has become now more vital and more actual than it has been at any time in the past'; 'the transfer proposal must be raised at every international forum'; it is possible to 'acquire supporters for the idea by its constant presentation'.[94] Shiloah's self-confessed advocacy of 'compulsory transfer' is expressed in the following statement: 'Some claim that I have spoken for voluntary transfer: Who wants to leave his home voluntarily?' And in justification of outright expulsion he says, 'In 1948, we deliberately, and not just in the heat of the war, expelled Arabs. Also in [19]67 after the Six Day War, we expelled many Arabs.'[95] Two years later Shiloah wrote an article in *Haaretz* (19 March 1990), arguing that there is absolutely

... no remedy to the demographic problem ... either in the Whole Land of Israel ... or within the Green Line boundaries apart from population transfer in order to create a homogenous Jewish state. Such a solution is likely to come after a Lebanese-style civil war or through peace agreement ... population exchange in the Land of Israel would have to take place within a wide regional framework. This is a very realistic forecast ... The State of Israel would have to think how to join this process, and it is possible that because of its grave existential situation it is likely to be the pioneer of that.

Shiloah believes, like many exponents of total transfer, that a future war should be exploited to bring about Arab removal; 'The big question is how we should be prepared when the [opportunity] of crisis time will come ... Since the days of Rome this slogan has been accepted: he who wants peace prepares for war. And we should paraphrase this: he who wants true peace must think about transfer.'[96]

In 1988, Shiloah became the ideologue of the Moledet Party, the single-minded 'transfer' party of Rehava'am Zeevi, who was minister without portfolio in the Likud Cabinet until 1992. In fact, Moledet was conceived at a meeting held at Shiloah's flat in Herzliyah in March 1987 which was attended by Generals Zeevi and Yehoshu'a Saguy (formerly a Likud MK), Professors Yair Sprintzak (later a Moledet MK) and Eli'ezer Schweid of WLIM, and Tzvi Bar, the mayor of Ramat Gan.[97] Shiloah was also offered the number two place, after Zeevi, on the Moledet list for the 1988 election to the Knesset, but he turned it down, preferring to concentrate on the propagation of his maximalist ideas in writing and to be treated as the ideologue of the new party. One of his recent books, *The Guilt of Jerusalem* (1989), which dwells on Greater Israel and ethnic cleansing, and rehashes many standard Zionist arguments in justification, was described in the official bulletin of the Moledet Party as an 'obligatory' book for all party activists and sympathisers.[98]

The planning and financing of the earliest Jewish settlement in the West Bank – the Hebron/Kiryat Arba'a settlement which was established in the spring of 1968 under the leadership of the future leaders of Gush Emunim – was provided by WLIM.[99] However, after the 1973 war, WLIM was rapidly eclipsed by Gush Emunim, which aspired to lead a mass movement for the purpose of not only influencing government settlement policies in the occupied territories, but also of transforming the cultural and ideological foundations of Israeli society by its Neo-Zionist orientation. Formally founded in 1974 and often seen as its natural successor, Gush Emunim absorbed many participants from WLIM. Encouraging the participation of secular ultra-nationalists in its settlement and 'redemption of the whole Land of Israel', Gush Emunim emerged as the focus of organised Israeli territorial maximalism and Jewish fundamentalism from the mid-1970s onwards. By 1977, WLIM and its newspaper, *Zot Haaretz*, had virtually ceased to exist. Much of its programme and many of its supporters were later incorporated into the Israeli secular and religious right, including the Tehiya, Moledet and Tzomet parties, the National Religious Party and the Likud, in addition to Gush Emunim.

2
Zionist Revisionism and the Likud: From Jabotinsky to Netanyahu

JABOTINSKY'S LEGACY

The main division within Zionism has been between the Labour and the Revisionist movements. The latter, the forerunner of the present-day Likud, was established by Vladimir (Zeev) Jabotinsky in 1925 and advocated the 'revision' of the Palestine British Mandate to include Transjordan as well as Palestine.[1] Many Israeli and pro-Zionist authors still propagate the myth that the Palestine Mandate had encompassed both Palestine and Transjordan, an area within which the 'promised' 'Jewish National Home' of the Balfour Declaration of 1917 might be established. The myth of the so-called 'partition of Palestine' in 1921–22, encouraged mainly by Revisionist Zionists,[2] instilled the belief that in 1921–22 the British 'betrayed' the Zionist movement by 'separating' Palestine from Transjordan (the East Bank of the Jordan River), and by establishing the Arab Hashemite Emirate on 80 per cent of the 'Jewish National Home'.[3] However, while most Labour Zionists came to terms with the Hashemite state in Transjordan and sought a tacit alliance with its ruler, among these the commitment remained strong to the principle of establishing a Jewish state in all Mandatory Palestine – in Zionist terminology, 'the western Land of Israel', that is, from the Jordan River to the Mediterranean Sea.

In contrast to the pragmatic and gradualist expansionism of Labour Zionism, with its perception of political reality and what was possible under local, regional and international conditions, Revisionist Zionism has always been known for its maximalist political aims, which during the Mandatory period included the establishment of a Jewish state ('Malchut Yisrael' or the 'Kingdom of Israel') on both sides of the Jordan River. While Labour Zionism concentrated on numerous objectives at the same time, the

Revisionists focused on one idea: the 'territorial integrity of *Eretz-Yisrael* in its biblical boundaries', which was the hallmark of Jabotinsky's largely 'monistic' ideology, an ideology which also embraced militant right-wing nationalism and the celebration of military prowess. In 1935, the Revisionist Party, bitterly protesting at the so-called 'separation' of Transjordan from Palestine and violently opposing the idea of any sort of partition, left the World Zionist Organisation and declared its unswerving devotion to the principle of establishing Jewish sovereignty on 'both banks of the Jordan'.

With regard to the ultimate solutions related to the 'Arab problem' in Palestine, Jabotinsky (1880–1940) frequently accused Labour Zionism of hypocrisy; in his view, the creation of a Jewish state had always meant imposing the will of Zionism on the Palestinian Arabs, and the resistance of the latter to the former was but the natural and logical consequence of Zionist objectives. In the 1920s, Jabotinsky wrote that Zionist settlement had always been carried out against the wishes of the Arab majority in Palestine:

> Zionist colonisation, even the most restricted, must either be terminated or carried out in defiance of the will of the native population. This colonisation can, therefore, continue and develop only under the protection of a force independent of the local population – an iron wall which the native population cannot break through. This is, *in toto*, our policy towards the Arabs. To formulate it any other way would be a hypocrisy.

Jabotinsky propagated his concept of an 'iron wall' of Jewish military might which would protect Greater Israel. He also argued that Zionists believed in an 'iron wall': 'In this sense, there are no meaningful differences between our "militarists" and our "vegetarians". One prefers an iron wall of Jewish bayonets, the other proposes an agreement with Baghdad [that is, Faysal I's Iraq], and appears to be satisfied with Baghdad's bayonets – a strange and somewhat risky taste – but we all applaud, day and night, the iron wall.'[4]

The 'iron wall' concept was to form a central plank in the Revisionists' attitude towards the Palestinians from the 1920s to the present-day Likud. Jabotinsky consistently ignored the nationalist aspirations of the Palestinians (the 'Arabs of the Land of Israel', in Revisionist terminology): agreement with them was neither desirable or necessary; on the contrary, confrontation with them was natural and inevitable and would be resolved only by the creation of an 'iron wall', that is, a militant, homogenous and organic Jewish state on both sides of the Jordan River.[5] In Jabotinsky's mind, to conclude an agreement with the Palestinians allowing the creation of a predominantly Jewish majority and eventual statehood in Palestine – which Labour Zionism publicly advocated in the 1920s – was neither possible nor desirable. Only an 'iron wall', of a Jewish armed garrison, would be able to secure Jewish sovereignty over Greater Israel.[6]

Jabotinsky was, evidently, a proponent of 'population transfer'. In a letter, dated November 1939, to one of his Revisionist colleagues in the United States – and written against the background of the German–Soviet pact of August 1939 – he wrote: 'There is no choice: the Arabs must make room for the Jews in Eretz Israel. If it was possible to transfer the Baltic peoples, it is also possible to move the Palestinian Arabs', adding that Iraq and Saudi Arabia could absorb them.[7] Jabotinsky also alluded in a number of articles to the Greco-Turkish 'transfer' in the early 1920s, describing it as a brutal, coercive action imposed by the victorious Turks but which proved ultimately beneficial to the Greeks.[8]

Typically, Jabotinsky expressed racist contempt towards the indigenous inhabitants of Palestine, and, unlike the leaders of Labour Zionism, he did not mince his words: 'We Jews, thank God, have nothing to do with the East ... The Islamic soul must be broomed out of Eretz-Yisrael.'[9] On another occasion Jabotinsky described Arabs and Muslims as a 'yelling rabble dressed up in gaudy, savage rags'.[10]

The Revisionist movement founded by Jabotinsky went through an ongoing process of fragmentation and coalescence. The authoritarian and militarist tendencies and the cult of personality which Jabotinsky absorbed from the growth of the far right in Europe during the interwar period were transmitted to, and enthusiastically received by, his disciples in Betar, the Revisionist movement's youth group.[11] Jabotinsky's ideological legacy found expression in two offshoots. The first was the Irgun Tzvai Leumi (National Military Organisation, or the Irgun), an underground military organisation formed in 1931 and commanded from 1943 to 1944 by Menahem Begin (later to become Prime Minister), who assumed the leadership of Revisionist Zionism with Jabotinsky's death in 1940. The Irgun became closely associated with the bombing of the King David Hotel in 1946, the hanging of British Army sergeants and the massacre of Palestinians at Dayr Yasin in April 1948. The second offshoot was Lehi (Lohamei Herut Yisrael, also known as the Stern Gang after its founder, Avraham Stern), which broke away from the Irgun in June 1940. From 1942 onwards, Lehi was co-commanded by Yitzhak Shamir – later to become Likud leader and Prime Minister – who had arrived in Palestine in 1935 and had become the chief of operations of Lehi. Shamir's belief in the importance of political assassination is evident from the fact that his work involved the planning and carrying-out of numerous assassinations and individual terrorist attacks: between September 1942 and July 1946, when Shamir was finally arrested by the British and exiled to Eritrea, there were 14 assassination attempts, including seven attempts on the life of the British High Commissioner for Palestine, Sir Harold McMichael, and several more were planned, for example, against Ernest Bevin, the British Foreign Secretary. One successful attempt on the life of the Cairo-based British Minister Resident in the Middle East, Lord Moyne, was carried out in 1944.[12]

The founder of Lehi, Avraham Stern (1907–42), had emigrated to Palestine in 1925; in the late 1920s, he went to Florence on a scholarship, returning to Palestine in the early 1930s as a fascist. Until his death in 1942, Stern was firmly convinced that the Axis powers were going to win the war. In 1940–41, he contacted Italian and German agents in the Middle East, proposing collaboration for solving the 'European Jewish problem', outside Europe.[13] Stern had also instilled in Lehi the notion that the 'Land of Canaan' had been conquered by the ancient Israelites' sword. Like Jabotinsky, Stern's right-wing orientation regarded a clash between the Hebrew and Arab worlds as unavoidable. He also described the Palestinian Arabs as 'beasts of the desert, not a legitimate people'.[14] 'The Arabs are not a nation but a mole that grew in the wilderness of the eternal desert. They are nothing but murderers,' wrote Stern in 1940.[15]

Stern's maximalist territorial ambitions and mystical inclination led him inevitably to the Bible rather than to the British Palestine Mandate when defining the boundaries of the envisioned Jewish empire in the Middle East. His 'Eighteen Principles of National Renewal', which was written in 1941, and became the ideological basis of Lehi, proclaimed a Jewish state from 'the great River of Egypt' (the Nile) to the Euphrates in Iraq and the rebuilding of the Third Temple in Jerusalem.[16] In this document, under the heading, 'Principles of Rebirth', the borders of the Land were defined by a quotation from Genesis (15:18): 'To your seed, I have given this Land from the River of Egypt to the Great River, the Euphrates ...' The third principle in the document stated: 'THE NATION AND ITS

HOMELAND: The Land of Israel was conquered by the Jews by the sword. It was here they became a nation and only here can they be reborn. Not only has Israel the right of ownership over the land but this ownership is absolute and has never been or can ever be rescinded.'[17] The fourteenth principle proposed 'ethnic cleansing': 'DEALING WITH ALIENS [that is, the Palestinian Arabs]: This will be done by means of exchange of populations.' The sixteenth principle envisaged the establishment of a new Jewish imperial power in the region: 'Strengthening the nation by developing it into a major military, political, cultural and economic power in the East and on the shores of the Mediterranean'.[18] Lehi also advocated that any Arab resistance to Zionist objectives should be crushed mercilessly. Moreover, in its memorandum to the United Nations Special Commission on Palestine (UNSCOP) in 1947 as well as in its political programme of July–August 1948 in preparation for the first Israeli Knesset election,[19] Lehi called for the compulsory evacuation of the entire Arab population of Palestine, preferably to Iraq, and declared it 'considers an exchange of the Arab population and the Jews of Arab countries as the best solution for the troubled relationship between the Jewish people and the Arabs'.[20]

The Revisionist groups were instrumental in exacerbating Jewish–Arab tensions and violent clashes during the Mandatory period. Jabotinsky himself endorsed the terrorist campaign launched in the late 1930s by the Irgun, a campaign that involved such actions as placing bomb-loaded vegetable barrows in crowded Arab markets in Haifa and Jerusalem and firing indiscriminately on Arab civilian houses.[21] While Irgun's bombing attacks of the late 1930s and 1948 were aimed at Palestinian civilians, the group also launched attacks against the British from 1944 to 1948. Lehi, it has already been shown, specialised in political assassinations. Later, during the 1948 war, these campaigns were intensified and played an important role in the exodus of the Palestinians from what became the State of Israel. The most infamous outrage carried out jointly by the Irgun and Lehi was the Dayr Yasin massacre of 9 April 1948, in which some 250 Palestinian villagers were murdered in cold blood. The Dayr Yasin massacre was perhaps the most important single factor precipitating the 1948 Palestinian exodus.[22] Dr Yisrael Eldad, who was in charge of Lehi's ideology and propaganda, regarded the Dayr Yasin massacre as an authentic expression of Lehi as a right-wing political movement. Eldad explained that the massacre articulated the need to 'transform Jerusalem into the

Archimedean point of the Hebrew revolution' and more specifically he was convinced that 'without Deir Yasin [sic] the State of Israel could never have been established.'[23]

THE PROPOSALS OF JABOTINSKY'S DISCIPLES

The following will discuss proposals and plans put forward by two close associates of Jabotinsky in the period leading to the Palestinian exodus of 1948–49.

Eliahu Ben-Horin's Proposal and Campaign, 1943–49

Eliahu Ben-Horin was a Revisionist publicist, a close associate of Jabotinsky, and an editor of the Yishuv's Hebrew newspaper *Doar Hayom*. In 1935, when the Revisionists seceded from the World Zionist Organisation, Ben-Horin was elected to the world executive of the New Zionist Organisation led by Jabotinsky, operating out of London from 1937 to 1940 and from New York from 1940 to 1943. After the Second World War, Ben-Horin served as adviser to the American Zionist Emergency Council, which was then chaired by Abba Hillel Silver, and continued to lobby for Zionist causes in the United States.

In 1943, three years after Jabotinsky's death, Ben-Horin's plan for Arab 'transfer' to Iraq or a 'united Iraq–Syrian state', was publicly put forward in his book *The Middle East: Crossroads of History*.[24] The plan was important mainly because it served as the basis of former US President Herbert Hoover's own transfer plan of 1945.[25] Not surprisingly, Ben-Horin's arguments bear the stamp of his mentor, Jabotinsky. As a maximalist Revisionist Zionist who believed in the establishment of a Jewish state on both sides of the Jordan River, Ben-Horin wrote:

> I suggest that the Arabs of Palestine and Transjordania be transferred to Iraq, or a united Iraq-Syrian state. That means the shifting about 1,200,000 persons. A larger number were involved in the Greco-Turkish exchange of population; many more in the internal shifts in Russia ...
>
> The Palestinian Arabs will not be removed to a foreign land but an Arab land ... The distance between their old and new homelands

is small, involving no crossing of oceans or seas, and the climatic conditions are the same. If the transfer and the colonization project are well planned and systematically carried out, the Palestinian fellah will get better soil and more promising life conditions than he can ever expect to obtain in Palestine. The city Arab, too, can find a much wider field for his activities and ambitions within the framework of a larger and purely Arab state unit.[26]

Ben-Horin suggested that the 'shifting' of the Arab populations of Palestine and Transjordan to Iraq, and the simultaneous transfer of Iraqi, Yemeni, and Syrian Jews to Palestine, could be executed within 18 months: 'Should the above course be adopted, western Palestine [that is, west of the Jordan River] alone would offer to Jewish immigration all the land at present cultivated by the Arabs', and 'then there is Transjordania with considerable areas of fertile soil, and good irrigation possibilities.' Both the speedy transformation of Arab Palestine into a Jewish state and the evacuation of its Arab inhabitants into Iraq could be achieved with active international assistance.[27] The evacuation project should be carried out with 'firmness'. He added:

... such a solution being both just and practicable, the Jews and the Arabs will soon develop good neighborly relations ... The one imperative pre-requisite to such a happy development is the absolute determination on the part of the major nations that will dictate the peace [at the end of the Second World War] and lay the foundation for future world-order – that this and no other solution of the Arab Jewish problems be adopted and carried into effect.[28]

Ben-Horin appealed to the US administration to support the Zionist drive and 'dictate' Arab evacuation. His efforts appeared especially to focus on obtaining the support of Herbert Hoover, the former US President, a well-known Zionist sympathiser. Ben-Horin first met Hoover in late 1943. According to him, the meeting led 'to a close contact with a great American ... Hoover's interest is aroused in one idea outlined in my book ... It is the plan for an Arab–Jewish exchange of populations between Palestine and Iraq.'[29] Hoover apparently agreed to join the Zionist campaign in support of the Ben-Horin plan. Two years later, on 19 November 1945, the so-called 'Hoover Plan' – in fact, a repackaging of Ben-Horin's initiative – was published in the *New York World-Telegram*.

Until the late 1940s, Ben-Horin was still active in the attempt to relocate the Palestinians to Iraq. In May 1949, during the last stage of the Palestinian exodus, *Harper's* magazine published an article by Ben-Horin entitled 'From Palestine to Israel'. The editor noted that in an earlier article in the magazine's December 1944 issue, Ben-Horin had advocated a plan which at the time 'looked far-fetched ... that the Arabs of Palestine be transferred to Iraq and resettled there. Now, with thousands of Arab refugees from Palestine facing a dismal future, the transfer idea appears to be a likely bet ... in view of the sound character of Mr. Ben-Horin's earlier judgments and prophecies, we feel we can bank on his word about present-day Israel: "It works."'[30]

Joseph Schechtman's Plan, 1948

Dr Joseph Schechtman (1891–1970) was involved in Zionist activity in Russia from his early youth. He left Soviet Russia in 1920 and became co-editor of the Russian Zionist weekly *Rassviet* in Berlin (1922–24) and Paris (1925–34), co-edited with Vladimir Jabotinsky. A very close associate of Jabotinsky for three decades, Schechtman was a founder of the Zionist Revisionist movement, and the New Zionist Organisation. Schechtman served on the Revisionist executive in Paris, London and Warsaw, and was a member of the Actions Committee of the World Zionist Organisation (1931–35, 1946–70). He was also a deputy member (1948–51) and member (1963–65, 1966–68) of the executive committee of the Jewish Agency for Israel, chairman of the United Zionists-Revisionists of America, and a member of the executive of the World Jewish Congress.

Schechtman published numerous books, many of which reflected his maximalist Zionist Revisionist outlook and his obsessive preoccupation with population 'transfers'/movements. These books included *Transjordan within the Framework of the Palestine Mandate* (in German, 1937); a two-volume biography of Jabotinsky, *Rebel and Statesman* (1956) and *Fighter and Prophet* (1961); *Jordan: A State That Never Was* (1969); *History of the Revisionist Movement* (vol. 1, 1970); *European Population Transfers 1939–1945* (Oxford University Press, 1946); *Population Transfers in Asia* (1949); *Postwar Population Transfers in Europe, 1945–1955* (1963); *The Refugee in the World: Displacement and Integration* (1963); *The Arab Refugee Problem* (1952); *On Wings of Eagles: The Flight, Exodus and Homecoming of Oriental Jewry* (1961).

In 1941, Schechtman had settled in New York. He had served as a research fellow in the Institute of Jewish Affairs, 1941–43, as Director of the Research Bureau on Population Movements, which he had helped to establish, and as consultant for the United States Office of Strategic Services in Washington, DC, as specialist on population movement, 1944–45. With this background in mind, members of the Israeli government's 'Transfer Committee' of 1948 had invited Schechtman to contribute to their efforts of encouraging Palestinian exodus. Members of the Transfer Committee had met Schechtman during his visit to Israel in September 1948 and hired him to carry out research and advise them on the question of the Palestinian refugees' resettlement in Arab states.

More significantly, sometime in early 1948, Schechtman had worked out his own plan entitled 'The Case for Arab–Jewish Exchange of Population', and submitted it in May 1948 in the form of a 'study' to Eliyahu Epstein (in Hebrew, Elath), Israel's ambassador to Washington, who later forwarded it to the Israeli Cabinet Secretary, Zeev Sharef, and to the head of the Transfer Committee, Yosef Weitz.[31] Schechtman explained that his 'study' was not merely a descriptive and historical explanation of the facts; rather he believed 'that many important conclusions for the future can and must be drawn from the experience of past transfer and that the underlying idea of any transfer scheme is basically a preventive one'. If a problem of an ethnic minority cannot be solved within the existing territorial frame, then 'timely recourse must be taken to the essentially preventive devise of transfer'. According to Schechtman, 'the case of Palestine seems to offer a classic case for quick, decisive transfer action as the only constructive possibility of breaking the present deadlock' and 'no constructive solution can be arrived at without a large-scale [Arab] transfer'.[32] In addition, 'The only workable solution is an organised exchange of population between Palestine and the Arab states mainly to Iraq of Palestine Arabs', and the transfer to Israel of the Jewish communities in Arab countries.[33]

Schechtman's scheme called for the 'compulsory transfer' of the Palestinians to Iraq and cited Ben-Horin's plan of Arab transfer to Iraq of 1943 as justification.[34] Both Revisionist men, Schechtman and Ben-Horin, appealed to the US administration to support the Zionist cause and 'dictate' Palestinian evacuation to and resettlement in Iraq. In November 1945, the so-called 'Hoover-plan' – in fact, a repackaging of Ben-Horin's initiative – was launched in the *New York World-Telegram*.[35] Schechtman's plan of early 1948, which was directly inspired by the 'Ben-Horin–Hoover plan' of 1945, was supplemented by a brief additional section written in the wake of the Palestinian refugee exodus of the spring of 1948. In this addition to his plan, he observed 'unmistakable indications to the effect that the Israeli Government begins earnestly to weigh an Arab-Jewish exchange of population as the most thorough and constructive means of solving the problem of an Arab minority in the Jewish state'. As evidence of transfer discussions in Israeli government circles, he cited remarks by Arthur Lourie, the head of the Israeli United Nations Office and the representative at the Lake Success talks in New York, in an interview that appeared in *The New York Times* on 20 July 1948.[36] In the spring of 1948, Schechtman had written to Israel's ambassador to Washington, Eliyahu Epstein, saying that the Arab flow out of the area of the Jewish state 'only strengthens the case for the organised Arab transfer' to Iraq.[37]

In his ethnic cleansing plan, Schechtman maintained that, although it was evident that the Palestinian Arab leaders would never agree to any plan of this kind, 'which provoked on their part limitless indignation',[38] 'once uprooted, they [the Arabs] would probably be responsive to any plan of their resettlement in Iraq, with full compensation by the state of Israel for their property left behind'.[39] The working of the transfer/resettlement scheme would be underpinned by an interstate treaty between the governments of Israel and Iraq and possibly other Arab states. These treaties 'would provide a compulsory, but not all-inclusive, ethnic sorting out. As a rule, every Arab in the Jewish State and every Jew in Iraq would be subject to transfer; no specific option to this effect would be necessary.'[40] For Schechtman, 'the equality of numbers on both sides' of the so-called exchange of population 'in this particular case was of no importance whatsoever, since the prospective Palestine Arab transferees in Iraq' would be resettled 'not on land vacated by the Jewish evacuees', but on land provided by the Iraqi state. As a result 'the amount of land ... would be sufficient in Palestine where millions of dunams would be left behind by the departing Arabs'.[41]

Schechtman wanted formal Israeli government acknowledgment about the research he was carrying out for the Transfer Committee. In mid-October 1948, he asked Arthur Lourie of the Israeli United Nations Office in New York whether Foreign Minister Sharett

... could sent him [Schechtman] a note stating that you [Sharett] are glad to learn that he has been in touch with friends in Israel who are interested in this matter of resettlement of Arabs, particularly in Iraq, and that you could be pleased if he would continue with his investigations. On the basis of such a letter, Schechtman would approach men like [former US President Herbert] Hoover with a view of interesting them further in this work.[42]

Two weeks later, on 27 October 1948, Schechtman received a cable from Cabinet Secretary Sharef: 'Approve your proposal collect material discussed. Danin [and] Lifschitz will refund expenses five hundred dollars.'[43] Schechtman's urgent assignment on behalf of the Israeli government and its Transfer Committee included collecting material and conducting further 'study' on Palestinians' resettlement in Iraq. On 17 December, Sharett himself wrote to Schechtman from Paris telling him how 'glad' he was to hear that he was pursuing his 'studies with regard to the resettlement possibilities of Palestinian Arab refugees. Now that Mr [Zalman] Lifshitz [sic] is in the United States I am sure that you two got together and pooled your knowledge on the subject.'[44]

In December 1948, Lifschitz arrived in the United States to lobby for the Israeli policy to resettle the Palestinian refugees in Iraq. On the initiative of the Israeli ambassador to the United States, Eliyahu Epstein, a meeting was held in mid-December in the ambassador's office in Washington, in which Epstein, Schechtman, Lifschitz, Edward Norman, a New York-based Jewish millionaire who had devoted much of his fortune to supporting the Jewish Yishuv in Palestine and had been secretly lobbying for his plan to transfer the Palestinians to Iraq between 1934 and 1948,[45] and Elish'a Friedman, economics consultant from New York and member of the Ben-Horin–Hoover team which was active from the middle to the late 1940s in the attempt to resettle the Palestinians to Iraq.[46] Epstein had been in close contact with Schechtman throughout 1948 and had received a copy of the typescript of Schechtman's plan in early May 1948. On 18 May, three days after the proclamation of the State of Israel, Epstein had written from Washington to Schechtman in New York telling him that he had read his manuscript 'with great interest and found it to be an important and constructive contribution to the subject of Jewish–Arab exchange of population':

The events in Palestine are developing meanwhile in such a way that if not your conjectures, at least certain of your conclusions will have to be modified in view of the Arab flow out of the area of our State. Certain problems, however, in the exchange of population will remain, especially in view of the necessity of a transfer with possibly a very short time of the Jews living in the Arab countries to Israel.[47]

Epstein and Schechtman had also met in New York in mid-June 1948 to discuss the subject. In mid-December 1948, Lifschitz told the gathering in the Israeli Ambassador's office in Washington about the activities of the official Transfer Committee and suggested that Schechtman, Norman and Friedman

... might be of very great help in this matter, in two directions in particular. The first that he [Lifschitz] mentioned was in the presentation of ideas and supporting data, on which a plan to be adopted by the Government of Israel might be based. The second was to mobilise the leaders of public opinion in this country [US] to speak out in support of such a plan as soon as the Government of Israel would make public announcement of it. It was agreed that the three of us who were present, who are American citizens, would be considered a sort of advisory committee, with myself as chairman, working in close cooperation with Mr Epstein. It is our purpose now to produce a more or less detailed plan, which presumably will be forwarded to you [Sharett] for your consideration and possible presentation eventually to your government.[48]

Like Eliahu Ben-Horin, Edward Norman and former US President Hoover, Schechtman appealed directly to the US administration and the White House to support the Israeli policy and 'dictate' Palestinian resettlement in Iraq. A revised version of his 'study' of early 1948, in which he outlined his plan for the removal of virtually all the Palestinians to Iraq, appeared in Chapter III of Schechtman's book *Population Transfers in Asia*, published in March 1949.[49] At the same time, the actual research carried out by Schechtman on behalf of the Israeli government and its Transfer Committee in late 1948 and early 1949 appeared in his polemical work *The Arab Refugee Problem* (1952).[50] In his letter to Hoover, dated 9 April 1949, Schechtman wrote:

I take the liberty of sending you the enclosed copy of my study *Population Transfers in Asia* whose chapter on the Arab-Jewish population transfer owes so much to the inspiration provided by your plan for the resettlement of Arabs from Palestine in Iraq, published in 1945 ... Recent events in the Middle East have pushed this idea into the foreground of public attention, and have impelled me to publish this study of the transfer issue against the background of similar transfer movements elsewhere in Asia ... As one of the world's elder statesmen who helped originate the transfer idea as a way out of the Palestine conflict, and from whom the public hopes to receive further wise guidance in this issue, you will – I sincerely hope – be interested in this book of mine.[51]

THE POST-1967 PERIOD

The 1967 war reopened the question of Israel's territorial ambitions and borders and helped Revisionist Zionists to escape from the political wilderness into Israeli mainstream politics. Within roughly a decade, Menahem Begin became Israel's first right-wing Prime Minister, heading a Likud coalition, dominated by the Herut movement. His political ascendance was a result of his charisma, his huge appeal to the deprived Sephardic masses of Israeli society and the inability of Labour Zionism to offer a remedy to Israel's mounting problems. Prime Minister for seven years, Begin did not introduce a fresh ideology; concern for the territorial integrity of 'Eretz-Yisrael in its biblical boundaries' was the main content of his rigid *Weltanschauung*. Employing impassioned biblical and East European rhetoric, he always believed that his mission was to see that all the 'biblical Land of Israel' would be under Israeli rule[52] and that the Zionist goals could be achieved only by force.[53] This was in large measure an adherence to Jabotinsky's 'iron wall' philosophy and the 'monistic' ideology of Greater Israel. Begin, the caretaker of Jabotinsky's ideas, believed in a Jewish state with a Jewish majority on both banks of the Jordan River and a strong Jewish army to defend it.

The Arab–Israeli Rhodes talks, leading to the armistice agreements of 1949, were accompanied by a public debate in Israel, which reached its climax in the election campaign for the first Knesset. Menahem Begin, then leader of the newly formed Herut, objected to giving up any part of the 'historical Land of Israel', and certainly any part of the territory west of the Jordan River. Begin's Knesset speeches were full of typical emotional rhetoric: 'They have carved up not the territory, but our very soul!'[54] Other more extreme members of Herut spoke in terms echoing the Sternist conception of Greater Israel. The poet Uri Tzvi Greenberg, then a member of the first Knesset, stated: 'Right now we might – without exaggeration, if we had only been ready in time – be across the Jordan and on the slopes of Lebanon and en route to the Nile. And then, instead of a worthless armistice, we would have obtained peace on very comfortable terms to us ...'[55]

In Knesset debates in May 1950, Begin again argued that the West Bank was part of the biblical Land of Israel and as such belonged to the Jewish people,[56] and rejected a suggestion to federalise Palestine on the pattern of Switzerland's cantons based on ethnic lines. Also in the early days of the Israeli state, he advocated a war to achieve the 'liberation of parts of the occupied homeland'.[57] In the spring of 1957, following the first occupation of Gaza and Sinai by Israel, Begin attempted to rally world Jewish opinion against the decision of the superpowers to impose a withdrawal on Israel. In a press conference held in Canada, Begin stressed that peace in the Middle East would become a reality only when both banks of the Jordan River and the Gaza Strip became part of the Jewish state.[58] Two and a half years later, in 1958, the issue of the 'lost territories of Eretz Yisrael' was raised at the Fifth National Conference of Herut, which by 1955 had become Israel's second largest parliamentary party. Begin spoke about 'shlemut historit' – the 'historic completeness' of Eretz Yisrael – and pointed out that there were at least three other political parties in the country which did not recognise the Green Line with the West Bank as the final border of Israel. A year later, Herut leaders such as Ya'acov Meridor publicly claimed both sides of the Jordan River: 'The primary goal of foreign policy is to re-create historic Israel – by liberating Transjordan. Israel can never rest until this is accomplished.' [59]

Shortly before the outbreak of the 1967 war, Begin was co-opted into Levi Eshkol's cabinet as a full partner in a National Unity government. He became a minister without portfolio, but this was an important step in his political ascendancy, legitimising Herut's struggle for political power and paving the way for the future electoral successes of right-wing groups led by Herut. During the years 1967–70, Begin served as the head of various committees in the National Unity government. He proposed the establishment of Jewish quarters in Arab cities in the occupied territories. In 1970, when the US Secretary of State William Rogers proposed his second peace plan to end the War of Attrition between Egypt and Israel, Begin and five Gahal ministers (drawn from Herut and its right-wing liberal allies) resigned, calling the plan a 'Middle Eastern Munich'.[60]

MOSHE DOTAN'S PROPOSAL, NOVEMBER 1967

Moshe Dotan was the chairman of the editorial board of *Haumah* ('The Nation'), a quarterly, published by Misdar Jabotinsky (the 'Order of Jabotinsky'). *Haumah* is the most important journal of the Revisionists, the Likud camp and the supporters of Greater Israel. Dotan's 'transfer' plan was published in *Haumah* in November 1967[61] in the euphoric period which followed the June war's spectacular conquests. Predictably, he found it necessary to remind his compatriots that the 'whole Land of Israel', which the Revisionist movement claimed, stretched beyond the newly 'liberated' territories: 'Our claim for a homeland on both banks of the Jordan [River] is a just matter and it has a chance of being realised if it is accompanied by force. The Israel Defence Force is a powerful force and is used for a just matter. The Arabs, perhaps more than other peoples, appreciate force and are bound to take it into consideration.' More immediately, however, Dotan's preoccupation was with the 'demographic time-bomb which is activated non-stop against us' in the newly conquered territories, which overnight quadrupled the Arab population to 1.3 million in comparison with 2.3 million Israeli Jews.[62] Such a large Arab minority could not be 'digested' and in order to 'prevent the creation of a bi-national state' and to maintain an exclusive Hebrew state in Greater Israel, 'one must be industrious [ensuring] that it has a decisive Hebrew majority and as tiny a minority as possible.'[63]

In justification of his ethnic cleansing plan, Dotan cites the 'transfer' campaign of Israel Zangwill – one of the most outspoken and vociferous of early Zionists on the subject – before and after the First World War, as well as the proposal of Baron Rothschild to transfer Palestinians to Iraq in the 1920s.[64] In order to ensure that 'the Arab minority within the boundaries of our state would be as small as possible', Dotan suggests:

'We had to adopt a policy which promotes and speeds up the organised emigration of the Arab minority. Towards the Arabs of Israel [including the Arab citizens], refugees as well as residents, we need to adopt a new approach ... it is possible to entice and ensure the exodus of individuals and groups to countries overseas, in which the absorption conditions are convenient. Those [departees] who would strike roots in the new countries in need of farmers – and the Arabs have acquired in this field no little knowledge from our agriculture – are likely to receive large tracts of land, houses, water and equipment. Every family, whose emigration has brought it benefit, would attract its relatives who remained in villages, or the sons of landless farmers, or the disappointed among their friends. The encouragement of emigration will come from two sides: from the inside and from the outside. We are capable, through the exploitation of our great experience ... in organising Jewish immigration to turn the emigration of refugees and youth to an efficient non-profitable humanitarian project.[65]

For Dotan, every Palestinian on either side of the Green Line is a potential candidate for 'transfer/emigration':

In the emigration of the refugees there is a humane, healthy and just element. This is an act of preventive medicine: we must not leave [this] population ... in a small plot of land that is poor in natural resources and its ownership controversial ... every young worker from the 'Triangle' villages [in Israel], who comes to a [Jewish] city in search of work is a potential candidate for emigration. It is known that his purpose in the town, in addition to satisfying his needs, is to collect a respectable sum (6000–8000 Israeli lira) for paying the dowry for his bride's father. Within a few years he establishes a family with many children in his birthplace village, and because there is not sufficient land in his village, also his children, the number of whom has doubled and tripled, are bound to come to the city. It is worthwhile for our state to ensure the emigration of the young man who comes to the market-place of our city even at the price of paying his dowry at once and recompensing him for his part in the village land, so it would become [Jewish] national property.

Moreover, 'by creating adequate conditions for orderly emigration we would be able to stop the relative growth of the Arab minority and constantly remove the undesirable and dangerous elements ...'

Dotan believes that this emigration 'policy should be carried out at the initiative and encouragement of the government, but not implemented by it – just as the Jewish Agency deals with [Jewish] immigration. It would not be difficult to work out agreements with the governments absorbing the emigration, and indeed the few initial contacts have certainly proved themselves as having great chances.' Would the Palestinian Arabs accept this mass, organised exodus? Dotan's answer: 'This thing depends, of course, on the conditions and means we would mobilise and on the skill and wisdom we would be able to direct for the success of the emigration project.' As for the sceptics and critics 'who will doubt the practical value of the mass emigration plan of Arabs', he suggests they should be simply ignored. The destination of the government-initiated, mass, organised Arab exodus should be, according to Dotan, South American countries such as Brazil, Colombia, Paraguay and Venezuela:

> All these countries, as well as Canada and Australia, are looking particularly for migrants who are from the white race, Christians or other monotheists, workers at a certain level who could be absorbed and migrants who would be ready to work in agriculture ... Indeed for the refugees in our country these conditions are good ... [the Arab emigrants] would be given the opportunity to start a new life overseas with our guidance and assistance, until they stood on their own feet in the wide open spaces of Australia, Canada, and Latin America which need settlers.[66]

The plan of Dotan envisaged an officially orchestrated, carefully planned and massively organised operation:

> In addition to our settlement experience in this country, we have proved that we possess great organisational, planning, technical and economic forces which are successfully operating already for years in Africa and Latin America. If we do harness them for the project of emigration and resettlement we could ensure its success. It is not impossible that other international, national and public bodies would agree to take part in the planning – and perhaps not only planning – of this humanitarian project.

As for the financial cost of this project, Dotan explains:

> The financial problem of putting into effect emigration on a large-scale should not deter us in spite of the large sums we would have

to allocate. It is possible to imagine that even if the emigration countries would participate (the allocation of land, housing, etc.), we would have to spend a sum estimated at 5000 dollars approximately for the emigration of a family with six to seven persons on average. This sum would cover the cost of the flight, and the remainder (not an insignificant sum for an ordinary Arab family) would be handed over to the exclusive control of the emigrating family. The initial reasonable price would be as the following: for the emigration of 100,000 families, 500 million dollars would be needed. Let us suppose that the emigration would be implemented over five to six years (it must not be executed too slowly otherwise the weight of the natural growth would increase), this means one hundred million dollars annually. If we did not receive foreign aid to finance this plan we would have to be compelled in the worst case to shoulder the entire burden of expenditure. Clearly we would have to care about acquiring long-term loans from financial elements abroad ... Understandably, it is possible that the sums set are too high, and the allowance per capita will be much lower. However, we must be prepared for every effort to solve once and for all the 'refugee problem' and the Arab 'demographic time-bomb'.[67]

The mass 'emigration' of 100,000 Arab families – 600–700,000 persons – within a few years, Dotan (whose figures echo the figures of Eli'ezer Livneh's proposal of 1967, discussed in Chapter One) envisages, 'is likely to change our demographic balance unequivocally and be most valuable in many respects ... We are likely to look forward to the start of 1975, at the end of the five-year plan of programmed emigration, to the following composition in the population of the Land of Israel in its present borders: instead of 1.3 million Arabs (today) there will be about 600–700,000 Arabs against over 3 million Jews.' With such a decisive Jewish majority of five to one in Greater Israel, it would be possible to maintain an exclusive Jewish state.

In conclusion, Dotan argued in November 1967 that the Israeli leaders should treat his plan as a top priority of their national agenda; mass Arab 'emigration' is perhaps 'a brutal solution ... but it is anyway an extreme and efficient [one] for all.' Consequently it is vital that 'our public opinion exercises constant and consistent public pressure on the leaders of our state ... for the execution of a project which has political, demographic and humanitarian implications and whose results are likely to ensure the future and character' of Greater Israel.

There is no evidence to suggest that Dotan has changed his views on the territorial and transfer issues since November 1967. In May 1981 he wrote again in the journal *Haumah* – which has since been turned into a platform for many other advocates of 'transfer' – suggesting that after the 1967 war, 'it would have been preferable to open [the Jordan River] bridges only in the exit direction and to encourage the emigration of labourers to neighbouring Arab states abundant in petro-dollars. We have lost years, in which dangerous thorns, that have greatly weakened the state, have grown.'[68]

THE LIKUD IN POWER

In May 1977, Labour Zionism was finally defeated by the disciples of Jabotinsky. The Likud assumed power and remained effectively in government for 15 years until 1992. In 1996, after four years in opposition, the Likud returned to power for another three years. Menahem Begin, labelled by his supporters 'Begin, melech yisrael' ('Begin, King of Israel'), maintained loyalty to the traditional slogan of the Revisionist movement, still officially valid: 'Both banks of the Jordan – this one is ours and that one is also.' Begin never abandoned Jabotinsky's claim to both sides of the Jordan River and indeed he was the only Israeli Prime Minister who refused to meet King Hussein of Jordan, even clandestinely.[69] Apparently this attitude led President Jimmy Carter to believe that Begin laid claim not only to the West Bank, but also to the East Bank, that is, the Hashemite Kingdom of Jordan.[70] When Begin assumed power in 1977, he decided that the occupied territories of the West Bank and Gaza were to be called 'liberated land', as opposed to the 'administered territories', an expression coined by the Labour government. In a press conference in Kaddum, a Jewish settlement in the West Bank, established shortly after he came to power, he said: 'We don't use the word annexation. You annex foreign land, not your own country.'[71]

Until 1977, the Labour governments had sought a political solution which would allow Israel to retain control over parts of the occupied territories (under the Allon Plan). Under Begin's leadership, the Likud organised a coalition government with the National Religious Party dominated by the settlement movement of Gush

Emunim. Espousing a fundamentalist and emotional attachment to 'Judea' and 'Samaria', Begin and his coalition partners pursued a settlement policy with the highest priority of consolidating Israel's permanent control of the whole of Eretz Yisrael Hama'aravit (the 'western Land of Israel'). Under the Likud administrations of Menahem Begin, Yitzhak Shamir and Binyamin Netanyahu, Palestinians were subjected to a colonial policy designed to encourage emigration. Drastic demographic changes were also introduced. To fulfil its settlement/colonial goals, the Likud government rapidly increased the number of Jewish settlements in the occupied territories.

In September 1977, Ariel Sharon, the new agriculture minister and head of the ministerial committee on settlement, announced a plan to settle more than one million Jews in the West Bank within twenty years. The following year Mattityahu Drobless, Chairman of the Land Settlement Department of the Jewish Agency, who, like Sharon, was closely associated with Gush Emunim, issued the first version of a similar document: the 'Master Plan for Judea and Samaria'.[72] From 1977 until the end of the Likud second term in August 1984, two Likud governments poured more than $1 billion into Jewish settlement in the West Bank and Gaza Strip and various support activities.[73] By August 1984, some 113 settlements were spread over the entire West Bank, including a half-dozen sizeable towns. By 1990, the Jewish population of the West Bank settlements had grown to 140,000 (excluding expanded East Jerusalem).[74] Today, over 160,000 Jewish settlers live in the West Bank with a similar number in Arab East Jerusalem; the number of settlers in the Gaza Strip has remained relatively small. Up to 1987, only 2,500 Jewish settlers resided in the Gaza Strip and by 1993, this number had reached 3810.[75] In the Syrian Golan Heights, at least forty settlements were established. Sweeping land confiscation and zone restrictions were implemented to provide a land reserve for current and future Jewish settlement. The increasing number of Jewish settlers' areas was intentionally planned by the Likud to make it difficult for future Israeli governments to remove the settlements in any future agreements with the Arabs. Many settlements were built by members of the fundamentalist movement of Gush Emunin which, with the support of the Likud government, was able to utilise economic incentives as well as ideological motives.

It would be misleading to take a simplistic and monolithic view of Israeli politics since 1967. Labour Zionism has remained more sensitive to Western public opinion and its style has been more subtle, more politic and above all more pragmatic on the territorial issue than Zionist Revisionism. However, until the Oslo Accords of 1993, the political programmes of both the Likud and the Labour Parties had much in common. Although, following the 1967 conquests, neither Likud nor Labour advocated outright and legal annexation of the West Bank and Gaza, both parties were deeply opposed to Palestinian nationalism and ruled out Palestinian self-determination and statehood in the West Bank and Gaza. Both parties categorically refused to negotiate with the PLO and unconditionally opposed the establishment of an independent Palestinian state in the occupied territories. In essence, both major groupings have taken the position that Jordan is a Palestinian state – the 'Jordanian Palestinian Arab state', in the official parlance of both the Likud and the Labour Parties. On 5 October 1981, Yitzhak Shamir, then Israel's Foreign Minister, gave a speech at the Foreign Policy Association in New York:

> Public opinion in the West is being exposed to loud clamors in support of the Palestinian cause ... Arab propaganda is calling for a homeland, as they put it, for the homeless Palestinians ... It is important to understand the 'Jordan is Palestine' aspect and that the conflict is not, and never was, between Israel and a state-less people. Once this is understood, the emotional dimension that evokes problems of conscience in some minds will be removed. If it is perceived in this light, you have on the one hand a Palestinian–Jordanian Arab state, and Israel on the other, then the problem is reduced to a territorial conflict between these two states. The conflict will then have been reduced to its true and manageable proportions. [76]

It was General Ariel Sharon as Defence Minister in the second Begin government who promoted the idea that the Palestinians already had a homeland – the Hashemite Kingdom of Jordan. Interestingly the foundation of this view had been laid a decade earlier by Labour Prime Minister Golda Meir, who, while dismissing the existence of the Palestinian people, suggested on occasion that 'they had a state in Jordan anyway.'[77] However, the idea of Transjordan as a 'Palestinian homeland' has been used extensively by Likud leaders largely for polemical purposes and as a propaganda exercise aimed at delegitimising the Palestinians. Most prominent members of

Herut, including Begin and Shamir, had an abiding ideological aversion to surrendering formally Jewish sovereignty claims over large portions of the East Bank. For Shamir, in particular – with his emotional and ideological attachment to the Sternist conception of 'a Land from the Nile to the Euphrates' – there could be no compromise on the issue of the borders of the 'Land of Israel'. In April 1974, a few months after his election to the Knesset, he appealed to Prime Minister Golda Meir to annex formally the Golan Heights, some seven years before Begin actually carried it through.[78] Even when he became the head of the Likud and Prime Minister in September 1983, having been chosen because he came from the same ideological background as Begin, Shamir was still at heart a loyal member of the 'Stern Gang'. Shamir remained in office until 1992, with a hiatus of two years as Deputy Prime Minister in the National Unity government of 1984–88. With the exception of Ben-Gurion, no other Israeli Prime Minister has served longer. He had strongly opposed the Camp David Accords and the return of Sinai to Egypt. Throughout his long tenure, he stubbornly adhered to an approach which was based on a coupling of Stern's maximalist philosophy to Ben-Gurion's perception of political reality of what was possible under current local, regional and international conditions.[79]

According to Labour's pre-Oslo 'Jordanian option', some densely populated Arab sections of the West Bank were to be returned to Jordanian control[80] (these sections are not contiguous but made up of three areas totalling about 60 per cent of the West Bank territories) and that would take the bulk of the Palestinian population out of the Jewish state. Labour has always ruled out withdrawing from occupied East Jerusalem and the Jordan valley and has backed 'security settlement' in the Jordan valley and elsewhere in the West Bank.

On the other hand, after 1977, the Likud governments moved fast towards settling the West Bank and Gaza and unilaterally annexed the Golan Heights. Already during Begin's premiership the Knesset had passed a law prohibiting the evacuation of any Jewish settlement from the West Bank and Gaza, which was tantamount to *de facto* annexation.[81] This move was in line with the Likud party manifesto:

> The right of the Jewish people to Eretz Yisrael is eternal and indisputable, and linked to our right to security and peace. The State of Israel has a right and a claim to sovereignty over Judea,

Samaria and the Gaza Strip. In time, Israel will invoke this claim and strive to realise it. Any plan involving the handover of parts of western Eretz Yisrael to foreign rule, as proposed by the Labour Alignment, denies our right to this country.[82]

Prime Minister Yitzhak Shamir, restating the Likud policy at a meeting of the Knesset's Foreign Affairs Committee in June 1991, declared: 'We think that Judea, Samaria and Gaza are an inseparable part of the State of Israel, and will fight to put that thought into practice.'[83] Five months later, in December 1991, Shamir, while participating in a rally of the 'Shorashim Society' in Tel Aviv (a rally held in honour of Yisrael Eldad, the ultra-nationalist ideologue who was Shamir's comrade-in-arms before 1948 in the leadership of Lehi) affirmed the core objective of the camp of Greater Israel:

This is it; this is the goal: territorial integrity. It should not be bitten or fragmented. This is an *a priori* principle; it is beyond argument. You should not ask why; this is the be-all and end-all. Why this land is ours requires no explanation. From as far back as the pre-state days, I have not been able to abide by such words. Is there any other nation in the world that argues about its motherland, its size and its dimensions, about territories, territorial compromises, or anything similar? What may be forgiven when it comes from people in the diaspora cannot be forgiven in this land, from the people ruling it.[84]

In fact, the Likud administrations have not called for legal comprehensive annexation of the West Bank and Gaza. Instead, Likud pursued the formula of *de facto*, creeping integration, which would have enabled Israel to settle the land, while restricting the Palestinian inhabitants to ever-shrinking enclaves or Bantustans, and at the same time finding ways to remove part of the population. Outright, comprehensive legal annexation, on the other hand, would sharply raise the question of citizenship for the residents of the territories, while a *de facto*, creeping annexation appeared to be widely supported in Israel. In any event, the logic of the Likud's extensive settlement policies seemed to be that the Arab population must be reduced one way or another. As Danny Rubinstein, the Israeli journalist who has covered the occupied territories for the daily *Davar* for many years, put it as early as January 1979:

Regarding those [people] who on no account want Israeli withdrawal from Judea and Samaria – these [transfer] ideas are very logical. Anyone who aspires to and claims Israeli sovereignty over Judea, Samaria and Gaza – including the Begin government – must understand that there is no way out save the removal of the Arabs from the territories. With over one million Arabs Israeli rule will not be established in Nablus and Hebron, and all the settlement will not help. The supporters of the Likud government know this secretly in their heart. The Gush Emunim people and the 'Whole Land of Israel's Faithful' are talking about this, some privately and some publicly. Whereas Rabbi Kahane is not interested in the refined tactic. He and his followers bring the principles of the government policy to absurd truth.[85]

It is hardly surprising, therefore, that some important Likud leaders have, both openly and privately, voiced support for Arab 'transfer'. Immediately after the 1967 conquests, at a secret meeting of the Israeli Cabinet, Menahem Begin, then minister-without-portfolio, recommended the demolition of the refugee camps of the West Bank and Gaza and the 'transfer' of their residents to the Sinai Desert, which had been captured from Egypt.[86] In the early 1980s, during the negotiations between the Likud and Tehiya over the latter joining the Begin government, a member of the Tehiya delegation, Tzvi Shiloah, asked Begin whether his 'government is thinking about the transfer of refugee camps in southern Lebanon to northern Lebanon, thus reducing their danger to peace in Galilee?' Begin's reply was: 'The question of refugees is indeed a serious question. I am about to appeal in a statement to Saudi Arabia, Libya, Iraq and other Arab countries to absorb in their countries the refugees of the camps in Lebanon. What, Iraq has no lands and water and Saudi Arabia and Libya have no oil revenues?'[87]

Some of the men around Menahem Begin were even more extreme than the Prime Minister. There were two senior advisers of Begin, Shmuel Katz and Dr Moshe Yegar, who publicly declared their advocacy of Arab 'transfer'. Yegar was also an adviser on 'hasbarah' (information) in the Prime Minister's Office in 1979. Formerly he was a Consul in Los Angeles, General Consul in Philadelphia and New York, Director of the Instruction Division and the Information Division in the Foreign Ministry and Deputy Director General of the Foreign Ministry. He was also Israeli Ambassador to Sweden from 1988. Yegar revealed his advocacy of 'transferring' the Palestinians, including those citizens of Israel, in an article, published in the Revisionist periodical *Haumah*, in May 1979,[88] while he was still serving as an adviser in the Prime Minister's Office. His article, entitled 'Zionism, the State of Israel and the Arab Question', discusses the views and transfer campaign of Avraham Schwadron (in Hebrew, Sharon), a Zionist journalist and publicist and a proponent of the theory of 'Cruel Zionism', who openly campaigned in the 1940s for the total 'transfer' of the Palestinians and, significantly, continued to do so in the 1950s with the aim of removing the remaining Arab citizens of Israel. Having researched into, and described, Schwadron's views on Greater Israel, Jewish organic nationalism and Arab 'transfer', Yegar concludes: 'It seems there is an actual importance, whether Zionist theoretical or publicly educational, for the reconsideration of his writings and the bringing up of their content to public knowledge.' In his sympathetic summing-up of Schwadron's campaign, Yegar writes that Schwadron

... demanded from the Arabs [including Israeli Arabs] to evacuate the land of Israel which is not their country. Because he was convinced that there is no chance of coexistence with them. The solution is that the Jews leave their diaspora ... and immigrate [to Israel], while the Arabs cross to neighbouring countries, to live with their brothers. This solution seemed to him humane, fair and ensuring the prevention of trouble in the future. Historical examples of population exchange strengthened his opinion that this is the right solution. There is no other alternative ...

Yegar's conclusion, which is not less important than his description of Schwadron's philosophy, includes the following:

Sharon [Schwadron] would have said that all these events [the radicalisation among Israeli Palestinians in the 1970s, the Land Day on 30 March 1976, etc.] are no more than a confirmation of his opinion that there is no remedy for the problem, in spite of what Israel has invested in the Arab minority, and that the only alternative is the complete separation between peoples by encouraging the Arabs to emigrate. Among the first he would have wanted to see departing are of course, the [Israeli] Arab students who do not recognise the state ... It is reasonable to assume that if Sharon [Schwadron] had lived after the Six Day War he would have supported the annexation of the regions conquered and liberated in this war, while encouraging their Arab residents to get out, and he would have demanded that the emigration matter be included in the peace agreements signed between Israel and whatever Arab country. Reading today Dr Avraham Sharon's articles, one stands surprised in front of the actuality of his analysis, his views, ideas and the solutions proposed by him.[89]

Shmuel Katz, a Revisionist publicist and publisher, served as an adviser for hasbarah to Prime Minister Begin in 1977–78, but resigned his post in protest against the peace negotiations with Egypt. He was a member of the High Command of the Irgun in the Mandatory period, a co-founder of the Herut Party, a member of the First Knesset and a co-founder of the Whole Land of Israel Movement in 1967. Apparently Katz was a proponent of the geopolitical and imperialist ideas of Professor Karl Haushofer (1869–1946), whose intellectual influence on the geopolitical conceptions of Adolf Hitler and the Nazi *Lebensraum* doctrine of territorial expansionism remain controversial. Haushofer defined *Lebensraum* in practical terms as the right and duty of a nation to provide ample space and resources for its people. Limited resources and population growth among nations guaranteed constant friction in the international power structure; it was thus the duty of the stronger state to expand at the cost of the weaker.[90] Katz preached that history was shaped by space and political geography, not economics. Israel needed the territories occupied in 1967 as 'living space', and should not give up any of the occupied territories, including Sinai.[91]

Remaining loyal to Jabotinsky's philosophy, Katz dismissed the legitimacy of Palestinian nationalism: 'The Arabs of Palestine are not a nation. There is no 'Palestine Arab' nation. They were and have remained a fragment of the large Arab people. They lack the inner desire, the spiritual cement and the concentrated passion of a nation.'[92] In an interview in the periodical *Haumah* in the summer of 1989, Katz was asked the following question: 'Do you see transfer as a humane solution?' His unequivocal answer was

... certainly a humane and logical [solution], it is possible to create acceptable conditions, compensation, etc., if they want to leave. Also in America there is a movement of citizens from one end of the continent to another. Also in this country a little transfer has already taken place. During the years [19]48–67, 382,000 Arabs left Judea and Samaria. In these years, a Jewish body operated which gave financial support to Arabs who wanted to get out. The activities of the body were stopped at the end of the [Prime Minister] Eshkol government.

Katz added in sorrow that when Begin came to power in 1977 the heads of this 'Jewish body' for transfer submitted a memorandum to him requesting the renewal of their activities, but Begin took little notice.[93] It is not clear to what 'Jewish body' Katz was referring or whether he was himself involved in that organization. It is clear, however, that Katz was also advocating the transfer of the Israeli Arab citizens and that as a founder, publisher and manager of the Karni Publishing House, he was responsible for the publication of Tzvi Shiloah's book, *The Guilt of Jerusalem* (1989), cited above, in which the author devotes a large section to the argumentation in justification of Arab expulsion within the context of Greater Israel.[94]

Another veteran Irgun commander and an associate of Begin, Dr Shlomo Lev-'Ami, openly preached Arab 'transfer' in 1988. Lev-'Ami had joined the Haganah in 1936, rising to the rank of company commander. Two years later, he moved to the Irgun and took part in 'retaliatory' strikes against the Arabs. In the Irgun he rose to the rank of chief training officer. In 1973 he was appointed head of briefing in the Ministry of Education for state schools' biblical and 'Jewish consciousness' teachers. He also lectures at academic institutions and at Histadrut Ha'ovdim, the Israeli 'non-socialist' labour organisation which upholds the idea of a Jewish state within the 'historic' boundaries of the Land of Israel. He is also a co-founder of the institute for research on Zionist pre-state underground movements at Bar-Ilan University.[95] In his book, *Did Zionism Fail?* (1988) Lev-'Ami argues that 'one hundred years of Zionism prove that so long as too many Arabs exist in the western Land of Israel [that is, Palestine] the future of Israel will be in danger'. Ben-'Ami devotes a section to what he calls the Arab 'Return to Arabia', a recurrent slogan in the Zionist-transfer apologia, that is, the transfer of the Palestinians to their so-called 'historical homeland' in Arabia or other Arab countries; there is no

> ... escape from the re-adoption [of the transfer plan] ... the return of the Arabs from the Land of Israel to Arab states, as an exchange for Jews who have departed from Arab states, is just and logical. This plan of return to Arabia is more necessary than that plan of

exchanging the minorities on behalf of the League of Nations in
Europe was vital ... There is no comparison at all between the
necessity of return to Arabia with the expulsion of Jews from
various countries in the world.[96]

Lev-'Ami believes that Israel must extend its sovereignty at least from
the Mediterranean to the River Jordan, leading logically and
inevitably to the 'return' of the Palestinians 'to Arabia':

> In their exodus from the Land of Israel to their historic homeland
> in the Arabian peninsula or any other Arab country, the Arabs
> would be likely to receive full assistance from Arab countries and
> the United Nations. In the framework of a settlement of
> population and property exchange between Arab states and Israel
> the Arabs of the Land of Israel would be able to receive the
> appropriate assistance, also from Israel.[97]

While he was still Prime Minister, Begin sent to New York Hagai Lev
as leader of the Herut Party in the United States. Following an
interview with Lev in 1982, Robert Friedman, an editor for the pro-
Zionist magazine, *Present Tense*, explained:

> Neither Lev nor Begin ... advocates forcibly evicting the
> Palestinians from their homes in East Jerusalem and the West Bank
> ... But, pointing out that Israel has a particular problem in the
> occupied territories – for Judea and Samaria could hardly be Jewish
> with a population of nearly 1 million Arabs and only some 20,000
> Jews – Lev suggested that the Arabs would eventually get fed up
> with life under Israeli rule and leave 'voluntarily'. In fact, in a way
> that is already happening, Lev noted with some enthusiasm, for
> the number of Arabs in the West Bank has remained constant since
> 1967, even though the area has the highest birthrate in the world.[98]

Begin remained faithful to Jabotinsky's concept of an 'iron wall' of
Jewish military might which would secure Greater Israel. On 6 June
1982, a massive Israeli expeditionary force began the long-planned
for and expected invasion, 'Operation Peace for Galilee', with the
aim of rearranging the Middle East map to suit Israel's imperialist
interests. Begin's attempts to delegitimise the PLO by branding it a
'terrorist organisation akin to the Nazis' and to destroy the PLO in
order to facilitate the absorption of the West Bank and Gaza into

Israel were central to his initiation of the invasion of Lebanon in 1982. Begin originally endorsed the 'big idea', while leaving the details to his Defence Minister Ariel Sharon, allowing the latter to develop the war into catastrophic proportions[99] – resulting in the death of some 20,000 Palestinian and Lebanese civilians and over 600 Israeli soldiers. There were, however, Israeli commentators and critics who said the ultimate aim of the Israeli invasion of Lebanon, ordered by the Israeli Cabinet and overseen by Sharon, was to bring about forcible 'transfer' of the inhabitants of the occupied territories. Professor Yesha'ayahu Leibovitz of the Hebrew University said that the invasion of Lebanon was the consequence of a 'phenomenon of Judeo-Nazism', which resulted from Israel's control over the occupied territories.[100] The American-based Israeli historian and strategic analyst and biographer of Begin, Amos Perlmutter, wrote in *Foreign Affairs*:

> Begin and Sharon share the same dream: Sharon is the dream's hatchet man. That dream is to annihilate the PLO, douse any vestiges of Palestinian nationalism, crush PLO allies and collaborators in the West Bank and eventually force the Palestinians there into Jordan and cripple, if not end, the Palestinian nationalist movement. That, for Sharon and Begin, was the ultimate purpose of the Lebanese war.[101]

Three weeks before the start of the Israeli invasion, Perlmutter wrote in the *New York Times* that Sharon 'hopes to evict all Palestinians from the West Bank and Gaza and drive them to Jordan'.[102]

During the invasion, Ya'acov Meridor, a long-time associate of Begin and the then minister-without-portfolio, visited the Sidon area and, on being asked what to do with the Palestinian refugees, he replied: 'You must drive them east, towards Syria ... and let them not return.'[103] (Shortly afterwards, Meridor became Minister of Economic Cooperation and Planning until 1984). Writing in the same issue of *Foreign Affairs*, Harold Saunders, Assistant Secretary of State for Near Eastern and South Asian Affairs under President Jimmy Carter and former member of the National Security Council with responsibility for Middle Eastern affairs, explained:

> With a fragmented and dispersed PLO, Israeli leaders foresaw the Palestinian population in the West Bank and Gaza – deprived of outside moral support – coming to accept permanent Israeli

control there, in a situation in which much of the Palestinian population could be induced (or gradually coerced) to migrate across the Jordan River into Jordan ... The Israeli invasion of Lebanon ... was designed to break any final resistance to total Israeli control and to pave the way for making life so difficult for those who valued their freedom and political self-expression that they would eventually leave for Jordan.[104]

Before becoming Defence Minister and presiding over the invasion of Lebanon in 1982, General Sharon, as Minister of Agriculture and Chairman of the Ministerial Committee on Settlement, was at the heart of the Likud's intensive settlement policies in the West Bank, whose trends and evolution since 1977 have been extensively documented by many researchers.[105] Though the Likud government cited security arguments in defence of its settlement policies, it is clear that the government's position was founded on the abstract, uncompromising ideological claim of the 'whole Land of Israel' for the 'Jewish people'. To all intents and purposes, the settlement policies of the fundamentalist movement of Gush Emunim and of the Israeli state had become one and the same after Begin's/Sharon's rise to power. Sharon, who had used the 'iron fist' to smash Palestinian resistance in Gaza in 1970 and to evict, ruthlessly, thousands of the Arab inhabitants of the Rafah salient from their homes around the same time, believed that the blitzkrieg strategies he had employed on the battlefield could be applied to the political and demographic problems of the West Bank and Gaza. In the opinion of General Mattityahu Peled, who subsequently became a Knesset member, Sharon (then, in 1981, Defence Minister) would try to thin out the Arab population of the territories 'by a variety of measures which will fall short of forcible deportation or open atrocities'.[106]

The creation of economic distress and economic discrimination against the Arab population of the occupied territories has long been deliberate and systematic, and growing ever worse. Mass expulsion, however, was never, for understandable reasons, a publicly stated policy of the Likud governments between 1977 and 1992, and 1996–1999. The *Jerusalem Post* reported in 1982 that more than 100,000 people had emigrated from the West Bank since 1967.[107] While the colonisation and increasing Judaisation of the occupied territories vastly increased the tensions between settlers and the Palestinians, economic migration has, in part, been precipitated by the seizure of Arab land. 'The seizure of Arab land does not increase friction with the Arab population,' Sharon argued, 'it will prevent such friction in the future.'[108] But the creation of economic hardship was not the only measure taken to make people leave 'voluntarily'. Israeli journalist Amnon Kapeliouk, writing in the Hebrew daily *Al-Hamishmar* on 6 June 1980 (p. 3), described the growth of pro-'transfer' groups in Israeli society as well as within the Likud government. These ruling circles were proposing a 'final solution' for the Palestinian problem:

> There are also people in official posts who are prepared to create a situation which would force most of the population of the territories to leave their homes and to wander off to Jordan ... The instrument for creating such a situation is collective punishment. The policy of collective punishment is not new. We saw it in its full glory in the days when Moshe Dayan served as 'the emperor of the territories'. But the difference between the policy pursued then and the one carried out under the Likud government is that now it is done with the clear purpose of making the inhabitants' life unbearable [and making them want to leave]. The curfew in Hebron, which lasted over two weeks, was not the end of the story. The daily harassment of the inhabitants and the cutting of all the elementary services – such as the disconnection of all the telephones in the town, even those in doctors' clinics – all of these are not designed to deter the inhabitants ... and not to punish them ... but to make life unbearable so that the inhabitants will either rise up and be expelled by the instruments that have been prepared for this (as revealed by General Yariv, who condemned these horrific plans), or they will prefer to leave voluntarily.

Kapeliouk was referring to public remarks made two weeks earlier by MK Aharon Yariv, a former chief of military intelligence, at the Leonard Davis Institute for International Relations of the Hebrew University of Jerusalem, that 'there exists widely held opinion in favour of exploiting a [future] situation of war to expel 7–800,000 Arabs – things are being said to this effect and the means are being prepared'.[109]

It is not clear from Yariv's remarks whether this 'expulsion plan' had been prepared by the army itself, or put forward by senior officials and ministers in the Begin government. However if such a plan was conceived and prepared by elements in the military establishment, then it is inconceivable that the then Chief of Staff Raphael Eitan was not privy to its formulation. In any event, however, Yariv's critical remarks were also part of an ongoing public debate about the transfer solution beginning in the late 1970s and intensifying as the 1980s progressed and drew to a close, and in turn generating outspoken condemnations from a small, though significant, group of liberal academics, journalists and members of the peace movement. Arguing against the Likud's annexationist policies, Dr Arieh Ya'ari, a political scientist and academic director of the International Centre for Peace in the Middle East, wrote in 1984: 'Formal annexation is liable to dangerously arouse the population in the territories, who will see in this move a plot to deny them their national independence. This uprising would, in turn, provoke a bloody repression and might be exploited for a mass expulsion of the West Bank residents – an idea that has gained momentum in recent years, not only among the masses but among some higher-ups as well.'[110] Ya'ari also took issue with Meron Benvenisti, arguing that nothing was more reversible than a military occupation. As we shall see, much of the Likud held similar latent views in favour of transfer.

Throughout the 1980s, General Sharon was among the most powerful 'higher-ups' who promoted public debate on the transfer solution within the framework of Greater Israel. In 1982, while he was Defence Minister, Sharon implied, shortly before and perhaps while contemplating his planned invasion of Lebanon, that the Palestinians might have to be expelled, warning that they should 'not forget the lesson of 1948'.[111] 'The hint is clear,' Amnon Kapeliouk commented, citing Sharon's statement.[112] Sharon's threat of a new mass expulsion if the Palestinians did not mind their manners also seemed to be directed towards the Palestinians as a whole (those citizens of Israel as well as the inhabitants of the occupied territories). Upon becoming Defence Minister in 1981, Sharon initiated the most brutal period of repression in the West Bank and Gaza and set about crushing all opposition to the Israeli occupation. Shortly after Sharon's threat was made, the *Middle East International* correspondent Amos Wollin reported from Israel that intensive preparations were continuing in the West Bank and Gaza for much harsher measures to combat their Arab inhabitants' opposition to the Likud's settlement policies. Wollin, hinting at Sharon's threat, commented:

Palestinian residents have been warned that resistance to occupation, colonisation, and the civil administration's effort [launched by Sharon] to impose Begin's version of 'autonomy for the Arabs of the land of Israel', or eventual territorial annexation, may easily lead to a repetition of the 1948 tragedy, when the local Arab population was forced into permanent exile in the neighbouring states. In the same way hundreds of thousands of 1948 refugees in the West Bank and Gaza camps would again be required to move east-wards, this time to Transjordan, which Israeli government leaders describe as 'the already existing Palestinian state.' Repeated hints of such a scenario becoming reality (thus also solving demographic and land problems in Israel's interest) may be meant to reduce Palestinian resistance and encourage the 'moderates' to cooperate with the autonomy plan.[113]

As we have seen, and will show, there were many threats of new expulsions if the Palestinians in Israel and the occupied territories did not mend their ways, made from the late 1970s onwards. Several threats were made during the intifada (the Palestinian popular uprising in the occupied territories which began in December 1987) by Prime Minister and then Defence Minister Yitzhak Rabin, President Haim Hertzog and the then Likud minister Gide'on Patt. Earlier on in January 1979, Sharon's mentor and cabinet colleague Foreign Minister Moshe Dayan, who had been involved in and responsible for numerous expulsions during the 1948 war, threatened the Palestinians with another tragedy if they rebelled: 'they would better remember and have in mind what happened with the Arab people in 1948 ... they find themselves, some of them, as refugees in Lebanon and this should serve as a lesson.'[114]

General Sharon was greatly inspired by Ben-Gurion's and Dayan's thinking and action. In an attempt to legitimise his open transfer advocacy, Sharon was among the first to reveal publicly, in November 1987, the transfer plan of Dayan which discreetly operated between 1967 and 1970. He told a Tel Aviv audience: 'For several years after the Six-Day War, assistance was given to Arabs who wished to emigrate from here. There was an organisation [set up by the Ministry of Defence] which dealt with it.'[115] Sharon is not usually known for speaking in euphemisms as to how the Palestinians should be dealt with, and he had no hesitation in openly describing the Palestinian citizens of Israel as 'foreigners'.[116] However, Sharon, then one of Yitzhak Shamir's challengers for the

Likud leadership, was fully aware, like other Likud leaders, of the highly sensitive nature of the transfer issue. In an interview in 1988, Minister Sharon put it more delicately: 'You don't simply bundle people on to trucks and drive them away ... I prefer to advocate a positive policy, like enhancing the level of technical education in the [occupied] areas – to create, in effect, a condition that in a positive way will induce people to leave.'[117] Moreover, shortly before the eruption of the intifada, a Morasha Minister in the Shamir government, Yosef Shapira, raised the transfer issue, proposing that Israel actively promote mass Palestinian emigration, especially among the intelligentsia. (Morasha was a Knesset faction within the National Religious Party in the 1980s.) Shapira suggested that the Israeli government pay $20,000 to each Arab who agreed to depart. Sharon, then Minister for Industry and Trade, repeated Shapira's proposal but added that Israel should stop talking about transfer and instead put it into action.[118]

After the eruption of the intifada, several prominent Likud members called for the appointment of Sharon to a key ministerial post with direct responsibility for dealing with the Palestinian uprising. Among these figures was Rafi (Raphael) Eitan, a former adviser to the Prime Minister and then Chairman of the Board of Directors of Israel Chemicals. Rafi Eitan urged the government 'to declare all the parts [of the territories] in which the intifada is active as zones in which a war situation exists. This would enable me legally to do things that today I cannot do; for instance to transfer population from one place to another in Judea and Samaria, to expel inciters without a prolonged legal process, to confiscate for security needs land and property.'[119] Eitan had already urged ten years earlier that

... every Israeli who enters the territories, and even the Old City of Jerusalem, should carry arms and know how to use them. In my judgement more Israeli civilians must be allowed to carry weapons. Some claim that such a state of affairs will be exploited for the worst purposes. My answer: already at this time several thousands of weapons are in the hands of the IDF personnel, the police and Israeli civilians.[120]

Clearly statements made by key Likud politicians in favour of mass expulsion of Palestinians from the West Bank and Gaza began long before the eruption of the intifada in December 1987. As early as

May 1976, Knesset Member Amnon Linn – an old-timer of the Mapai Party and a self-styled 'expert' on Arab affairs who had joined the Likud in the 1970s – had this to say in a Knesset debate on Palestinian protests against the Israeli occupation: 'We should begin mass expulsion of entire communities which took part in demonstrations and riots – and to transfer them across the border. This applies to women, men and children.' [121] Commenting on Linn's statement, Meir Pa'il, of the small left-wing Sheli Party, reacted indignantly in the Knesset debate of the following day: 'I think that the proposal of MK Linn to expel the Arabs causes [huge] ... damage [to Israel's image]. Generally, I am astonished by the insolence of such a man.'[122] More importantly, on 16 March 1983, Deputy Speaker of the Knesset Meir Cohen-Avidov expressed support for Arab mass transfer at a meeting of the Knesset Foreign Affairs and Defence Committee. Cohen-Avidov added that 'Israel had made a great mistake by not expelling 200,000 to 300,000 Arabs from the West Bank' in 1967.[123] The *Jerusalem Post* commented at the time that the failure of the Begin Cabinet to reprimand Cohen-Avidov and dissociate itself from his remarks 'inevitably' created the impression that 'he articulates the tacit premises of official policy.'[124] Cohen-Avidov was cited on another occasion to the effect that Arab 'terrorists' should have their eyes torn out.[125]

These remarks represented a growing tendency in the 1980s among Likud MKs and stalwarts towards a more blunt and less guarded attitude when publicly discussing Greater Israel's 'demographic problem' and the transfer solution. A senior colleague of Cohen-Avidov, Michael Dekel, who was Deputy Defence Minister in the 1980s, was among the most consistent public proponents of transfer. Since the early 1980s, a group of Likud party activists, campaigners and senior figures congregated around Dekel; they openly argued that a mass transfer was 'the only way to solve the Palestinian problem'.[126] A very 'worrying' problem for Zionism, Dekel declared in October 1982, is the 'frightening natural growth of the Israeli Arabs within the Green Line, which is among the highest in the world'. As for the population of the West Bank and Gaza, which the Likud government would never give up, 'there is nothing left to them, apart from looking for their future in [countries] overseas,' Dekel said. With a 'mocking smile', he added that Israel should set up 'schools for construction work for the Arabs of Judea and Samaria in order to encourage them to emigrate to Arab countries while equipped with Israeli certificates'.[127] Dekel and his colleagues argued that the West Bank and Gaza can be radically transformed by a combination of massive Jewish settlement, and the mass dispatch of hundreds of thousands of Palestinians across the Jordan River, starting with the residents of the refugee camps. Was Deputy Defence Minister Dekel articulating the tacit premises of Likud government policy towards the Palestinian population? It should be pointed out that Dekel was known to be a close associate and stalwart of Prime Minister Shamir who had never dissociated himself from the public statements of his protégé. Tzahi Hanegbi, Geula Cohen's son, who was an assistant to Prime Minister Shamir – and subsequently became a minister in the Binyamin Netanyahu government of 1996–99 – had close connections with Rabbi Meir Kahane, the co-founder of the Jewish Defense League and campaigner for Arab expulsion from the early 1970s until his death in 1990, and was said to hold similar views.[128]

It has already been shown that threats of mass Arab expulsion made by senior Likud figures were becoming more frequent in the late 1980s against the background of the continuing Palestinian intifada. During the same period, Gide'on Patt (Minister of Housing, 1977–79; Minister of Industry and Trade, 1979–84; Minister of Science and Development, 1984–88; Minister of Tourism between 1990 and 1992) warned the Palestinian citizens of Israel that if they did not behave themselves they would be put on trucks and in taxi cabs and sent to the border.[129] Patt's colleague Yitzhak Moda'i (Minister of Energy and Infrastructure, 1977–84; Minister of Finance, 1984–86; Minister of Justice, 1986–88; Minister of Economy and Planning between 1988 and 1992) suggested that 'it would be possible to destroy the intifada by a combination of military, economic and social means', including the 'evacuation' of Arab neighbourhoods to other regions.[130] Another senior Likud figure, Binyamin Netanyahu, then Deputy Foreign Minister, told an audience at Bar-Ilan University, according to the *Jerusalem Post* of 19 November 1989, that the government had failed to exploit internationally favourable situations, such as the Tiananmen Square massacre in June 1989 when world attention and the media were focused on China, to carry out 'large-scale' expulsions at a time when 'the danger would have been relatively small'. Later, when Netanyahu denied making these statements, the *Jerusalem Post* produced a tape recording of his speech at Bar-Ilan University.[131] Was Netanyahu speaking just for himself or was he revealing the Likud government's hidden agenda?

Moreover, on 16 November 1989, the Ministry of the Interior gave a certificate approving the registration of a voluntary organization ('Amutah), whose single-minded aim is the 'transfer' of the Arabs from Israel and the occupied territories. Avner Ehrlikh (who in the early 1970s was a member of the executive of the Whole Land of Israel Movement), based in Tel Aviv, placed an advertisement and article in the name of 'Amutah, the management of this 'transfer', which stated: 'Its principal aim is explicit in the registration certificate: a lobby for explaining the necessity of transferring the Muslim Arabs of the Land of Israel, because this is the most humane and just way for achieving peace in the Middle East.' The only way to prevent the development of a bi-national state in Greater Israel is to

> ... implement the plan of evacuating the Arabs of the Land of Israel outside the boundaries of the Land of Israel ... we have reached the 12th hour and we should know that this country would be either for us or for the Arabs. And if we want this country [Greater Israel] a decision should be taken immediately to set up a parliamentary lobby, the aim of which is to bring about that the state of Israel, the whole Jewish people and most peoples understand that peace in the Middle East will be established ... only if the transfer of the Arabs of the Land of Israel is carried out to Arab countries ... if the evacuees decide on another destination, it would be the role of the United Nations to provide it for them. I am convinced and certain that the United States could absorb 300–400,000 of them; France, England, Italy, Germany and Canada would have to absorb the rest of the evacuees. Only thus would the problem of the Arabs of the Land of Israel be solved in a humane way.

Other Likud activists such as Aharon Pappo (also a member of the Israeli Broadcasting Authority Executive) have argued that expulsion would be a humane and practical solution.[132] Like many Likud members, Aharon Pappo is not a recent convert to the transfer doctrine. In 1973, Pappo acted as a solicitor for Rabbi Meir Kahane who had been indicted by an Israeli court for his letter-writing campaign urging Arab citizens to emigrate from Israel. The line of defence Pappo intended to employ during the trial – which in the event was postponed indefinitely – was that Kahane's campaign was perfectly legitimate since it was in line with the attitudes espoused

by the founding fathers of the State of Israel, including Chaim
Weizmann, David Ben-Gurion, Berl Katznelson, Yitzhak Tabenkin,
Zeev Jabotinsky, Moshe Sharett and Golda Meir.[133] Pappo pointed
out that the then Prime Minister Golda Meir used to confide to her
close entourage that she was apprehensive about waking up every
morning and hearing that another Arab baby had been born in
Israel.[134]

In the early 1990s, Pappo, while remaining a Likud member,
became closely associated with two groups of the extreme right
which campaigned for Palestinian expulsion: 'The National Circle' of
Ora Shem-Ur and the Moledet Party led by General Rehava'am Zeevi.
In an article entitled 'Moledet is the Message', published in the mass-
circulation daily *Yedi'ot Aharonot* during the second Gulf War and
shortly after Moledet joined the Shamir cabinet in January 1991,
Pappo wrote:

> The Moledet movement's joining of the government is important
> and has a significance because of the latest events which proved
> ... that there is no possibility of 'living together' with the Arab
> residents of the Land of Israel ... the joining of the government
> by Gandhi [that is, Zeevi] will give legitimisation to the possibility
> that indeed, in certain circumstances ... the solution of their
> transfer to Arab countries in general, and the desert of Iraq in
> particular, is possible and legitimate.

He added that Israel should follow the example of Czechoslovakia
which 'expelled' three-and-a-half million Germans after the Second
World War.[135]

The atmosphere created by the Iraqi invasion of Kuwait in August
1990 and second Gulf War of 1991, coupled with the general Israeli
tendency to blame the Palestinians for Saddam's actions as well as
public statements made by Israeli ministers and Likud MKs who
exploited the Gulf crisis to threaten the Palestinians, greatly
heightened the Palestinians' fear of mass expulsion. In August 1990,
shortly after the Iraqi invasion of Kuwait, a confidant of Prime
Minister Shamir told the daily *Haaretz* that 'if ... Israel is forced into
a war and if the Palestinians in the territories are as a result
emboldened enough to cause us a problem, they will find themselves
outside Israel's borders'.[136] Emil Habibi, a leading Israeli Palestinian
writer and former editor of the Israeli Communist Party daily *'al-*

Ittihad, explained in an interview with the Israeli periodical *New Outlook* (September/October/November 1990, pp. 22–23):

> We have a real fear that an atmosphere of chaos and hatred might develop which would allow the resumption, and completion of the 'job' of 'transfer' begun in 1947–48. We have 'seen death' – expulsion from the homeland – twice in our lifetime: in the 'great catastrophe' of 1948 ...
>
> We may argue with the Palestinian leadership over the justification of some of the positions they have taken during the crisis. But to place the stress on blaming them would divert attention from the substantial danger Palestinians now face. The appearance of new 'Arab refugees' – the expulsion of hundreds of thousands of Palestinians and other Arabs from the Gulf Arab states – is again putting us face to face with the danger of expulsion from our homeland. Focusing on Palestinian guilt will only help the 'transferists' in Israel create a smokescreen for hiding, or even worse, justifying, their intentions. No honest individual has the right to forget the fate of the Palestinians in 1947–48, a fate which became possible because of just such a smokescreen.

The more the Likud became entrenched in power in the 1980s, the more many of its government officials and ministers became persistent in their public support for a radical solution to Greater Israel's 'demographic problem'. In 1990, the Likud dissolved its coalition partnership with the Labour Party and formed a coalition government with the far-right parties – including the Tehiya, Tzomet, Moledet and the National Religious Party; this coalition lasted until 1992. The leaders of these extreme-right parties were among the most vocal advocates of territorial maximalism and Arab 'transfer'. In January 1991, General Zeevi, the leader of the Moledet Party, with its single-minded transfer platform, joined the Likud coalition as a minister-without-portfolio and member of the policy-making inner cabinet.[137] Shamir's last government (1990–92) was a right-wing radical administration in which the extreme right exerted unprecedented influence, but there was a sense of fatalism about its prospects of longevity. Shamir told the Knesset that his new government contained 'all the national forces which have fought for the sake of Eretz Israel, for settlement in all parts of Eretz Israel'.[138]

With the Likud entrenchment in power and the subsequent rise of extreme right-wing forces in Israel, the most far-reaching imperialist proposals were now entering mainstream Zionist thinking and official circles. Such proposals, including Arab population removal, were outlined in an article entitled 'A Strategy for Israel in the 1980s', which appeared in the World Zionist Organisation's periodical *Kivunim* in February 1982, a few months before Israel's invasion of Lebanon. The article was authored by 'Oded Yinon, a journalist and analyst of Middle Eastern affairs and former senior Foreign Ministry official. The importance of the article's contents lie in the fact that *Kivunim* is published by the World Zionist Organisation's Department of Information and it may have expressed the view of some elements within official circles. 'Oded Yinon analyses the weaknesses that characterise the national and social structures of Arab states and concludes that Israel should work to bring about their dissolution and fragmentation into a mosaic of ethnic and confessional groupings. In the short term, Yinon proposes, Israel should bring about the 'dissolution' of Jordan:

> There is no possibility that Jordan will exist in its present shape and structure in the long-term, and the policy of Israel, whether in war or in peace, must be to bring about the dissolution of Jordan under the present regime [and the consequent] termination of the problem of the [occupied] territories densely populated with Arabs west of the [River] Jordan, whether in war or under the conditions of peace; emigration from the territories, and economic-demographic freeze in them ... we have to be active in order to encourage this change speedily, in the nearest time ... It is no longer possible to live in this country in the present situation without separating the two peoples, the Arabs [including the Arab citizens of Israel] to Jordan and the Jews to the territories west of the [Jordan] River ... [The Palestinian Arabs] can only have security and existence in Jordan.

Yinon believes, like many advocates of transfer in Israel, that 'Israel has made a strategic mistake in not taking measures [of mass expulsion] towards the Arab population in the new territories during and shortly after the [1967] war ... Such a line would have saved us the bitter and dangerous conflict ever since which we could have already then terminated by giving Jordan to the Palestinians.'

The long-term objectives, Yinon suggests, encompass the whole Arab world, including the imposition of a *Pax Israela* on, and the determination of the destiny of, Arab societies: reinvading Sinai and 'breaking Egypt territorially into separate geographical districts'. As for the Arab East:

> There all the events which are only our wish on the Western Front [that is, Egypt] are happening before our eyes today. The total disintegration of Lebanon into five regional, localised governments as the precedent for the entire Arab world ... the dissolution of Syria, and later Iraq, into districts of ethnic and religious minorities, following the example of Lebanon, is Israel's main long-range objective on the Eastern Front ... Syria will disintegrate into several states along the lines of its ethnic and sectarian structure ... As a result, there will be a Shi'ite 'Alawi state, the district of Aleppo will be a Sunni state, and the district of Damascus another state which is hostile to the northern one. The Druze – even those of the Golan – should form a state in Houran and in northern Jordan ... Oil-rich but very divided and internally strife-ridden land of Iraq is certainly a candidate to fit Israel's goals ... Every kind of inter-Arab confrontation will help us to prevail in the short run and will hasten the achievement of the supreme goal, namely breaking up Iraq into elements like Syria and Lebanon. There will be three states or more, around the three major cities, Basra, Baghdad and Mosul, while Shi'ite areas in the south will separate from the Sunni north, which is mostly Kurdish ... The entire Arabian Peninsula is a natural candidate for dissolution ...[139]

Given the auspices under which Yinon's proposals were put forward, this article generated wide echoes in Arab countries[140] giving the impression that the World Zionist Organisation was endorsing a detailed plan for Zionist territorial expansionism, including the destruction of several Arab countries and Arab transfer. Regardless of whether Yinon's transfer proposal was endorsed by official circles in the World Zionist Organisation, the Palestinians, as has already been demonstrated, have good reason to fear mass transfer from the occupied territories. To the Palestinians, the massive immigration of Russian Jews into a small country in 1990–91, which was channelled by the Likud government into 'creating facts on the ground' in the form of Jewish settlements, aroused the gravest fear of a 'new 1948 exodus'. 'One million newly arrived Jews dropped into the laps of Shamir and Sharon ... will destroy the (demographic) argument of the Labor Party and strengthen support for transfer,' stated Saeb

'Erakat, professor of politics at the al-Najah University in Nablus, and later member of the Palestinian delegation to the Middle East peace talks. Hanna Siniora, the editor of the East Jerusalem-based *al-Fajr*, said in a similar vein: 'In the context of the lack of a political initiative to end the conflict and reach a solution, the Palestinians see Soviet immigration as a threat and part of a plan to transfer them from their homeland.'[141] The Palestinians viewed this large-scale immigration as giving further impetus to the whole dimension of Greater Israel and wreaking havoc on the views of Israel's 'demographic doves'[142] and the supporters of the Israeli Zionist peace camp, who stood to lose the basis of their whole 'demographic' argument used to stave off increasing settlement and annexationism. Such fear has been evidently expressed in rumours of impending mass expulsion widely circulated in the West Bank and Jordan in 1990. On 9 January 1990, an Arab newspaper claimed that 'the PLO has a report on a plan endorsed by the US administration calling for the expulsion of half a million Palestinians from the occupied West Bank and Gaza Strip within two years.'[143] It is very questionable whether the US had ever endorsed such a plan. However, such a report appears to have been taken very seriously in Jordan. Four days later, on 13 January, a Jordanian newspaper warned against the mass transfer of Palestinians from the West Bank across the Jordan River:

> We must, through awareness and decisive clear measures, differentiate between opening the bridges to keep the economic veins alive and opening them to fulfil the enemy's desire to uproot and deport the Palestinians and drive them to emigrate or seek work outside the land of Palestine. Hence, attention should be paid – for strategic, national and Pan-Arab reasons in the interests of the Palestine question and Jordan – to standing firmly against the desire by any Palestinian citizen to reside in Jordan after the decision to disengage ties with the West Bank, taken on 31 July 1988. It follows that those who came to visit and failed to return, hoping to stay, should not be allowed to stay. Nor should there be silence over the large number of people who came but failed to return.[144]

In the event, however, only a minority of the 800,000 new Russian immigrants who had arrived from the former Soviet Union between 1990 and 1998 found themselves in Jewish settlements in the West

Bank, despite the price incentives. Although many Russian Jews were encouraged to settle in Greater Jerusalem, most opted for a quieter life in Israeli cities and towns on the Mediterranean coast. But those new Russian immigrants who settled in new Jewish neighbourhoods in East Jerusalem or settlements on the West Bank tended to display the same hard-line and territorially maximalist Zionism found in the Likud and other parties of Greater Israel. Many of the new immigrants did not identify themselves with most other secular Ashkenazis and supporters of liberal Zionism, but gravitated to the Israeli right. For instance, Binyamin Netanyahu received the votes of 60 per cent of the Russian immigrants in the general election of 1996.[145] Among these immigrants, there was also solid support for both Natan Sharansky, the former Soviet Zionist dissident whose Yisrael b'Aliya party was an essential component in Netanyahu's cabinet until May 1999, and Avigdor Lieberman, Prime Minister Netanyahu's former lieutenant who in 1998 was planning a new Russian party further to the right of Likud.[146]

Throughout the 1990s, the Russian vote was generally seen to be the wild card of Israeli politics. In mid-1998, however, the Russian votes remained solidly on the Israeli right. 'Most of the Russian immigrants have a strong imperialist sense from the Soviet Union. For them what counts is control of maximum territory,' remarked the editor of the Russian-language *Vesti* newspaper, Eduard Kuznetsov.[147] Some Russian immigrants have even drifted to the extreme right. In June 1997, one woman, aged 25, set off weeks of Palestinian protests and rioting on the West Bank by drawing cartoons of the Prophet Muhammad as a pig and pasting them to walls in the West Bank city of Hebron.[148]

Moreover, with the Likud entrenchment in power there was, in conjunction with the increase in public support for radical solutions to Greater Israel's 'demographic' problem and territorial disputes, a coarsening of political rhetoric towards, and a stirring up of racism against, the Palestinian population.

NETANYAHU AND THE OSLO PROCESS

Binyamin Netanyahu served as Prime Minister from 1996 to May 1999. His Likud Party returned to power in the post-Oslo period which followed the conclusion of a series of agreements on Palestinian autonomy in the West Bank and Gaza between the

Labour government and the PLO – agreements whose frameworks and contents were largely shaped by Labour Zionist premises and fundamentals. A master of the sound-bite and tough on rhetoric, the American-educated Netanyahu envisaged a model of the Likud shaped in the image of Jabotinsky's 'iron wall' philosophy and Israel's pragmatic politics of the post-Oslo period. Netanyahu's father, Ben-Tzion, is an academic and long-time Revisionist, and the strong Revisionist legacy was passed from father to son. However, Netanyahu sought to modernise and change the hitherto crude approach of the Revisionist old guard and mould it using the political vocabulary of the 1990s.

In the 1980s, Netanyahu had believed it was a political imperative to block off any discussion of the Palestinian case in the West. During his time in the United States, he had developed Israel's hasbarah (public relations industry/propaganda) to a new level. Netanyahu, then seeking to delegitimise the Palestinians, developed the idea that 'Jordan is Palestine' as a purely propaganda tool to the extent that a network of 'Jordan is Palestine' committees were established linking most major Jewish communities in the West.[149] Netanyahu had also referred to Jordan as 'eastern Palestine' (that is, eastern Eretz Yisrael) in an article in the *Wall Street Journal* of 5 April 1983. He argued that the demand for 'another Palestinian state in Erertz Yisrael' had nothing to do with Palestinian self-determination; it simply provided the basis for an irredentist drive to destroy the State of Israel. The 'Jordan is Palestine' hasbarah line gained wide currency among Jews and non-Jewish Zionist sympathisers, even spawning an entire conference in Jerusalem. It was a diversionary measure in support of Likud policy, with the aim of marginalising the Palestinians and delegitimising them as negotiating partners.[150] The Likud's acceptance of the peace treaty with Jordan signed in October 1994 suggested they were *de facto* ideologically reconciled to the so-called 'loss' of the East Bank, even though they did not shout it out loudly for the party faithful to hear.[151] While the subsequent abandonment of the Jabotinskite notion of Jordan as part of the 'homeland' was crucial to the Likud prospects in the 1990s, Netanyahu still remained the intransigent opponent of the slightest concession regarding the West Bank – 'the old biblical lands of Judea and Samaria', in which there was no room for a real Palestinian autonomy, let alone a Palestinian state.

Throughout his tenure as Prime Minister, Netanyahu – like his predecessor Shamir – pursued a policy which admitted little deviation from Jabotinsky's 'iron wall' concept, believing that the international community and the Arab world would acquiesce in the continuation of the Israeli hold on the West Bank and Gaza. Moreover, it was assumed that the situation would become more permanent with each new Jewish settlement. The strategy of seeking peace with the Arabs on these terms, it was argued, would minimise the degree of interference from the West. It was therefore in the Likud's interests to reject or drag out any political initiatives which hinted at the possibility of withdrawal and the renunciation of Israeli sovereignty over the occupied territories. Netanyahu also shared with Shamir an enforced political immobility and lack of ability to manoeuvre. Indeed, the more the prospect for a decision on the future of the West Bank and Gaza drew closer, the more difficult it became to contain emotions towards the West Bank within the Likud.

Netanyahu's effort to establish himself as Likud leader had received a severe jolt when the Oslo Agreement suddenly emerged and Yitzhak Rabin hesitantly shook Yasir 'Arafat's hand on the White House lawn in September 1993. Given the psychological assault which embracing the PLO entailed, Netanyahu had no other choice if he wished to maintain his position as Likud leader.[152] In the post-September 1993 period, Netanyahu's approach to the Oslo process was, at root, ideological and hard-line, repeating the pattern of decades by embracing undiluted Revisionism. Netanyahu emulated Begin and Shamir in making common cause with the far-right parties. His espousal of a radical populist approach was the path chosen to confront the Oslo process. This was highly reminiscent of Menahem Begin's tactics of the past. Netanyahu called the Oslo process 'an enormous lie' and 'a crime against Zionism' and demanded a national referendum. In the Knesset debate, he went further and stated that the Likud might not honour the Oslo Agreement if they were returned to power.[153]

Under the settlement-backing, land-grabbing, new-right Likud government of Netanyahu, which came to power in June 1996, things got much worse. Confidential Israeli documents leaked to the *Observer* in June 1996 showed that Netanyahu's government had drawn up plans to 'devour Arab East Jerusalem and reduce its Arab community to an insignificant minority'. The godfather of the master plan was Jerusalem's Likud deputy mayor, Shmuel Meir, who believes the Palestinians have no rights in the holy city. His ideas include the demolition of at least 2,000 Arab homes which he claims have been built without planning permission, and the construction of some 7,000 new homes exclusively for Jews in Arab East Jerusalem – which has already 160,000 Jewish settlers in ten major settlements ringing the Arab sector. 'Every time he [Yasir 'Arafat] says Jerusalem is his, we will respond by building a thousand homes for Jews,' explained one of Netanyahu's advisers.[154]

Netanyahu fervently embraced the cause of undermining the Oslo process. However, under intense American pressure, in October 1998, he and the head of the Palestinian Authority (PA), Yasir 'Arafat, signed the Wye Memorandum at the White House. In essence, the Wye Memorandum was a long-overdue mechanism to implement aspects of earlier agreements, notably the Interim Agreement (Oslo II) of 28 September 1995 and the Hebron Protocol of 15 January 1997. The overarching principle that governs the Wye agreement is the concept of security/reciprocity. The sections on security consume about 60 per cent of the memorandum, while the rest is taken up with further redeployment and unresolved interim issues, including Israel's commitments to negotiate safe passage between the West Bank and Gaza, as well as the opening of the Gaza airport and eventually a seaport.

Under the Memorandum, Israel agreed to turn over 13 per cent of area C (currently under full Israeli control) in a combined first and second stage of further redeployment; 1 per cent will go directly to area A (under PA control), 12 per cent to area B (though 3 per cent will be 'nature reserves' in which new construction is banned). Israel will maintain full security control in the nature reserves, but PA security forces may enter with prior Israeli approval. Israel will also turn over 14.2 per cent of land currently in area B to area A, leaving the PA at the end of twelve weeks with full control of 18.2 per cent of the West Bank and in partial control of 21.8 per cent. Israel also committed itself to carry out a third stage of further redeployment. Under Wye, Israel's other responsibilities were open-ended. They included: a) to open the Qarni industrial estate in a 'timely' manner; b) to revive talks of safe passage between Gaza and the West Bank; c) to resume talks on the Gaza airport, and d) to address outstanding legal disputes with the PA. The PA and Israel also agreed to prevent acts of terrorism, crime, hostilities, and incitement against people and property.

Under Wye, the PA's specific obligations were concrete and to be met by specific dates. These included pledges: a) to submit and implement a work plan to the US on combating 'terrorist organisations'; b) to resume full security cooperation with Israel; c) to outlaw organisations or wings of organisations that incite violence; d) to apprehend specific individuals suspected of violence; e) to prohibit and collect illegal weapons; f) to issue a decree prohibiting all forms of incitement, and g) to provide a list of all PA police 'in conformity with prior agreements'. Concerning the PLO charter, the Memorandum stated that the PLO Executive Committee and Central Council should reaffirm Arafat's 22 January 1998 letter to President Clinton, listing the 26 out of 33 articles of the charter annulled on 22 April 1996, after which Arafat should invite members of the Palestinian National Council, the Palestinian Legislative Council, and heads of the PA ministries to a meeting to reaffirm their support for the Executive Committee and Central Council's decisions.

Both sides also agreed to resume final status talks immediately, with the goal of concluding an agreement by 4 May 1999, and to refrain from taking unilateral steps that would change the status of the West Bank and Gaza. Following the signing of the Memorandum, the PA immediately began taking steps to meet its obligations, sometimes sparking riots and prompting accusations of human rights abuses in its areas. Meanwhile, on 27 October, Netanyahu postponed Cabinet and Knesset ratification of Wye on the pretext that the PA would not meet its obligations on security issues. While delaying Wye, Netanyahu proceeded with settlement expansion, declaring on 26 October that he had not agreed at Wye to halt settlement construction or confiscation of Palestinian lands. Around 28 October, Netanyahu approved the addition of a thousand new units to existing West Bank and Gaza settlements within 18 months. Also, the Israeli government approved the fortification of 33 settlements near the expanded area A prior to redeployment, on 13 November it approved the construction of 13 bypass roads requiring the confiscation of large tracts of Palestinian lands. When Netanyahu's Cabinet finally reconvened on 11 November, under intense US pressure, and ratified the Wye Memorandum (8–4, with 7 abstentions), it set up so many conditions on its approval that more disputes and delays were inevitable. At the close of 1998, it was uncertain where Wye implementation was headed. With the peace process apparently dead, the right-wing government began disintegrating.

Netanyahu's term of office as Prime Minister had been marked by incessant acrimony and the Likud itself was wracked by bitter infighting. Netanyahu's credibility was in shreds among his own colleagues. Two-and-a-half years after coming into office, Netanyahu underwent the humiliation of being forced to support an opposition motion dissolving the Knesset and calling for early elections, scheduled for 17 May 1999. But it was not the parliamentary opposition that toppled the Netanyahu government. The ruling coalition simply imploded under the burdens of its own contradictions – above all, the tension between a professed commitment to the peace process and its compositions of factions and individuals implacably opposed thereto.

The vote to dissolve the Knesset did not put an end to the Likud's disintegration. Netanyahu's leadership was challenged by senior Likud figures, including Benny Begin, whose father Menahem Begin was a long-time standard bearer of the 'Greater Israel' cause. In January 1999, Defence Minister Yitzhak Mordechai was dismissed by Netanyahu, after he had met with leaders of the emerging Centre Party, Amnon Shahak (a former army chief of staff) and Dan Meridor, a former Likud finance minister (together they were joined by the outgoing mayor of Tel Aviv, Roni Milo, another erstwhile ally of Netanyahu). Humiliated by Mordechai's move and his evident intention to leave the Likud, Netanyahu struck first. During his 31-month tenure, Netanyahu had parted company with two ministers of finance (Ya'acov Neeman and Dan Meridor), one defence minister (Mordechai) and one science minister (Benny Begin). Netanyhau's former foreign minister, David Levy, had gone even further, crossing the lines to ally himself with Ehud Barak of the Labour Party. Mordechai (born in Iraqi Kurdistan) became a major boost to the fortunes of the new Centre Party, which aimed to capture Israel's middle ground, appealing to well-to-do, secular and middle-class voters. However, Mordechai, who was running against Netanyahu as candidate for prime minister for the Centre Party, entered the increasingly crowded arena of contestants for the post of prime minister.

This mass defection decimated the Likud leadership. Netanyahu proved a bitter disappointment to significant sectors of his own constituency – that is, settlers and other hard-liners – and the Russian immigrants were equally disillusioned. Furthermore, Netanyahu had never enjoyed much sympathy in the Israeli media and most journalists disliked his manipulative rhetoric. He had done no better with other elite groups, including the academic and business communities. Despite an enthusiastic espousal of globalisation and Reaganite free-market dogma, much of the business community laid the blame for economic recession in equal measure on his sabotage of the peace process and his espousal of the monetarist dogma. The stalled peace process continued to take its toll on the Israeli economy. In October 1998, the Finance Ministry had reported that 1998 had been Israel's worst year in the past decade, with real foreign investment in the Tel Aviv stock exchange down to 73 per cent for the first six months, according to the Bank of Israel. The Central Bureau of Statistics had reported a 'considerable' economic slump in the second half of 1998.

As the countdown for the general election of 17 May began, Netanyahu stepped up his efforts to woo right-wing voters. His hard-line Foreign Minister Ariel Sharon, within weeks of the Wye Memorandum's signing, had publicly called upon settler groups to 'grab' as much West Bank land as possible to prevent it from remaining in Arab hands. On 9 January, Netanyahu threatened to annex the bulk of the West Bank if the head of the PA, Yasir 'Arafat, declared Palestinian statehood when the Oslo process expired on 4 May. Netanyahu's tough rhetoric was combined with the escalation of settlement expansion in the West Bank and East Jerusalem. In early January, he gave the go-ahead for the construction of the Har Homa settlement at Jabal Abu Ghunaym on Jerusalem's southern outskirts, a step which triggered fierce Palestinian opposition. The new settlement will effectively complete the cordon of Jewish settlements around East Jerusalem, virtually cutting off the city from the rest of the West Bank. Jabal Abu Ghunaym was one of several settlement expansion schemes the Israeli government was putting into effect, to take advantage of the election atmosphere in Israel. Since the Wye agreement was signed, Israel had established 17 new 'hilltop' settlements in the West Bank, all located close to areas slated for transfer to the PA under the terms of Wye. Their aim was not only to swell the West Bank settler population from its current 160,000 to a potential 200,000, but also to enclose the existing Palestinian autonomous areas to prevent their expansion much beyond the 10 per cent of extra territory granted them in Wye's 'second further redeployment', if and when implemented.

On 17 May, the Israeli electorate summarily booted the incumbent Prime Minister Netanyahu out of office and elected One Israel Party leader Ehud Barak, a former army chief of staff, in his place. Barak, of the opposition Labour Party, won the prime ministerial elections by a landslide, taking 56.8 per cent of the vote compared to 43.1 per cent for Netanyahu. In the second ballot to the Israeli Parliament,

Likud's strength fell from 32 to 19 seats in the 120-member Knesset. In an unprecedented action, Netanyahu conceded defeat less than 40 minutes after the polls closed, when exit polls clearly pointed to a sizeable defeat for the Likud candidate. He immediately resigned the leadership of the Likud Party. Subsequently, the senior leaders of Likud recommended that the outgoing 71-year-old Foreign Minister, Ariel Sharon, become acting chairman of the party in place of Netanyahu. A new Likud leader is expected to be elected in three months to a year. The outgoing Finance Minister, Meir Shitrit, has announced that he intends to run for leader of the Likud but the Jerusalem mayor Ehud Olmert appeared the clear front-runner for the leadership. However, even the most 'moderate' and pragmatic of these Likudniks aspire to a reconciliation between Israelis and Palestinians which would include acceptance of the Israeli presence in the 'entire historic Land of Israel'.

3
Jewish Fundamentalism, Greater Israel and the Palestinians

GUSH EMUNIM, SETTLEMENT AND THE NATIONALIST-RELIGIOUS MESSIANIC TREND

Since 1967, the cutting edge of imperial Israel has been provided by Jewish fundamentalism. The founding fathers of modern Zionism and the State of Israel were almost all of them atheists or religiously indifferent, although their legitimisation of the Zionist enterprise in the biblical narrative and record was always a powerful driving force to gain international support. The founder of political Zionism, Theodor Herzl, had been little concerned with the exact location of the 'Judenstaat' and the scope of its boundaries. Since 1967, however, the new religious Zionism, often described as the messianic redemptionist or fundamentalist trend, has transposed the rhetoric of Herzlian Zionism from a secular aspiration to create a sovereign 'state for the Jews' to the apocalyptic redemption of the 'whole Land of Israel'. Arising in the wake of Israel's 1967 territorial conquests and accompanying the success of Zionism, Jewish fundamentalism has developed into a major political and cultural force on the Israeli scene, with a considerable influence on the attitudes, commitments and votes of a large number of Israelis. Its organised focus is the highly influential settlement movement of Gush Emunim ('The Bloc of Faithful'), which activates the entire panorama of Jewish fundamentalists and secular ultra-nationalists, including some of Israel's most powerful leaders.[1]

Jewish fundamentalism has spawned Jewish terrorism in the occupied territories from the late 1970s and through the 1980s and 1990s (examples include the anti-Arab Jewish Underground in the early 1980s and the Hebron massacre in February 1994 and, indirectly, the assassination of Prime Minister Yitzhak Rabin on 4 November 1995). For the Neo-Zionist fundamentalists, who embrace the supremacist notion of Jews as a divinely 'chosen people' ('am segula'), the indigenous Palestinians are no more than illegitimate tenants and squatters, and a threat to the process of messianic redemption; their human and civil rights are no match for the divine legitimacy and the religiously ordained duty (or 'mitzvah') of 'conquering, possessing and settling the Promised Land'. For the Gush Emunim settlers in the West Bank, Israel must continue the ancient biblical battles over settlement of the 'Land of Israel', to be won by a combination of religious faith and military might. The devotion of an increasingly powerful trend to the total possession of 'the biblical Land of Israel' and to messianic redemption has effectively turned the Palestinians into resident aliens on their own soil.

As a settlement/colonial movement and a pre-eminently ultra-nationalist-religious political force, Gush Emunim emphasises both the 'holiness' and 'territorial wholeness' of Eretz-Yisrael. In its ideology, national identity is not just a sociocultural reality, it is a geopolitical and territorial ideal. Israeli-Jewish national identity is born both out of a cultural self-understanding and out of the actual land that the Jews inhabit.[2] The popular slogan of the movement reflects this: 'The Land of Israel, for the People of Israel, According to the Torah [Bible] of Israel'. As Rabbi Kook put it, 'The Land was chosen before the people.' Hanan Porat, one of the most influential leaders of the movement, echoed the same perspective:

> For us the Land of Israel is a Land of destiny, a chosen Land, not just an existentially defined homeland. It is the Land from which the voice of God has called to us ever since that first call to the first Hebrew: 'Come and go forth from your Land where you were born and from your father's house to the Land that I will show you.'[3]

Given this view, it is hardly surprising that questions of the geo-national borders of 'Greater Israel', automatically assume cosmic proportions.

The Gush Emunim philosophy is based on several components: messianic fervour related to the belief in the 'sanctity' of Greater Israel; the establishment of Jewish sovereignty over the 'whole Land of Israel' and the building of the Temple in Jerusalem; the ethos of a religious utopia, reflecting the desire to build a nationalist Jewish state based on the 'halacha' (code of Jewish law) as a substitute for Western-style liberal democracy; the claim of pioneering settlement inspired by the Labour Zionism and its Kibbutz movement of the pre-state era, and political activism inspired by maximalist Revisionist Zionism.[4] Although at present the settlement drive of Gush Emunim is confined to the post-1967 occupied territories (so-called 'Judea', 'Samaria' and Gaza), according to Ehud Sprinzak, a renowned expert on Gush Emunim, 'When Gush ideologues speak about the complete [whole] Land of Israel they have in mind not only the post-1967 territory, but the land promised in the Covenant (Genesis 15) as well. This includes the occupied territories – especially Judea and Samaria, the very heart of the historic Israeli nation, and vast territories that belong now to Jordan, Syria and Iraq.'[5]

Traditionally, Transjordan – where, according to biblical stories, the Israelite tribes of Reuven, Menashe and Gad were supposed to have resided – has been the primary focus of Gush Emunim's expansionist ambitions,[6] although other expansionist aspirations in all sorts of directions across the Fertile Crescent have also been openly expressed. In the judgement of the late Rabbi Tzvi Yehuda Kook (1891–1982), the paramount spiritual leader of Gush Emunim, the destined borders of the Jewish state will stretch broadly across the whole area: Transjordan, the Golan Heights, the 'Bashan' (the Jabal Druze region in Syria), are all part of the 'Land of Israel'.[7] Echoing the same vision of geopolitical ambitions, Yehuda Elitzur, one of the most influential scholars in Gush Emunim, considered the 'promised' or 'patriarchal' boundaries extending to the Euphrates River, southern Turkey, Transjordan and the Nile Delta; the lands which Israel is required eventually to conquer, 'redeem', 'inherit' and settle include northern Sinai, Lebanon and western Syria, the Golan Heights and much of Transjordan.[8]

Israel's military invasion of Lebanon in 1982 encouraged many religious Jews to discuss '*halachic* imperatives' towards territorial expansion in the direction of Lebanon, regardless of the price. These religious Jews claimed large tracts of Lebanon to be the domain of the biblical tribe of Asher. Beirut was even Hebraicised to Beerot – the Hebrew for 'well'. Members of the Israeli Army's rabbinate issued a leaflet which quoted the 'inheritance of Asher' in the Book of Joshua.[9] In September of that year, the Gush Emunim journal *Nekudah* ('Point') published 'a study' by Yehuda Elitzur, claiming that the most serious distortion of Israel's borders was in the north – in Lebanon.[10] The following month a paid advertisement of Gush Emunim in support of the invasion of Lebanon asserted that South Lebanon was part of Eretz-Yisrael and that the 1982 war 'brought back the property of the tribes of Naftali and Asher into Israel's boundaries'.[11] In the same month, Jewish fundamentalists reiterated the same claim in a book entitled *This Good Mountain and the Lebanon*. Rabbis Ya'acov Ariel, Dov Leor and Yisrael Ariel, as well as other fundamentalists, declared southern Lebanon to be the lands of the Israelite tribes of Zevulon, Asher and Naphtali. Yisrael Ariel went even further by asserting that the boundaries of the Land of Israel included Lebanon up to Tripoli in the north, Sinai, Syria, part of Iraq and even part of Kuwait.[12] In the same month he called for the annexation and settlement of most of Lebanon, including its capital Beirut, to Israel, at any price:

> Beirut is part of the Land of Israel – about that there is no controversy, and being that Lebanon is part of the Land of Israel we must declare that we have no intention of leaving. We must declare that Lebanon is flesh of our flesh, as is Tel Aviv and Haifa, and that we do this by right of the moral power granted to us in the Torah. Our leaders should have entered Lebanon and Beirut without hesitation, and killed every single one of them. Not a memory or a trace should have remained ... We should have entered Beirut at any price, without regard to our own casualties, because we are speaking of the conquest of the Land of Israel ... We should immediately divert the waters of the Litani to the Jordan [River].[13]

Forty American rabbis, who had been brought to the hills surrounding Beirut to view the the Lebanese capital besieged and bombarded by the Israeli Army, declared that Operation Peace for Galilee was, Judaically, a just war and a 'milhemet mitzvah', a 'commandment war' or an obligatory war. A leading American Jewish scholar, Rabbi J. David Bleich, suggested that a verse from the biblical Song of Songs supported the acquisition of southern Lebanon. Bleich interpreted this as another step towards complete redemption.[14] The Ashkenazi Chief Rabbi of Israel, Shlomo Goren, went even further, and following Maimonides, cited various categories of obligatory wars, which included Joshua's battle to clear Eretz-Yisrael when the ancient Israelites crossed into Canaan, the battles against the Amalekites and the contemporary war in Lebanon.[15] The Lubavitcher Rebbe, the Hasidic leader who held court in Brooklyn, New York, and popularised the messianic idea, fiercely opposed Israel's partial withdrawal in 1985 from southern

Lebanon, describing the area as Israel's 'North Bank' which had been part of biblical Land of Israel.[16]

Back in 1982, shortly before Israel's invasion of Lebanon and immediately after Israel's evacuation of the settlement of Yamit in northern Sinai, leading Gush Emunim figures, such as Beni Katzover and Rabbis Moshe Levinger and Haim Druckman, formed an organisation called Shvut Sinai ('Return to Sinai'), dedicated to campaigning for the reconquest of Sinai by Israel and Jewish rule over it.[17] Two years later, in 1984, Ya'acov Feitelson, a Tehiya Party member and the former mayor of Ariel, the largest Jewish settlement in the northern part of the West Bank, echoed the same Jewish imperial vision of a Jewish state stretching across the entire Arab East:

> I am speaking of a tremendous vision. We are only in the infancy of the Zionist movement ... Israel must squarely face up to the implementation of the Zionist vision – a vision that has not changed since the days of Herzl. As is known, Herzl never indicated what the borders of the state were to be ... in his time the settlement [by Jews] of the Syrian desert was discussed. I say that Israel should establish new cities throughout the entire area. I mean really the whole area of the Middle East, without limiting ourselves: we should never say about any place: 'here we stop'.[18]

In the same year (1984), Rabbi Eli'ezer Waldman expressed opposition to the idea which was then propagated by Likud leaders, such as Ariel Sharon and Yitzhak Shamir, that Jordan has become the Palestinian homeland. Waldman and the majority of Gush Emunim opposed any final agreement to relinquish the East Bank of Jordan to non-Jewish rule.[19]

This geopolitical vision of territorial expansion across the region can only be ensured by military campaigns and 'wars of liberation'. In fact, the actual settlement drive in the West Bank is viewed and planned as nothing less than a military campaign. Military might, war and warfare are desired and often eagerly sought by many Neo-Zionist groups. War simply represents a time of testing, a sign of strength, a necessary means by which the will of Providence is worked out. Territorially ambitious rabbis and leaders of Gush Emunim share the same attitude to war. Within Gush Emunim, war, leading to Jewish rule over the 'whole Land of Israel,' is a central component of the purgative process that will bring about messianic times. Emphasising expansion by military means, Rabbi Tzvi Kook advised the following:

> We are commanded both to possess and to settle [the land]. The meaning of possession is conquest, and in performing this *mitzvah*, we can perform the other – the commandment to settle ... We cannot evade this commandment ... Torah, war, and settlement – they are three things in one and we rejoice in the authority we have been given for each of them.[20]

In a similar vein Rabbi Shlomo Aviner writes: 'We have been commanded by the God of Israel and the creator of the world to take possession of this *entire* land, in its holy borders, and to do this by wars of defence, and even by wars of liberation.'[21] Hanan Porat, a leading Gush Emunim figure, spoke in 1982 in terms of practical preparations for future opportunities that will arise: 'We must prepare ourselves in terms of our consciousness and by establishing new settlement nuclei, to settle those portions of the Land of Israel that today are still not in our hands ... nuclei for the Litani area [in south Lebanon], Gilead, Transjordan and Sinai.'[22]

Gush Emunim has been the most successful extra-parliamentary movement to arise in Israel since 1948 and has had a profound influence upon the Israeli political system.[23] Its practical settlement of the West Bank has been the main vehicle of the political success of Jewish fundamentalism inside Israel. Gush Emunim, Sprinzak writes, 'is a very dynamic force, by far the most viable component of the radical right. It may also be the most effective social movement that has emerged in Israel since 1948.'[24] A large measure of its huge success has been due to the symbiotic relationship it forged with the Likud, Israel's major right-wing political party, which (unlike Labour Zionism) had no strong settlement movement of its own. Consequently, after May 1977, the practical expertise and settlement zeal of thousands of fundamentalist settlers provided the Likud administrations with an indispensable resource in the implementation of their annexationist policies.[25] Formally established in February 1974 and wielding tremendous influence over the Likud administrations of Menahem Begin, Yitzhak Shamir and Binyamin Netanyahu, the movement has played a key role in establishing dozens of Jewish settlements throughout the occupied West Bank. The establishment of numerous Jewish settlements is also designed to prevent any territorial concessions in the West Bank or any other areas deemed as being part of the 'divinely ordained Land of Israel'. The creation of the State of Israel in 1948 and the conquest ('liberation') of additional territories in the 1967 war are both perceived as constituting part of the divine process of messianic redemption – a process that, according to the Gush Emunim leaders, should not be stopped or altered by any elected government of Israel.[26]

Seen as a successor to the Whole Land of Israel Movement, Gush Emunim underwent several stages of development. Its roots are embedded in the post-1967 reality. It had evolved into an organised and dynamic force of settlers from the youth branch of the National Religious Party (NRP, or Mafdal), which in the last three decades, has epitomised the nationalist-religious messianic trend in Israeli politics. The NRP has been a member of all Israeli governments since 1948, with the exception of short periods in 1958–59 and in June 1992–June 1996, and is currently represented in the government of Ehud Barak. Until 1967, the NRP's main interest had been in advocating legislation of a religious nature and its role in Israeli external affairs had been limited. However, in the post-1967 period, the NRP came to be dominated by its Young Guard: those elements committed ideologically to the practical settlement by Jews of the 'whole Land of Israel' and its permanent incorporation into the State of Israel. Until 1977, the NRP remained a coalition partner with the pragmatic ruling Labour Party. However, its commitment to Greater Israel and its close identification with Gush Emunim meant that its natural partnership lay with maximalist Revisionist Zionism, with the Likud and Israel's secular radical right.

Indeed after 1977, the NRP, dominated by its hawkish Young Guard, joined all Likud coalition governments and was until May 1999 a major partner in Binyamin Netanyahu's Cabinet. In the 1996 elections, the NRP increased the number of its parliamentary seats to nine (out of 120) and its vote share to 8.6 per cent, and joined the largest religious voting bloc in Israeli parliamentary history. Moreover, from 1986 to January 1998, the party was led by Zevulun Hammer, the founder of the Young Guard, who, more than any other office-holder, epitomised the influence of the religious right on both the state's education system and Israeli politics in general. A former leader of the Bnei 'Akiva youth movement, Hammer served in most Israeli Cabinets since the mid-1970s: Minister of Welfare 1975–76, Minister of Education and Culture June 1977–84, Minister of Religious Affairs October 1986–June 1990, Minister of Education and Culture June 1990–June 1992, Minister of Education June 1996–August 1997, and finally Minister of Religious Affairs and Deputy Prime Minister from August 1997 until his death in January 1998. In 1990, then Minister of Religious Affairs, Hammer proposed openly that the Israeli citizenship of those Israeli Arabs who were campaigning peacefully against Soviet Jewish immigration to Israel should be revoked.[27]

Three years earlier, in October 1987, another prominent office-holder from the religious right, Yosef Shapira, a former member of the NRP and a Morasha minister in the Cabinet of Yitzhak Shamir, referred to 'transfer' as a reasonable and viable solution, suggesting that a sum of $20,000 should be paid for a Palestinian family ready to leave permanently.[28] In support of his proposal, Shapira cited a survey his party conducted among rabbis in the West Bank and Gaza Strip, in which 62 per cent of them responded that 'we must force them to do so by any means at our disposal and see in it an exchange of population'; 13 per cent favoured the encouragement of voluntary emigration.[29] The current leader of the NRP is Rabbi Yitzhak Levy, a founder of Matzad (the Religious Zionism Camp), an extreme-right faction within the NRP, who has previously made clear his opposition to allowing Israeli Arab Knesset members the right to vote on the Oslo Accords of 1993 and who, according to the daily newspaper *Haaretz* of 25 February 1998, was reputed to have supported 'exiling Arabs' in the occupied territories to other Arab states.[30] Rabbi Levy is also known to be close to former Sephardi Chief Rabbi Mordechai Eliyahu, another advocate of Greater Israel, who has called for the rehabilitation of Yigal Amir, Yitzhak Rabin's assassin.[31] In 1983, while serving as Sephardi Chief Rabbi, Eliyahu had sponsored a conference with 'Ateret Cohanim Yeshiva on the rebuilding of the Third Temple in Jerusalem. He believes that the Third Temple would descend from heaven amid flames of fire – at that point the Muslim shrines, the Dome of the Rock and al-Aqsa Mosque, would be burnt and the Third Temple be built in their place.[32]

Since the 1967 'miraculous' conquests, the NRP youth, the religious youth movement of Bnei 'Akiva ('Sons of 'Akiva'), which gave birth to Gush Emunim, has been imbued with an explosive mixture of Zionist territorial expansionism, militant nationalism and religious fundamentalism by their nationalist-religious yeshivot (talmudic seminaries and high schools); these yeshivot are funded by the state's Ministry of Education. However, the Gush Emunim's single most influential ideologue was Rabbi Tzvi Yehuda Kook, head of Merkaz Harav Yeshiva in Jerusalem, and the son of the Chief Ashkenazi Rabbi of the Jewish community in Mandatory Palestine, Rabbi Avraham Yitzhak HaCohen Kook (1865–1935) (Rabbi Kook the Elder). The ideas and teachings of the Kooks, father and son, integrated the traditional, passive religious longings for the land with the modern, secular, activist and expansionist Zionism, giving birth to a new comprehensive ideology of Jewish nationalist-religious fundamentalism.[33]

'Kookist' Neo-Zionism saw the 1967 war as a turning-point in the process of messianic redemption and the deliverance of Eretz-Yisrael from what it termed the 'Sitra Achra', the 'evil (Arab) side'.[34] Tzvi Kook himself rushed with his biblical claims towards the West Bank immediately after the 1967 conquests: 'All this land is ours, absolutely, belonging to all of us, non-transferable to others even in part ... it is clear and absolute that there are no "Arab territories" or "Arab lands" here, but only the lands of Israel, the eternal heritage of our forefathers to which others [the Arabs] have come and upon which they have built without our permission and in our absence.'[35] Kook's politics were described by the Israeli journalist David Shaham as 'consistent, extremist, uncompromising and concentrated on a single issue: the right of the Jewish people to sovereignty over every foot of the Land of Israel. Absolute sovereignty, with no imposed limitations. "From a perspective of national sovereignty", he [Kook] says, "the country belongs to us ... ".'[36] Immediately after the 1967 war, Rabbi Kook demanded the annexation of the occupied territories, in line with explicit halacha provisions.[37] He also said at a conference after 1967: 'I tell you explicitly ... that there is a prohibition in the Torah against giving up even an inch of our liberated land. There are no conquests here and we are not occupying foreign land; we are returning to our home, to the inheritance of our forefathers. There is no Arab land here, only the inheritance of our God – the more the world gets used to this thought the better it will be for it and for all of us.' These statements were made in the presence of over a thousand people, including the Israeli President Zalman Shazar, ministers, members of the Knesset, judges, chief rabbis and senior civil servants.[38]

For the followers of Rabbi Kook, continuing territorial expansion, combined with the establishment of Jewish sovereignty over the entire, biblically described, Land of Israel, and the building of the Temple in Jerusalem, are all part of implementing the divinely ordained messianic redemption. Rabbi Shlomo Aviner, the former

Rabbi of Bet El settlement on the West Bank and currently the Rabbi of the 'Ateret Cohanim Yeshiva (which belongs to a fundamentalist group campaigning for rebuilding the Jewish Temple on the ruins of the Muslim mosques on the Haram al-Sharif in East Jerusalem), called for further territorial expansionism beyond the current occupied territories: 'Even if there is a peace, we must instigate wars of liberation in order to conquer additional parts of the Land of Israel.'[39]

The Palestinians are viewed by many Gush Emunim spiritual leaders as well as the settlers as temporary alien residents, and as a population living, at best, on sufferance. Gush Emunim stalwarts strongly opposed the idea of Palestinian autonomy in any sort in the occupied territories. A Gush Emunim spokesman, Meir Eindor of Kiryat Arba'a, was quoted as saying in 1980: 'The Arabs must know that there is a master here, the Jewish people. It rules over Eretz-Yisrael ... The Arabs are temporary dwellers who happened to live in this country. There are commandments in the Bible concerning such temporary dwellers and we should act accordingly.'[40] According to the Gush spiritual leaders, there is no need to take into consideration the Arab inhabitants, since their residence in the country for hundreds of years was prohibited and was based on theft, fraud and distortion; therefore now the time has come for the Arab 'robbers' to depart. As Rabbi Shlomo Aviner explains:

> To what can this be compared[?] It resembles a man entering his neighbour's house without permission and residing there for many years. When the original owner of the house returns, the invader [the Arab] claims: 'It is my [house]. I have been living here for many years.' So what? All of these years he was a robber! Now he should depart and pay housing rent as well. A person might say there is a difference between a residence of thirty years and a residence of two thousand years. Let us ask him: Is there a law of limitation which gives a robber the right to his plunder? ... Everyone who settled here knew very well that he was residing in a land that belonged to the people of Israel. Perhaps an Arab who was born here does not know this, none the less the fact that a man settled on land does not make it his. Legally, 'possession' serves only as evidence of a claim of ownership, but it does not create ownership. The Arabs' 'possession' of the land is therefore a 'possession that asserts no right'. It is the possession of territory when it is absolutely clear that they are not its legal owners, and this possession has no legal and moral validity.[41]

In a similar disposition, the afore-mentioned Rabbi Kook, who apparently inspired Aviner's apologia, wrote: 'We find ourselves here by virtue of our forefathers' inheritance, the foundation of the Bible and history, and there is no one that can change this fact. What does it resemble? A man left his house and others came and invaded it. This is exactly what happened to us. There are those who claim that these are Arab lands here. It is all a lie and falsehood. There are absolutely no Arab lands here.'[42] This imagery of the homecoming Jew and the Arab invader permeates the writings of the spiritual leaders and ideologists of Gush Emunim, particularly the religious extremists, and implies that the Jew has the right to evict the 'alien' Arab 'invader'. Moreover, these ideologues interpret the Zionist assertion of 'historical rights' to the land as meaning that the very fact of Arab residence on, and possession of, the land is morally flawed and legally, at best, temporary – therefore the Arabs must evacuate the land for the 'legal owners' of the country and depart.

In 1980, the Gush Emunim movement's Department of Information published an article written by the above-mentioned Yisrael Eldad recommending that the best course of action would be to bring about large-scale Arab emigration through the deliberate creation of economic hardship in the West Bank and Gaza. Similar views have been expressed at every level of the Gush Emunim movement by both leaders and rank-and-file members, most of whom are religious extremists. Elyakim Ha'etzni, of Kiryat Arba'a, is a prominent secular figure in the settlers' movement, who later became a Tehiya Party Member of the Knesset and was until the early 1950s a member of the Mapai Party. He spoke at a settlers' conference attended by fifty leading activists from settlements in the occupied territories and held in Moshav Bnei-Tal in the Gaza Strip in 1980 (only a few weeks after the maiming of the West Bank mayors) to discuss the future of Arab–Jewish relations in Eretz-Yisrael. According to the account of the conference, published by the official Gush Emunim bulletin *Hamakor* (August 1980), Ha'etzni stated:

> We must get rid of the real obstacle to peace, which is the Hashemite royal house, and we must not leave Amman [after the IDF has occupied it] except in exchange for an agreement stipulating the elimination of the Hashemite royal house and the elimination of the refugee problem. We must help the Palestinian Arabs to set up their own state on the East Bank of the Jordan ... The Arabs living on the West Bank, in Judea and Samaria, and in

the Galilee and the Negev will then elect the Jordanian Parliament, and the Jews will settle on the East Bank [and] will elect the Knesset.

Ha'etzni – who, like many supporters of Greater Israel mentioned earlier, makes little distinction between the Palestinian citizens of Israel and those of the West Bank and Gaza – added: 'Today there is no plan to make Hebron into a Jewish town ... but if you ["the Arab neighbour"] think that Kiryat Arba [*sic*] will disappear, you had better remember Jaffa [the Arab town which was largely depopulated in 1948] ...' Another speaker from the Gush Emunim settlement of 'Ofra named Aharon Halamish was much more straightforward: 'It is not necessary to throw bombs into the casbah or expel the Arabs. There is nothing wrong, however, with making their life difficult in the hope that they will emigrate ... Perhaps in the end only those will remain who genuinely want to be loyal citizens of Israel, and if they really do, let them convert.'[43] Clearly this settler did not believe that many Arabs would agree to 'convert' and therefore he suggested the encouragement of Arab emigration.

This and other evidence, which will follow, illustrates the hardly surprising fact that most Gush Emunim settlers and protagonists would like to drive out the Palestinians of the West Bank and Gaza. David Grossman, a *Jerusalem Post* correspondent covering the West Bank, described a meeting of Gush Emunim in the settlement of Alfei Menashe at which Ha'etzni urged the authorities to take steps against PLO activities and anyone who opposed the settlement policies. Grossman writes: 'I make out the words "expulsion", "closure", "imprisonment", "death penalty", "destruction", and for a short, mad moment I see Haetzni [*sic*] prancing happily through a West Bank completely emptied of people.'[44]

Many leading Gush Emunim figures sought to legitimise discussions of mass Arab expulsions. In an article entitled 'In Defence of the Transfer', published in *Nekudah* 14 April 1987 (pp.16–17), Moshe Ben-Yosef wrote: 'It is kosher to discuss the idea of transfer, and even to put it into effect ... It is kosher not only because it is an "actual solution", but also because it is required for the vision of the whole Land of Israel ... The idea of transfer has deep roots in the Zionist movement.' Yisrael Harel, a Gush Emunim activist and the editor of *Nekudah*, wrote in January 1988: 'Half a year ago, 90 per cent of people would have objected to transfer. Today 30 to 40 per cent would argue that it's not a dirty word or an inhuman policy. On the contrary, they would argue it's a way to avoid friction.'[45] David Rosentzweig of Kidumim wrote in an article in *Nekudah* in December 1983: 'We should urge them [the Arabs] to get out of here. The Arab public must feel that the land (really the land) is being pulled from under its feet ... the very fact of their presence endangers our life every day ... For our own safety there is no place for the Arabs with us in this country ... we must seek a new and revolutionary way to deal with the Jewish–Arab conflict.' In November 1990, the leader of Karnei Shomron (in the West Bank) regional council, Beni Katzover, (who is also a leading Gush Emunim figure and was a candidate for the Tehiya in the 1992 elections), wrote in an article in *Nekudah*, under the headline: 'The Jews are Coming, the Arabs are Going': 'The only outlet open to them [the Arabs] is to leave, to emigrate, and it does not matter to where. They have not achieved a state and will not ... and with no choice and no livelihood, the process of "no choice" will drive the Arabs out.' As a result of this Arab evacuation, the demand for housing by the new immigrants from the Soviet Union 'would find its partial and substantial solution in the many houses which the Arabs of Judea, Samaria and Gaza would leave behind'. According to the prominent leader of Gush Emunim and the Tehiya Party, Israel should not wait until the Palestinians give up hope and depart: 'Now [is the time] to come out with a concentrated offensive. Now is the time to break finally their spirit. Now is the time to crush the leadership of the intifada and to expel the fifty main leaders of the rioters. Now is the time to expel the five thousand inciters and central rioters ... Now is the time to instruct the IDF to shoot without hesitation in order to hit every rioter.'[46]

The newspaper *Nekudah*, which has been assiduously popularising the 'transfer'/ethnic-cleansing idea, appeared first in December 1979. By 1986, its circulation reached 10,000 copies, sent to subscribers in the occupied territories and in Israel, including public institutions and public and academic libraries. *Nekudah* also appears in the form of pamphlets with a circulation of 50,000.[47] The November 1987 issue of *Nekudah* discusses the results of a recent questionnaire on 'security matters' conducted among rabbis, yeshiva students and directors in the settlements of 'Judea', 'Samaria' and Gaza. Eighty-six per cent of the respondents to the questionnaire from the Tzomet Institute in Elon Shvut settlement supported the imposition of collective punishment – on a refugee camp, hamulah (clan or extended family) or family – for Arab inhabitants. Sixty-four per cent were of the opinion that the collective punishment should be expulsion. Seventy-seven per cent of the respondents believed that 'Arab emigration should be encouraged', while 85 per cent thought that the death penalty should be imposed on Arab 'terrorists'.[48] Israeli journalists, who have covered the West Bank for over three decades, provide some of the best accounts of the ideology of the settlers' movement and its anti-Arab racist concepts, as well as amply documenting its violence in the occupied territories. In his seminal work *On the Lord's Side: Gush Emunim* (1982), Danny Rubinstein concludes that the majority of the Gush Emunim settlers are in favour of expelling the Arab population, describes the anti-Arab feelings that permeate the Gush Emunim meetings and provides excerpts from the settlers' movement's pamphlets and bulletins: 'Hatred of the [Arab] enemy is not a morbid feeling, but a healthy and natural phenomenon'; 'The people of Israel have a legitimate national and natural psychological right to hate their enemies'; 'The Arabs are the Amalekites of today'; 'The aim of the settlements in the Nablus area is "to stick a knife in the heart of the Palestinians".'[49] For the right-wing religious fundamentalists, Jewish sovereignty over the 'whole Land of Israel' was divinely ordained, since the entire land had been promised by God to the Jewish people. Moreover, for many settlement leaders, particularly those religious figures and extremist rabbis, the ideological conflict with the Palestinian Arabs had its roots in biblical injunctions, regarding the Amalekites (see 1 Samuel 15:2–3). At least some leading rabbis interpreted this biblical injunction to justify not only the expulsion of local Arabs but also the killing of Arab civilians in the event of war.[50]

In 1980, Israeli journalist Amnon Kapeliouk, of *'Al-Hamishmar*, described vividly the attitudes of the Hebron region settlers towards the local Arabs: 'It ranges from utter contempt to wishing that they would vanish. When one of the settlers was asked why they want Hebron after having established Kiryat Arba'a, the reply was: "It is not theirs, it is ours ... it is ours by the power of the Bible. It was ours 2000 years ago and it always belonged to us. If they do not like it let them leave."'[51] The Gush Emunim settlers viewed the escalating violence between Arabs and Jews in the territories as a positive thing. As a prominent Gush Emunim leader, Hanan Porat, of Kfar 'Etzion – who was later in 1984 elected to the Knesset on the Tehiya list – put it: the violence will prove that 'the two cannot co-exist', and 'will bring about the expulsion of the Arabs'.[52] More recently, in mid-1990, David Forman, of the *Jerusalem Post*, commented on how any visitor to the West Bank could not fail to notice Jewish graffiti: 'Death to the Arabs' and 'Transfer is the answer.' He added that no Jewish settler had been awakened at 3 o'clock in the morning to whitewash these pejoratives[53] – as opposed to what the authorities do when Palestinian graffiti appear.

In practical terms, the Gush Emunim settlers and activists – mostly well-educated Ashkenazi, middle-class Israelis who have close and often personal ties with Israel's traditional ruling groups and powerful figures in the Likud and the NRP – perceive themselves as continuing the process of early 'pioneering Zionism', particularly within the field of establishing new Jewish settlements. For much of the larger camp of the Israeli right and the supporters of Greater Israel, Gush Emunim now fulfils the role that the kibbutz movement fulfilled for Labour Zionism in the pre-state period.[54] And, like early Zionist settlers in Palestine, who engaged in actual 'redemption' and 'conquest' of land ('kibbush haadamah') and the creation of irreversible 'facts', the Gush Emunim settlers have always had a disproportionate impact on the official policies of successive Israeli governments, even when the settlers have acted independently, or in ostensible or real defiance, of the government, such as during the last few years of the Labour era in the 1970s, when three settlements were established in heavily-populated West Bank areas: Kaddum, 'Ofra and Elon Moreh. The three settlements were allowed to remain by the Rabin government, and various Labour ministries provided material assistance for these three settlements. In fact it was the post-1967 Labour governments which pioneered settlement policies, establishing settlements such as Kiryat Arba'a, neighbouring Hebron, and the Gush 'Etzion settlements. These were extremely important not just because land and resources were appropriated from the occupied West Bank, but also because these settlements provided the Gush Emunim fundamentalists with a territorial base from which they could grow, mobilise more supporters and exert pressure for further expansion into heavily-populated areas. The Gush settlers' disproportionate impact on official policies stemmed also from their dogged religious determination as well as from their dynamism and practical pursuit of their objectives.

Following the Likud assumption of power in May 1977, Gush Emunim settlement aspirations were given an enormous boost. From 1977 through the early 1980s, it became public knowledge that the Gush Emunim movement enjoyed the crucial support of Prime Minister Menahem Begin, the Agriculture Minister and Chairman of the Ministerial Committee on Settlement and later Defence Minister Ariel Sharon, and the army Chief of Staff Raphael Eitan.[55] Under the Likud, settlement activities in areas densely populated with Arabs acquired official authorisation and were carried out as government policies. New settler groups were assisted in establishing numerous settlements throughout the West Bank in accordance with settlement blueprints prepared jointly by the Gush Emunim and the Settlement Department of the World Zionist Organisation under its new co-chairman, Likud appointee Mattityahu Drobless. After 1977, the principal financial support of the settlement movement and its activities has been the Israeli government, the World Zionist Organisation and the Jewish Agency.[56] These official bodies provided the Jewish settlers with material resources; and the Israeli Army gave them weapons and explosives and protected them, while ensuring the Arab population remained defenceless.

The core of Gush Emunim is the more than 150 settlements established in the West Bank, the Gaza Strip and the Golan Heights since 1967. By April 1988, the settlement branch of Gush Emunim, Amana ('Covenant'), had been instrumental in controlling 48 community settlements in the occupied territories.[57] Many of the Gush settlements are socially homogeneous community villages ('kfar kehilati') whose inhabitants mostly commute to Israeli cities for employment.[58] Gush Emunim also claimed to enjoy support from secular settlers, who (in 1996) made up approximately 60 per cent of the total settler population in the occupied territories.[59] Its settlements are organised within Yesha', the Association of the Local Councils of Judea, Samaria, and the Gaza District. Mo'etzet Yesha' ('the Yesha' Council') gives Gush Emunim a semi-official governing body, considerable economic and administrative resources, and direct involvement in the implementation of government settlement policies in the occupied territories.[60]

Although institutionalised with thousands of full-time devotees, Gush Emunim has no formal membership list or an elected leadership. Nevertheless, it maintains an organisational network that spans the 'Green Line', the 1949 armistice line dividing Israel from the territories occupied in 1967. At the party political level, the movement also remains an unaffiliated movement, although many of its leading personalities are formally members of both the NRP and the Tehiya. However, Gush Emunim's real power lies in its extensive settlement network, its thousands of highly devoted and motivated settlers, its dozens of settlements, with their huge financial and material assets, and above all in the activities of its leading personalities in all the political parties of the right. Gush Emunim has drawn crucial support from the Likud, the NRP, Tzomet, Moledet, Tehiya and Matzad. Knesset members of these parties identified with Gush Emunim objectives and openly campaigned for their implementation. In 1987, members of the Knesset faction Matzad, all of whom were closely identified with Gush Emunim, succeeded in capturing key positions within the NRP. Furthermore, several leading Gush Emunim personalities, including Hanan Porat, Rabbi Eli'ezer Waldman, and Rabbi Haim Druckman have been Knesset members.[61] In addition, through dynamic leading figures like Daniella Weiss, a religious activist in the Tehiya Party who was appointed general secretary of the Gush Emunim Secretariat in 1985, the settler movement runs an effective public relations machine in Israel and the occupied territories.[62]

THE POLITICS OF 'AMALEK'

Direct Action and Violence: Activities of the Jewish Underground, Terror Against Terror, the Sicarites and Temple Mount Groups

The ideas of the religious fundamentalist-messianic current in Israel are not confined to the realm of doctrines and sermons; from the outset their ideas began to accommodate and sanctify the use of violence as a proactive means of forestalling any moves that might retard the 'messianic process' of territorial 'redemption' and land conquest. From the beginning of the occupation and especially since the late 1970s, the settlers – whose ideo-theology grants them the divine right to judaise the territories and who reject the very existence of the Palestinians – were deliberately seeking to foster clashes between Arabs and Jews and to create conditions that would precipitate a gradual Arab depopulation.

After 1977, with the encouragement of successive Likud governments, the militant settlers in the West Bank and Gaza Strip effectively organised themselves into a private and highly motivated army. In 1979, at the behest of the Army Chief of Staff, General Raphael Eitan, the settlers were integrated into regular reserve units responsible for patrolling the streets of local Arab towns and villages.[63] With weapons, ammunition, and training readily available, and a sympathetic political climate created by superhawks Chief of Staff Eitan and Likud Defence Minister Ariel Sharon, attacks on Arab civilians and Arab property became commonplace. From 1980 and through 1984, the Israeli press reported more than 380 attacks against individual Arabs, in which 23 were killed, 191 injured, and 38 abducted. Hundreds more attacks were directed at Arab property, such as cars, homes and shops. Forty-one attacks on Muslim and Christian institutions were also recorded.[64] In 1981, Yehuda Litani of *Haaretz* daily warned: 'The West Bank settlers constitute military units ... They will disrupt any political move towards concessions to the Arabs ... Their well-stocked ammunition stores in the West Bank will be of great help in this struggle.'[65] Having organised themselves into a militant, well-disciplined, private army, and having always regarded themselves as being subject to divine laws and above the conventional laws of the state as far as Eretz-Yisrael is concerned, the Gush Emunim settlers would represent the severest challenge to any Israeli government which might consider ceding West Bank territory to Arab sovereignty.

Gush Emunim was also reported in the Israeli press to be harbouring a whole range of violent groups which either planned or actually carried out attacks against Arab civilians. These militant groups included Kach, Temple Mount-related groups, Terror Against Terror (TNT) – a shadowy group or groups related to Kach which claimed responsibility for a long series of attacks against West Bank Palestinians, Christian missionaries in Jerusalem and dovish Israeli Jews – and the Sicarites, a group which vowed to avenge tit-for-tat the stabbing of Jews by militant Palestinians.[66] On the eve of the 1977 elections, Rabbi Kook, Gush Emunim spiritual leader, spoke explicitly in praise of Rabbi Meir Kahane and his overtly racist Kach list which was standing for the Knesset.[67] Also Gush Emunim had ties with Kach, the Temple Mount Faithful and the 'Ateret Cohanim group which apparently on various occasions tried to blow up the two mosques on the Haram al-Sharif in East Jerusalem, so as to herald the building of the Jewish Temple and the advent of the Messiah.[68]

From 1967 and through the mid-1980s, at least five separate, Temple Mount-related groups, with a total estimated membership of 1500, sought to change (sometimes violently) the status quo on the site of the Haram al-Sharif in Jerusalem. Their objectives ranged from building a Jewish synagogue on the site, to restricting the Muslim access area, and even replacing the Muslim shrines with a rebuilt Temple. More recently, a Miami-based American Jewish millionaire, Dr Irving Moskowitz, apparently offered twelve million dollars for Jewish groups seeking to replace the Muslim shrines with a rebuilt Temple.[69] Back in May 1980, the Israeli police discovered a plot to blow up al-Aqsa Mosque. A large cache of explosives was unearthed on the roof of a yeshiva in the Old City of Jerusalem. Those involved were two soldiers with links to Gush Emunim and Kach. In March 1983, several dozen yeshiva students and soldiers from Kiryat Arba'a and Jerusalem were arrested after they were found digging under the mosques. Equipped with weapons, shovels and diagrams of the underground passageways, they seemed to have planned to seize the site and hold public prayer services there. Apparently leading Gush Emunim figures, including Hanan Porat, Moshe Levinger and Eli'ezer Waldman, had prior knowledge of the operation and expressed support for the conspirators' objectives. On the night of 27 January 1984, another group of Jewish religious zealots was reported in the immediate vicinity of the Muslim shrines. The group managed to escape, leaving behind 30 pounds of explosive, fuses, detonators, and 22 grenades.[70]

But by far the best organised effort to destroy al-Aqsa Mosque and the Dome of the Rock was planned by a secret group of Gush Emunim leaders and activists known in the Hebrew press as 'Hamahteret Hayehudit', the 'Jewish Underground'. The plot to blow up the Muslim shrines in Jerusalem in January 1984 was developed carefully and systematically over several years. It involved a group of 25 men from Jewish settlements on the West Bank and the Golan Heights, including an army officer with a high level of expertise in explosives and sufficient ammunition to carry out the operation stolen from the Israeli Army.[71] Their widely documented terrorist activities also included attacks on the lives of the mayors of Nablus (Bassam Shaka'a) and Ramallah (Karim Khalaf), on 2 June 1980, in which both mayors were maimed; an attack on the Islamic College in Hebron in July 1983, killing three students, and an attempt to place bombs under five Arab buses in Jerusalem in April 1984.[72] The network of Jewish terrorists, which was given assistance by two senior officers in the Civilian Administration, included several army reserve officers and one career officer; most of the terrorists held key positions in Gush Emunim and the settlers' organisations. These included the assistant editor of the settlers' monthly *Nekudah*, a former general secretary of Gush Emunim, four people who had been members of the Gush Emunim Secretariat, committee chairmen in settlers' institutions, a former chairman of the Kiryat Arba'a local council and his deputy and settlement secretaries.[73] Spokesmen of Gush Emunim drew satisfaction from the result of the attacks on Mayors Shaka'a and Khalaf: 'Well organised, very good work'; 'I hope that Jews did it.'[74] In a similar vein, Rabbi Haim Druckman, then MK for the NRP and a settlers' leader, declared: 'Let all thine enemies perish thus.'[75] Haggai Segal, a prominent Gush Emunim settler from 'Ofra on the West Bank, who had served three years in prison for his part in the car-bomb attacks on the two West Bank mayors in June 1980, said several years later: 'You can't make a big roundup and put them on buses, but you must make conditions bad for the Arabs – and if they continue the war [the intifada], you must make them leave. I drove by the American consulate in East Jerusalem yesterday and saw a long line of Arabs waiting to get visas. The situation is very hard for them now, and it must get harder.'[76]

Initially, the discovery and arrest in April 1984 of members of the Jewish Underground and their conviction in July 1985 spurred the Gush Emunim movement into debate over 'failures in education' and internal discipline. But the movement soon became active in the campaign for their release.[77] This campaign was particularly helped by the fact that members of the Jewish Underground were applauded in the top echelon of Israeli society. Individuals who had been directly involved in Underground terrorist activities, such as Uri Maier, Zeev Friedman and Yossi Eindor, had been arrested in 1984. While on trial they had been pampered by judges and jailers; politicians from the Likud, the Tehiya and Morasha had flocked to the prison where the accused were held to express their sympathy and support. At the conclusion of the trial, a number of prominent members of the right, such as Likud MK Yigal Cohen-Orgad and General Rehava'am Zeevi, who advocated 'transferring' the Palestinians out of the occupied territories, appeared as character witnesses to the defendants. Two Likud Knesset members, Meir Cohen-Avidov and Dov Shilansky, were extremely active from the beginning in support of the Jewish Underground.[78] Although they had been convicted for planting the bombs which maimed the West Bank mayors and for the assault on the Islamic College in Hebron where Palestinian students were murdered, Israeli Television was forbidden to call them convicted 'murderers'; it was instructed by the government to call them only 'prisoners'. Moreover, the religious parties in the Knesset put forward a motion demanding that an amnesty be granted to them.

Support for an amnesty for these Underground members did not only come from the religious camp. On 19 June 1985, a public opinion poll conducted by *Haaretz* revealed the following results: 52.6 per cent of those interviewed supported an immediate release without trial; 4 per cent supported pardon after the trial; 35.5 per cent opposed a pardon; the remaining 7.9 per cent expressed no opinion. Also revealing, reputed 'moderate' Rabbi Likhtenstein, who heads a yeshiva in the occupied territories, voiced his opinion that these Jewish Underground murderers – though they should receive some punishment – should not receive the same penalty meted out to a Jew convicted of murdering another Jew because the soul of a non-Jew had a different value from that of a Jew.[79] The former Ashkenazi Chief Rabbi Shlomo Goren also expressed sympathy for the Underground members. And MK Yuval Neeman – Minister of Science in the Shamir government who supported Arab 'transfer' – defended the Underground network as acting in self-defence.[80]

In the autumn of 1986, the fundamentalist movement launched a national campaign on behalf of amnesty for the convicted members of the Jewish Underground. Some twenty members of the Knesset campaigned on the convicts' behalf and these included representatives of the right-wing and religious parties Tehiya, Ometz, the NRP, Shas, Agudat Yisrael and Morasha, as well as members of the Likud.[81] By the spring of 1987, some 300,000 signatures had been gathered. Forty members of the Knesset, including Prime Minister Yitzhak Shamir, Industry and Trade Minister Ariel Sharon, and Minister of Transport Haim Corfu, voted for a bill to grant a blanket amnesty to the Underground prisoners. Other Likud ministers, including Moshe Arens, David Levy, Yitzhak Moda'i, Moshe Nissim, and Moshe Katzav showed their sympathy for the measure by deliberately absenting themselves from the vote. Of the 27 men convicted in 1984, 20 were free by September 1986, eight as a result of presidential pardons. In April 1987, President Haim Hertzog permitted most of the remaining prisoners to enjoy a holiday leave from jail and reduced the sentences of the three who had been given life terms to a maximum of 24 years.[82] After serving only seven years in jail, the leader of the Underground, Menahem Levni – who in 1984 was found guilty of murdering Palestinians – was released under a presidential pardon.[83]

Likewise, the relatively light punishment of the Jewish Terror Against Terror (TNT) network in 1984 did nothing to discourage settlers' violence, which aims at precipitating Arab exodus, particularly when leading Israeli politicians describe those convicted murderers as basically 'good boys' acting in self-defence, or when those convicted murderers have their sentences reduced or are pardoned by the president, after the intervention of leading Israel rabbis. Sixty prominent Israeli rabbis including the two former Chief Rabbis, 'Ovadia Yosef and Shlomo Goren, intervened on behalf of, and supported the release of, the TNT detainees,[84] whom General Yehoshafat Harkabi, of the Hebrew University of Jerusalem, described in 1984 as

> ... serious people who occupy high positions among their public ... they have a rational state of mind and their chief motivation stems apparently from the awareness that annexation of the West Bank together with its Arab population would be disastrous and tantamount to national suicide – unless that population were thinned out and made to flee by terrorism. This reasoning is not moral, but it stems from the rational conclusion of the policy that aims at annexation. Such terrorism is neither a 'punishment' nor a deterrent; it is a political instrument.[85]

Ten years later, in January 1994, in an interview given to two researchers from the Ben-Gurion Research Centre in the Negev, Harkabi (who died in August 1994) predicted the assassination of Prime Minister Rabin at the hand of Jewish fundamentalists: 'There will be attempts on people's lives. Rabin will not die a natural death.'[86]

Liberal Israelis voiced criticism over the Jewish Underground's and TNT's disobedience to the state's authority and pointed to the Underground as an inevitable consequence of the philosophy and activities of Gush Emunim. But the actual reluctance of the state in general and the Likud administrations in particular to punish those settlers who murdered Palestinian civilians, as exemplified by the delayed publication of, and subsequent reticence over, the Karp report on settlers' violence against Palestinians, only encouraged militant Gush Emunim settlers and their radical right-wing supporters who were determined to drive the Palestinians out one way or another. The same reticence over settlers' violence against Arabs must also have encouraged those Jewish fundamentalists who were prepared to use violence against those perceived to be dovish Israeli Jews. In the wake of Rabin's murder by religious fundamentalist Yigal Amir in November 1995, two influential West Bank rabbis, Dov Leor and Nahum Rabinovich, were accused of issuing a religious edict, declaring the Israeli premier to be a 'rodef' – a person whose killing is permissible under halachic law.[87]

From Ger Toshav to the Annihilation of the 'Amalekites of Today'

The spiritual leaders of Gush Emunim – such as the late Rabbi Tzvi Yehuda Kook – are by no means a group on the lunatic fringe. Most of them are influential figures within the mainstream religious population and beyond, and their demand that the halacha guide official policies towards the Arab population is widely accepted in religious circles and parties. With the rise of the radical right and the nationalist political messianic trend in the last two decades, many far-reaching ideas, such as 'annihilating the Amalekites of today' (that is, the Palestinians), have entered mainstream Zionist religious thinking. Inspired by a literal interpretation of some of the traditions of the Old Testament Scriptures, especially the books of Exodus, Deuteronomy and Joshua, their discourse presents ethnic cleansing as not only legitimate, but as required by the Divinity. It has already been shown that the idea of 'ethnic cleansing', or 'transferring' the Palestinians, is widely supported by nationalist religious groups as well as the mentors of the Gush Emunim movement, both leaders and members. If the very idea of Arab residence in Palestine is based on 'theft', is morally flawed and legally temporary, according to the religious messianics, then Arab removal is the logical conclusion. Rabbi Yisrael Ariel bluntly and explicitly demands expelling the Palestinians as necessitated by Jewish religious commandments:

> On the one hand there is a commandment of settling Eretz-Yisrael, which is defined by our sages of blessed memory also as the commandment of 'inheritance and residence' – a commandment mentioned many times in the Torah. Every young student understands that 'inheritance and residence' means conquering and settling the land. The Torah repeats the commandment 'You shall dispossess all the inhabitants of the land' tens of times, and Rashi [Rabbi Shlomo Yitzhaki, a paramount Bible and Talmud commentator in the eleventh century] explains that 'You shall dispossess – You shall expel.' The Torah itself uses the term 'expulsion' a number of times such as: 'Since you shall expel the inhabitants of the country with my

help.' The substance of this commandment is to expel the inhabitants of the land whoever they may be ... This is also the opinion of Rashi in defining the commandment. In the same Talmudic passage which mentions the commandment pertaining to the land, Rashi interprets: 'Because [of the commandment] to settle Eretz-Yisrael – to expel idolaters and to settle [the people of] Israel there.' Thus according to Rashi the commandment to settle [the land] aims at the expulsion of the non-Jew from Eretz-Yisrael and that it be settled with Jews.[88]

In particular, these influential rabbis have demanded that the Arabs, Muslims as well as Christians, should be removed from, or at least discouraged from living in, Jerusalem. Rabbi Eli'ezer Waldenberg, the Israel Prize winner for 1976, stated: 'I, for example, support the application of the halacha prohibition on gentiles living in Jerusalem, and if we should apply the halacha, as it should be, we would have to expel all the gentiles [Arabs] from Jerusalem and purify it absolutely. Also we must not permit the gentiles to be a majority in any of Israel's cities.'[89] In his statement, Waldenberg implies not only the expulsion of the Arabs from Jerusalem but also that in other towns, such as Nazareth, Nablus, Hebron, Ramallah, etc.; the Palestinians, who should only be given the status of alien resident, must be reduced to a small minority. Rabbi Shalom Dov Wolpo – who bases his views on discussions with, and on the opinions of the rabbi from Lyubavich, the Habad Hasidic religious movement – agrees with Waldenberg: 'According to the halacha it is prohibited for a gentile to live in Jerusalem, and in the ruling of Maimonides it is forbidden to give a resident alien a place in Jerusalem ... True, this applies when Israel has a strong hand, but today, too, although it is not possible to expel them by force, this does not mean that they should be encouraged to live there.'[90] Rabbi Wolpo adds:

... if they [the Israeli leaders] had declared at the time of the occupation of Jerusalem and the territories [in June 1967] that they were going to leave alive the residents and give them financial compensation, but they must 'cross immediately to Trans-Jordan, they [the Arabs] would have been thankful for this until today ... yet what did the [Israeli] leaders do: they left the Arabs in their location ... but from the beginning they should have removed them from here.[91]

These fundamentalist ideas, which in the past were marginal, are becoming increasingly close to the centre of political thinking. For instance, 'Ovadia Yosef – the politically relatively moderate former Chief Rabbi of Israel, and spiritual mentor of the orthodox religious party of Shas currently represented in the government of Ehud Barak – ruled that the New Testament should be burned because Christianity is a form of idolatry.[92] The practical effect of this ruling was revealed in the Hebrew daily *Ma'ariv* in June 1985 when copies of the New Testament found in the library of the base of the Army's chief education officer were burned by the military rabbi of the base.[93] Three weeks later, *Ma'ariv* reported that the influential Knesset Foreign Affairs and Defence Committee had referred to the incident and one of its members (MK Rabbi Haim Druckman) had justified the New Testament burning.[94] The implication of these ideas and actions are crystal clear: if Christian Arabs are practising a form of 'idol worshipping', and if the Palestinians, Christian and Muslim, are to be discouraged from living in Jerusalem and are to be subjected to the Torah laws of 'resident alien' (a status that is extremely unlikely to be acceptable to the Palestinians) then expulsion becomes a logical conclusion for the political messianics.

Resisting the extension of Jewish sovereignty over the 'whole Land of Israel' by the Palestinians, according to many Jewish fundamentalists, will result in their uprooting and destruction. Frequently Jewish fundamentalists refer to the Palestinians as the 'Amalekites' or the 'Canaanites' of today. Although some refer to the local Arabs as 'Ishmalites' and to the circumstances under which biblical Abraham expelled Ishmael, many prefer to use Joshua's destruction and subjugation of the Canaanites as a model for the determination of Israeli policy towards the contemporary 'Arab problem' of Greater Israel. Reflecting on the appropriate policy for Jews to adopt towards the Palestinians, Rabbi Tzvi Yehuda Kook cited Maimonides to the effect that the Canaanites had three choices – to flee, to accept Jewish sovereignty, or to fight – implying that the decision by most Canaanites to resist Jewish rule justified their destruction.[95] According to the Old Testament, the Amalek were an ancient nomadic people, who dwelled in the Sinai Desert and southern Palestine, who were regarded as the Israelites' inveterate foe, whose 'annihilation' became a sacred duty and against whom war should be waged until their 'memory be blotted out' forever (Ex. 17:16; Deut. 25:17–19). Although the biblical stories mention that the Amalekites were finally wiped out during the reign of Hezekiah in the eighth century BC, rabbinical literature dwells on Amalek's role as the Israelites' permanent arch-enemy, saying that the struggle between the two peoples will continue until the coming of the Messiah, when God will destroy the last remnants of Amalek. Some of the political messianics insist on giving the biblical commandment to 'blot out the memory of Amalek' an actual contemporary relevance in the conflict between Israelis and Palestinians. In February 1980, Rabbi Yisrael Hess, the former campus rabbi of Bar-Ilan University, published an article in the student bulletin *Bat Kol*, the title of which, 'The Genocide Commandment in the Torah' (in Hebrew, 'Mitzvat Hagenocide Batorah') leaves no place for ambiguity. The article ends with the following: 'The day is not far when we shall all be called to this holy war, this commandment of the annihilation of Amalek.'[96] Hess quotes the biblical commandment according to which he believes Israel, in the tradition of Joshua from biblical times, should act: 'Go and strike down Amalek; put him under the ban with all that he possesses. Do not spare him, but kill man and woman, baby and suckling, ox and sheep, camel and donkey.'[97] Hess adds:

Against this holy war God declares a counter-jihad ... in order to emphasise that this is the background for the annihilation, and that it is over this that the war is being waged and that it is not a conflict between two peoples ... God is not content that we annihilate Amalek – 'blot out the memory of Amalek' – he also enlists personally in this war ... because, as has been said, he has a personal interest in this matter, this is the principal aim.[98]

Citing Hess's article, Professor Amnon Rubinstein, a Knesset Member representing the centrist Shinui Party and a lecturer in law at Tel Aviv University, commented: 'Rabbi Hess explains the commandment which instructs the blotting out of the memory of Amalek and says that there is not the slightest mercy in this commandment which orders the killing and annihilation of also children and infants. Amalek is whoever declares war on the people of God.'[99] Professor Rubinstein points out that 'no reservation on behalf of the editorial board, the students or the university were made after publishing this article which was also reprinted in other newspapers.'[100] However, a subsequent issue of *Bat Kol* (No. 2, 16 April 1980), carried articles written by Professor Uriel Simon and Dr Tzvi Weinberg severely criticising the article of Rabbi Hess. Clearly, for Hess, Amalek is synonymous with the Palestinian Arabs, who have a conflict with Israeli Jews, and they must be 'annihilated', including women, children and infants. His use of the Arabic term 'jihad' leaves no doubt as to against whom such a war of 'annihilation' should be waged.

These ideas were not confined to Rabbi Hess, who refers to the Palestinian Arabs as the 'Amalekites of today', who 'desecrate the Land of Israel'; in his book, *On the Lord's Side*, Danny Rubinstein has shown that this notion permeates the Gush Emunim movement's bulletins. *Nekudah* of 29 August 1980 (p. 12) carried an article written by Gush Emunim veteran Haim Tzoriyah, entitled 'The Right to Hate', which reads: 'In every generation there is an Amalek. The Amalekism of our generation finds expression in the deep Arab hatred towards our national revival in our forefathers' land.' The same notion propagated by the messianic trend regarding the synonymity of the Palestinians with the Amalekites was widely discussed in the Israeli daily press and even on television. It was also criticised in moderate religious circles.[101] But it was the late Professor Uriel Tal, who was a prominent biblical scholar at Tel Aviv University, and who conducted his study in the early 1980s, who did more than anyone to expose the 'annihilationist' notions preached by the strident messianic trend in Israel. Professor Tal, who had also done extensive research on anti-Semitism between the two World Wars, concluded that these messianic doctrines were similar to ideas common in Germany during the Weimar Republic and the Third Reich. The gist of Tal's research was presented to an academic forum at Tel Aviv University in March 1984 and was subsequently widely publicised in the Hebrew press and Israeli journals. Tal pointed out that the totalitarian political messianic stream refers to the Palestinian Arabs in three stages or degrees: 1) the reduction of the Arabs to the halacha status of 'resident alien'; 2) the promotion of Arab 'transfer', that is, expulsion; 3) the implementation of the commandment of Amalek, as expressed in Rabbi Hess's article 'The Commandment of Genocide in the Torah', in other words, 'annihilating' the Palestinian Arabs.[102] Like Uriel Tal, many liberal Israelis found the resurgence of this political messianic and racist trend a chilling prospect as Dr Yoram Peri, an Israeli political scientist, remarked in an article 'Expulsion is Not the Final Stage', in *Davar* on 3 August 1984: 'The solution of the transports and the trucks is not the end of the story. There is a further stage which the proponents of racist Zionism do not usually refer to explicitly, since the conditions for it are not ripe. But the principles are there, clear and inevitable. This is the stage of genocide, the annihilation of the Palestinian people.'[103]

The discovery of the activities of the Jewish Underground organisation in the mid-1980s showed that the ideas of the messianic trend were not confined to the realm of sermons. On 2 May 1985, the *Jerusalem Post* published an article by David Richardson which pointed out that at least seven rabbis, among them the prominent spiritual guide of the Gush Emunim movement, were privy to the violent campaign conducted by the Jewish Underground organization. According to the article, a statement confirming this was given to the Jerusalem police by the accused leader of the underground group, Menahem Livni, and his 27-page affidavit was presented to the Jerusalem District Court on 1 May 1985. These rabbis included the above-mentioned Tzvi Yehuda Kook, 'Ovadia Yosef and Shlomo Aviner, as well as Rabbi Moshe Levinger, a prominent veteran leader of Gush Emunim and the founder of the first Jewish settlement in Hebron, in 1968, and the adjoining Kiryat Arba'a, Rabbi Eli'ezer Waldman (then a Tehiya MK), Rabbi Yo'ezer Ariel and Rabbi Dov Leor. Waldman, Ariel, Leor and Levinger all took part in a meeting at which, after discussion, it was unanimously decided to wage a widespread campaign of violence against the inhabitants of the occupied territories. Rabbi Yisrael Ariel, who, as has already been shown, explicitly demanded the expulsion of the Arabs, justified the campaign of the Jewish Underground organisation, implying that the killing of an Arab was not murder:

> Anyone who searches through the code of Maimonides, which is the pillar of the halacha in the Jewish world, [and searches for] the concept 'you shall not murder' or the concept 'holy blood' with regard to the killing of a non-Jew – will search in vain, because he will not find [it] ... It follows from the words of Maimonides that a Jew who kills a non-Jew ... is exempt from the prohibition 'you shall not murder.' And so Maimonides writes in the halachas of murder: 'An Israelite who kills a resident alien is not sentenced to death in the court of law.'[104]

The ideology of the political messianics, including the theory of the 'Amalek of today', also found an echo in an article published by the Chief Military Rabbi of the IDF Central Command, Rabbi Avraham

Zemel (in Hebrew, Avidan) who, according to Professor Amnon Rubinstein, gave halacha justification for the 'murder of non-Jewish civilians including women and children, during war'.[105] Another soldier, who was also a yeshiva student, asked his rabbi about the subject of 'tohar haneshik' (the 'purity of arms'). From the answer of the rabbi the soldier concluded: 'During war I am permitted or even obliged to kill every male and female Arab that happens to be in my way ... I must kill them even if this involves complication with the military law.'[106] Professor Rubinstein, who cites in his book *The Zionist Dream Revisited: From Herzl to Gush Emunim and Back* many references made by the spiritual mentors of Gush Emunim to the Arabs as the 'Amalek of today', wrote critically in an article in *Haaretz* daily on 3 February 1983:

> We are dealing with a political ideology of violence. It is needless to show how this ideology is expressed in the way the Arabs are treated. The Rabbis of Gush Emunim – except for the few brave ones ... publicly preach incitement to kill Arab civilians, and those who kill civilians, and are caught and brought to court, are later amnestied by the Chief of Staff [General Raphael Eitan], who believes in the use of violence that the Arabs 'understand'. Those who think that it is possible to differentiate between blood and blood are wrong. The verdict on 'Amalek' can easily be extended to the enemies within, the traitors.

Rubinstein wrote his article against the background of the attacks carried out by the extreme right on the Peace Now demonstrators and the increasing violence in Israeli political life in general as well as the resurgence of the far right and the national religious chauvinists. There is good reason to suggest that the greater the role of the Jewish halacha in the political life of Israel becomes, the more vigorously will these messianics demand that the Palestinian Arabs be dealt with according to halachic regulations, including the imposition of the status of 'resident alien' on them; the insistence on diminishing Arab numbers by making life even more difficult; the revival of the command to 'blot out the memory of Amalek' and the insistence that the Arabs are the 'Amalekites of today' to be dealt with by annihilations, and the assertion that the killing of a non-Jew is not a murder.

THE PROPOSALS OF FUNDAMENTALIST ACADEMICS

Professor Mordechai Nisan

Professor Mordechai Nisan is a senior lecturer at the Hebrew University's school for overseas students, where he teaches the basic foundations of Zionism and Middle East politics to American Jewish students coming to Jerusalem, who are often enticed by the authorities to settle in Israel. He has published a number of books including *Israel and the Territories* (1978) and *The Jewish State and the Arab Problem* (1986, reprinted 1987).[107] In Chapter Five of the latter book, entitled 'The Separation Line: The Idea of Transferring Arabs from the Western Land of Israel [that is, Palestine]',[108] Nisan attempts to legitimise his advocacy of transfer with ample documentation of previous Zionist leaders' support for such a solution. After reviewing Zionist transfer ideas and proposals from Herzl to Ben-Gurion, Nisan quotes several statements made by leading Israeli politicians and Knesset members (including Yitzhak Rabin, then Prime Minister, Haim Hertzog, then President of Israel, Michael Dekel, a former Deputy Defence Minister (Likud), Meir Cohen-Avidov, a former Deputy Speaker of the Knesset and Yuval Neeman, leader of the Tehiya Party and former Minister of Science).[109] Among the well-known authors who expressed support for this solution, Nisan points out, is Yigal Mossenson.[110] The latter, an officer in the Palmah during the 1948 war, a military judge and author of 25 children's books and 20 plays for screen and theatre who has received top prizes, including the Ussishkin Prize, the Kinor David Prize and the Prime Minister's Creative Prize, published an article in the mass-circulation daily *Ma'ariv* in June 1985 in which he expressed support for the non-compulsory transfer of Arabs from Israel.[111] Nisan states that 'the idea of transferring the Arabs from the Land of Israel has not left the national agenda in Israel – in recent years books were written proposing explicitly the removal of the whole Arab population or at least most of it, from the Jewish state, in order to safeguard it from the Arab danger which is becoming stronger.' All these statements, books and articles in the Hebrew press in support of transfer 'are a few signposts which, perhaps, indicate a tendency in the Israel public to raise forcefully this ancient idea ... it seems to me that the time makes the idea relevant and vital now,' Nisan suggests.[112]

Nisan goes further, questioning the very possibility of Arab–Jewish coexistence, an attitude characteristic of many of the supporters of messianic Zionism and Greater Israel mentioned above. His justification of Arab removal rests on explicitly racist premises, echoing the strident arguments of Rabbi Meir Kahane, which have been discussed: 'It is likely that a sharp and extreme solution will be raised as a remedy to the Arab plague that afflicts the country. The idea of removing the Arabs from the western Land of Israel [that is, Palestine] radiates hope and arouses interest in the face of the hopelessness that the governments of Israel have shown in the recent period.' Nisan spells out three advantages for Israel 'if the country were to be emptied of the Arab inhabitants':

1. 'The internal security problem would disappear.'
2. 'The Arab claim over the land of Israel would lose its validity, and the Jewish people would be able to enjoy exclusive sovereignty without contestation' over the country.
3. 'The danger of assimilation, the blurring of the state being solely a Jewish state, mixed marriages, etc., would all disappear as a threat' to the Zionist/Jewish domination of Greater Israel:[113] 'These advantages in the security, political and cultural field would certainly contribute to the strengthening of the State of Israel and its turning into a more comfortable secure, quiet and Jewish place. The extreme solution of removing the Arabs from the country is surely tempting in its simplicity and its anticipated results of spoils (or gains). It appears as a positive and pragmatic measure that could solve once and for all the bitter conflict and thereby secure a good life for the people of Israel ... Is it a secret that among very many Jews in Israel this is the solution that has settled deep in their heart? Every person who is deeply rooted in the life of Israel, with its problems and dreams, knows this at first hand,' Nisan concludes.[114]

Notwithstanding the euphemistic terms used by Nisan, it is very likely that he advocates an outright mass expulsion of Arabs, as in the following letter written by him on 24 January 1986 and sent to Ora Shem-Ur, the author of the book *Greater Israel*, in which she calls for compulsory removal of the Arabs. Nisan writes: 'I enjoyed [reading] your book *Greater Israel* which has sharpened many facts and assumptions for me ... Of course the widest distribution of your new book would be very useful, because its basis, cast in demographic fact, could persuade many Israelis.'[115] Nisan, who has elsewhere expressed rationalisation and endorsement of Jewish terrorism against the Palestinians of the occupied territories, writes the following passages shedding further light on the religious-messianic fundamentalism and exclusionist premises underpinning his transfer imperative:

> At the very dawn of Jewish history, contact with the Land of Israel established the principle that the presence of non-Jews in the country is morally and politically irrelevant to the national right of the Jews to settle and possess the Land ... The Bible states the Jewish right regardless of non-Jewish presence. Much later, the Rabbinic sages expounded on the patriarchal promise and articulated the following principle: ... Dwelling in the Land is the Jewish priority and it is in no way restricted, let alone nullified, by a non-Jewish majority population in any given part of the Land. This principle was later codified by Maimonides in his legal work, thus lending his outstanding halachic [religious legal] authority to this Abrahamic national imperative ... [The view that questions the legitimacy of Jewish settlement in 'Judea' and 'Samaria'] is a direct denunciation of Abraham, the first Jew, the Father of the Jewish people ... [who] set the precedent and model for settling there in spite of the fact that the 'Canaanite was then in the Land'. The Jewish presence in the Land has always had to contend with, and at least partially overcome, an indigenous non-Jewish element in the Land ... The Land is the eternal possession of the Jewish people alone ...[116]

For Nisan, as for Yisrael Eldad, the Palestinians face the same predicament as the Canaanites of old and have little choice but to leave their native land. Hence the approval of Jewish terrorism on the part of Nisan is the logical and practical conclusion of the political messianic ideology of Greater Israel and is a political instrument designed to force the Arab population into evacuation.

Nisan, like many supporters of Greater Israel and Arab 'transfer', believed that the Gulf crisis of the second half of 1990 and the consequent war in early 1991 could and should be exploited to drive the Palestinians out. In an article entitled 'The Persian Gulf Crisis and the New Order in the Middle East',[117] Nisan argues that the gulf between Palestinian Arabs and Israeli Jews was growing steadily and 'this reinforced the call for separation – the idea of mass Arab transfer. Despair and fear led many Jews to this thinking in 1990. It is possible to arrive at such thinking also as a result of pure political analysis.' The 'new political order' and the redrawing of the Middle East map, proposed by Nisan, would be the result of a massive Israeli strike on Iraq which 'would not aim at the temporary military dismantling [of Iraq], but to ensure an achievement on the strategic level – and first of all – a fundamental change in the political and demographic balance of forces in the Arab-Israeli conflict ... inside and outside the country'. Other proposals put forward by Nisan during the Gulf War included the treatment of the entire population of the occupied territories as 'hostages':

> ... the Arabs in the areas of Judea, Samaria and Gaza are a problem, they are an enemy and a severe nuisance, but from an entirely different point of view: the Arabs of Judea and Samaria are hostages. This is a hostile and violent public and fifth column in our country. They identify completely with Saddam Hussein ... [We should carry out] a policy of limited expulsion of Arabs from the Land of Israel ... For every [Iraqi] missile, Israel should remove instantly from the country about 1000 Arabs or more ... We must carry out this quickly and accompany it with information as official statements of a state under siege.

If these expulsions of Arabs did not stop the Iraqi missile attacks, then at least the objective of thinning out the Arab population would have been achieved, Nisan explains.[118]

Professor Paul Eidelberg

Professor Paul Eidelberg is close in his political ideology and thinking to Mordechai Nisan. He is a professor of politics in the political science department of Bar-Ilan University, which is a stronghold of the supporters of political messianism and of the Gush Emunim settlers in the occupied territories. In his 'transfer' proposal, published in the journal *Haumah* in the spring of 1988[119] – while he was a visiting professor at Yeshiva University in New York – Professor Eidelberg is preoccupied mainly with the question of *how* to bring about Palestinian removal, rather than *whether* the Palestinians should be transferred. More specifically he outlines the steps which ought to be taken to press the Israeli government to drive out the Palestinians on both sides of the Green Line. Like most far right-wing supporters of Greater Israel (as we have already seen) Eidelberg makes no distinction between the Palestinian citizens of Israel and those of the West Bank and Gaza: both populations pose 'two demographic problems', he argues in his plan set out under the inflammatory title 'Neutralisation of the Arab Time-bomb: The Demographic Problem'.

He draws inspiration from the archetypal proposal of political Zionism's founder Theodor Herzl, who said that 'We must transfer the Arabs across the River Jordan, by finding employment for them there, and denying them employment in the Land of Israel.'[120] He also has good words to say for Rabbi Kahane's campaign for an outright mass Arab expulsion: 'his [Kahane's] book *They Must Go* is a humane and serious alternative, although it is not always realistic. I find none of his proposals turned down by the *halacha*.' Eidelberg puts it even more explicitly and bluntly:

> If the government has the courage to expel ['legaresh'] the Arabs ... the Arabs would have known this, and this alone would have accelerated many to leave voluntarily. Indeed if they had the moral courage to expel ['legaresh'] the Arabs from the Land of Israel, this thing would change fundamentally the psychological and political climate of the Middle East and even the whole world. This was likely to be the beginning of the end of not only the demographic problem – but I dare to say – the whole Arab–Israeli conflict.[121]

However, since the Israeli leaders – Eidelberg complains – lack the 'courage' and 'efficiency' to threaten mass expulsion of the Palestinians, he explains 'how to solve this problem by legal and political means'. First of all, there are the Arab citizens of Israel:

> It is impossible to pay these Arabs in order to make them leave and they will not be compelled to leave the country in the light of the convenient climate of public opinion. It almost certain that most Jews in Israel want these Arabs to disappear somehow, but they do not intend to call for a wholesale denial of [their] voting right [that is, citizenship] ... as the Kahane plan demands. Our problem is how to turn the will to see the Arabs leave into a clear public opinion, and politically an effective one, which would force the paralysed government of Israel to do everything required and

proper for neutralising the Arab time-bomb. It follows that our first task is to stir up and guide public opinion. Here I explain how to do this ... the plan I am thinking about is designed to overcome the demographic problem of Israel and to stir up and guide public opinion so that it would unite public support for the solution of this crucial problem.[122]

Eidelberg outlines the agitation campaign which should be launched, and the legal and legislative measures which should be pursued, in order to bring about the removal of citizenship from the Israeli Palestinians and their eventual transfer: the distinction between Jews and non-Jews according to the Law of Return 'can constitute the legal basis for the taking away of citizenship of every non-Jew who carries out subversive acts against the state. Because non-Jewish citizens of Israel hold citizenship as a privilege determined by state law, and not as a natural right, it is possible to lose this right as a result of disloyalty to the state.' As for the Independence Charter which promises equal civil rights to all citizens without distinction according to religion or race, he explains that this Charter 'does not carry any constitutional authority and cannot constitute a basis for real legal right at all'.[123]

The legal and legislative steps suggested by Eidelberg, which are designed to mobilise Israeli Jewish public opinion behind the plan to disenfranchise the Arab citizens and ultimately to remove them, begins with the following: an 'action group', made up of Jewish draftees or young Jews who are about to join the army, would submit a legal claim to the Supreme Court, complaining that the Jewish citizens are being treated unjustly and unequally because they have to serve in the army while the Arab citizens are exempt. Consequently, as a result of the wide publicity which would surround this case, 'the Jews would be made more aware of the problem and as a result would be prepared to overcome it in a more decisive and intelligent way, now.' If the Supreme Court imposes on the Arabs three years' 'national service in labour corps' and additionally one month of service annually, after that 'many Arabs would refuse to serve and therefore they would be liable for the legal punishment. Consequently many are likely to ask to leave the country, particularly if they and their families are spurred by the encouragement of compensation for the property they leave behind. Such a thing would not impose a burden on the public treasury, because it would be possible to sell by auction the houses of these

Arabs.' Professor Eidelberg's perverted logic, lack of intellectual integrity and utter cynicism lead him to argue that 'the principle of political equality is likely to serve in the education of public opinion in Israel [concerning the need for Arab removal] on the one hand, and to facilitate the emigration of Arabs from Israel on the other.' In parallel, Eidelberg suggests that a draft bill be submitted to the Knesset, imposing national service of three years and one month of annual labour on every Arab who passes the age of 18. Such a law is likely to be enacted if the Israeli public is 'educated' and 'guided' according to the above steps of Eidelberg's proposal. Once again, 'many Arabs would refuse to serve in labour corps' and then the punishment imposed would include taking away their citizenship. As a result, 'many Arab families are likely to leave the country, and their readiness would increase when they are encouraged by compensation for their property (which ... would be auctioned).' Other measures designed to reinforce this official policy of transferring Arab citizens, according to the Eidelberg proposal, include the abolition of allowances for large families.[124]

The second, more straightforward, part of Eidelberg's proposal sets out practical measures, to be implemented by a future government of Israel, designed to drive the Palestinians of the occupied territories out: 'First, in order to facilitate Arab emigration ... the government must reduce gradually the employment of the 100,000 Arabs working now in Israel and living in the administered territories (this is exactly, as we have seen, what Theodor Herzl recommended ... many years ago). Clear efforts should be made to find employment for these Arabs in other places', outside the land of Israel. Second, 'our future government ... must impose severe restrictions on the flow of money from Amman to Judea and Samaria'; third, the government must prevent financial aid coming from the US government to the Arab inhabitants of the territories and simultaneously 'must facilitate their emigration to free countries like the USA'. Fourth, the government must bring to an end the services and activities of foreign voluntary organisations in the territories; fifth, the Arab universities in the West Bank and Gaza 'must be closed down'; sixth, the Arab press in East Jerusalem must be turned into an instrument for 'providing information to Arabs on employment opportunities in other countries'.[125]

Eidelberg ends his plan with the following: 'Now, what we require is a small number of courageous Jews in Israel who would start the legal action and then the political action outlined in this article and

I dare to say that I can see the beginning of the end of the demographic problem.'[126]

Rabbi Dr Chaim Simons

Rabbi Chaim Simons is a settler residing in Kiryat Arba'a on the West Bank. Born in London in 1942, Simons received a PhD from London University. He is currently the director of the Nansen Institute, and of the Audio-Visual Centre for Education and Instruction, in Kiryat Arba'a, an institute whose name provides thin camouflage, and which works to propagate Arab 'transfer' from Greater Israel. This 'institute' is cynically named after Fridtjof Nansen, a Norwegian scientist and statesman. According to Simons, Nansen presided over the Greco-Turkish population 'transfer' in the 1920s and received the Nobel Peace Prize for that work. In fact, Nansen (1861–1930), who was appointed head of the Norwegian delegation to the League of Nations in 1920, took an active part in the repatriation of prisoners of war after the First World War and then directed a programme to bring relief to famine-stricken Russia and to Armenian refugees. For these works, he was awarded the Nobel Peace Prize in 1922. Nansen's involvement in the resettlement of Christian refugees (of the Greek Orthodox faith) in Greece, who had been expelled from Anatolia by the victorious Kemalists in 1920–21, was in the second half of the 1920s. The so-called 'population exchange' between Greece and Turkey was by and large the result of outright expulsions and had little to do with agreed 'population transfer': consequently Nansen's rehabilitation programmes for refugees on both sides were *post facto* and obviously his being awarded the Nobel Peace Prize had nothing to do with the Greco-Turkish affair.

Rabbi Simons preaches for the removal of the Palestinians in Israel and the occupied territories, writing in both Hebrew and English. He publishes regularly articles in this regard in the Hebrew monthly *Moledet*, the organ of the far-right party of Moledet. In 1988, a book entitled *International Proposals to Transfer Arabs from Palestine 1895–1947* (Ktav Publishing House, New Jersey), written by Simons, was published, which in spite of its dispassionate style and camouflaged message, had the underlying assumption that the 'transfer' of Arabs from Palestine was legitimate because it was widely supported by Zionist leaders and Western sympathisers. A year later, a less camouflaged and more polemical pamphlet, a collection of articles by Simons, was published entitled *Chelm or Israel?*[127] which carried an unambiguous message. In an article titled 'Israel, Three Years After Transfer: Letter from Israel, 17 August 2005', Simons writes: 'Three years have now passed since the summer of the year 2002, when the Arabs from both sides of the Green Line were transferred out of Israel. The Green Line is now a thing of the past, since three months after this transfer, the Knesset almost unanimously passed a law incorporating Judea, Samaria and Gaza into the State of Israel.'[128]

Simons goes on to explain the 'historical background' for such an ethnic cleansing:

> The idea of transfer was first put forward by Theodor Herzl over a century ago. At the same time that Herzl was writing his famous book *The Jewish State*, he confided to his diary plans for removing the non-Jewish population from the Jewish State: 'We shall try to spirit the penniless population across the border.' Following in the footsteps of Herzl, many if not most of the Zionist leaders including Ben-Gurion, Weizmann, Sharett, Ussishkin, Tabenkin and Katznelson were to propose such transfer. Even some members of 'Brit Shalom' – an organisation whose aim was for a bi-national Jewish-Arab state-would privately propose transfer ... Apart from a transfer of Arabs during the War of Independence and much more limited transfer following the Six Day War, the idea of transfer remained a dead letter [until the 1990s] ... The Arab problem was swept under the carpet by the Israeli Government who argued that transfer was completely unnecessary.

However, setting out his desired scenario for the ultimate mass Arab expulsion, Simons goes on in his letter of 17 August 2005: 'Over the years, voices advocating transfer increased', against the background of escalating Arab resistance in the territories. 'They began in the 1980s with the entry of the Kach Party' – with which Simons displays marked sympathy – 'to the Knesset. As the time went on, voices from the Likud, Mafdal and Techiya [sic] parties were added to this sole voice. Towards the end of the 1990s, almost the entire religious and right-wing parties were calling for transfer.' Pressure also began building up in the Labour Party:

> It was pointed out to them that their mentor, David Ben-Gurion, had enthusiastically welcomed the Peel Report recommendation

on compulsory transfer: 'We must expel Arabs and take their places,' he wrote to his son Amos in 1937. During the following year, he had told the Jewish Agency Executive: 'I favour compulsory transfer – I see nothing unethical in it.' As Prime Minister during the War of Independence, he was asked by his army chiefs what to do with the Arabs of Lod [Lydda] and Ramla [*sic*]. To this question he retorted 'Expel them.' He expressed anger at the fact that the Arabs of Nazareth had not been expelled. Ben-Gurion's record swayed the Labour Party and they joined in the chorus of transfer.

Having persuaded the Labour Party to espouse a mass expulsion policy, Simons turns, in his hypothetical scenario, to the remaining 'stubborn liberals': 'When however they heard that Chaim Weizmann had regarded the transfer of the Arabs [as] "absolutely essential" and had told the British Colonial Secretary that the Jews "will help in getting Arabs out of Galilee", these liberals dropped their opposition to transfer.'

Simon's most desired scenario culminates in the summer of 2002:

Having a broad consensus on transfer, the Israeli Government fully implemented it in the summer of 2002. It was planned with military precision – advice being gained from the retired generals ... and was completed within two weeks. The cost of the operation was relatively low, since it was felt that as long as the Jews who had left Arab countries following the establishment of the State of Israel had not received compensation ... payment to the transferred Arabs should be held in abeyance. The magnificent villas owned by the Arabs, were ... given to the Jewish refugees from Arab countries.

The letter of 17 August 2005 informs us that on al-Haram al-Sharif ['the Temple Mount'] 'a great synagogue is at present under construction', implying the destruction of the third holiest shrine of Islam. The letter concludes: 'Although over a hundred years were to pass from the time Herzl proposed transfer until its full implementation, his motto "If you wish it, this is no fairy tale", has once again been proved right.'

Simon's mass expulsion scenario was also underlined by the editor of *Chelm or Israel?*, Mark Braham of the South Head Synagogue, Australia, who wrote in the pamphlet's Foreword in July 1989:

I agree with Dr Simons: there is no future for Israel, as we know it, if the Arabs remain ... Nothing could better illustrate the double standards adopted over Israel than the current attitude to population transfer. Political realism demands that one compare Israel's situation in 1989 with Britain's in 1939, when she stood alone, threatened by a mighty Nazi empire. Britain immediately interned or transported all enemy nationals or potential enemies of the State. Israel must do the same.[129]

Apparently Simons and Braham believe that Israel is strong enough and can get away with expelling two and a half million Palestinians within two weeks.

OTHER RACIST GROUPS

Rabbi Meir Kahane and the Kach Movement

Rabbi Meir Kahane (1932–90) claimed that Jewish *Lebensraum*, stretching from the 'River of Egypt' to the 'River of Euphrates', is needed for Israel, and he, like other religious messianics of Gush Emunim, envisaged a theocratic regime for Israel and spurned universal, humanistic and liberal values.

Rabbi Kahane was the rabble-rousing founder of the Jewish Defense League in the United States and its Israeli counterpart, the Kach movement, established in the late 1970s, which has become the most outspoken exponent of the ethnic cleansing solution. Kach has also acquired a reputation for defining the outer limits of both right-wing fascism and overt racism in Israel. It had connections with Gush Emunim settlers and other associated extreme right-wing groups, such as the avowedly terrorist Jewish Underground and 'Ateret Cohanim.[130] The 'Kach' ('Thus') name was taken from the motto of the Irgun Tzvai Leumi, the Menahem Begin-commanded Revisionist military organisation of the 1940s, whose symbol was a hand holding a rifle over the map of Palestine and Transjordan, with the motto 'Rak Kach' ('Only Thus'). This fact also echoes Kahane's earlier membership of Betar, the Revisionist youth organisation in the US. In reality, however, Kahane's ideology was largely drawn from Jewish religious fundamentalism and has more in common with the political messianism of Gush Emunim's rabbis than with secular Zionist Revisionism.

Kahane's public campaign for maximum territorial expansion and the expulsion of the Arab population was launched in earnest in 1972, at a lecture delivered at Haifa University, shortly after his immigration to Israel (in 1971).[131] This was followed by a letter-writing campaign, letters mailed in late 1972 and early 1973, to thousands of Arab citizens of Israel as well as residents of the occupied territories, urging them to emigrate.[132] To this end, Kahane employed a Christian Arab from the western Galilee village of Fasuta, named Emanuel Naji Khouri, who had described himself as having worked for the pre-1948 Haganah intelligence services as well as having been an informer for the Israeli secret services and the military government after the establishment of the state.[133] The text of the letters, signed by the 'Jewish Defense League in Eretz Yisrael' and addressed to 'the Arabs of Hebron, Nablus, Ramleh, etc.' reads:

It is clear that the citizens of the Jewish state will never agree to surrender Eretz Israel or to partition it and dismember it. There is no possibility of a retreat from the territories of Eretz Israel which were liberated in 1967. This being the case, and since we respect the Arab national sentiment, we realize that a condition of perpetual tension is liable to be created between the Jewish majority and the Arab minority, as in Northern Ireland. It is desirable, for tranquillity and fraternity, to take steps, ahead of time, to prevent this danger. It is desirable that each people live in its own state, and not under the rule of another people. We therefore appeal to you, and propose that you emigrate from Eretz Israel. We are therefore establishing the 'Emigration Fund,' which will assist every Arab willing to leave the country. If you are willing to emigrate, we turn to you and ask that you inform us of:

1) the number of people in your family, so that we can work out a plan to pay each family, in accordance with its size;
2) if you are willing to sell your apartment to a Jew, and if so, when;
3) to which country you would prefer to immigrate.

Please inform us of your order or priorities. Please inform us of these details by return mail, and as soon as possible.
Sincerely yours.
The Jewish Defense League in Eretz Israel
P.O.B. 7287, Jerusalem.[134]

Contrary to the secretly guarded 'transfer' plans initiated by the Israeli government after 1967,[135] Kahane's strident public campaign thrived on media publicity, and concentrated, also, on the Arab citizens of Israel and not just on the inhabitants of the occupied territories. Kahane believed (as he was to put it later in the mid-1980s):

> We have a terrible problem in Israel. It's not the Arabs of the Occupied Territories who are the problem. We can get rid of those Arabs now. The real problem is that there are many Arabs in Israel who have Israeli citizenship. And these Arabs are making many, many children ... Once the Arabs have a majority in this country, they're going to do what any self-respecting nationalist would do. They are not going to accept living in a country called a Jewish state, in a country with a Law of Return that applies solely to the Jews. Once the Arabs have gained a majority, they'll change the laws and the nature of this state, and they'll be right. Completely right. And this is why I want to move them all out now.[136]

On 1 March 1973, Kahane held a press conference in Tel Aviv and introduced his colleague Dr William Perl, a Jewish Defense League leader based in Washington, DC. Like Kahane, Perl had a Revisionist background and in the late 1930s was a joint chairman of the Revisionist organisation in Vienna and working closely with the Irgun Tzvi Leumi in Palestine. At the Tel Aviv press conference, Perl claimed that he had set up a 'Committee for the Immigration of Arabs from Israel' in the US, with branches set up in Los Angeles and Washington and others in the process of formation in Miami and San Diego; the committee was designed to raise funds and promote the removal/ethnic cleansing of 'hundreds of thousands of Arabs'.[137] However, soon it became clear, Kahane's biographer Yair Kotler explains, that 'there was no operative plan for emigration, nor was there any corporation for raising funds'. Three years later, Perl was convicted by a US court for conspiring to shoot two Soviet diplomats in Washington.[138] Kahane himself received huge publicity but no Arab emigrants.[139] However, as we shall see, Kahane was not content with encouraging 'voluntary' Arab emigration; outright expulsion was at the heart of his platform. He often voiced the view, which is also held by other religious messianics in Israel, that it would have been possible to expel the Arab population of the West Bank and

Gaza immediately after the 1967 victory, but because of the Israeli leaders' weakness of will, a golden opportunity was missed.[140]

In 1973, Kahane's widely publicised campaign for Arab 'emigration' elicited strong local Palestinian reaction. His tactics were also to the aversion of the Israeli authorities who sought to prevent the outburst of protests among the Arab citizens. On 24 February 1973, the East Jerusalem-based *al-Fajr* newspaper sharply lambasted Kahane's ethnic cleansing campaign, describing him as a 'mass murderer, criminal, the devil Kahane'. Publishing a list of those who allegedly agreed to emigrate under the Kahane plan, the newspaper announced the establishment of a fund to assist those potential migrants who might be tempted by financial incentives.[141] The authorities were also nudged into action. On 20 April, Jerusalem's district attorney brought charges against Kahane, and against Yoel Lerner, a member of the Jewish Defense League's secretariat. The charges cited the letters sent by the organisation, calling for Arab emigration, which were described as 'incitement to rebellion'.[142] In the event, however, the trial of Kahane was allowed to drag on and eventually was postponed indefinitely without explanation. Also the files of the case were burned, as Israeli law permits the burning of files after seven years.[143]

Kahane was fully aware that the Palestinians were unlikely to remove themselves 'voluntarily', since they regarded Palestine as their homeland and were fighting to keep it as such. He concluded, however: 'I do not feel sorry for the Arabs of Eretz Yisrael, no matter how much they feel that the land is theirs. I do not feel for them because I know that the land is not theirs, that it is Jewish.'[144] He was usually explicit, revealing the real intent behind his campaign for Arab 'emigration' on countless occasions. In a letter to the *Jerusalem Post*, dated 3 August 1980 (p. 8), Kahane wrote: 'We of the Kach Movement are committed to a Knesset law to remove the Arabs. Those who wish to leave willingly will be compensated for their property, not given "large sums of money". Those who are unwilling would be removed without compensation. It is a Knesset law we seek.'[145] Kahane was more explicit in an interview he gave in the following year to the *Los Angeles Herald Examiner*. In an article entitled 'Portrait of a Zealot', in 1981, the *Los Angeles Herald Examiner* journalist Gary Rosenblatt reported that Kahane's ultimate means for solving Israel's problem is the use of force to drive the Arab population out: 'I'd go to the Arabs and tell them to leave ... I'd promise generous compensation. If they refused, I'd forcibly move them out.' To a question as to whether he would carry this out with 'midnight deportations in cattle cars?', Kahane answered, 'Yes'.[146] Around the same time, Kahane wrote in his book *They Shall be Strings in Your Eyes* that the election of a strong, iron-handed government, whose reputation and determination to implement the expulsion programme at all costs would be known to the Arabs, would keep resistance to a minimum. As Kahane declared on another occasion: 'No non-Jews can be citizens of Israel', seeking to rescind the citizenship status currently given to the Arabs inside the Green Line; if the Arabs refuse to accept the status of 'resident alien' (paying 'tribute' and living in 'servitude'), 'We'll put them on trucks and send them over the Allenby Bridge ... we'll use force. And if they fire at our soldiers, we'll kill them.'[147] In another interview given in 1986, Kahane stated, 'I want to make life hard for them. I want them to think: "It makes no sense to go on living here; let's take our compensation payment and leave"'; 'I would only use force for those who don't want to leave. I'd go all the way, and they know that.'[148]

He focused on the 'demographic debate' in Israel, using blatantly anti-Arab racist references. The cover of one of his inflammatory books, *They Must Go* (1981), demands: 'How Long Can Israel Survive Its Malignant and Growing Arab Population?' Kahane maintained that the Arab 'demographic threat' spurred him to launch his expulsion campaign: 'To sit back with arms folded and allow the Arabs to grow and destroy Israel from within is unreasonable.'[149] In a speech in Karnei Shomron settlement on the West Bank on 15 May 1985, Kahane declared: 'The Arabs are a cancer in the heart of the nation, they are growing at a frightening pace, six in the belly of one [woman].'[150] In Kahane's thinking, expulsion of the Palestinians would fulfil two main objectives: first, political, to prevent the Palestinian population from becoming a majority in Greater Israel and thereby undermining Israel as a Jewish state from within; second, religious, as a means of hastening messianic redemption:

The Arabs of Israel are a stark desecration of God's name. Their non-reconciliation to Jewish sovereignty over the Land of Israel is a rejection of the sovereignty of the God of Israel and of his kingdom. Their removal from the country is more than a political affair. It is a religious matter, a religious duty, a commandment to wipe out the desecration of God's name. Instead of worrying about the reactions of the Gentiles if we do act [to remove them], we should tremble at the thought of God's anger if we do not act.

Tragedy will befall us if we do not remove the Arabs from the country. Since redemption can come immediately and in its full glory, if we do that which God commands ... Let us hasten the redemption.[151]

The Statement of Principles of the Kach Movement, which provides further racist incitement against the Arabs and justification for their expulsion, goes a step further by implicitly calling for the destruction of the Muslim shrines in Jerusalem, the third holiest in Islam. Under the section 'Arabs to Arabia,' the statement demands:

The transfer of the Arabs from all parts of Eretz Israel. The Arabs' presence in Israel ensures hatred, disturbances, and bloodshed. It is a time bomb, threatening the existence of the Zionist enterprise. The Arabs living in Eretz Israel must therefore be transferred to the Arab countries. The danger of their becoming a majority in the State as a result of their natural increase is already a real danger now. The transformation of Israel to 'Palestine' in a 'democratic' manner must be prevented. Coexistence between Jews and Arabs is possible only by means of separation: Arabs to Arabia and Jews to Zion!!

The statement also calls for 'the removal of all foreigners [that is, Muslims] from the Temple Mount [al-Haram al-Sharif] ... The preparation of the infrastructure – material and spiritual – for the building, of the Temple, speedily in our days.'[152] Kahane was more explicit in an interview in 1986: 'I want to move the Arabs out from the two mosques [the Dome of the Rock and al-Aqsa Mosque] on Temple Mount. The Arabs have no right to be there.' To a question whether he would 'applaud it', if somebody blew up the Jerusalem shrines, Kahane replied: 'I certainly would.'[153]

Kahane stated frequently that he was not the only Israeli advocating expulsion and repeated his familiar slogan: 'I am only saying what you are thinking.'[154] While Kahane was publicly criticised by many prominent Israeli politicians and proscribed by the Zionist establishment in the US, his campaign in Israel remained vociferous. He frequently visited the US and his column was published in the wide-circulation American weekly the *Jewish Press*. The *Jewish Press* is owned and edited by Rabbi Shlomo Klass, a supporter of the American Friends of 'Ateret Cohanim'. With a wide circulation of 160,000, the *Jewish Press* has considerable influence in

New York and elsewhere in the US; for over three decades, the *Jewish Press* published three separate columns in every issue by Rabbi Kahane until his assassination in November 1990. Kahane also used the paper to launch his Jewish Defense League in the US and later his Kach Movement in Israel.[155]

In his book, *They Must Go* (1981), which was published by the well-known New York publisher Grosset and Dunlap, giving the impression that by 1981 Kahane's platform had become a sellable commodity. Kahane argues that because the Arab–Israeli conflict generates a constant state of tension and instability in the Middle East, potentially disrupting the 'orderly flow of oil' to the West, it is in the 'vital interests of the Western nations to receive Arab emigrants from *Eretz Yisrael*' who would also be 'willing to do the important but unsavory jobs that go begging for lack of local hands'.[156] In the Preface to *They Must Go*, written in 1980 in the Ramle prison,[157] Kahane bragged of the popularity of his views in Israel:

[The] average guard was overwhelmingly sympathetic to me. It was clear to all that I was not an ordinary criminal and that I had been imprisoned for my ideas – ideas that so many of these guards, as well as Jews throughout the country, privately espoused ... And that is the key to the writing of this book. It would have been impossible to write the manuscript, with all its facts, dates, incidents, quotes, and names, had the prison officials not allowed me to bring in all my private papers and clippings.

As expected, the most sympathetic feelings towards Kahane's message were expressed by Jewish settlers in the occupied territories, as one settler, Miriam Lapid, put it in February 1980: 'I think the most humanitarian solution, and mainly because I have a Jewish soul, is that two peoples shall not live here together. If Rabbi Kahane has opened an office and wanted to arrange one-way tickets for Arabs, should he sit in prison for that? ... It hurts me that they [the Arabs] are not regarded as something temporary.'[158]

Throughout the 1980s, Kahane used every opportunity to deliver his racist message, aiming it provocatively at Arab audiences. He led his followers repeatedly to Arab villages, addressing the residents as 'dogs' and warning them to leave the country.[159] He and his followers were responsible for numerous attacks on Arab individuals and Arab property and the relentless spreading of inflammatory agitation against them. In January 1980, Kach was responsible for a violent assault on Christian clergy in Jerusalem and some of its members were arrested;[160] three months later, in April, Kahane led a group of men on a rampage smashing the windows of 150 Arab cars and 30 houses and shops in the West Bank town of al-Bireh. Four days later, Kahane returned to the neighbouring town of Ramallah demanding the deportation of its mayor Karim Khalaf, while his followers distributed leaflets telling the local population to leave the country. The provocation had the 'desired effect' of sparking a large demonstration of local residents and students which ended in four protesters being sent to hospital after the army dispersed the demonstration with clubs and tear gas.[161] This incident had all the hallmarks of the Kach tactics which were described by two Israeli journalists as follows: 'Kahane, or another leader of the movement, sets out with a group of his followers to an area densely populated with Arabs, having previously notified the media of their intention, and when they arrive they tell the Arabs to leave the country, provoke them and pick quarrels with them in the hope that the security forces will do their "duty" against the Arabs for attacking Jews.'[162] The Kach leaders' reactions to the maiming of the West Bank Arab mayors Karim Khalaf and Bassam al-Shaka'a by Jewish terrorists in May 1980 revealed a great degree of satisfaction – Yossi Dayan declared that the attack was carried out by 'good Jews': 'We must make the Arabs aware that they have to leave ... anyone who thinks that Jews and Arabs can co-exist is kidding himself', stated a spokesman of the movement.[163]

In May 1980, Kahane was arrested and held in administrative detention by the Israeli authorities for six months, following the unearthing of caches of arms and explosives stored by the Kach movement in Hebron; he was held reportedly on suspicion of taking part in a plot to destroy the Dome of the Rock and al-Aqsa Mosque, the third holiest shrine in Islam. Other charges against Kahane included 'a plot to attack Arabs'. In the same year, Kahane was convicted for disorderly conduct in Ramallah and Nablus and for disturbing the peace at the Hebrew University; he served a prison sentence of several months.[164] Proposing laws that would forbid intimate contacts between Jews and Arabs, Kach called during the 1981 elections for a five-year prison sentence for any Arab found having sexual relations with a Jew. The weekly *Jewish Press* reported on 16 October 1981 that Kach activists put posters on the walls of the Hebrew University warning Jewish female students to 'Beware of Arabs, who seek only to shame you and take advantage of you.' In

They Must Go, Kahane warned that God's 'holy nation' was being corrupted by the 'ugliness of intermarriage, prostitution, and sexual contacts between the Arabs and Jewish women'. On 25 October 1982, Kahane's followers posted leaflets praising highly the massacres of Palestinian civilians in the Sabra and Chatilla refugee camps near Beirut.[165] In August 1984, Kahane used his Knesset immunity to lead a provocative demonstration in the town of Umm al-Fahm, urging the local Arab citizens to leave the country.[166]

By the early 1980s, the Kach movement was making inroads into Israeli politics by capitalising on the serious economic situation and growing unemployment as well as the increasing antagonism towards the Arabs; it could no longer be dismissed as a 'lunatic fringe'. It enjoyed a young membership, consisting of disgruntled, poor Sephardim and US immigrants (many of whom were 'ba'alei teshuvah', or newly orthodox Jews).[167] In July 1984, Kahane was elected to the Eleventh Knesset receiving 25,907 votes, 1.4 per cent of the vote.[168] A public opinion poll carried out by the Modi'in Ezrahi Research Institute one year after Kahane became a Member of Knesset found that the Kach movement would receive eleven seats in the Knesset, and would become the third largest party after Labour and Likud, if the general elections were held in that year.[169] The popularity of Kahane and the Kach movement seemed to be increasing particularly among the soldiers and youth, including high-school students. A 1985 survey carried out by Dr Kalman Benyamini, of the Hebrew University, among high-school students found that 50 per cent of the respondents were in favour of Kahane's solution.[170] However, the formal membership of Kach was not particularly large – one conservative estimate put it in November 1990 at around a thousand members.[171] The movement's strength was evident in the Jewish settlements on the West Bank, particularly in Kiryat Arba'a, overlooking Hebron, which was the home of Kahane. From the movement's strongholds in Kiryat Arba'a and Hebron, the Kach members set out on their shooting sprees and attacks against Arab property. In the 1985 municipal elections of Kiryat Arba'a, two Kach representatives were elected to the eight-member local council and joined a governing coalition with the Tehiya and Morasha national-religious faction. The coalition agreement stated that Arab labourers would not be employed by the local council and its municipal institutions.[172]

Kahane carried his expulsion platform and explicit racist rhetoric into the Knesset debates, shouting at an Arab Member of Knesset

'Shut up, Arab!'[173] He had always called for expulsive legislation to be enacted by the Knesset. Shortly after his election, Kahane submitted two draft bills to the Speaker of the Knesset Shlomo Hillel: the Proposed Law for Israeli Citizenship and for Jewish and Arab Population Transfer, and the Proposed Law for the Prevention of Assimilation between Jews and Non-Jews and for the Sanctity of the Jewish People. (This draft law would ban intermarriage and sexual intercourse between Arabs and Jews). According to the first bill, the right of citizenship is reserved exclusively for Jews; the Arab can only obtain the status of 'resident alien in Eretz-Yisrael', with no right to vote or hold office.[174] The bill defines a 'resident alien' as a non-Jew, who accepts upon himself the seven Halachic (Jewish religious law) Noachide laws: that is, the prohibition of idol worship, blasphemy, bloodshed, illicit sexual conduct, theft, and eating of limbs from a still-living animal, as well as the commandment to maintain the laws. The draft bill would also make the Jewish halacha prohibition on the residence of a 'resident alien' in Jerusalem the law of the state of Israel. A non-Jew who will not accept the status of 'resident alien' 'shall be removed from the country, either of his own free will, or against his will'.[175] Clearly, Kahane was of the opinion that only 'a small percentage [of Arabs] would agree to the conditions imposed on a resident alien, who would not have the status of a citizen. These would be mainly old people. They would remain';[176] the rest would be expelled.

Kahane's draft bill details the measures and proceedings for putting Arab removal into effect:

> In order to assist the non-Jew who willingly leaves Israel, the government shall establish information teams among Diaspora Jewry, in order to explain the problem of a hostile minority which is liable to become a majority within the State of Israel, and the important role of world Jewry in aiding the transferral of these people. Similarly, a fund will be established, with the assistance of world Jewry, to compensate those leaving for their property which shall be left in Israel. Special bonds will be issued for this purpose, similar to the Israel Bonds, and will be sold among world Jewry.
>
> ...
>
> A commission shall be established which shall investigate and determine the exact sum of the compensation to each non-Jew who prefers to voluntarily leave Israel. A certain sum shall be

deducted from each determination, which shall constitute a portion of the value of the property of the Jews of Arab countries who abandoned their property when they immigrated to Israel, for which they received no compensation. The sum which shall be deducted shall be placed in a special fund, and shall be distributed to Jews from Arab countries, as the commission shall determine.
...
Every non-Jew who will not be willing to assume the status of resident alien and the obligation of taxes and slavery and who will not be willing to voluntarily leave Israel, shall be forcibly removed from here.
...
A special government Ministry for Emigration shall be established, which shall be responsible for the implementation of the sections of this law. Special offices will be established within this Ministry to register non-Jews who will be willing to emigrate.

The second draft bill submitted by Kahane to the Knesset Speaker in 1984 would ban intermarriage and sexual relations between the 'resident aliens' (Arabs) and Jews. The bill states that a non-Jew who has any sort of sexual relations with a Jew shall be punished with three years' imprisonment. There is a clear discrimination in favour of Jews in the punishment for breaking such laws: 'A non-Jew who has sexual relations with a Jewish prostitute or with a Jewish male shall be punished with fifty years' imprisonment; a Jewish prostitute or Jewish male who has relations with a non-Jewish male shall be imprisoned with five years' imprisonment.'[177] Agitating against sexual relations between Arabs and Jews had always been obsessional for Kahane and his followers. In another book by Kahane, *Forty Years*, which is full of inflammatory incitement and racist references to the Arabs, the following is found:

Daily the Ishmaelite [the Arab] adds to Hillul Hashem [the desecration of the Name of God] that is expressed in the profanity of his roaming of land, seeking out Jewish women to bed and, sometimes, to wed them. The Jewish women who live as wives of the Ishmaelites in Arab villages are joined by the countless others ... who serve the Ishmaelite's sexual pleasures without benefit of bridal canopy ...[178]

The two draft bills of MK Kahane were disqualified by the Knesset Presidium (the Speaker Shlomo Hillel and his deputies) on 3 December 1984, although the Supreme Court later ruled that Kahane had the right to submit them for Knesset debates.[179]

The disqualification of Kahane's bills by the Knesset Presidium, however, could not stem Kach's extra-parliamentary activities, whose upsurge in the mid-1980s was bolstered by the political trend in Israel which moved towards right-wing extremism. The leading activists of Kach, who were scattered throughout Israel and in Jewish settlements in the occupied territories and were not a group on the fringe of society, were expressing confidence that the expulsion platform would be put into effect when Kach attained power sharing in a right-wing coalition in the near future. Avner Uzan was fourth on the Kach election list in 1984; he was born in Hadera in 1958, was active in the Revisionist Betar youth movement and resides in a Jewish settlement in the occupied territories. In September 1984, he said:

> The philosophy of expelling Arabs can be put into practice. When we have six seats in the Knesset, and we form a coalition with the Likud, the Likud will have commitments towards us. We will demand the establishment of a government body authorized to deal with the emigration of Arabs, Israeli Arabs. The official in charge of this department will travel to, say, Canada. He will deal with the absorption and settlement of the Arabs there. Everything will be done with compensation ... American Jews will also contribute ... Jordan is Palestine. It will be possible to transfer the Arabs there, or to disperse them throughout the world.

When questioned what would happen if the Arabs refused to leave, Uzan replied: 'We'll bring them to this'; 'The Arab only understands force.' Uzan explained in September 1984 that the mass expulsions would begin in five years, after the Arabs 'finish building Judea and Samaria for us'. Then the builders will be expelled, 'since we're degenerating due to them', that is, Jews were eschewing physical labour.[180] According to another leading activist in the Kach movement, Gad Servetman, who was born in Tel Aviv in 1959 and served as an aircraft technician in the Israeli Air Force, the Kach leadership has a single-minded goal: 'To remove the Arabs from the Land of Israel, if not in a good spirit, then in a not-good spirit'; 'What Rabbi Kahane says today, the others will say tomorrow'; 'If Kahane will be Defence Minister in 20 years, the Arabs will certainly want to leave Israel.' Kahane was not completely ostracised: 'Kahane and [Rabbi] Levinger [a Gush Emunim leader] danced together in Simhat Torah celebrations in Hebron in October 1984. Minister Ariel Sharon also danced with him.'[181] Yair Kotler, who interviewed Servetman after the Kach election success in 1984, wrote: '[Servetman] is convinced that the government will decide upon this course of action sooner or later, passing a law to this effect. He admits that this is not realistic today, but believes that when Kach has 10 or 16 representatives in the Knesset ... the movement will be asked to join the government.'[182]

MENA, Upper Nazareth and the Debate on Racism

The campaign of Kahane's representative in the Galilee, Kach activist Alexander Finkelstein in Upper Nazareth, exemplified the surge in popularity of the movement in the 1980s. Finkelstein, like Kahane, preached for the removal of Arabs, including those citizens of Israel, by force. He stated in an interview in the mid-1980s:

Let the Arabs [citizens] of Israel move to the Arab lands [that is, states], where they will assist in strengthening the economy ... We have to amputate the infected limb. Many ways have to be used for a population transfer ... We have to be sophisticated and careful to solve the problem. In order to win support, there will have to be intensive information and groundwork. The Arab minority is growing stronger, and sticks in our throat.[183]

In the summer of 1983, Finkelstein established MENA (an acronym formed from the Hebrew letters for 'Defender of Upper Nazareth'), which launched a notorious campaign for the eviction of the 4,000 Arab residents of Upper Nazareth and the exclusion of Arabs from access to housing in this largely Jewish, upmarket town. Avraham Cohen of MENA declared: 'The aim is to obtain a pure Jewish town.'[184] The same slogan of a 'pure Jewish town' was repeated at a debate between MENA activists and a group of Israeli Palestinians which was screened by Israeli television in December 1983.[185] In one instance, Finkelstein, heading a MENA delegation from the town, met the then army Chief of Staff Raphael Eitan, who lived in the neighbouring Moshav of Tel 'Adashim, for consultation. Eitan, who later set up the far-right Tzomet Party which won eight seats in the Knesset in June 1992 and advocates partial Arab expulsion, advised the Finkelstein delegation to appeal to David Levy, the then Housing Minister. The latter, however, after meeting the MENA delegation, demurred, telling them that Arabs could live in Upper Nazareth.[186]

The publicity surrounding the actions of MENA clearly inspired 'The Institute for Researching Social Problems in the Light of the halacha', at Mazkeret Batya, to come out in December 1983 with a halachic decision stating that Jews and non-Jews should not live together in the same building. The head of the institute, Rabbi Ephraim Zalmanovitch, also justified the demands of Jewish inhabitants of the 'Coptic Neighbourhood' in Jaffa, who were trying to prevent Arab inhabitants of the same town from being housed in a new building on Kiyoso Street in Jaffa. Rabbi Zalmanovitch also turned to the Housing Minister with the recommendations that the government should issue regulations prohibiting the purchase of flats by Arabs in houses, streets and neighbourhoods where Jews lived.[187] Clearly the pronouncements and actions of Kach, MENA, the Mazkeret Batya institute and other similar groups, with their manifest emphasis on racial purity and the propagation of thoughts of a 'Arabrein' ('pure of Arabs')[188] environment, contributed to the rise in public support for Arab transfer in the 1980s.

At the same time, however, the actions of such groups, exemplified by Upper Nazareth and elsewhere, sparked off a controversy and were promptly condemned by liberal journalists, writers and academics. Aharon Bakhar commented on the Mazkeret Batya institute decision:

... because what a Rabbi in Israel could say ... as a halacha decision was most serious. It was racism of the ugliest sort. This Rabbi from Mazkeret Batya claims in his Halachic decision that Israeli citizens who are Arabs should not be permitted to buy flats in houses where Jews live. On the other hand, he has nothing to say about Jews who buy flats in areas populated by Arabs, under the one condition that it is done in Hebron ... If such a decision was made by a Christian priest in New York against Jews, we could witness a scandal there. But when it is said here, and by a Rabbi there is no one to protest.[189]

The emphasis on racial purity, exemplified by the Mazkeret Batya institute's recommendations, prompted the writer Yehoshu'a Sobol to remark on how Judaism had long ago become an instrument for 'the theological and ideological justification of any outrageously racist act performed in this state, either by the authorities or by citizens imbued with racist ideology':

> After the rise of the Nazis to power in Germany, Alfred Rosenberg established a sort of 'Institute for Research on Judaism' in a castle near Frankfurt. Rosenberg's *'Einsatzstab'* was a sort of Institute established in order to research the dangers to Aryan society and its culture from Judaism. The Rosenberg institute stated that German property must not be sold to Jews and issued orders that Jews and non-Jews must not live in the same neighbourhood.[190]

Professor Yesha'ayahu Leibovitch of the Hebrew University, a former editor-in-chief of the *Encyclopedia Hebraica*, described this racist ideological trend as 'Judeo-Nazism'.[191]

There was a minority of liberal Israelis who saw the activities of MENA, Kach and other similar racist groups as the outcome of a deeply ingrained anti-Arab racism, which permeates and is part of the general brutalisation of society, which is sanctioned by the state, and which leads logically to the expulsion idea. Professor Dan Miron, an eminent scholar of Hebrew literature at Tel Aviv University wrote that the phenomenon 'grew out of the well-known' 'home-made' racism:

> It is definitely not a new phenomenon that Jews refuse to live together with Arabs in equality. Neither is the harassment which was supposed to drive away the Arabs from Upper Nazareth ... anything new. Such refusal and such actions exist in Tel Aviv and in Jerusalem and in other Israeli towns, Moshav and Kibbutz ... I believe that no part of the Israeli public can regard itself to be completely clear of the racist disease.

MENA 'exposed the ugly face of Israeli racism in its old essence and new ideological cover. This racism is not unique to them, but exists in all sections of the Israeli public ... it is part of the general brutalisation and behaviour of our society.'[192] Commenting on Finkelstein's (the MENA spokeman's) comparison of the Arabs to a 'cancer in the body of the state',[193] Professor Miron thought that Finkelstein's cancer metaphor echoed similar expressions repeatedly made by army generals, ministers and prime ministers: General

Yanush Ben-Gal, the Commander of the Northern Front (who said the Arabs were 'a cancer in the flesh of the country'), former Chief of Staff Raphael Eitan (who compared the Arabs to 'drugged insects'), Ariel Sharon (who ordered the army to 'tear off their balls'), and the Prime Minister Menahem Begin (who compared the Palestinians to 'two-legged animals' in the first days of the invasion of Lebanon):

> The source of the evil does not lie in the Finkelsteins from Nazareth, but in those in charge of leading Israel and showing examples of behaviour. Their metaphors were absorbed by people who were willing to accept them. If the Arabs are the 'insects' in our national home, then they should be removed. And what better way to get rid of insects than killing them with some drug? And dead insects should be removed from the house to avoid the bad smell. The one who claims that the Arabs are the cancer in the body of the state recommends an operation to remove the cancer in order to save the rest of the body. So after all this, what is so new in Finkelstein's demand to drive the Arabs across the border? His version is not even the most extreme, after what we heard from politicians and generals.[194]

The rise of the Kach movement and its offshoots in the 1980s, clearly indicating a trend in Israeli society rather than an aberration, had implications which were bound to arouse deep fears among the Palestinians in Israel. Commenting on the election of Kahane to the Knesset, attorney Muhammad Mi'ari, representative of the Progressive List for Peace in the Knesset and a member of the Secretariat of the Committee to Defend the Land, stated in 1984 that Kahane

> ... may, as a symbol, arouse some fears in some people. Actually, I should not say fear, because we live in our own country and no force on earth is going to make us leave; yet, I suppose fear is a possible response. The issue has more dangerous implications, when we understand that Kahane does not differ essentially from Tehiya and some of the religious parties. Nor is he different from Likud's Sharon and Shamir; the only difference is that Kahane is allegedly unbalanced and lacks political 'sophistication'. He says exactly what he thinks, while others, such as Likud or Tehiya members, try to disguise their real positions with more moderate ones.[195]

Racism, inherent in a state established exclusively for the members of one religious/national group, has frequently resurfaced in the way the Arab citizens of Israel are treated. Kahane did not create the public's racism. However, 15 years of Likud rule and annexationist policies encouraged constant political shift to the right and created a highly charged racist atmosphere with dangerous implications for Israeli Palestinians.

The rise of Kahane did galvanise liberal circles into action in 1984–85. To many supporters of the Peace Now movement, which was basically an Ashkenazi elitist protest movement, the Kach leader became a rallying point for their extra-parliamentary campaigning against the messianic religious and right-wing groups.[196] A section of the MKs was also nudged into action. On 18 December 1984, the Knesset Committee voted to restrict Kahane's parliamentary immunity. The Likud, Tehiya and the National Religious Party MKs voted against the motion.[197] However, even within the Likud, there was unease about Kahane's exhibitionist style, his tactics and strident undisguised racism. One Likud MK, Michael Eitan, found similarities between Kahane's draft bills and the two Nazi laws enacted in September 1935 (the 'Nuremberg Laws'), the 'Reich Citizenship Law' and the 'Law for the Protection of German Blood and Honour', which underpinned the whole structure of Nazi legislation.[198] In February 1987, MK Amnon Rubinstein, of the centrist Shinui Party, requested that legal measures be taken against the Kach movement because of letters sent to Arab citizens, calling on them to leave Israel. As a result of the letters, Attorney General Yosef Harish decided to indict Kahane for racial incitement.[199] On 5 October 1988, the Central Election Committee decided not to approve the Kach list in the election to the Twelfth Knesset.[200] Apparently, the Likud representatives on the election committee agreed to such a disqualification on condition that the Progressive List for Peace, which advocates a two-state solution and negotiation with the PLO, also be disqualified. Kach then appealed to the Supreme Court but failed to overturn the Central Election Committee's disqualification.[201]

In spite of this disqualification, Kahane's strident campaign for Arab expulsion went on unabated. In May 1990, two days after an Israeli named 'Ami Popper cold-bloodedly massacred seven Arab workers from Gaza whom he had never seen before in Rishon Letzion, Kahane held a 'mass solidarity meeting in Rishon to celebrate the deed'. He addressed his audience: 'Good evening, good

Jews and filthy traitors. What's all the crying about? ... A Jew kills seven Arabs, Ishmaelites, haters of Israel – and that's bad?'[202]

Kahane himself was assassinated by an Arab gunman in New York in November 1990. Only a few hours after his death, two innocent Palestinians, a man and a woman from Lubban al-Sharqiyah village, near Nablus, were reportedly murdered by Kach members in revenge for Kahane's death. Two Arab MKs were also forced to flee Jerusalem in the night out of fear for their safety. At the same time the Israeli government saw fit to issue mourning notices for Kahane.[203] One Israeli journalist remarked on 'the orgy of mourning for Kahane, and the legitimation he suddenly received after his murder from the political establishment and the [Israeli] media', which exemplifies the extent to which racism and support for 'transfer'/ethnic cleansing has been implanted in Israeli minds.[204] In spite of the departure of Kahane, Kahanism remains very much alive. A senior editor of the *New Outlook* monthly wrote in January 1991:

> His frenzied funeral in Jerusalem shows how many disciples he left behind, with cry of 'Death to the Arabs' as a trademark. But this is only the tip of the iceberg. Belief in Israeli racism and 'transfer' is equally strong in Rehavam [sic] Ze'evi's Moledet (Homeland) party and Raful Eitan's Tsomet (Crossroads) party, which together have four Knesset seats. The same goes for the three mandates that went to Yuval Ne'eman and Geula Cohen's Tehiya (Revival) party. Much of the Likud holds similar views, as expressed by MK Tsahi [sic] Hanegbi (Cohen's son), as do many in the religious parties. By the way, all these belong to or support the current Shamir coalition. It is generally assumed that were there to be elections today these groups would increase their strength, and it is not so important if the name of Kahane does or does not appear.[205]

Kahanism remained alive in Israel after the assassination of Rabbi Kahane. In 1991, Rabbi Avraham Toledano became the leader of Kach, but he was later replaced by younger men, such as Baruch Merzel and No'am Federman, Kach's operations expert. Kahane's son, Binyamin Zeev, founded another smaller group with an identical platform, called Kahane Hai (the 'Kahane Lives' party). The Israeli High Court rejected the appeals of these two lists to be permitted to run in the elections of 1992 on the grounds that their platforms were still supportive of open racism.[206] Many supporters of the two groups live among Jewish settlers in Kiryat Arba'a and Hebron, on the West Bank. One of these zealots was Dr Baruch Goldstein, who carried out the massacre of 29 Muslim worshippers at the Ibrahimi mosque in Hebron on 24 February 1994.[207] After the Hebron massacre, the two groups were banned outright. Nevertheless, prominent figures of Kach continued to receive funds from supporters in the USA and resurfaced in other groups such as Eyal[208] – whose member Yigal Amir was responsible for the assassination of Prime Minister Yitzhak Rabin on 4 November 1995. No'am Federman is currently active in the Committee for Safety on the Roads, a right-wing pressure group, led by a former Tehiya Member of Knesset, whose *raison d'être* is to keep the West Bank roads safe for passage by Jewish settlers and whose members have been accused of acts of violence against Palestinians.[209]

Meanwhile several Kach policies (notably 'transfer' of Palestinians from the occupied territories) were openly adopted by still-legal parties of the far right, such as Tehiya, Tzomet and Moledet.[210] Also many former supporters of Kahane were dispersed among the far right parties, which adhere basically to Kach's Arab removal goals but, as we shall see, articulate them in a less shrill and more 'respectable', middle-class and politic style.

4
The Secular Ultra-nationalists: Parties and Movements of the Far Right

It was the conquest of the West Bank, Gaza, Sinai and the Golan Heights in 1967 which resurrected the dormant far right in Israel. Between 1948 and 1967, few had been willing to follow figures such as the Lehi veteran Yisrael Eldad into the wilderness of confrontational ultra-nationalism which sought a Land from the Nile to the Euphrates.[1] Unlike the far right, Menahem Begin adopted a pragmatic attitude towards the question of Sinai and the Peace Treaty with Egypt; he also believed that Sinai did not belong to the 'biblical Land of Israel'. It was in part his sponsorship of the Camp David Accords in the late 1970s and his decision to return Sinai to Egypt which consolidated the radical right. The formation of the Tehiya Party – mainly from the Likud's radical right wing in 1979 – and, subsequently, of Tzomet by General Raphael Eitan in 1983 from Labour Zionism's adherents, was symptomatic of the growing influence of the far right in Israeli politics and its moving away from the official Revisionist umbrella.[2]

In the 1980s, the Tehiya, Tzomet and Moledet became the leading parties of the extreme right. Situated further to the right of the Likud, the three parties, along with substantial sections of the Likud and the National Religious Party, are generally considered part of the influential parliamentary radical right. In comparison with the stridency of these extreme right-wing parties on the territorial issue, the policies of the current Labour coalition of Ehud Barak towards the Palestinians look like the epitome of pragmatism. It should be pointed out, however, that these radical right-wing parties are also rooted in basic Zionist-Israeli values and principles that have guided the Israeli leadership in the pre-state and state period. The Israeli far right basically supports the Greater Israel position of the mainstream right-wing Likud, only more so. An appropriate description of the radical right parties is provided by Ehud Sprinzak:

The radical right should not be seen as an isolated extremist faction that stands in diametrical opposition to both Israeli democracy and the moderate right, but rather as a very influential school that has been pushing the entire Israeli right toward greater ultra-nationalism, greater extra-legalism, greater militarism, greater ethnocentrism and greater religiosity. The radical right is neither separated historically nor detached politically from the larger Israeli right. It is instead the right pole of the nationalist continuum ... It is a political and ideological camp of the true believers whose values and ideas are sometimes shared by large numbers of Israelis who are usually not considered radical.[3]

The three parties of the far right are also open proponents of the 'transfer' solution. According to Sprinzak,

The difference between the manifest transfer of Moledet and the 'latent' transfer of the Tehiya is that the former recommends the removal of all the Arabs of the occupied territories while the Tehiya only speaks about the refugees. Tzomet, while similarly avoiding the transfer concept, also sees the political expediency of the removal of the Arab population of the refugee camps from the occupied territories. Its 1987 Kiryat Shmone Convention passed a resolution supporting 'an exchange of population as a way to terminate violent confrontations and hostile operations'. Its platform leaves no doubt that 'as a part of every peace agreement, the residents of the refugee camps inside Eretz Yisrael will be rehabilitated *in the Arab countries* and the remaining Jews in the Arab countries will immigrate to Israel.' [original emphasis][4]

The 1980s began with a clear rise in the parliamentary representation of the parties of the extreme right but the 1990s ended with their marked decline. In 1984, parties running on explicitly ultra-nationalist (both secular and religious fundamentalist) platforms (the Tehiya, the National Circle, Morasha and Kach) received 150,000 votes, electing eight (of 120) members of the Knesset.[5] In the early 1990s, the three parties of the extreme right – the Tehiya, Tzomet and Moledet – were all represented both in the Knesset and the ruling Likud coalition. Together the three parties had attained seven seats in the Knesset in the 1988 elections, while the National Religious Party had five seats; together these four parties received twelve parliamentary seats and 10.5 per cent of the vote. In the 1992 elections, the Tehiya declined, but many voters moved further from the Likud to the far right; Tzomet increased its parliamentary representation to eight seats, Moledet gained three seats and the National Religious Party six seats; together these three parties gained 17 seats. In the 1996 elections, the National Religious Party gained nine seats, Tzomet five seats and Moledet two seats; the three parties gained collectively 16 seats. However, the May 1999 elections marked a clear decline in the parliamentary representation of the extreme right's parties: Tzomet lost all its Knesset seats, while the National Religious Party gained only five seats. However, taking into account the fact that the radical right was fully represented in the Israeli government until 1992, and between June 1996 and May 1999, by a number of highly influential ministers in the Israeli Cabinet, its general political influence until May 1999 was much greater than its actual vote percentage would suggest.

THE TEHIYA PARTY

The ultra-right Tehiya ('Revival') Party was founded in October 1979 to oppose the Camp David Accords and the return of Sinai to Egypt, and to demand outright Israeli sovereignty over the occupied territories. The founders were two Knesset members who broke away from the Likud: Geula Cohen,[6] a long-time associate of Menahem Begin and member of the pre-state Irgun Tzvai Leumi (the Irgun), the para-military underground organisation founded by Vladimir Jabotinsky, and the afore-mentioned Moshe Shamir, a leader of the Whole Land of Israel Movement which operated between 1967 and 1977. The Tehiya was joined by Professor Yuval Neeman, Israel's leading nuclear physicist (then also president of Tel Aviv University) and a secular ultra-nationalist, who came from Labour Zionism and was closely associated with Ben-Gurion and Dayan in the 1950s, and Eliykim Ha'etzni and Hanan Porat, two prominent settler leaders who were subsequently elected as members of Knesset on the Tehiya list. (Later the secularist emphasis in Tehiya drove Hanan Porat to return to his former party, the National Religious Party.)

Steeped in mystical Zionism and having much in common with classical European fascism, the Tehiya pursued a vision of maximum territorial expansion with the destined borders of the Jewish state stretching across the Arab Middle East. Its commitment included Jewish sovereignty over the 'whole Land of Israel' and Israel's

reconquest of Sinai, an Egyptian territory which the party, unlike
Menahem Begin, considered as an integral part of 'biblical Eretz-
Yisrael.[7] In a recent article in the Hebrew daily *Yedi'ot Aharonot* of
26 December 1997, Geula Cohen wrote:

> True, in 1948 we accepted a state *de facto* within the (UN) partition
> borders, borders which left out most of Eretz-Yisrael. However, no
> Israeli government to this day has ever voluntarily given up, *de
> juri*, our right and legal ownership of most of historic Eretz-Yisrael
> which is not yet in our hands by signing an agreement to this
> effect. (Menahem Begin, sadly, did not regard Sinai as part of
> Eretz-Yisrael).[8]

Earlier in 1983, the leader of the Tehiya, Yuval Neeman, envisioned
an Israeli domain stretching across the region and called for the
annexation of southern Lebanon to Israel and for the use of the
waters of the Litani River. He also advised the following:

> If we are attacked by Jordan, I would annex the Red Mountain
> (east and south of the Dead Sea), which is relatively unpopulated,
> and which has great importance for the development of the
> southern part of the country. We would also thereby create a
> border with Saudi Arabia from which we could threaten the oil
> fields ... In the North, if the conflict in Lebanon should begin
> again, I advocate maintaining control over the Litani.[9]

The Tehiya advocated the abrogation of the Peace Treaty with Egypt,
opposed the Begin 'Plan of Administrative Autonomy for the Arabs
of Judea and Samaria', and, unlike the Likud, demanded the outright
imposition of Israeli sovereignty on, and the legal annexation of, the
West Bank and Gaza, over which the 'Jewish people has exclusive
and eternal right'.[10] The Tehiya political platform for the 1988
election described Jordan as a '*de facto* Palestinian state', however,
'if this state initiate war in the future against Israel the territories
which it will lose in such a war will not be returned to it'. The
implication of this statement is that Jordan, which, according to the
Tehiya, constitutes part of the Land of Israel, over which Jews have
'exclusive and eternal right', would be targeted for the next stage of
territorial expansion. The same election platform also calls for the
'confiscation of the control over the Temple Mount [al-Haram al-
Sharif] from the Muslim Waqf' and its handover to Israeli hands, as

well as the 'building of a Jewish place for prayer on the Temple Mount in the place permitted according to the halacha'. Apparently Geula Cohen was pinning her hopes on the high frequency of earthquakes in the region which would perhaps cause the destruction of the Muslim shrines in Jerusalem.[11] This position seems to conceal a latent position in favour of a partial or even complete dismantling of the Muslim shrines, the al-Aqsa and Dome of the Rock Mosques and it is close to the position of the Kach movement, although, as has already been shown, Kach explicitly demanded the 'rebuilding' of the whole Temple and not just 'a place for prayer on the Temple Mount'. Moreover, the followers of Rabbi Kahane did not satisfy themselves with messianic hopes of this kind: they explicitly announced their intention to blow up the mosques. Moreover, as we shall see below, the territorially maximalist and 'ethnic cleansing' positions of the Tehiya – which declared in 1980 that it would not accept non-Jewish members[12] – reveal not only a latent but rather an explicit pro-'transfer' stand.

A major parliamentary success of the Tehiya Party in 1980 was the passage by the Knesset of the Basic Law: Jerusalem. Proposed by the Tehiya, the so-called Jerusalem Law declared the city to be Israel's capital. A second law proposed by the Tehiya, calling for the application of Israeli law to the Golan Heights, was adopted by the Knesset the following year. In the spring of 1982, the three Tehiya Members of Knesset led the unsuccessful campaign in Yamit in the Rafah salient to halt Israeli withdrawal from Sinai in the wake of the Egyptian–Israeli Peace Treaty.

In September 1982, shortly after the Israeli invasion of Lebanon, the Tehiya joined the Likud coalition government. Its chairman, Professor Yuval Neeman, was appointed Minister of Science and Development, and Deputy Chairman of the Ministerial Committee on Settlement which subsequently authorised more than forty new settlements, most of them on the West Bank.[13] Prior to the 1984 elections, General Raphael Eitan, the army Chief of Staff during the invasion of Lebanon, joined the Tehiya with the political movement he had set up called Tzomet ('Crossroads'). In the elections of 1984, the Tehiya-Tzomet joint list received five Knesset seats, emerging as the third largest party after Likud and Labour, although remaining outside the National Unity Government. This growth in strength was a clear sign of the rise in public support for the extreme right in Israeli politics. However, in November 1987, as a result of an internal power struggle combined with a personal feud between Geula Cohen and General Eitan, the party split into its original components of the Tehiya and Tzomet, and in the elections of the same year, the Tehiya emerged with three Knesset seats while Tzomet received two seats, thus together retaining the same electoral strength obtained in 1984. The Tehiya chairman, Neeman – who is one of the most persistent, vocal advocates of Arab 'transfer' – did not come from a 'lunatic fringe' group of the far right, but rather from the Israeli Labour establishment. Neeman had served in the Israeli Army in planning and intelligence posts, rising to the rank of colonel; in early 1950s, while serving as a senior intelligence officer, he formulated a strategic plan which subsequently became instrumental in shaping Israel's territorial ambitions; as a professor of nuclear physics, Neeman held key posts in Israel's nuclear planning and was acting chairman of Israel's Atomic Energy Committee; he has been chairman of Israel's Space Agency since 1982; he served as Senior Adviser and Chief Scientist to the Ministry of Defence, 1975–76, when Shim'on Peres was Defence Minister and he was closely associated with the Labour Party; President of Tel Aviv University 1971–75; Minister of Science and Development 1982–84; and Minister of Science and Energy in Shamir's Cabinet, until January 1992. Having held key posts in Israel's military and nuclear planning, Neeman seems to consider that the deterrent power of Israel's nuclear weapons and conventional army can ensure maximum territorial expansion and Arab 'transfer', as well as enabling Israel to accept the burden of permanent war with the Arabs. When the security arguments behind his approach of territorial maximalism are questioned, Neeman resorts to nationalist and ideological reasons to justify his arguments in favour of Greater Israel.[14]

The pro-transfer position of the Tehiya leaders has been expressed on numerous occasions. In August 1981, the Israeli journalist Amnon Kapeliouk wrote that Neeman considered the failure of the Israeli Army to exploit the October 1973 war for 'emptying the Gaza Strip of all its Palestinian inhabitants, once and for all' constituted 'great laxity' and a missed golden opportunity.[15] Already in June 1967, two weeks after the war, Professor Neeman had suggested that Israel could 'now' solve the problem of Arab refugees by 'organising their emigration'.[16] Expressing a rather transparent position in favour of 'partial' transfer in his book *The Policy of Sober Vision* (1984), Minister of Science and Development Neeman asserted that Israeli citizenship and the right to vote must not be given to the Arabs of the territories – who were, in effect, resident aliens[17] –

except for those individuals 'who would identify with the Zionist state of Israel, be examined in Hebrew and Zionism, do national service, and pay taxes ... some of the Arab population (350–400 thousand in Judea, Samaria and Gaza) who hold a refugee passport ... will have to find for themselves a permanent home ... Such a home will not be here, and just as we absorbed the Jews of Arab countries, the Arab countries will have to absorb the refugees.'[18] At the Tehiya Party conference in the spring of 1986, Neeman demanded the transfer of at least 500,000 Arab refugees out of the Land of Israel as a precondition for a peace settlement.[19] At the end of the conference, the Tehiya called on the government to encourage the inhabitants of the West Bank and the Gaza Strip to 'emigrate', and to expel the 'subversives'.[20] Neeman's colleague, MK Geula Cohen, explained that 'inducing the Arabs to leave would be humane as Jordan is part of the Land of Israel, so going there would not be emigrating'.[21] In a similar vein, the Tehiya political platform for the 1988 election states: 'A condition will be set in any peace negotiation with Arab countries that the Arab residents of the refugee camps of Judea, Samaria and Gaza be rehabilitated in Jordan and other Arab countries.' Here the Tehiya advocates the clearing out of over half a million refugees under the thinly disguised formula of 'rehabilitating the refugees in Arab countries and not in Israel'. Also 'Israel [should] encourage and assist in the emigration of the Arabs of Judea, Samaria and Gaza, who will not agree to live [as mere residents and not citizens] under Israeli rule'.[22] However, since Jordan is considered as territory of the Land of Israel destined for a future stage of territorial expansion, it is very likely that the Tehiya leaders would prefer the 'evacuation of the camps and the deportation of all the refugees to Saudi Arabia and the oil-producing countries which have urgent manpower needs'.[23]

One of the more vociferous advocates of transfer among the Tehiya leaders is Avi Farhan, a former spokesman for the party and currently a member of its Centre, and who had served as an assistant to Neeman, the science and energy minister,[24] when he held this post until January 1992.

The thinly disguised pro-expulsion political platform of the Tehiya for the 1988 election does not exclude the Arab citizens of Israel who have expressed solidarity with their brothers in the territories since the beginning of the intifada: 'The intifada, which exposed manifestations of lack of loyalty also among respectable parts of the Arabs of the State of Israel, necessitates a new political arrangement towards the Israeli Arabs.' This new arrangement includes: 1) that the right to vote and be elected to the Knesset, currently enjoyed by the Arab citizen, be revoked and made conditional on doing three years' 'national service'; 2) that the 'national insurance' allowance (currently an Arab citizen receives half of the allowance given to a Jewish citizen) 'be made conditional on the fulfilment of all the citizens' duties and a test of loyalty to the state of Israel'; 3) 'any Israeli [Arab] who takes part in subversive activities against state security and in collaboration with the enemy will have his citizenship taken away and he will be liable to be expelled from the country'.

The eruption of the intifada in December 1987 prompted the Tehiya leaders to urge that *en masse* deportation measures be taken, targeting initially Palestinian leaders and activists in the territories. 'To break the intifada' the Tehiya proposed, *inter alia*: the deportation of 'terrorists' and 'inciters', the evacuation of the casbahs and other residential parts of the town centres, and the creation of wide traffic routes.[25] On 29 March 1989, MK Geula Cohen, together with four other members of the influential Knesset Foreign Affairs and Defence Committee, toured the Arab towns of Nablus, Ramallah and al-Bireh and she repeated her party's proposal 'to destroy the casbahs', and evacuate their Arab residents.[26] The *Jerusalem Post* reported on 11 September 1988 that the Tehiya leaders maintained that all that was needed was to expel 1,200 Arab leaders and activists and the 'intifada would die'. Eliyakim Ha'etzni, a settler leader and a fiery Kiryat Arba'a veteran (and then a Tehiya Knesset member) proposed a much higher figure:

> When the intifada erupted I immediately called for the expulsion of five thousand persons. The leaders. I would then open all the Ansars [that is, the detention camps in which, according to one estimate, 11,000 Arabs are detained without trial] and they would all [be registered] on my computer. Anyone who throws a stone would be expelled ... otherwise there would be no alternative ... there would be another war like 1948 and then the Left would have to carry out the expulsion order.[27]

The long list of Arab leaders targeted by lawyer Ha'etzni includes moderate figures such as Mubarak 'Awwad of the Center for the Study of Non-Violence (who was in fact deported in 1987), Hanna Siniora, editor of *Al-Fajr* daily, and Faysal al-Husayni of East Jerusalem.[28]

Ha'etzni claims that his proposal of expelling thousands of Arab leaders and activists in order to bring about the suppression of the intifada is an 'antithesis of the transfer' advocated by the Moledet Party of Rehava'am Zeevi and the Kach movement of Rabbi Kahane.[29] But, as has already been shown, the Tehiya positions of territorial maximalism contained an explicit ethnic cleansing agenda. Moreover, the fact that Ha'etzni, as a Tehiya member of the Kiryat Arba'a Municipal Council, formed a municipal coalition which included Kahane's Kach party after the municipal election in 1985, and signed a coalition agreement stating that Arab workers would not be employed by the Kiryat Arba'a council,[30] shows how close he and his Tehiya Party are to the pro-transfer position of Moledet and Kach. Furthermore, in his bid to justify the annexationist policies of the right and the activities of the Jewish settlers, Ha'etzni – who had been a member of the ruling Mapai Party in the 1950s – criticises the hypocrisy of left-wing Zionism and its attempts to beautify the past: in 1948 the Yishuv 'did things to them beyond Kahane's most terrible dreams ... The Jewish community expelled Arabs with mortars. Afterwards we killed Arabs who infiltrated at night to collect the remnants of their property, which they had abandoned at the height of the battles'; 'Many of those "missing" ['nifkadim' or absentees is the official Israeli term used to describe the Arab refugees of 1948] were expelled. And if they fled during the height of the war, was there any sin in that? We wiped them out and divided their property'; 'We didn't stop with the theft of lands. We also enacted laws for the expropriation of Arab lands which had been abandoned, and the High Court of Justice was quick to approve after the fact the expropriations which had been carried out in the field. In this manner we took Nazareth's land reserves ...';[31] '... the Land of Israel for the Jewish people. Arabs [who say that the occupied territories are Palestine] ... and who reveal hostilities towards us in their actions, must be removed from here.'[32] Ha'etzni wants to remove 'only' those Palestinians who do not accept his 'axiomatic' position that the 'Land of Israel belongs to the Jewish People' and who oppose settlement and annexation and do not accept the legal status of 'resident alien' (deprived of the right to vote) in their own homeland – in effect such a removal would encompass the bulk of the Arab population.

Public statements in favour of 'forcible transfer' were made by the Tehiya leaders shortly after the Iraqi invasion of Kuwait in August 1990. These leaders were, also, reportedly rejoicing as the Gulf crisis escalated. Geula Cohen, then Deputy Minister in the Shamir government, was reported in August as telling a group of supporters from the United States, Europe and South Africa that if 'the crisis keeps escalating and if Jordan crosses certain red lines, we will immediately respond by annexing Judea and Samaria and extend our sovereignty there. Shortly after we will forcefully transfer the Arabs of Judea and Samaria ... to Jordan.' She went on: 'This means that the King of Jordan would thus lose both territory and his kingdom. Only Israel can settle the Palestinians there and it will be done in a way that suits us best.'[33] The chairman of Cohen's Tehiya Party and Minister of Energy Yuval Neeman was reported in the Jerusalem Hebrew newspaper *Kol Ha'ir* as making similar statements to the same Zionist group.[34] In a *New York Times* leader of 6 September 1990, former MK Uri Avenery (perhaps having in mind these statements of the then Cabinet Minister Neeman and Deputy Minister Cohen as well as statements made by a confidant of the then Prime Minister Shamir to *Haaretz* daily) warned that as a result of the Gulf crisis, 'certain influential Israeli circles betray eagerness for an Israeli invasion of Jordan'. Avenery also noted, as has been mentioned elsewhere, that many right-wing Zionists have not abandoned their advocacy of expansion into, and conquest of, the East Bank territory of Jordan. He also warned that a war with Jordan and Iraq might be exploited by these influential circles to 'transfer' the West Bank Arabs as well as to invade and annex part of Jordan.[35] Like Avenery, many liberal Israelis have warned that the temptation for men in high official positions to exploit a war as a cover for mass transfer was growing in Israel.

In the elections of 1981, the Tehiya received 44,500 votes and placed three deputies in the Knesset. In 1984 its vote total rose to 83,000 (receiving 23 per cent of the votes cast in Gush Emunim settlements)[36], resulting in a parliamentary representation of five seats. In the elections of 1992, however, the party's three deputies all lost their Knesset seats. Part of its 1992 election failure is ascribed to confusion caused by Rabbi Moshe Levinger of Kiryat Arba'a purporting to stand for a united radical right.[37] Since then the party has disintegrated, with former members drifting into other radical right-wing parties and pressure groups, such as Zo Artzienu ('This is Our Land'), which first came to prominence in 1995 by organising 15 'hill-top protests' by Jewish settlers in the occupied territories who opposed the policies of the Labour government.[38] Tehiya co-founder Geula Cohen, after years in the wilderness since the collapse of her party in 1992, has returned to the Likud. Although failing to secure a safe seat in the Likud list for the 1996 election, Cohen could take comfort from the fact that her son, Tzahi Hanegbi, is a prominent Likud politician who served as a minister in the government of Binyamin Netanyahu between 1996 and May 1999.

GENERAL EITAN AND TZOMET

Founded in 1983 and led by former chief of staff, General Raphael (Raful) Eitan, Tzomet ('Crossroads') surprised many political analysts with its good showing in the 1992 elections, raising its total number of seats in the Knesset from two to eight, making it the third largest party after Labour and Likud. The party is dominated by the authoritarian personality of Raphael Eitan, a controversial but popular figure who was chief of staff in 1982 and together with General Ariel Sharon masterminded Israel's invasion of Lebanon that year. Born in 1929 in Moshav Tel 'Adashim, Eitan comes from the Spartan militarist tradition of the Palmah, strike force of Labour Zionism in the 1940s and he still commands considerable respect in the army. The political agenda of Tzomet is dominated by one issue: the commitment to Jewish sovereignty over the whole Land of Israel, including the Golan Heights. However, unlike Gush Emunim and other religious fundamentalist groups, Tzomet is staunchly secular in outlook and its roots are in the activist Zionist Labour movement; the 1,300 activists who formed it in 1983 were drawn from the ranks of the Labour cooperative and collectivist sectors, moshavim and kibbutzim.[39] Although Tzomet shared hard-line positions with the Tehiya on a whole range of issues related to the Palestinians, including the annexation of the occupied territories and the harsh treatment of the Arab citizens of Israel, it did not share the mystic or religious fervour of many Tehiya supporters; on occasion Tzomet has lambasted the ultra-orthodox for 'sponging off the state' while not contributing to Israel's defence.[40]

The leading members of his party come neither from a fringe group nor a religious background. Tzomet's Greater Israel positions, which are similar to those of the Tehiya,[41] largely reflect the militant nature and super-hawkish views of its leader; Eitan justifies his views on territorial maximalism by pragmatic, strategic considerations and practical necessities; he preaches that the main task is to inculcate the 'spirit of the first [Zionist] pioneers' in the youth for winning the struggle with the Arabs of the 'Land of Israel'.[42] Upon assuming office as Chief of Staff in 1978, 'Eitan not only identified with Begin's views ... but even outdid Begin in supporting Gush Emunim and its policy of settlements on the West Bank', the Israeli political scientist Yoram Peri writes.[43] Eitan's deeply sympathetic approach to the Gush Emunim settlers on the one hand and his openly bigoted views towards the Palestinians on the other have already been referred to elsewhere, as has his widely publicised metaphor, comparing the Palestinians to 'drugged insects'. During his tenure as chief of staff, Eitan also issued orders to Israeli officers and soldiers to rough up Arab students in order to 'deter' further protests,[44] and reduced the sentences of soldiers who had been found guilty of crimes against Arab civilians, including two notorious cases in which he pardoned convicted murderers.[45] Later, in mid-1984, Eitan visited members of the Jewish Underground while on remand and expressed understanding for their violent campaign. He also told them: 'I know about one case in the Galilee in which Arabs uprooted a [Jewish] plantation, and then [Jews] went and uprooted three times as much [of an Arab plantation] ... this is not legal, but it did help. No more [Jewish plantation] was uprooted [by Arabs].'[46]

Eitan's solution for the intifada, which the Israeli Army has found difficult to suppress, was very simple: instead of chasing after the Arabs with clubs, 'we should be shooting them in the head. I have no doubt that this will happen in the end';[47] '... a bullet in the head of every stone thrower'.[48] He also urged a 'mass deportation' of leaders and activists ('rioters') 'without taking into account what the rest of the world says'.[49] During a visit to Jewish settlements in the occupied territories in February 1988, Eitan proposed to expel 20 to 30 persons from every village from which stones were thrown at Israelis: 'We must carry out a policy of expulsion and collective punishment. We must expel propagandists, inciters, young children who riot. First of all, to expel, at once, the whole political and information system of East Jerusalem.'[50] Moreover, 'we must pressurize them economically, how[?], that they will not be allowed to work in Israel, that the supply of basic commodities such as oil and cement, be prohibited to them, and heavy fines be imposed on them', Eitan proposed on another occasion.[51] It should be noted that some of these proposals have since then indeed found their way into the actual policy of the Israeli government.

In its thinly disguised pro-transfer Political Platform for the 1988 election,[52] Tzomet urges that 'the Israeli law be imposed on Judea,

Samaria and Gaza' which are the 'land of the Jewish people'; it 'views the solution to the Palestinian problem [to be] to the east of the [River] Jordan' and demands that 'the refugee camps' dwellers within the boundaries of the Land of Israel be rehabilitated in Arab countries as part of any peace settlement'. After the legal annexation of the territories, their Arab inhabitants 'would remain Jordanian citizens', in effect, with the legal status of 'resident alien'. Moreover, in order to achieve the 'national objective ... of increasing the demographic gap between the Jewish population and the Arab minority in the Land of Israel', Tzomet urges, *inter alia*, the encouragement of high birth rates among the Jews and that 'the state of Israel facilitates the emigration of the Arab residents of Israel to any place they would choose.'

It has already been shown that most advocates of the whole Land of Israel, and virtually all extreme right-wing Zionists view Arab 'transfer/emigration' as the only solution to the perceived 'demographic problem'. And like all the far-right parties, Tzomet makes little distinction between the Palestinian citizens of Israel and those of the West Bank and Gaza. Tzomet asserts – echoing the notoriously racist document of Koeing in the mid-1970s – that a 'demographic time-bomb' exists in 'the impressive increase in the weight of the non-Jewish community within the Green Line that numbers today [late 1988] approximately 800,000'; 'the [statistical] data of the last 20 years indicates clearly that this community constitutes the real "demographic bomb"'.[53] As a result, Tzomet wants additional restrictions to be imposed on the Israeli Arabs as well as deportation measures and an active state policy to encourage emigration; among these restrictions: a) the banning of Arab political parties which undermine and do not recognise the State of Israel as the state of the Jewish people; b) 'the transfer of state lands to the Jewish National Fund as a means of ending the Arabs' takeover of state lands'; c) 'any Arab in the Land of Israel who acts on behalf of the terrorist organisation or on his independent initiative to undermine the state's existence will be considered as enemy, his Israeli citizenship (if he holds one) will be revoked, his property confiscated and he will be expelled from the country'; d) 'the Arab population in the Land of Israel must know that its residence in the country is conditional on its full upholding of the state's laws and in case of uprising it risks revocation of citizenship and the transfer of this population to outside the country's borders'; e) 'the State of Israel [would] facilitate the emigration of the Arab residents of Israel [including the Arab citizens] to any place they would choose'.[54] If these 'transfer' proposals were to find their way into the government's policies, particularly the revocation of the citizenship of Israeli Arabs and their deportation, they would constitute a radical new departure from the existing approach of avoiding the use of administrative and forcible means to remove Arab citizens from the country.

Eitan has been a MK since 1984 and a member of the influential Knesset Foreign Affairs and Security Committee and the State Control Committee. He served in the Shamir Cabinet from 1990 to early 1992, when, together with Moledet, he left the Likud coalition, in protest at perceived concessions to Palestinians. In 1994, three Tzomet MKs, led by Gonen Segev, broke away to form a new party, Ye'ud, which subsequently joined the Labour coalition. On 8 February 1996, Eitan and Likud leader Binyamin Netanyahu announced a pact between the two parties. Under the terms of the agreement, Tzomet would be guaranteed eight seats (of the first 42 slots) in a joint Knesset list; while Eitan would get a leading cabinet post. In return, Eitan agreed not to stand in the first direct elections for the prime ministership; instead he would throw his weight behind Netanyahu's candidacy.[55]

From mid-1996 to May 1999, Eitan served as minister of agriculture and environment in Netanyahu's Cabinet. In the 1999 elections, Tzomet failed to get elected to the Knesset. However, it is still too early to judge whether Tzomet's decline will bring an end to Eitan's political career.

GENERAL ZEEVI AND MOLEDET

Moledet ('Homeland') is the most radical right-wing party in Israel. The party was established in the summer of 1988 by General Rehava'am Zeevi then aged 65, and since then it has been waging a single-minded, strident public campaign for the removal of the Palestinians from the 'entire Land of Israel'. The party appears to have been first conceived in March 1987, several months before the Palestinian intifada erupted in November of that year, at a meeting held in the town of Herzliyah, which was attended by Zeevi himself, Reserve General Yehoshu'a Saguy (Likud MK 1988–92), Professor Yair Sprintzak (the son of a former Secretary-General of the Histadrut and the first Speaker of the Israeli Parliament and subsequently a Moledet Member of Knesset), Eli'ezer Schweid, a Hebrew University professor and one of the most articulate publicists of Greater Israel, Tzvi Bar, the mayor of Ramat Gan and Tzvi Shiloah, who later became a co-founder and ideologue of the new party upon its formal establishment.

Inspired by the increasing polarisation of the Israeli public since the beginning of the intifada, Zeevi then organised a symposium to debate the 'transfer' solution at the Zionist Organization of America House in Tel Aviv on 22 February 1988. Initially Zeevi wanted the conference to be held secretly, and the guests were requested not to transfer their invitation cards to other people; cameras and tape recorders were banned at the conference. However, the attempts to keep the conference confidential failed and even the IDF radio 'advertised' it one day before it was held.[56] Among the 150 to 200 people who attended the conference were former General Officer Commanding Northern Command (1983–86) General Uri Orr (who has been Director General of the Jewish National Fund since 1987), and the former head of the prison service, General David Maimon, a former Intelligence chief, Shlomo Gazit and Professor Arnon Sofer of Haifa University. Gazit, Sofer and Orr, however, made it clear during the conference and later that they did not identify with Zeevi's call for large-scale expulsions because these were impractical. On the other hand, other speakers such as Tzvi Shiloah and Aharon Pappo argued that expulsion would be a humane and practical solution.[57] Another participant, the historian Professor Yoav Gelber of Haifa University maintained that 'transfer' was a legitimate solution; he was annoyed by the attempt of some people to delegitimise it beforehand: 'When I come to consider other alternatives, I still don't see them as more practical than transfer.'[58] The super-hawkish organiser of the conference Zeevi announced triumphantly: 'We have lit the torch – and it shall burn.' Seeking legitimisation for his pro-expulsion views in Israeli history, Zeevi reminded the participants that more than 400 Arab villages and towns had been replaced by Jewish settlements in and after 1948. He also added that it was the Labour Prime Ministers David Ben-Gurion and Levi Eshkol who had established official bodies to deal with the question of transfer: Ben-Gurion set up a Transfer Committee in 1948, and Eshkol a special unit after the 1967 war.[59]

Zeevi, however, was vague as to how the mass expulsions should be carried out. When pressed by other participants, he advocated making life difficult for the Palestinian Arabs, in the first stage; if they face economic hardship, unemployment, shortage of land and water, then 'in a legitimate way, and in accordance with the Geneva Convention, we can create the necessary conditions for separation.'[60] The Israeli journalist Hagai Eshed, criticising Zeevi's proposal, wrote in *Davar* on 17 July 1987:

> ... the very idea of raising this proposal ... [very serious]. Its argumentation is more important than the operational conclusions. First of all, they accustom public opinion – at least part of it – to the idea that it is impossible without the territories and impossible with their [Arab] inhabitants.[61] It is forbidden to give up Judea and Samaria and it is impossible to continue the occupation of their Palestinian residents forever against their will. Moreover, large [Jewish] immigration which would change the 'demographic map' is not seen on the horizon. Another solution must be found. The proposal of 'Gandhi' [that is, Zeevi] – even if he does not mean that – is in fact the code-name of the military operation in the coming war, whose combined aim would be to solve the problem of Judea, Samaria and Gaza and our 'demographic problem'... raising the idea of 'voluntary transfer' now is within the advance emotional preparation ... for the forcible expulsion of the inhabitants of the territories in the coming war ... this is a latent or open proposal to prepare now the required 'operation plans' in order not to miss the opportunity when the time comes.

In fact, in his article in *Davar*, Eshed was responding to earlier proposals made by Zeevi in support of transfer, which were published in the Israeli press.

At a conference on the future of the territories, organised by Bamah, a group of supporters of the late Moshe Dayan, in Tel Aviv, on 3 July 1987 (on the 20th anniversary of the Israeli rule in the West Bank and Gaza), Zeevi stated that a possible solution to the Palestinian problem was the transfer of the Arabs from the country.[62] These statements sparked off a public uproar and some Members of Knesset as well as liberal figures called for the resignation of Zeevi from his position as chairman of the Tel Aviv-based Land of Israel Museum, a post Zeevi had held since 1981. Zeevi, however, refused to resign and the mayor of Tel Aviv, Shlomo Lahat, refused to sack him. Moreover, two weeks later, on 16 July 1987, Zeevi published an article in the mass-circulation daily *Yedi'ot Aharonot*, in which he criticized his detractors as hypocritical, explaining that there was nothing new in advocating 'transfer,' since the concept had already been adopted by his mentors: the founders of Labour Zionism. He also reiterated his position in favour of the annexation of the West Bank and Gaza and the transfer of their Palestinian inhabitants as the only solution to the Arab–Israeli conflict.

Ever since the February 1988 symposium, the tough-talking Zeevi has repeatedly stated that in pursuing an 'agreed transfer' policy he was following in the footsteps of his 'mentors', the leaders of labour Zionism: 'Ben-Gurion's memoirs and documents are imbued with reports and thoughts about transfer. See the Ben-Gurion *War Diary* [of 1948], the details on evacuating [the Arab] population, and on his hope that with the occupation of Judea and Samaria we would acquire a territory from which its inhabitants have fled.'[63] In fact, Zeevi, like Raphael Eitan of Tzomet and Yuval Neeman of the Tehiya, and Yigal Allon and Yitzhak Rabin of the Labour Party, came from the Palmah, the elite strike force of Labour Zionism in the Mandatory period. Zeevi remained closely associated with the Labour government until its election defeat in 1977. Joining the Palmah at the age of 17, Zeevi served about thirty years in the army, rising to the rank of major general. Between 1968 and 1973 he was the OC of the Central Command. During the 1973 war he served as a special assistant to the chief of staff and tried to persuade his army colleagues that Israel should use non-conventional weapons.[64] From 1974 to 1977, Zeevi served as adviser on anti-terrorism to Prime Minister Yitzhak Rabin. (Zeevi maintained in an interview with Israeli television on 4 June 1980 that the maiming of the West Bank mayors Bassam al-Shaka'ah and Karim Khalaf had been carried out by Arab 'terrorist' groups.) Since 1981, Zeevi has been a chairman of the board of the Eretz Yisrael museum in Tel Aviv.[65]

Encouraged by the publicity surrounding the Tel Aviv symposium and the public's response to his call for the mass expulsion of Arabs, Zeevi set up the new ultra right-wing Moledet Party one hundred days before the elections of November 1988 – Moledet won about 45,000 votes and two seats in the Knesset. While some analysts of the election observed that Moledet appeared to be replacing the Kahane-led Kach Party,[66] which had been banned from taking part in the November election, other researchers found that the majority of the supporters of Kach voted for the Likud.[67] Moledet's voters, unlike the Kach supporters, appear to come from a broad ethnic and social background, and although its 1988 electoral support in Jewish settlements in the occupied territories was above its national rate, its highest electoral rate – 45 per cent – was given by Kibbutz Beit Guvrin, in the south of Israel.[68] It is also worth noting that Beit Guvrin, founded in 1949, is affiliated with the Labour movement of Hakibbutz Hameuhad which was closely associated with the Palmah, from which Zeevi came. After the elections of 1988, the support for Moledet appeared to be growing steadily. In the elections of 1992, Moledet won 90,000 votes.[69] A survey carried out by the Modi'in Izrahi research institute for the newspapers *Ma'ariv* and *Mabat* in February 1989 found that Moledet would obtain four Knesset seats if elections were held that month. Another poll by the same institute in August 1989 found that Moledet would receive five seats in a general election.[70] The Modi'in Izrahi polls of October and December 1990 found that Moledet would receive eight and nine seats in the Knesset respectively, if elections were held at the time, and would become the third largest party in Israel after Likud and Labour.[71] In 1989–90, support for the Moledet Party seemed to be particularly high among the new Russian immigrants to Israel. Surveying the views of 1,123 new Russian immigrants and employees of the Hebrew University, a poll carried out in 1990 found that 21.5 per cent of them would vote for Moledet, putting it in second place after Likud.[72] In June 1990, the newspaper *Yerushalayim* carried out a survey at random among new Russian immigrants living in Neve Ya'acov, a Jewish neighbourhood in East Jerusalem, and found many of them were in favour of 'transferring' the Arab inhabitants of East Jerusalem. Alexander Fieldman, who had arrived in Israel three months earlier, said in broken Hebrew: 'There are many Arab countries: Jordania [*sic*], Morocco, Iraq. The Arabs can go there.' Two other new immigrants Igor and David put it less delicately: 'They must be seized by the tip of their penis, and hanged by it. It would be much better if transfer were carried out ... this is a Jewish state, so only Jews must remain here.'[73] However, many new immigrants from the former Soviet Union seemed to have voted for the Labour Party in the elections of 1992 in protest against the immigration absorption policies of the Likud coalition (including Moledet) which resulted in high unemployment among the new immigrants.[74]

The increased public support for Moledet after the success of its list in the elections of 1988 was, in part, due to the fact that the Knesset provided the new party with constitutional immunity and an ideal pulpit for propagating its message, consequently bolstering the 'legitimacy' of its solution in the public eye. Indeed, the Moledet

MKs Rehava'am Zeevi and Yair Sprintzak made very effective use of this pulpit for hammering home the issue, making endless statements in defence of Arab removal in numerous Knesset debates. Examples include Zeevi's statement in a debate on 22 December 1988, calling for Palestinian transfer to Jordan and other Arab countries,[75] in another debate on 18 January 1989,[76] on 8 February 1989,[77] and on 12 March 1989, in which Zeevi cited as justification the expulsion being carried out by the Romanian dictator Nicolai Ceausescu, who had just 'transferred from his country 1.8 million Hungarians and Germans among them those who had been living in Romania for 400 years'.[78] In January 1989, when MK 'Abdul-Wahab Darawshe of the Arab Democratic Party raised in a Knesset debate the problem of unemployment among Israeli Arabs with academic qualifications, Zeevi retorted that these Israeli 'Arab academics should depart to other Arab countries, which are thirsty and longing for a skilled and professional workforce'.[79] This proposal to deny the Arabs employment in Israel in order to encourage their departure has been repeatedly put forward by the two Moledet MKs.[80] The ending of employment of the territories' Arabs in Israel would aggravate their economic situation and bolster the transfer idea. In a Knesset debate in the summer of 1989, Sprintzak stated:

> This [transfer] task cannot be carried out in one day and it requires thinking and planning ... the government of Israel must be the initiator of this humanitarian operation, should take part in its planning and accompany it at least in its first stages. Together with the gradual reduction in the employment of the territories' workers ... the government should begin their [Arab refugees'] orderly transfer to Arab states, with international funding and with the cooperation of the United States and other friendly states.[81]

In the same vein, Zeevi wrote in May 1991 (after becoming a minister in the Shamir government): 'There is nothing which can contribute to the emigration tendency of the Arabs of Judea and Samaria ... more than the lack of work. These must provide for themselves and their families, and when they are banned from working in Israel they will turn to the neighbouring Arab countries.'[82] However, it is not as though Moledet was content with 'voluntary' emigration of individuals or communities as a result of the denial of employment. As Sprintzak put it, 'in the "political programme of Moledet", emphasis has been put on agreed transfer, and we are talking about agreement between governments and international funding.'[83] As for individuals and indeed the whole Palestinian population, their 'agreement' would not be necessary; they would have to be forcibly removed. The Moledet MKs do not provide any original argument in justification of such forced removal but rather rehash standard Zionist apologia in this regard. As Zeevi put it in an open letter to Prime Minister Yitzhak Shamir in May 1989: 'The majority of the Arabs of the Israel arrived in our country and multiplied following the Zionist settlement. They came from Arab countries and to these they must return.'[84]

The Moledet Party has branches in all major Israeli cities. While its actual membership is not known, the number of its youth movement's activists was estimated in March 1989 as being between 200 and 400, operating in 21 towns and settlements, including Tel Aviv, Jerusalem, Beersheba, Petah Tikva and the West Bank. In the Tel Aviv youth branch, there were fifty activists, who came largely from affluent, middle-class Ashkenazi backgrounds.[85]

The above proposals were published in *Moledet*, the official organ of the Moledet Party. Written in an inflammatory style of anti-Arab agitation, *Moledet* often carries disinformation articles such as the following written by Dr Irving Moskowitz,[86] a Miami-based American Jewish millionaire, who is currently financing the construction of a new Jewish neighbourhood being built on Arab land in Ras al-'Amud in Arab East Jerusalem. This housing programme, designed exclusively for Jewish settlers, was approved by the Netanyahu government in December 1996.[87] Moskowitz, who is a regular contributor to *Moledet* and a supporter of transfer, wrote in February 1990: 'A pro-Israeli source in the American Congress leaked lately to the Jewish lobby people that American officials are secretly discussing a new approach to the Arab–Israeli conflict. According to this approach population transfer should be carried out between Israel and its Arab neighbours.' According to Moskowitz, 'only one sole option has been left to American policymakers: to come up with a completely new approach.' This so-called new approach is euphemistically termed by Moskowitz as 'population exchange';

> The idea of population exchange is currently being rediscussed by the State Department (Foreign Ministry) policy makers. This is the only realistic way for bringing bloodshed to an end. The American dependence on Arab oil has decreased substantially and the US is

in a position which enables it to exercise pressures on Arab countries regarding the question of refugees. The resettlement of the refugees from Judea and Samaria in Jordan as well as Syria and Iraq, in a well-planned form and with international financial assistance, will neutralise the Arab–Israeli conflict, because it will remove the hostile Arab elements from the theatre of conflict. What remains for us is only to hope that the discussions currently conducted in Washington will bear fruit, because a humanitarian pattern for the [Palestinian] Arab refugees [in Arab countries] is the real hope for a durable solution of the Arab–Israeli conflict.[88]

Moledet's open campaign for Arab removal intensified in the second half of 1990 against the background of the unfolding crisis in the Persian Gulf in the wake of the Iraqi invasion of Kuwait in August. In October 1990, Zeevi stated that the impending war in the Gulf 'has also chances which are worthwhile considering already now', and that the forthcoming war should be exploited to get rid of the Palestinians: 'We must make preparations for carrying out the transfer of the Arabs from Judea and Samaria to east of the [River] Jordan, if we are attacked [by Iraq]. And if this deterrent will not work and we are attacked from the East it will be a supreme operational need to get rid of the fifth column – the Palestinians of the intifada.'[89] The same proposal was reiterated by Zeevi in a Knesset debate on 16 January 1991: if Iraq attacks from the East 'we would have no option but to drive the Arabs of Judea and Samaria out ... as we have done in war-time ... We also have a fifth column called Palestinians ... the achievements of the war would be the removal of the Iraqi threat and evacuating the Arabs from Judea and Samaria, so that the Land of Israel would remain an inheritance of the people of Israel, and only the people of Israel.'[90] The appointment of Zeevi as a minister-without-portfolio and member of the Ministerial Committee for Defence (effectively a policy-making inner cabinet) in the Shamir government in January 1991 gave an added impetus to the single-issue campaign of Moledet, which had by then become a fully-fledged 'legitimate' member of the Israeli establishment. The *Moledet* magazine reported that 'the Prime Minister asked MK Rehava'am Zeevi upon joining the government to engage in the preparations for setting up a team which the Prime Minister will run for permanent professional advice in fields of national security'.[91]

Several months earlier, on 22 August 1990, Zeevi's colleague Meir Lifschitz had revealed that Prime Minister Shamir had offered the Environment portfolio to Zeevi but the latter demurred, insisting on being entrusted with the Police portfolio. Lifschitz was even more euphoric regarding the prospects of exploiting the forthcoming Gulf War for driving the Palestinians out, and believed that Prime Minister Shamir was best placed to preside over such mass expulsion. Shamir, the commander of Lehi (the Stern Gang) in the 1940s, Lifschitz wrote, had not changed and had remained a 'transferist' ever since; although he did not reveal the secrets of his heart publicly, there was sufficient evidence for proving his general tendencies. According to Lifschitz:

For many years the picture of the next war has been set in his [Shamir's] mind. He has no doubt or illusion. This is our opportunity to solve once and for all the [demographic] problem. Together with the trampling of tanks and the aircraft engines' thunder, the trucks will be put in operation. The big and final transfer will acquire acceleration. The territories' Arabs will be the first evacuees and after them will come [the Arabs] who hold Israeli identity cards.

Shamir, Lifschitz went on, is an 'original' Zeevi: 'If this thing were to be dependent on him, he would not only carry out the idea of voluntary transfer, but would work out a method of forcible expulsion. Give him only a sufficient pretext and you will see how Jordan would be turned overnight into the only Palestinian state.' Lifschitz thought that Saddam Hussein's actions were 'serving Zionism's aims in a wonderful way. In the next stage he [Saddam] ought to deploy an army in Jordanian territory and threaten Israel.' For Lifschitz:

A war against Iraq is a real [religious] duty. If it is possible to make provocation, we must carry this out immediately. Such a golden opportunity in a convenient international situation falls into our hand once every hundred years ... No one will busy himself with the triviality of transfer which we will carry out in parallel at the same time ... Who exactly would be interested in the fate of two million Palestinians, who supported the butcher of Baghdad and are settled on the lands of the little king [King Hussein]?[92]

The gist of Lifschitz's argument is that war against Iraq should be provoked if only so it could be utilised for the forcible mass expulsion of the Palestinians. Zeevi pulled out of the Likud coalition in January 1992, together with the Tehiya, in protest at the mention of the idea of Palestinian autonomy at the Madrid track of the Middle East peace talks.[93] Several months later, Moledet gained an extra seat in the 1992 elections, winning 62,269 votes, but the party was deeply split over Zeevi's dictatorial style of leadership; in 1994 one of its three MKs (Shaul Gutman) defected to form a one-man Knesset list. In the 1996 elections, the number of votes for Moledet rose to 72,002, but its Knesset representation was down to two seats, occupied by Zeevi himself and Rabbi Benny Elon, a leader of Zo Arzteinu, an influential extreme right-wing pressure group led by Jewish settlers in the occupied territories.

Since the signing of the Oslo Accords of September 1993 between Israel and the PLO, Zeevi and other Moledet activists have joined extra-parliamentary protests led by the Jewish settlers in the occupied territories. Zeevi has also threatened to shoot any Palestinian Authority's policeman who tries to arrest him.[94]

Despite his openly fascist views and extremist vision, Zeevi has retained his position as chairman of the Land of Israel Museum in Tel Aviv. Clearly, despite their openly racist views, members of Moledet are still being recruited into the Israeli state bureaucracy, including the Mossad secret service. For instance, Yehuda Gil has been a senior Mossad operative. Gil joined Mossad in 1970 – for many years he maintained his contacts with his semi-imaginary Syrian opposite and fed his organisation with false information on the allegedly belligerent intentions of the Syrian regime against Israel and provided Israeli decision makers with alarming reports about President Asad's intentions. This almost led to skirmishes with Syria which could have exploded into a real war. Four years ago, Gil retired from the secret agency and became the organisational secretary of the Moledet party. Gil's association with Moledet's extremist views did not prevent Mossad chiefs from re-employing him. Gil deliberately misled his Mossad bosses and the Israeli government and made a war with Syria more likely. Gil had told his Mossad colleague Gad Shimron that 'not even one Arab wants peace with us, the only solution is transferring them across the border'.[95]

ORA SHEM-UR AND THE NATIONAL CIRCLE

Ora Shem-Ur is a well-known Polish-born journalist in Israel and contributes a regular column to the mass-circulation daily *Yedi'ot Aharonot*. Although she describes herself as a secular Zionist, for her – as for other non-religious ultra-nationalists such as Yisrael Eldad and Tzvi Shiloah – Israel's proper geopolitical ambitions and her concept of Greater Israel are defined by the boundaries of the 'biblical promise' from the Nile to the Euphrates including the Syrian cities of Damascus and Tadmur (ancient Palmyra): 'These boundaries have always constituted the framework for the national aspirations of the Jewish people,' she writes in her book *Greater Israel*, published in 1985.[96] 'We must never give up our historic rights and [must] exploit the options when these are created in certain circumstances in the future.'[97] Shem-Ur even criticises the right-wing camp in Israel, which claims that a Palestinian state already exists in the Kingdom of Jordan, and its willingness to give up Transjordan in order to hold on to and annex the West Bank and Gaza to Israel; this camp 'must surely be aware that the territory of Jordan is the Land of Israel'. She believes that Israel is the 'dominant military power in the region, there is no constraint on us to give up to the Arabs'.[98] On the contrary. She believes that Israel could and should invade and annex the state of Jordan and from there threaten the Middle East oil resources.[99] In the next 60–70 years, Shem-Ur writes, Israeli military force is likely to be used to block the Strait of Hormuz as well as several Arab ports.[100] She recounts that her preoccupation with the 'compulsory transfer'/ethnic cleansing solution dates back to 1975:

> Why don't we annex at once Judea, Samaria, Gaza and the Golan [Heights]? ... And why didn't we empty these territories from Arabs, as we did in 1948? Why don't we follow the example of Poland, which, after the victory of the Allies, emptied the province of Silesia of ten million Germans, who had lived on these lands for tens of generations? Or the example of Czechoslovakia ... its government did not hesitate to order two million Germans, who had lived for many generations in the Sudeten province, to leave their houses within a month? There are also other historical precedents ... there was 'population transfer' between Greece and Turkey ... it is possible to add the two million Hungarians being expelled lately [1989] from hundreds of villages in Romania.[101]

Three years later in 1978 Shem-Ur's super-hawkish views on Arab removal were expressed in her book *Israel: A Conditional State*,[102] in which she called for the 'transfer' of the majority of the Arabs to 'outside the state's borders ... there is no other way' (p. 110). For Shem-Ur – who denies the existence of a Palestinian people – 'it is not only that the Arabs have no political rights over the Land of Israel. They have no [individual ownership] rights over the land they are residing on. All these lands were once the lands of Jewish farmers ... the holding of these lands [by Arabs] is like the holding of absentee property ... the moment that the legal owners return home, the ownership over these lands must also be returned to them' (p. 112). (The notion that the Arabs have not even individual legal rights over the lands they possess is, as we shall see, a recurrent argument among the proponents of Arab expulsion.) Consequently, while 'the [would be] evacuated Arabs' would no doubt experience 'temporary inconvenience', they would not be the victims of any 'wrongdoing,' according to Shem-Ur (p. 111). Notwithstanding the euphemism of 'evacuation', Shem-Ur is explicitly talking about dispossession and outright mass expulsion. Her great admiration for David Ben-Gurion stems from the fact, as she puts it, that 'Ben-Gurion expelled from here 600 thousand Arabs [in 1948] in the midst of establishing a state. This is a glorious merit';[103] 'Yes we dispossessed [them in 1948] ... We had no alternative but to dispossess. And in this way we rose on the ruins of their cities ... Acre, Haifa, Beersheba, Ramle, Jaffa, Jerusalem were Arab cities' in the pre-1948 period;[104] 'I stand for the transfer of the Arabs from the country without their agreement.'[105]

Soon after the publication of her book *Israel: A Conditional State*, Shem-Ur emerged as one of the most extremist public campaigners for Arab expulsion from Israel and the occupied territories. A self-styled 'expert' on the 'Arab demographic problem', she relentlessly promoted her campaign in public speeches throughout the country under the slogan 'the Arabs must be transferred to Arab countries, there is no other way'. These forums were attended by thousands of people.[106] Around the same time, Shem-Ur also preached for her ethnic cleansing solution in an appearance on Israeli television.[107] Shem-Ur's data on, and conclusions regarding, the Arab 'demographic problem' brought the Likud MK Dov Shilansky, a former Speaker of the Knesset, to ask Prime Minister Menahem Begin, in a private question in the Knesset, on 20 December 1978 whether his government was 'alert to the demographic problem in the Land of Israel'.[108] Shem-Ur's book and conclusions were also welcomed by various supporters of Greater Israel including Dr Yisrael Eldad,[109] Professors Binyamin Aktzin (of the Hebrew University) and Moshe Atar,[110] Rabbi Yehuda Kook and Shalom Dov Wolpo. Avraham Orren, the headmaster of the state comprehensive school in Migdal Ha'emek, a 'development' town near Nazareth, wrote in a private letter to Shem-Ur: 'I see in your book great educational value for the youth in Israel and I would be pleased to cooperate in bringing it to high school students throughout the country.'[111] Shem-Ur's *Israel: A Conditional State* was also translated into English and published, with minor changes, by the New York-based Jewish publishing house Shengold Publishers in 1980 under the title *The Challenges of Israel*. This English version was sent to the US President Ronald Reagan by the author, who explained in an enclosed letter to the President that 'the policy advocated is – I am convinced – not only the sole way to secure the continuous existence of Israel in an alien environment but might also lead to the repulsion of the Arabic-Islamic threat to the West.'[112]

Shem-Ur articulates the standard arguments of the radical right advocates of Greater Israel and Arab transfer/ethnic cleansing: that the Palestinian Arabs are a 'cancer in our body', which must be removed,[113] and that Israel is very powerful militarily and able to do what it wants in the whole region, including Arab removal. Simultaneously, however, the same protagonists argue, paradoxically, that the Zionist/Jewish state would be undermined or weakened badly if the Palestinian Arabs were to remain in large numbers, or even as a large minority, in Greater Israel. Hence the obsessive preoccupation with the Arab 'demographic threat' among the most vocal campaigners of transfer/ethnic cleansing, such as Shem-Ur. Moreover, it is not only that Shem-Ur makes no distinction between the Arab citizens of Israel and those of the occupied territories: she asserts that the 'demographic problem' emanating from the existence of the Arab citizens of Israel is far more 'threatening' and would continue to be so even if Israel gave up the territories in order to avoid such a problem. These extremist arguments form the core of her book *Greater Israel* which came out in 1985 (and reprinted in 1988):

> There exists ... a latent danger lying in wait for Israel as a Jewish state – and this is the speedy increase of the Arab minority in Israel ... this natural Arab growth will necessarily bring about the

abolition of the Jewish character of Israel, and is likely at the end of the process to create an Arab majority in the State ... the continuous growth of the Arab sector in Israel constitutes, consequently, the most burning problem, and its solution must be given a prime national priority. On this solution our future depends: either Israel will continue as a Jewish State or it will be a passing episode in history and disappear ... the State of Israel will, at best, be turned into a bi-national state.[114]

In a letter to Minister of Industry and Trade Ariel Sharon, dated 26 October 1985, accompanying a copy of her book *Greater Israel*, Shem-Ur wrote:

The Arab citizens of Israel within the Green Line borders constitute the real electoral danger, who, because of their natural growth, could already in seven years send twenty representatives to the 13th Knesset. Such a number of Arab MKs will determine the character and composition of the government which will stop being Jewish and become bi-national ... if you would want to use the data given in my book, it would be desirable – for national reasons – that you mention the book in order to create awareness of the relevant facts among the public at large.[115]

Shem-Ur's book, it should be pointed out, was written before the recent influx of Soviet Jews to Israel, and cited the annual statistic of the Israeli government which forecast that in the year 2000 the Arab citizens of the state would constitute 22 per cent of the population.[116] And 'when the official annexation of Judea and Samaria and the Gaza province to the state of Israel comes ... the Arabs would constitute immediately 37 per cent of the total population; and if the citizenship of the state were to be granted to the Arabs of Judea, Samaria and Gaza, they would constitute the majority in the state in 30 years,' she wrote.[117]

The underlying assumption of Shem-Ur's preoccupation with the 'demographic threat' and its ethnic cleansing solution is predicated on explicitly racist thinking and discriminatory ideology. Contrary to her denial that she is motivated by racism or Arab hatred in advocating a transfer/ethnic cleansing solution for the Palestinians including those citizens of Israel, she writes Arab culture is 'based on the savage desert laws ... which stand for limb-amputation for a minor thief, for enslaving women, for blood revenge and for slavery'.[118] Of the Arab citizens of Israel, she writes: they are 'more aware than us of their ever-growing weight. A new generation of educated leaders has emerged among them, heads of councils and mayors, professors and students, who insist on equal rights for the "Palestinian people" in Israel.' Twenty-five Arab members of the Knesset in the future could thwart the state's policies regarding

... settlements, transfer of land [from Arab to Jew], the division of water, etc. They would demand and receive their proportional share in manning the most senior posts: ministers, deputy ministers, judges, chief executives, ambassadors, deans, etc. They would use their weight in [deciding] media policies, radio and television. They would have substantial influence on cultural life, art and information. And most importantly: they would pass a law in the Knesset which would oblige each young Arab to serve in the army, and would oblige the integration of the Arab officers in the IDF command.[119]

'What should be done to prevent this development?' Shem-Ur asks, that is, what should be done to prevent the Israeli Palestinians from becoming equal citizens? And what should be done in order to prevent the Arabs, with a high birthrate, from becoming a majority in Greater Israel and the Zionist/Jewish state becoming a bi-national state? Shem-Ur's answer is 'the transfer of the bulk of the Arab population to outside the boundaries of Israel'.[120] Her compulsory transfer/ethnic cleansing plan is predicated on a number of assumptions: first, a 'voluntary' transfer plan is doomed to failure: 'The plan of persuading the Arabs to emigrate in exchange for financial incentives is unrealistic. Not only have we not got the resources for that, but very few [Arabs] would respond to this solution.' 'Voluntary agreed' transfer 'was and will never be applicable: for its implementation the agreement of the two parties is required, and the Arab states, which even refused to absorb the [refugee] camps' residents, would never adopt it',[121] and moreover 'the Palestinians themselves would never agree to this.'[122] Second, no Arab state would be prepared to absorb the would-be evacuees. Third, such pressurised 'relocation'/'resettlement' 'could only be, in our conditions, to regions that would be at the same time under Israeli control'[123] – implying the need to conquer new Arab territories in order to put Arab 'relocation' into effect. Fourth:

The majority of the Arab population in Israel is rural, and therefore, in order to thin out this population there would be a need to settle the Arab farmers, with their equipment, outside the boundaries of the Land of Israel [that is, outside the boundaries from the Nile to the Euphrates]. This plan constitutes merely a principle, and does not point out the details of implementation. This, since such a type of plan could only be carried out by a governmental-political echelon, according to a decision of the Israeli government and in accordance with a master plan, [would be implemented] in a number of years, and its details would be worked out by experts. It is reasonable to assume that such a plan could be operated within the framework of agrarian reform, which means the re-division of the agricultural lands ... such a plan is not dependent on the agreement of any external factor ... The population transfer operation could only be carried out by government agencies and according to the state laws. I have reservations about any religious-fanatic partisan act to solve this problem. Such partisan acts ... have no practical purpose and they are likely to cause damage to the orderly implementation of the operation.'[124]

It is worth noting that the term 'agrarian reform' used by Shem-Ur is a thinly disguised device for additional confiscation of Arab land, and that the same suggestion to engineer a mass Arab evacuation by the 'legal' and administrative means of expropriating Arab lands was generally advocated in the pre-1948 period and prominently figured in the official Jewish Agency transfer schemes in 1937–38. Moreover, in Israel proper, after four and a half decades of seizure and appro-priation of land, Zionist state institutions are now in absolute control of nearly 93 per cent of the land, while nearly half of the land in the West Bank and a third of the land of the Gaza Strip have already been taken over by the state and allocated to Jewish settlement.

For Shem-Ur – like some Zionist Israelis – the higher Arab birth rate is an obsessional problem. Nearly half of the Palestinians in the occupied territories and Israel are below the age of 25. For Shem-Ur, only an ethnic cleansing plan can provide a fundamental remedy. This transfer plan 'would be gradual and would apply especially to the youth'; 'middle-aged Arabs' would be allowed to stay in Israel.[125] On another occasion, she proposed that only a minority of Arabs 'who had passed the age of fertility, people aged 50 to 60' would be allowed to remain.[126] Moreover the 'Arab evacuees in the new regions [outside the boundaries from the Nile to the Euphrates], to which the inhabitants of the refugee camps would also be transferred, could choose – as they wished – self-determination, political or economic cooperation with Israel, or annexation to neighbouring Arab states.'[127] Shem-Ur assumes, correctly, that a section of the Israeli Jewish public 'would see in compulsory transfer of Arabs an anti-democratic act',[128] and might attempt to oppose it. There is also a technical-legal obstacle which should be removed, thus paving the way for the 'forcible transfer'/ethnic cleansing /expulsion of the Arab citizens of Israel, who would also be bound to put up strong resistance to such policies. Consequently, she proposes additional legislation to safeguard the Zionist/Jewish character of the state and stem the natural growth of the Arab citizens in Israel as well as their demands for equal citizenship. She proposes the modification of a clause in the Independence Charter, which promises equal social and religious (though not national) rights to all citizens without distinction on the grounds of religion, race and gender, and the insertion of a revised clause which includes, *inter alia*: 'the transfer of the Arabs from the boundaries of the Land of Israel is our democratic and legitimate right, in order to safeguard Israel as a Jewish state.'[129]

Evidently Shem-Ur believes, like many protagonists of Greater Israel, that Israel, as the dominant military power in the region, should not be deterred from carrying out mass 'transfer' by international pressures or even the possibility of the imposition of economic sanctions. In an interview in the Jerusalem weekly *Kol Ha'ir* on 26 March 1986, Shem-Ur declared: 'what will the Americans do if we carry out transfer? In the worst case they will send an army, and even this I don't believe.' And that 'in the end the Arabs would reconcile themselves – in the absence of any choice – to the facts that would be created in the region',[130] making transfer a *fait accompli*.

Shem-Ur's *Greater Israel* gained wide coverage in the Israeli press in late 1985 and early 1986. The journalist Yaron London commented in the Tel Aviv-based weekly *Ha'ir* on the similarity between Shem-Ur's plan and that of Meir Kahane, but also observed the fact that the author 'avoids explaining how the transfer would be carried out: by trucks, as proposed at one time by [the Minister] Gide'on Patt, or by other transport means'.[131] Shortly after her book was published, Shem-Ur was interviewed on the state-run Voice of Israel radio by David Margalit and was asked: 'Should we buy trucks and expel the Arabs in them?' Shem-Ur replied: 'If Hitler had removed the Jews in trucks we would have been grateful to him ...'[132]

Seeking maximum publicity for these ideas, Shem-Ur sent hundreds
of copies of her book to MKs, cabinet ministers, journalists,
television and radio producers and public figures.[133] She also
mentioned the names of several MKs and ministers (mostly from the
Likud and Mafdal), who agreed to meet her and discuss the
'demographic problem' with her. These figures – whose reactions are
not revealed by Shem-Ur – included Zevulun Hammer (Minister of
Education and Culture, 1977–84, Minister of Religious Affairs
1984–92), Yigal Hurvitz (a Likud MK), Yehuda Ben-Meir, Meir Shitrit
(former Treasurer of the Jewish Agency and MK since 1981), Dan
Meridor (Minister of Justice 1988–92),[134] Amnon Linn, Miriam
Ta'asa Glasser (MK since 1981 and formerly Deputy Minister of
Education and Culture), 'Ovadia 'Eli (a Likud MK), Eli Kolem and
Beni Shalita. 'I think, in the course of years I personally talked about
the demographic problem with at least half of the MKs. They and
all the others also received my books and additional information
material,' Shem-Ur wrote,[135] and added that in October 1985, 'the
Minister [of Industry and Trade] Ariel Sharon had shown great
interest in the [demographic] subject [in the book *Greater Israel*], and
he was interested in reading the book as quickly as possible, in order
to prepare the demographic subject for discussion at a Cabinet
session.'[136] Six months later, Shem-Ur declared in an interview with
the Jerusalem weekly *Kol Ha'ir*: 'I pin great hopes on him [Ariel
Sharon] because when the time comes he is the man who is likely to
carry out this plan very efficiently.'[137]

Shem-Ur was not satisfied in influencing public opinion and
lobbying MKs and ministers to endorse her mass expulsion platform.
Already in 1977, she had founded a movement called the 'First
Circle', which called for an immediate stop to all contacts with Arab
leaders interested in promoting a settlement of the Arab–Israeli
conflict.[138] Nine years later, in January 1986, Shem-Ur, riding the
rising tide of racism in Israel, founded another movement, this time
called the 'National Circle.' This movement, like the Kahane-led
Kach Party, was preoccupied with a single-minded platform of Arab
expulsion, which was presented, however, in more delicate terms:

The only solution which ensures our national interests is the
'Polish' solution – the evacuation of eight million Germans from
Silesia after its annexation to Poland. The transfer idea which is
being heard lately is conditional upon the agreement of the party
which receives the evacuees, an agreement which we will never

get. The National Circle will work for the transfer, administratively
[that is, compulsorily], of the residents of the refugee camps to
[new] areas [beyond Transjordan] which will be under our control
[in the future], and for the gradual resettlement of other Arab
sectors.[139]

In an interview with the Tel Aviv weekly *Ha'ir* in 1986, the leader of
the 'National Circle' was asked about the destination of the evacuees.
She replied: 'In territories that will be in our hands during the period
in which we will decide to carry out the transfer ... We can always
occupy [these territories], enter a country, in the same way we
entered Lebanon, [and] transfer the Arabs there, and come back as
we came back from Lebanon.'[140] When pressed by the interviewer
for further elaboration on this administrative/military operation of
ethnic cleansing, Shem-Ur shows reluctance to go into detail: when
'the government decides that this is the only way, it will set up teams
and committees, and [these] will work out plans. I am also not saying
that all the Arabs should be removed. I am explicitly in favour of
allowing those Arabs who have passed the age of fertility [50–60
years old] to live here quietly.'[141] In another interview in the
Jerusalem weekly *Kol Ha'ir* on 26 March 1986, Shem-Ur was pressed
again by the journalist Haim Bara'am: 'How according to your plan
would the transfer of the Arab population be carried out?' Her reply
was: 'First of all we must make sure that such a plan is moulded and
be ready for an opportune moment.' To a question as to whether she
would wait for a future war, she replied '... correct. We are not
initiating a war, but clearly it will break out. Every few years there is
a war ... I am in favour of exploiting the war situation and the fog of
war for carrying out plans prepared in advance. We must in advance
earmark for the [Palestinian] Arabs a territory in an Arab state, whose
name I don't want now to mention, but not next to Israel.'
Apparently the destination of the Palestinian transferees should be,
according to Shem-Ur, not Jordan, but one of the 'Fertile Crescent'
states, that is, either Syria or Iraq.[142]

   According to Shem-Ur, the objective of the membership of the
'National Circle' movement was to 'pull' the Israeli public in the
direction of supporting mass expulsion of Arabs and 'within a short
time to capture the government'; however, their numbers never
exceeded a thousand.[143] The actual number of activists was reported
in early 1986 to be around 250, mostly young people aged 20 to 30.
At the same time, the movement had branches in Haifa and its

satellite towns and in Beersheba.[144] Shem-Ur and her movement decided, however (for reasons which are not entirely clear), not to run in the Knesset election of November 1988.[145] Its main activities since its foundation in 1986 have concentrated on press publicity, lobbying MKs and ministers and public agitation carried out through billboards and posters. In September 1986, the Tel Aviv municipality permitted the displaying of National Circle broadsheets, which called for the transfer of Israel's Arab citizens, on its billboards throughout the city.[146] Inciting anti-Arab hostility, one street poster of the movement declared: 'The Arabs who live in the Land of Israel are settled on and holding stolen property, which they must return to its owners ['the Jewish people'].'[147] The Jerusalem municipality's Director-General Aharon Sarig, however, refused in August 1986 to permit the display of this poster on the grounds that it was likely to stir up conflict in the mixed city.[148] Other posters of the National Circle were approved for displaying on billboards by the municipalities of Tel Aviv, Rehovot and Ashdod.[149] Interestingly, also, when the Jerusalem municipality refused to display the above-mentioned poster and the National Circle took its case to the High Court, the lawyer Aharon Pappo, a Likud activist and a supporter of Arab transfer (and who had been involved in a similar legal case in the 1970s defending Rabbi Kahane's campaign of Arab expulsion) offered his legal services to the National Circle.[150] However, Pappo was deemed too expensive a solicitor by the movement, which instead employed attorney Akiva Nof, a former Likud MK, to contest the Jerusalem municipality's decision in the High Court.[151] In the event, the same court upheld the municipality's decision; moreover, the then liberal Legal Adviser to the government, Professor Yitzhak Zamir, expressed in a letter to Shem-Ur his private opinion that 'the call to expel the whole or part of the Israeli Arabs to outside the state borders is racial incitement.'[152]

5
The Public Opinion Debate: Evolving Jewish Attitudes, the Palestinians and Greater Israel

Studies on Israeli public opinion have often emphasised the salience of the Palestinian issue, the territorial controversy and demographic debate in defining the dovish-hawkish divide and the Israeli Jewish population's attitudes towards Greater Israel.[1] This chapter will largely concentrate on the evolving Israeli-Jewish population's attitudes towards both the one million Palestinians living in Israel proper, often described as 'Israeli Arabs', who are Israeli citizens and constitute nearly 20 per cent of the state's total citizens, and the three million Palestinians living in the occupied West Bank and Gaza Strip, who are still subject to military rules and regulations. Since 1967, a large number of studies of Israeli public opinion towards the Palestinian issue have attempted to address a number of questions: Are trends in Israeli public opinion stable over time, and if not, what is the scope of change? What is the relation between public opinion and official Israeli policies? And, to what extent is the Israeli public opinion manipulated by the Israeli establishment/political elite? Clearly, public attitudes change with changing political reality; the change of attitudes in Israel towards Egypt that followed the dramatic visit of Anwar Sadat to Jerusalem in 1977 is often cited as an indication of the flexibility and constant evolution of Jewish public attitudes in Israel.[2] Moreover, public opinion surveys should be interpreted with caution; different sampling techniques might produce different results. It is generally assumed, however, that public attitudes related to national consensus are far more stable than other attitudes.[3] Also the attitudes and decisions of political leaders do reflect (and help to articulate) the country's political culture and principal social and political myths.[4]

The discussion below will attempt to address these questions as well as show that, throughout the 1970s and most of the 1980s, studies on Israeli public opinion, most of which focused on the

Palestinian issue and the fate of the West Bank and Gaza, observed a relatively stable hawkish trend. However, several recent studies have also observed a greater polarisation of the Israeli public and a growing dovish trend over time since the end of the 1980s, primarily a result of the general impact of the Palestinian intifada on Israeli society.[5] Since then, the Israeli public has displayed a greater willingness to negotiate with the PLO and, in particular since the Oslo Accords of September 1993, there has been a greater inclination to part with some of the occupied territories. None the less, despite the significant changes occurring over time in the Jewish population's attitudes on certain questions relating to the occupied territories and the Palestinians in general, the anti-Arab attitudes of the Israeli public remain deeply worrying.

Throughout the 1970s and most of the 1980s, there was relative stability in the Israeli public's attitudes on most issues relating to the Palestinians in the West Bank and Gaza Strip, with the exception of the 'transfer' issue for which population support rose from a quarter in 1967 to around one in two in the late 1980s. At the same time, however, polls conducted in the mid-1980s detected rational and strong scepticism among the Jewish public regarding the feasibility of such a solution; for example, in 1987, one public opinion poll showed that only 14.4 per cent believed that this solution was practicable.[6] The data discussed in this chapter will also show that much of the Jewish population has been closely behind the policies pursued by all Israeli governments towards the Arab citizens of Israel: land alienation, the 'Judaisation of Galilee' project, exclusionary domination, economic dependency and political control.

The public opinion/'transfer' debate has figured prominently in the post-June 1967 period. The importance of this public debate lay not in the likelihood that any of the proposals of mass transfer would soon be implemented, but rather in the widening of the parameters of acceptable political discourse to include the mass expulsion of Palestinians as a publicly discussible option.[7] Prior to 1948, the issue of 'transfer' was discussed largely behind closed doors, in the inner sanctums of the Zionist leadership bodies; but in the 1980s, it entered the domain of the Hebrew press and public political speeches. Thus, leading right-wing figures and supporters of Greater Israel, some of whom were members of the Israeli politico-military establishment, openly pronounced themselves in favour of mass transfer of the Palestinians from the occupied territories (Ariel Sharon, Raphael Eitan, Michael Dekel, Rehava'am Zeevi, etc.). The

Greater Israel camp graduated from whispering and hinting to discussion of this solution in closed meetings and even open forums. Public opinion polls carried out in the mid- to late 1980s also showed that close to 50 per cent of the Jewish population pronounced themselves in favour of expelling the Palestinians of the West Bank and Gaza. This proportion was particularly alarming in view of the asymmetrical power relationship between the Israelis and the Palestinians.

It is extremely important to remember, however, that, although the 1980s witnessed a sharp increase in public support for the 'transfer' of the Palestinians from the West Bank and Gaza Strip, that support was not entirely the result of the Likud coalition's domination between 1977 and 1992, as many liberal Zionist writers in Israel and the West would like us to believe. Opinion polls conducted in the mid-1960s (at the height of the Labour Party's domination) and published in the early 1970s, showed that a staggering majority of 90 per cent of the Jews sampled preferred to see fewer Arab citizens remain in Israel; about the same proportion said that the 'Arabs understand only force' and 80 per cent believed that 'Arabs will not reach the level of progress of the Jews.'[8] Another survey was conducted by Dr George Tamarin among pupils in primary schools in March 1967 (three months before the June 1967 war), on 'the Influence of Chauvinism on Moral Judgement'. The 1,066 pupils (aged 10–14) who took part in this poll, were required to answer two questions: a) Had the Israelites in the days of Joshua done well by exterminating all the inhabitants of a city after they had captured it? b) Would it be right for the IDF (Israeli Defence Force), during the occupation of an Arab village, to deal with its inhabitants in the same way Joshua had done? In answering the first question, 66 per cent of the pupils totally agreed, 8 per cent agreed with reservations, and 26 per cent were completely against. As to the second question, 32 per cent agreed completely, 7 per cent partially agreed, and 61 per cent were completely against. The conclusion drawn by Tamarin was that a considerable number of pupils in Israel had extreme prejudices bordering on racism.[9] Another poll conducted by the Israeli Institute for Applied Social Research (IIASR) three weeks after the June 1967 war revealed that 28 per cent of the Israeli-Jewish electorate was in favour of expelling the Palestinian citizens of Israel, and 22 per cent endorsed the same solution for the Palestinians in the newly-acquired territories.[10] However, as we shall see below, the option of 'transfer' of the Palestinian citizens of Israel did not become the focus of public debate in Israel until the 1970s, when the late Rabbi Meir Kahane became active in Israeli politics. Over the years, a relative stability in the Jewish public's attitudes on certain questions relating to the Palestinian citizens of Israel was much in evidence. An opinion poll carried out in the early 1970s revealed that a majority of 74 per cent of the Jews sampled would be worried if their children befriended an Arab, 84 per cent would be bothered if a relative or a friend married an Arab, and 49 per cent if an Arab moved next door.[11] Several years later, the Israeli-Jewish attitudes surveyed had changed little, as a 1980 survey by Dr Mina Tzemah for the liberal Van Leer Institute in Jerusalem showed that a majority of 60 per cent believed that the Arab citizens should not be accorded full, equal rights.[12] Tzemah's findings were confirmed by another 1980 survey carried out by Professor Sammy Smooha of Haifa University (a sociologist and a leading authority on Arab–Jewish relations in Israel, see below), which showed that 96.6 per cent of the Jews sampled believed that it 'would be better if there were fewer Arabs in Israel'; 83.1 per cent felt that it was 'impossible to trust Arabs in Israel'; 87 per cent said that 'surveillance over Arabs in Israel' should be increased; 70.8 per cent believed that 'Arabs will not reach the level of progress of Jews', and 76.1 per cent expressed 'reservations or unwillingness at working in a position subordinate to an Arab'. Smooha (whose survey was based on interviews with 1,267 Jews, a sample representing the entire adult population of Israel) concluded: 'These findings furnish a clear-cut empirical indication for the general impression that the policy of control [over the Arab citizens], far from being arbitrary, enjoys wide acceptance among the Jewish population.'[13]

The discussion below will show that support for the 'transfer' of the Palestinians of the occupied West Bank and Gaza Strip was not only widely held in Israel throughout the 1980s but also remained considerable throughout the early 1990s. At the same time, however, the Israeli-Jewish public remained polarised and deeply divided on this controversial and highly explosive issue. Since the early 1980s, several professional Israeli pollsters have extensively and continuously surveyed the attitudes of Israeli Jews towards the Palestinians, both those living in Israel and those in the occupied territories, involving a wide range of related subjects, including Jewish settlement, annexation, transfer, territorial compromise and partial territorial withdrawal, Jerusalem, Palestinian state, the PLO, peace settlement, civil and human rights, etcetera. These pollsters include the IIASR, Public Opinion Research of Israel (PORI), Hanokh Smith Institute, Dahaf research institute in Tel Aviv and Modi'in Ezrahi Applied Research Centre. The findings of some of the polls conducted by these professional bodies will be presented and analysed in the following discussion, while focusing on the anti-Arab and 'transfer'/'demographic' debates rather than assessing the attitudes of the Israeli public on a whole range of related questions at the heart of the Palestinian–Israeli conflict.

THE 'DEMOGRAPHIC THREAT' DEBATE

Since the occupation of the West Bank and Gaza, with their solid Palestinian population, demography and the so-called Arab 'demographic threat' has obsessed leaders in Israel. After June 1967, there was a slight rise in net immigration and in 1990–1991 there was a mass immigration of Jews from the former Soviet Union. Yet the demographic concern remained an ever-present subject in public debates and political speeches. Some Israelis openly proposed a blatant discriminatory approach on demography and Arab birth control; in an editorial in *Ma'ariv*, Israel's largest circulation newspaper, Shmuel Schnitzer, a prominent journalist and supporter of Greater Israel, suggested on 29 September 1967 the encouragement of large Jewish families and birth control measures for the Palestinians in Israel and the occupied territories, as well as the adoption of an open policy of encouraging Palestinians to emigrate to countries overseas.

Since 1967, the recurring theme in the 'demographic threat' debate in Israel has been that a large Arab proportion could not be integrated into the Israeli state. Some Israeli leaders have even viewed the natural increase of the Arab minority in Israel as an obstacle to Jewish immigration and to the settlement and dispersion of a Jewish population throughout the country, and consequently as a threat to the Zionist-Jewish character of the state. The declining Jewish birth rate is often contrasted with the high natural growth among the Arab citizens of Israel. Israeli Labour politicians have also warned about the 'demographic threat', implying that annexation of the densely populated areas of the West Bank and Gaza would mean the end of the Jewish state.[14] Yet Zionist Labour 'demographic threat' arguments only reinforced the notion that an integralist Jewish state with few Arabs was and remains Zionism's basic aim, and that the cardinal problem of annexation and Greater Israel was that it might bring more Arabs into the Jews' midst. These arguments only exacerbated the alienation of Palestinian citizens of Israel, who now make up about a sixth of the population, and who will, according to various forecasts, be 20 to 25 per cent by 2020. Moreover, Zionist liberal 'demographic' criteria not only made the values of secularism and democracy irrelevant but also contributed to the fact that part of the Israeli public's comprehension of this racist notion led it to favour the further consolidation of the apartheid system and the 'alien residency' status of Palestinians in the occupied territories and 'transfer', rather than compromise and withdrawal from the territories.

Throughout the 1980s, demography remained a major topic of public debate in the Hebrew media and in political speeches. A very 'worrying' problem for Zionism, declared Michael Dekel (who was deputy defence minister in the Likud government in the 1980s) in October 1982, is the 'frightening natural growth of the Israeli Arabs within the Green Line, which is among the highest in the world'.[15] The journalist Ora Shem-Ur, a well-known secular ultra-nationalist and campaigner for maximum territorial expansion-cum-Arab-expulsion, claims that in October 1985 Minister of Trade and Industry Ariel Sharon 'had shown great interest' in the subject of her book *Greater Israel* (1985), which dwells largely on the 'Arab demographic threat' and the transfer solution, 'and he [Sharon] was interested in reading the book as quickly as possible, in order to prepare the demographic subject for discussion at a cabinet session'.[16] In 1993, the leader of the Likud Party, Binyamin Netanyahu, later to become prime minister, wrote: 'If the statistics suggest any demographic "threat" at all, it comes not from the Arabs of the territories but from the Arabs of pre-1967 [that is, the Israeli Arab citizens].'[17]

In May 1986, the Israeli Cabinet and the Knesset held open discussions on Jewish and Arab birth rates.[18] On 11 May 1986, the Israeli government devoted a special session to the 'demographic problem' of Jews and Arabs in Israel. Shortly after, the government established an official working group whose members included representatives of various ministries and the Jewish Agency and coordinated by the Demographic Centre (first located in the Prime Minister's Office, and later in the Ministry of Labour and Welfare) to prepare a programme for demographic policies.[19] Moreover, in all the proposals that successive prime ministerial advisers on Arab

202 Imperial Israel and the Palestinians

affairs put forward in recent years, with the aim of formulating policies towards Israel's Arab citizens, these citizens are perceived as constituting a 'demographic danger'.[20]

This openly racist 'demographic' debate also contributed to the rise in Israeli public support for transfer ideas in the 1970s and 1980s. By the 1980s, the pro-transfer camp of Greater Israel (including Tehiya, Tzomet, Moledet, many leaders of Gush Emunim, and several leading politicians in the Likud and the National Religious Party) had been emboldened by the fact that the solution of transferring the Palestinians of the occupied territories was not only widely held in Israel, but was steadily growing throughout most of the 1980s. Already in 1982, a survey carried out by the Dahaf research institute, and based on a representative sample composed of 1,182 respondents from 30 Jewish localities in Israel, revealed that 37.9 per cent of the Jewish population were in favour of 'annexation of the territories without [population] transfer', while 26.7 per cent of the Jewish population viewed 'annexation of the territories with population transfer' as 'acceptable'.[21] Two years later, in the spring of 1984, a survey commissioned by the Jerusalem-based Van Leer Institute showed that Rabbi Kahane's views on the Palestinians in Israel and the occupied territories were acceptable to a large section of the Israeli youth. Kahane himself won a parliamentary seat in 1984 and his views were generally described in Israel as outright racist. As many as 42.1 per cent of the Israeli adolescents interviewed were in favour of Rabbi Kahane's solution of expelling the Palestinians, including those Arab citizens of Israel. The survey revealed that the Jewish youth were even more intolerant than their elders. The liberal Van Leer Institute, which appeared to consider these findings abhorrent and embarrassing, decided to suppress them, but they were leaked to the Hebrew daily *Yedi'ot Aharonot* which broke the story. The same newspaper conducted its own poll which confirmed the Van Leer's findings.[22]

In the wake of these revelations in *Yedi'ot Aharonot*, the Van Leer's findings were also raised and discussed in Israel Television's weekly programme 'Moked'. *Yedi'ot Aharonot* of 28 June 1985 published an investigative article by three Israeli journalists (Elie Tabor, Nitza Aviram and Nehama Doek), entitled: 'The Youth is Swept Towards Kahanism'. After surveying opinions of students in a variety of high schools in Jerusalem and Tel Aviv, the three journalists found a sharp rise in support for Kahane's expulsion solution among Jewish youth. In one survey by *Yedi'ot Aharonot* in a vocational high school in

Jerusalem, in which 75 students (aged 16) took part, 58.7 per cent said that they agreed with Kahane's views towards the Arab citizens in Israel, while 41.3 per cent disagreed. In another survey in three high schools in affluent north Tel Aviv, in which 64 students (age 17–18) took part, 27.7 per cent said that they agreed with Kahane's views towards Israel's Arab citizens, while 72.3 per cent disagreed. In his book *The Tragedy of Zionism*, Bernard Avishai cites a paper by Dr Mina Tzemah and Ruth Tzin, presented to the Van Leer Institute in conjunction with the Dahaf research institute in September 1984, showing that 57 per cent of the Israeli youth interviewed, aged 15–18, thought that the inhabitants of the West Bank and Gaza who refused Israeli citizenship should be expelled and that 60 per cent would support the curtailment of the rights of the Arab citizens of Israel.[23] Only marginally improved results were produced by a public opinion survey conducted among 612 Jewish youth in May 1987 by the Dahaf research institute for the Van Leer Institute. The findings, which were published by the Van Leer Institute in October 1987 in a report entitled 'Political and Social Positions of Youth – 1987', showed that, while 80 per cent of the Jewish youth supported a democratic government in principle, about 50 per cent wanted to reduce still further the rights of the Israeli Arab citizens; about 40 per cent did not support the right of the Arab citizens to vote; about one-third said that 'they agreed with the ideas of Rabbi Kahane and his movement', and 50 per cent supported the legalisation of his party, Kach.[24]

A number of polls carried out by the Hanokh Smith Institute over a two-year period indicated that in August 1985, 35 per cent of those questioned agreed with the statement: 'I support any one who acts to get the Arabs to leave Judea and Samaria.' This proportion dropped to 29 per cent in February 1986, before rising to 34 per cent in June 1986 and rising again to 38 per cent in September 1986.[25] Also, several Israeli politicians and respected personalities, including General Rehava'am Zeevi, Likud's Michael Dekel (Deputy Minister of Defence), Minister of Trade and Industry Ariel Sharon, Gide'on Altschuler, Yuval Neeman, Geula Cohen of the Tehiya, Yosef Shapira and several other NRP politicians, joined in a sustained public debate over how to contain Greater Israel's 'Arab demographic problem' and what sort of 'voluntary' or forcible transfer might be implemented.[26]

Rabbi Kahane's Kach list was disqualified for the 1988 general election after the 1985 amendment to the Knesset Basic Law barred any list from Knesset elections if its aims or actions point to 'the denial of the democratic nature of the state' or to 'an incitement to racism'. Apparently, the immediate impetus for the amendment was concern over increasing support for Kahane, particularly among the Israeli youth.[27] Barred from Knesset elections, Kach continued to agitate for Arab expulsion as an extra-parliamentary movement until it was outlawed by the Israeli authorities in the aftermath of the massacre of 31 Palestinian worshippers at the Ibrahimi Mosque in Hebron by an Israeli settler and Kach activist, in March 1994.

The level of public support for Zionist territorial maximalism and annexationist Israeli policies appeared to be very solid throughout the mid- to late 1980s and this fact had been confirmed by scores of polls during this period. In a poll taken in April 1987, some 62 per cent of Israeli Jews interviewed indicated that they were 'against the evacuation of settlements in Judea and Samaria, even in exchange for a peace agreement'. Also significantly, 45–50 per cent expressed support for the key Gush Emunim demand that the West Bank and Gaza Strip be permanently and unconditionally incorporated into Israel.[28] Furthermore, public support for the idea of transfer/ expulsion increased during the same period. A survey conducted by Tel Aviv University in early 1988, several months after the eruption of the Palestinian intifada, revealed that 40 per cent of the Jewish electorate supported the transfer proposal.[29] The Hebrew daily *Ma'ariv* of 5 August 1988 revealed the results of a survey carried out by the Modi'in Izrahi institute for political scientist Dr Yoav Peled of Tel Aviv University; the survey found that in the 'development towns', which are inhabited largely by economically and socially deprived populations of Sephardic background, 68 per cent supported transfer compared with 41 per cent among the public at large. Earlier, in mid-1987, a survey conducted by the Tel Aviv Teleseker institute suggested that 50.4 per cent of the respondents supported the transfer idea propagated by General Rehava'am Zeevi. The same poll, however, detected strong scepticism among the respondents regarding the feasibility of such a proposal, as only 14.4 per cent believed that this solution was practicable.[30] Another 1987 study conducted by two Israeli scholars: Ephraim Yucktman-Ya'ar of Tel Aviv University and Michael Inbar of the Hebrew University revealed that the Israeli annexation of the West Bank and Gaza and a 'transfer' of the Palestinians to elsewhere in the Middle East was the 'most desirable' solution among 30 per cent of the Jewish public and 'acceptable' to 42 per cent of Israeli Jews. The same study also showed that a majority of the West Bank Palestinians would accept a Palestinian state in the occupied territories alongside Israel. In contrast, the survey, in which 2,000 people were polled, indicated that the Israeli Jews were deeply divided, and that no solution mustered a clear majority among them.[31]

In 1988, a new radical right-wing party, Moledet, was launched, for which the transfer of Palestinians was central. Moledet not only won seats in the Knesset elections of 1988 and 1992 but was also part of the coalition that governed Israel between 1990 and 1992, thus (unlike Kach) gaining legitimacy as a respectable parliamentary party. Also in 1988, a 'highly reputable' poll, conducted by the Israeli Institute of Applied Research and the Hebrew University Communication Institute, found that 50 per cent of Israeli Jews thought that the population of the West Bank should be 'caused to leave' in order to preserve Israel's Jewish character. The survey also revealed that a third of those saying they supported the 'transfer' solution described themselves as Labour Party voters. Commenting on these findings, the moderate Labour MK Abba Eban said that the results 'represent a disturbing movement in Israeli public perception away from both reality and morality'.[32] This was another indication as to how widely the transfer concept was held in Israel and the fact that it was not merely confined to supporters of the right and the radical right (Moledet, Tehiya, Tzomet, etc.). Another survey by the pollster Hanokh Smith carried in *Haaretz* on 9 November 1989 suggested that the proportion of Israeli Jews supporting transfer had risen to 52 per cent. Eight months later, on 6 June 1990, the daily *Ma'ariv* revealed the results of another poll which showed that 59 per cent of Israeli Jews supported transfer, the highest proportion ever recorded.[33] A year later a survey carried out by the Institute of Applied Research found that 43 per cent of those questioned were in favour of transfer.[34] However, two years later, in March 1993, ten months after the election of the Labour-Meretz government, a public opinion survey regarding Israel's handling of the Palestinian intifada, carried out by the Israeli political scientists Gad Barzilai and Efraim Inbar, found that public support for the 'massive uses of force against the entire Palestinian population and their expulsion' did not exceed 30.7 per cent. In socioeconomic terms, respondents in this extreme hawkish group were generally less educated, non-secular, of lower income, Sephardi and, more often, male.[35]

From the findings of these numerous polls it would be possible to suggest that from the mid-1980s until the eruption of the intifada in late 1987, there existed a solid public quorum of between 30–40 per cent in favour of transfer, and from then up to 1992 that proportion rose to about one in two Israeli Jews, but by 1993 had declined to about 30 per cent. The general rise in Israeli public opinion's support for transfer during the 1980s and the proximity of such development with frequent statements from some Likud government officials and ministers (including ministers from the junior partners in the Likud coalition, such as Yosef Shapira, Yuval Neeman, Geula Cohen, Rehava'am Zeevi, Raphael Eitan), in favour of Arab removal is noteworthy.

Moreover, since Likud assumed power in 1977, there has been, in conjunction with the growing polarisation of the Israeli public (particularly after the 1982 Israeli invasion of Lebanon) and the increase in public support for transfer, a coarsening of political rhetoric towards, and a stirring up of racism against, the Palestinian population. The relative proximity of hostile public attitudes towards the Palestinians, including those who are citizens of Israel, to the government's repressive and discriminatory policies is also reinforced by the countless number of remarks from ministers and army generals referring to the Palestinians as 'two-legged animals' (Begin's statement shortly before the 1982 invasion of Lebanon); 'drugged insects' (by Raphael Eitan, then Army Chief of Staff, later a minister in the Shamir government until 1992, and subsequently Minister of Agriculture in the Netanyahu government); 'a cancer in the flesh of the country' (by General Yanush Ben-Gal, Commanding Officer of the Northern Command, who later joined the Labour Party); 'Arab scum' (by the head of the council of Rosh Pina settlement in the Galilee); 'foreigners' and 'aliens' (by Minister Ariel Sharon, who was describing Israel's Arabs). When Defence Minister, Sharon ordered army officers 'to tear off [Arab male demonstrators'] balls';[36] Binyamin Gur-Arie, a former Prime Minister's adviser on Arab affairs stated that 'this disease [that is, the Palestinisation of the Arab minority in Israel] cannot be cured as the war continues and the PLO rises on an international level.' This propagation of dehumanising and contemptuous anti-Arab attitudes, replete with racist metaphors and overtones, against the intended Arab victims, became increasingly pronounced after the Lebanese war of 1982; it also had a pernicious influence and was a prerequisite for public support for, and acquiescence in, the apartheid system in the occupied territories. Against the background of this political culture and the constant erosion towards the right, even the extreme right, the view that there was no room for two peoples in Greater Israel was heard increasingly in Israel throughout the 1980s.

In her book *Land or Peace: Whither Israel?* (1987), Israeli political scientist Yael Yishai showed that opinions regarding the West Bank remained generally very hawkish, although some changes in the direction of moderation did occur over time. A 1972 poll indicated that 91 per cent of the Jews supported settlement in the Jordan valley of the West Bank. In 1974, there was still a huge majority of 85.9 per cent backing settlement in the Jordan valley. In the same year, at the height of the clashes between the Labour government and the Gush Emunim settlers, almost two-thirds of Israeli Jews (63.5 per cent), approved settlement activity in the West Bank. In 1976, this support rose to 65 per cent. When the Likud came to power in 1977, an average of 76.3 per cent approved the settlement policy in the West Bank. The 1978 peace process with Egypt had only a slight moderating effect on public opinion: support for settlement declined to 65.5 per cent. A year later, in 1979, support for settlements rose to 72.7 per cent, confirming the hawkish mood of the public. In 1987, Professor Yishai wrote: 'The public clung tenaciously to those lands regarded as either vital to Israel's security or sanctified by divine promise.'[37] She concluded: 'For the time being public opinion in Israel inclines sharply toward hawkish attitudes. Although changes have occurred over time ... most people continue to cling to the remaining territory and are unwilling to hand it over even in return for peace.'[38]

The opinion polls conducted during the 1980s have generally shown not only a drift of the Israeli public towards the transfer solution – at least in connection with the Palestinians of the West Bank and Gaza Strip – but also particularly a growing popularity for this programme among the younger generation and in the army. As shown by opinion polls, the younger generation was in fact more vociferous in its support for mass transfer of Palestinians from the West Bank and Gaza. This younger generation, which was born into the reality of different norms and standards for Jews and Arabs and an official policy of Arab-bashing, accepted anti-Arab attitudes as a way of life. Moreover, the Israeli public had for a long time been accustomed to its government's iron-fist policy in the occupied territories to the point where a large section of the public regarded the transfer solution as only a logical extension of the official policy.

SAMMY SMOOHA'S ATTITUDINAL DATA

Recent works by Professor Sammy Smooha (who carried out four surveys of public opinion in Israel, both Jewish and Arab, in 1976, in 1980, and more recently in 1985 and April 1988) show that the Israeli-Jewish public was somewhat conflicted on the subject of Palestinians in Israel and the occupied territories. At the same time, however, the findings of Smooha (whose primary method of studying Arab–Jewish relations in Israel has been the attitudinal approach rather than a structural-institutional-legal approach) were extremely worrying.[39]

In his 1980 survey, which drew on interviews with 1,267 adult Jews, representing the entire adult Jewish population of Israel within the pre-1967 borders, Smooha found that, in spite of the differences among Israeli Jews, much of the Jewish public was behind the official Israeli policies and actions in the occupied territories. Seventy-two per cent lent at least some support for settlement in the West Bank and a clear majority favoured unrestricted settlement in the occupied areas, while 47 per cent of the public backed fully the policy of the Likud government in the territories. It was clear that the Jewish public was close to the views of hawkish Israeli leaders: only one-tenth of the Jewish population was prepared to withdraw to the pre-1967 frontiers and 86 per cent opposed the handing back of Arab East Jerusalem even if this concession was deemed vital for a peace settlement. Moreover, only 10 per cent of the Jewish public was prepared unconditionally to accept Israel's recognition of a Palestinian people and 84 per cent of the public was totally opposed to recognising the PLO as the Palestinians' representative. Similar opposition was also expressed regarding the creation of a Palestinian state in the West Bank and Gaza. On these questions, the public was very much behind the official positions taken by all Israeli governments since 1967.[40]

Regarding the Palestinian citizens of Israel, the 1980 poll carried out by Smooha revealed that around two-thirds of Israeli Jews were unwilling to have an Israeli-Arab citizen as their own personal doctor or a superior in a job; most Israeli Jews thought that most Arabs in Israel were 'primitive'. In addition, 41 per cent of Israeli Jews regarded the Arab citizens as a 'real danger'; 43 per cent a 'certain danger'. Only 16.5 per cent of the Jewish public saw no danger. Moreover, 65 per cent felt that Israel should increase its surveillance over the Arab citizens, while 68 per cent wanted further 'security restrictions' imposed on them as long as the Arab–Israeli conflict continued. Twenty-five per cent of Israeli Jews wanted some restrictions imposed on the Arab citizens, while only 7 per cent were against such restrictions.[41] According to Smooha, the Jewish public feared, among other things, that the high birth rate among, and population growth of, Israeli Palestinians might undermine the dominant Jewish majority; that Arab land holdings hinder the state settlement policies; that the Arab citizens might 'subvert' Israel's 'ethnic democracy'. 'To avert these undesirable possibilities,' Smooha explained, 'most Jews in the [1980] survey support or at least do not oppose' such measures as a ban on Rakah (a communist party largely supported by Arabs), 'seizure of opportunities encourage [Israeli] Arabs to leave the country, and expropriation of Arab land for Jewish development projects [such as the 'Judaisation of Galilee' project].'[42]

While Smooha observed in the 1980 poll a growing polarisation among the Jewish public as well as the political parties on the question of the Arab minority in Israel,[43] his data was still very alarming; 50.3 per cent of the Jewish population believed that 'Israel should seek and use any opportunity to encourage Israeli Arabs to leave the state' while 30.8 per cent had 'reservations' about this and only 18.8 'disagreed'.[44]

The Israeli Palestinians themselves acknowledge that the Israeli element in their cultural identity has increased; they function easily in Hebrew and tend to read it as much as Arabic. Their political identity is cast increasingly in joint Palestinian-Israeli terms. However, they feel quite alienated from the Israeli state which continues to treat them as second-class, unwanted citizens. As Smooha showed in 1980, over two-thirds of the Israeli Palestinians felt they could not be equal citizens, and believed Zionism was racist or at least immoral.[45]

With the aim of continuously monitoring developments among the Israeli public (both Arab and Jewish citizens), Smooha conducted two polls, in 1985 and more recently in April 1988, that is, about four or five months after the eruption of the Palestinian intifada. The 1985 poll drew on interviews with 1,205 Jews as well as 144 Israeli-Jewish public figures and the April 1988 survey consisted of 1,209 Jews, but it did not include leaders.[46] The attitudinal data of the 1985 and April 1988 surveys show that the Jewish public is somewhat divided on the question of Palestinians in Israel and the occupied territories.

Israeli-Jewish views on settlements in, and annexation of, the West Bank in the 1985 survey conducted by Smooha were as follows: 50.5 per cent of the Jewish public was in favour of settlement in the West Bank, 27.4 per cent had 'reservations' and 22.1 per cent were against; 41.2 per cent were in favour of immediate annexation and 26.5 per cent were in favour of future annexation, while 32.2 per cent were against annexation.[47] It is quite clear from these data that support for settlement dropped from a clear majority in 1980 to about half of the population in 1985.

According to Smooha's 1985 data, the Jewish public was confused, divided and ambivalent on the crucial questions of whether the Palestinians constituted a nation and whether they had a right to self-determination and an independent state in the West Bank and Gaza Strip, to which all Israeli governments had always been strongly opposed. Between 1980 and April 1988, there was some softening of the Jewish public's hard-line views on territorial concessions in the West Bank and Gaza Strip; opposition to a Palestinian state alongside Israel fell from 77 per cent in 1980 to 71 per cent in 1985 to 54 per cent in April 1988. However, the April 1988 poll, carried out a few months after the outbreak of the intifada, revealed that only 18 per cent of the Jewish public favoured a two-state solution and the establishment of a Palestinian state in the West Bank and Gaza. The Jewish population remained internally divided on the questions of settlement and annexation, but was still largely united in rejecting the Palestinians' demands for self-determination and the establishment of an independent state in the occupied territories. Consequently, according to the 1988 poll carried out by Smooha, basic stands had not been fundamentally changed regarding the overall solution to the Palestinian problem.[48] Commenting on the data of the 1988 survey, Smooha writes, 'It is noteworthy that 56 per cent of the Jews would prefer continued Jewish domination with a possibility of driving out those Palestinians who resist their rule.'[49]

With regard to the question of the Arab citizens of Israel, Smooha's 1985 poll revealed that 70 per cent of the Jewish public (and 74 per cent of the leaders from the Likud camp) favoured the continuation of the status quo of Jewish domination or even its reinforcement by increasing the state's surveillance over its Arab citizens.[50] In comparison in the 1980 poll, 65 per cent of the Jewish public felt that the state should increase its surveillance over the Arab citizens. In the 1985 survey, 21.9 per cent of the Jewish public believed that 'the most appropriate solution to the Arab minority problem' was that the 'Arabs will be forced to live outside Israel' (a euphemism for the endorsement of expelling the Arab citizens). In the same survey, 33.5 per cent of the Jewish public (as well as 66.7 per cent of Likud camp leaders and 12.5 per cent of Labour leaders) thought that 'the Arabs will live in Israel only if they are resigned to their minority status in a state designed for Jews.' In Smooha's April 1988 survey, 20.4 per cent of the Jewish public believed that the 'Arabs will be forced to live outside Israel' and 23.6 per cent thought that 'the Jews will rule, and Israeli Arabs who refuse to accept this will have to keep quiet or leave the country', showing only a marginal softening of views in this respect. At the same time '43 per cent endorse the principle of offering the minority a choice between subordination and voluntary transfer.'[51]

Smooha's data of 1985 and 1988 showed that most Israeli Jews approved of the state's active discrimination against the Arab citizens; in the 1985 survey, between 56 per cent and 87 per cent were against the idea of equal budgets for Arab and Jewish local authorities and schools. A striking majority of the Jewish public was in favour of an increase in the restrictions imposed on Israeli Arabs which would result in further discrimination against them: 'A majority of three quarters of the Jews partly or fully endorse the outlawing of Rakah and the Progressive List for Peace, the seizing of any opportunity to encourage Arabs [citizens] to leave the country, and the expropriation of Arab lands within the Green Line for Jewish development.'[52]

On the other hand, according to Smooha, Israeli-Jewish leaders were divided on this question and all opposed the banning of Rakah (the communist party). Labour and Likud leaders, Smooha writes, disagreed on 'the need to continue expropriating Arab lands, and the propriety of pushing Arab citizens to resettle outside Israel'.[53]

On the whole, both the Israeli public and the Israeli leaders were divided on the question of whether Israel should pursue an active policy of 'encouraging' the Arab citizens of Israel to leave the country. In the 1985 survey, 42.4 per cent of the Jewish public agreed that 'Israel should seek and use any opportunity to encourage Israeli Arabs to leave the state', while 33.7 per cent had reservations and 23.9 per cent disagreed. Israeli Jews who favoured 'without reservations' an active policy of 'encouraging' the Arab citizens to leave the country seemed to have declined from about 50 per cent in 1980 to about 40 per cent in 1988.[54] However, this fact was of little consolation, since the figures throughout the 1980s were still very alarming indeed. Both in the 1985 and April 1988 polls, a majority of three-quarters of the Jews with and without reservations (partly or fully) endorsed the idea that Israel should 'encourage' its Arab citizens to depart. Only a minority of less than a quarter clearly disagreed.[55]

According to Smooha, among Israeli-Jewish leaders, however, the picture was less grim; they were much more divided and expressed relatively less hard-line views on this question than the Israeli public. In the 1985 poll, 20.6 per cent of the Likud camp leaders 'agreed' that 'Israel should seek and use any opportunity to encourage Israeli Arabs to leave the state'; 50 per cent had 'reservations' and only 29.4 per cent 'disagreed'. On the other hand, among Labour leaders, the vast majority (84.2 per cent) 'disagreed', while only 2.6 per cent 'agreed' and 13.2 per cent had 'reservations'. As expected, the best results came from the leaders of the small Mapam-Citizen Rights Movement (CRM) camp, which currently forms the bulk of Meretz: 88.2 per cent 'disagreed', while 11.8 per cent had 'reservations'.[56]

However, when it came to the question of confiscating lands from the Arab citizens for the benefit of Jewish settlements (such as in the case of the project of 'Judaisation of Galilee'), the views among Jewish leaders got worse. In the 1985 survey, 37.5 per cent of the Likud camp leaders approved of 'expropriation of Arab lands within the Green Line for Jewish development'; 43.8 per cent had 'reservations', while only 18.8 per cent 'disagreed'. Regarding the same question, 15.8 per cent of Labour leaders approved; 50 per cent had 'reservations' and 34.2 per cent 'disagreed'. As for the leaders of the small liberal camp of Mapam-CRM, 14.7 per cent 'agreed', 17.6 per cent had 'reservations' and 67.6 per cent 'disagreed'. The views of the Jewish public on this issue are closer to Likud's than to Labour's.[57] According to Smooha, both Labour and Likud were clearly divided on this issue.

There was a methodological problem with the way Smooha used the responses to his questions, which consisted of three categories: 'agree', 'with reservations', and 'disagree'. The 'with reservations' category was both problematic and ambiguous, and was used by Smooha with either of the first or the third category whenever it suited his conclusions that the Jewish population was becoming more accommodating and less intransigent in the 1980s. In fact, the conclusions deduced depended on how one interpreted and used the 'with reservations' category: if 'with reservations', as opposed to 'disagreeing', meant partial approval of land seizure from the Arab citizens for Jewish use, then there was in the mid-1980s a clear majority among both Labour and Likud leaders approving 'with and without reservations' the premise of land appropriation from Israeli-Arab citizens, who between 1948 and 1990 lost close to one million acres of land.[58] On the other hand, if this category is incorporated with the 'disagree' one, then the opposite conclusion is deduced.

It should be pointed out that there was a general consensus among all Zionist parties in Israel, left, right and centre, behind the project of 'Judaisation of Galilee' and the confiscation of the lands of the Negev Bedouin in the late 1970s and the 1980s.[59] In essence, this consensus stems from Zionist ideological premises that the state's policies are designed to fulfil the Jewish majority's aspirations, not those of the Arab citizens. The Jewish majority's attitudes, which tend to endorse land confiscation from the Arab minority, are closely linked to the state's land policies and administrative-legal drive to ensure total control of land for meeting the needs of the Jewish settler population. While Smooha is reticent about the general consensus mentioned above, the data of his April 1988 survey showed that as many as 58 per cent of all Israeli Arabs and 75 per cent of all land-owning Israeli Arabs reported having lands expropriated by Israel. Moreover, the proportion of Israeli Arabs reporting land confiscation had risen sharply, from 57 per cent in 1976 to 75 per cent in April 1988.[60] This sharp rise was due to two main reasons: first, the continuation of the 'Judaisation' policies in the Galilee, including the establishment of more than fifty settlements since the late 1970s and the setting up of Jewish regional authorities with jurisdiction over large tracts of Arab lands in Galilee. Second, the massive seizure of Bedouin lands in the Negev in the late 1970s and early 1980s in the name of building new military airfields in this area on the eve of, and after, the withdrawal from Sinai in 1982 following the Israeli–Egyptian peace treaty.

According to Smooha's poll of April 1988, the intifada had a mixed (though generally adverse) effect on the attitudes of the Israeli-Jewish population towards the Palestinians in Israel (who are at the same time Israeli citizens and Palestinian in their ethnic and national affiliation); on the one hand the growing polarisation among the Jewish population reduced slightly its political intolerance, and on the other hand demonstration of solidarity by Israeli Palestinians with their brothers and sisters in the occupied territories shocked many Israeli Jews to the point that support for disenfranchising the Israeli Palestinians increased dramatically from 24 per cent in 1985 to 43 per cent in April 1988.[61]

In his 1992 book *Arabs and Jews in Israel*, Vol. 2, Smooha argued that since the late 1980s the Jewish public had become more tolerant and less intransigent towards the Palestinians in general and Arab citizens in Israel in particular. There are, however, some discrepancies between the figures mentioned in the second volume of *Arabs and Jews in Israel*, and the figures revealed by Smooha himself in a symposium held on 4 June 1990 at Haifa University entitled 'Education Against Hatred', which were cited in the Hebrew daily *Hadashot* on 5 June 1990. According to the figures cited in *Hadashot*, the April 1988 survey showed that 58 per cent of the adult Jewish population (as opposed to 43 per cent, the figure mentioned in *Arabs and Jews in Israel*, Vol. 2) would disenfranchise all Israeli-Arab citizens; 74 per cent were in favour of active discrimination by the state against the Arab citizens in all areas of life; 75 per cent would not be prepared to work under an Israeli-Arab boss, and 59 per cent supported the 'transfer' of Palestinians.[62] However, whether Smooha's figures were 43 per cent or 58 per cent for those who would disenfranchise all the Arab citizens, this proportion was very alarming, especially taking into consideration that at the same time (in April 1988) about 40 per cent of the Jewish public believed that 'Israel should seek and use any opportunity to encourage Israeli Arabs to leave the state.'[63]

Hadashot of 5 June 1990 quoted Smooha as explaining at the Haifa University symposium that 'The intolerance [towards the Arab minority] stems from the structure of the state, from the centrist forces, not from the periphery.' According to *Hadashot*, Smooha also suggested a number of conditions which were reinforcing the Jewish population's hostility towards the Arab citizens:

1) Jewish society lives in a hostile environment, and it is only natural that hatred towards the Arab citizens should develop.
2) In order to rule over the occupied territories, Israel has no alternative but to deny the Palestinians human and civil rights.
3) Israel was still an ideological [Zionist] society with no room for compromise.
4) Israel is a 'second-class democracy' with no civil rights anchored in law and it is a state in which the Jews have a privileged position.[64]

Looking carefully at the tables produced by Smooha in *Arabs and Jews in Israel*, Vol. 2, clearly the situation was only marginally better in 1988 than in 1980. In 1988, 57.5 per cent of the Israeli Jews were still not prepared to accept an Israeli-Arab citizen as their personal doctor and as many as 68 per cent, as their superior in a job.[65] However, Smooha himself argues that during the 1980s the Israeli Jews became (though not consistently) somewhat more tolerant, less certain and more confused in their attitudes towards the Palestinian citizens of Israel. A confirmation of Smooha's conclusion may also be found in a 1989 survey by the Palestinian scholar Nadim Rouhana, of 570 Jewish students in eleven (socio-economically diverse) high schools and 323 Jewish students in five universities in Israel. This survey revealed that the option of 'full equality' between Arabs and Jews in Israel is 'undesirable' to 47.6 per cent of Jewish university students and 56.8 per cent to Jewish high-school students. But it also showed that the percentage of Jewish respondents who found 'full equality' or 'civic equality' 'desirable' (18.3 per cent and 27.3 per cent of the high-school and university students respectively) was higher that the figures revealed in the (above-mentioned) 1980 survey carried out by Dr Mina Tzemah for the Van Leer Institute.[66]

The above account clearly shows that opinion polls carried out in 1989–91 revealed that between 40 and 60 per cent of the public was in principle in favour of 'transferring' the Palestinians of the West Bank and Gaza Strip, the highest proportion ever recorded, although, at the same time, the vast majority of Israeli Jews remained sceptical about the practicability of such a solution. This shows clearly that the Jewish public has remained largely intransigent, rather than accommodationist, at least on the question of Palestinians in the occupied territories. It is also not certain that the Labour Party coalition's (including Meretz's) success in the June 1992 election, which captured close to one-half of the electorate and espoused a more pragmatic approach than the previous Likud coalition, signalled a major turning-point as far as the drift of the Israeli public in support of the transfer concept is concerned. An opinion poll conducted on 17 December 1992 by Dr Mina Tzemah of the Dahaf research institute, on Israeli-Jewish attitudes towards the mass expulsion of the 413 Palestinians from the West Bank and Gaza in mid-December 1992, showed that Prime Minister Rabin enjoyed the support of 91 per cent of the Jewish public for the biggest single mass expulsion carried out since June 1967. Only 8 per cent of the public were against the expulsion.[67]

The menacing trend of coarsening political rhetoric and of prevailing anti-Arab racism and public xenophobia, which has been on the rise since the late 1960s, is very much in evidence today. In December 1992, on the eve of the mass deportation of the 413 Palestinian men, a telephone survey was initiated by the moderate Labour MK Avraham Burg, in his capacity as chairman of the Knesset's Education Committee; the survey indicated that 28 per cent of the Jewish population would prefer a 'pure' Jewish state, without Arab citizens, and a quarter of the public supported putting pressures on the Arab citizens in order to 'induce' them to leave the country.[68] Commenting on the findings of this poll, some liberal Israelis advanced typically apologetic arguments against Burg's conclusions. For journalist David Pedahtzur, for instance, the evident anti-Arab feelings had nothing to do with racism; they stemmed from Israeli-Jewish anxieties and fears of Israeli-Arab citizens.[69] Burg's findings were another indication as to the extent of anti-Arab racism in Israel and its alarming implication for the future of the Palestinian minority in Israel. More recently, Israeli journalist Arie Dayan has cited in an article in *Haaretz* of 19 December 1999, the findings of a recent academic study, showing that 68 per cent of Israeli Jews were unwilling to have an Israeli-Arab citizen as a superior in a job. These and Burg's findings are particularly worrying in view of the asymmetrical power relationship between the dominant Jewish majority and the politically controlled and economically dependent Arab minority.

THE IMPACT OF THE 'PEACE PROCESS'

The hawkishness of the Israeli public towards the West Bank, in particular, was once again confirmed in May 1993, when the ninth round of the Madrid/Washington 'peace process' was taking place. An opinion poll by Gallup Israel published in *Ma'ariv* in early May 1993, showed that 51 per cent of the public thought that the Labour government of Yitzhak Rabin was making too many concessions; 69 per cent favoured the continuation of Israeli jurisdiction over settlements in the West Bank, and 89 per cent were opposed to changing the status of any part of Jerusalem, that is, they were fully behind the unilateral annexation of Arab East Jerusalem.[70] This public support for land annexation has never meant integrating the Palestinians of East Jerusalem and the West

Bank into Israel. When the Rabin government sealed off Israel's borders with the occupied territories on 30 March 1993, thus throwing at least 100,000 Palestinians out of work, the Israeli-Jewish public was strongly behind it. Judging by opinion pollsters and commentators, although the Rabin government relaxed the initial ban on Palestinians crossing into Israel proper, both this government and the overwhelming majority of public opinion support social and economic separation between Israeli Jews and the Palestinians of the territories.[71] Support for both land annexation and economic and social separatism could increase public endorsement of 'latent and discreet transfer', such as in the case of the current policies in Arab (East) Jerusalem. On the other hand, real progress in the Israeli PLO talks, leading to a recognition of the Palestinians' right to self-determination and a readiness on the part of Israel to withdraw from the West Bank and Gaza, could potentially have the effect of diminishing public support for territorial expansion-cum-'transfer', at least as far as the Palestinians of the occupied territories were concerned.

On the whole it would be impossible to predict the effects of the establishment of a Palestinian entity in the West Bank and Gaza on the status and future of the large and increasing Palestinian minority in Israel, which by 2020 is expected to be at least a quarter of the total population and could reach 35 to 40 per cent of the population by the middle of the twenty-first century.[72] In any event, however, because the desire for 'more land and less Arabs' is so deeply rooted in Zionism, there is little hope that the themes of territorial expansion and Arab 'transfer' would completely disappear from public debate. Indeed, the findings of a recent public opinion survey, broadcast on Channel Two of Israeli Television on 18 January 1998, show that the situation remains extremely worrying. The survey (which was carried out on behalf of the municipalities' education authorities and drew on interviews with 400 students) showed that 19 per cent of all Jewish students support the 'transfer' of Israeli-Arab citizens from Israel; 44 per cent of those interviewed backed reduction in civil rights for Israeli Arabs; 32 per cent opposed any equality of rights, while 24 per cent were in favour of equality on condition that the Arab citizens did military service. Predictably, the survey also showed that support for anti-Arab racist views was much higher among students of religious schools than secular ones.[73]

Over the years, Israeli Jews have become more realistic and more pragmatic in their attitudes towards the Palestinians residing on both sides of the Green Line. Israel's prolonged political and cultural crisis has been most expressive in a polarisation of sentiment and opinion on the most profound questions affecting Israeli society. The Oslo 'peace process', in particular, which resulted in the Israeli–Palestinian agreements of September 1993, the Cairo Accords of May 1994, as well as the establishment of the Palestinian Authority in the West Bank and Gaza, has had a moderating, though mixed, impact on Israeli public attitudes towards the Palestinians. Six years into the Oslo process, many Israelis, according to a number of recent opinion polls, have come to believe that there will eventually be a Palestinian state in the West Bank and Gaza. However, the Israeli public has remained polarised and deeply divided on a whole range of issues relating to the Palestinians and the occupied territories and there is still a wide public consensus about keeping a sizeable part of the West Bank and all of greater Jerusalem.[74] On the other hand, in the present circumstances, the idea of mass expulsion seems unrealistic and impractical. The sizeable support for the idea among the Israeli public and its open legitimisation in several radical right-wing parties and by the supporters of Greater Israel is outweighed by mainstream public opinion and political forces that oppose such an option for pragmatic and moral reasons. No less significant is the fact that both the Palestinian Authority in the West Bank and Gaza and the international community would strongly oppose such an option.[75]

Epilogue

There have been continuous debates and struggles over the ever-changing definitions and actual borders of the Israeli state. Outside influences, regional wars and Arab resistance – the Anglo-Zionist-Hashemite secret diplomacy during the 1948 war, the tough attitude taken by the two superpowers against the tripartite collusion during the Suez War of 1956 and the then Israeli occupation of Sinai, the October war of 1973 with its huge human costs for Israel, President Jimmy Carter's mediations in the late 1970s and the Israeli–Egyptian negotiations culminating in the Camp David Accords of 1979, and the current resistance by the Hizbullah guerrillas in south Lebanon – have all had a huge impact on Zionist territorial aspirations and expansionist instincts and the tendency to lay claims to the whole area of Mandatory Palestine and its environs. Moreover, in addition to Arab resistance and pressures from the international community, the high cost of maintaining direct occupation has had an enormous impact on the concept of Greater Israel and Zionist territorial ambitions.

Zionist territorial ambitions of expanding into the so-called 'whole Land of Israel' were greatly influenced by the outcome of wars and military campaigns. Generally speaking, military successes gave a huge impetus to expansionist ambitions, and this was particularly evident during two major periods: between 1948 and 1956, and between 1967 and 1973. In early 1957, Israel was forced by the United States to evacuate Sinai and the Gaza Strip and consequently between 1957 and 1967, the Green Line evolved into a semi-permanent border. Israeli irredentist ambitions receded into the background until the spectacular military victory of June 1967. The military failures of the 1973 war, with its huge costs in human casualties, led to the interim agreements of 1974–75 with Egypt and Syria, with partial Israeli withdrawal from the Golan Heights and Sinai. Ultimately, Israeli willingness to withdraw from Sinai, in the wake of the Camp David Accords and the Israeli–Egyptian peace treaty of 1979, can be traced to the military and political outcomes of the 1973 war, in which thousands of Israeli soldiers were killed. Once again, the 1982 invasion of Lebanon temporarily gave encouragement to Jewish fundamentalist irredentist sentiments towards Lebanon. However, the subsequent sharp rise in the human cost of maintaining direct occupation of south Lebanon led Israel to scale down its expansionist ambitions in the north.

Indeed, there has been a clear link between the high cost of maintaining direct occupation by Israel and its readiness to redeploy or even withdraw its troops. The example of the so-called 'security zone' in south Lebanon is one case in evidence. The south Lebanon occupation zone was born in 1978 after Israel invaded Lebanon up to the Litani River and the United Nations Interim Force in Lebanon came in for an initial six-month period to oversee its withdrawal. Twenty-one years on, the Israeli Army is still there, though the occupation zone has grown. In 1982, the Israelis invaded Lebanon all the way to Beirut, driving out the PLO leadership. The occupation zone is essentially what they retained of Lebanon after the second withdrawal, completed in 1985. It stretches from the foothills of Mount Lebanon down to the Mediterranean. More than ten kilometres wide, until June 1999 it included a salient, offensive in nature, running north to the mountain resort of Jazzin. The 'zone', populated overwhelmingly by Shi'ite Muslims, comprises about 10 per cent of Lebanon, with about 150 small towns and villages.[1]

In the one major change of actors, the Palestinian guerrilla forces in Lebanon have been replaced as Israel's adversary by the Lebanese Shi'ites of Hizbullah, the Iranian-backed 'Islamic resistance'. In view of the growing unpopularity of Israel's highly costly occupation of the 'zone', in the general election of May 1999 most Israeli parliamentary candidates pledged efforts to end it, but ruled out unilateral withdrawals. On the night of 22–23 February 1999, three Israeli Army officers, one a major from an elite unit, were killed and five wounded during a three-hour battle with Hizbullah guerrillas inside Israel's south Lebanon occupation zone. These were Israel's first fatalities in 1999; 23 Israeli soldiers in the zone were killed the previous year. On 2 March 1999, four more Israelis, including Brigadier-General Erez Gerstein, were killed by a Hizbullah roadside bomb while travelling along a road inside the occupation zone. This particular loss was a major psychological blow to the Israeli Army, which responded by launching its heaviest air raids and bombardments since the April 1996 'Grapes of Wrath' operation and reinforcing its troops in the north with tanks and armoured personnel carriers. The two sides teetered on the brink of another major clash. However, the then pragmatic Likud Defence Minister

Moshe Arens said Israel had no plans to escalate the confrontation as long as the Syrians refrained from encouraging Hizbullah's rocket attacks on northern Israel.

Although Israel continued to stress that the 'address' of Hizbullah's resistance was Damascus, the Likud politicians lacked the will to resume negotiations with Syria on withdrawal from the occupied Golan Heights – Syria's price for peace in south Lebanon. As Israeli casualties in south Lebanon mounted, public opinion polls showed a sharp swing in favour of withdrawal. In March, Labour's Ehud Barak pledged that, if elected prime minister, he would have the army out of Lebanon 'within a year' and would revive the Israeli–Syrian negotiations track, which had remained dormant throughout Netanyahu's tenure. From mid-1998 onwards, the Israeli Army began debating a plan involving a withdrawal from the Jazzin salient and a redeployment to new fixed positions along the south bank of the Litani River. As this would concentrate troops along a shorter front and reduce the number of outposts, fewer Israeli troops would be targets of Hizbullah's guerrillas. On 3 June 1999, Israel's local proxies, the 2,500-man South Lebanon Army began its withdrawal from the Jazzin enclave, north of Israel's occupation zone.

The issue of territorial expansion is the most concrete expression of a highly parochial brand of Jewish organic nationalism – a world-view that stands a sharp contradiction to liberal democratic values. The establishment of Jewish political sovereignty over Greater Israel constitutes the vital focus of Israeli right-wing and fundamentalist action. The supporters of the 'Whole Land of Israel' see Israel perpetually embattled, on the defensive, territorially expanding in all directions, and with a historic and religious/'divine' mandate. Among these supporters, however, there existed two major trends. One trend, which was made up of the radical right (Tzomet, Moledet, Tehiya, Gush Emunim, large sections of the Likud and the National Religious Party and some Labour Zionist 'activists'), was little influenced by pragmatic considerations and believed that Israel was strong enough to do whatever it wanted, including maximum territorial expansion through war if necessary. Certainly the radical right in Israel would like to expel the Palestinians of the West Bank and Gaza. One of the justifications for this open, strident advocacy of 'transfer' is the 'logical' conclusion that annexation of the West Bank and Gaza with their millions of Palestinian inhabitants would be detrimental if not disastrous to the whole concept of the 'greater

Jewish state'; hence the conclusion that the Arabs should be made, one way or another, to depart. The second, relatively pragmatic trend, while believing that settlement and annexationist policies should continue and even be intensified, believed that strategic cooperation or at least a working relationship with the US government – which would oppose maximum territorial expansion – must be maintained as a vital Israeli interest. According to one conservative estimate, US economic aid to Israel is $4 billion annually; between 1948 and 1992 American aid to Israel totalled $77 billion.[2] A much higher figure was even suggested by US Ambassador to Israel Martyn Indyk who stated in 1997 that the total of 'US loans, grants and loan guarantees' to Israel came to $13 billion per annum.[3] Israel's dependence on the United States for economic and military assistance, particularly while still seeking to accommodate the Russian Jewish immigrants, the pragmatists argued, made the scenario of maximum expansion impracticable.

Yet for the caretakers of Jabotinsky's Revisionist philosophy (Begin, Shamir, Netanyahu), the secular radical right and the fundamentalist settlers of Gush Emunim, the Jewish state has always meant 'unpartitioned Eretz-Yisrael', 'the whole Land of Israel', 'the old biblical lands of Judea and Samaria', in which there is no room for real Palestinian autonomy, let alone an independent Palestinian state. For instance, on 14 January 1998, the government of Binyamin Netanyahu voted to hold on to large segments of the West Bank under any peace deal with the Palestinians. The Israeli Cabinet did not publish a map of the area Israel planned to retain its hold on, but said that it would include areas surrounding all the 148 Jewish settlements set up in the West Bank since 1967, a buffer zone ringing the territory, in addition to roads crisscrossing the area. Also included were a wide zone around Jerusalem, military bases of 'strategic importance' or necessary for 'deterrence', water resources, electricity networks and 'historic sites sacred to the Jewish people', an eastern 'security zone' along the Jordan Valley, a western 'security zone' along the divide line, north–south and east–west roads, and vital installations. If these components were translated into percentages, what would remain is an area of 12 per cent of the West Bank, which would be handed over to the Palestinians.[4]

Despite his personal victory in the election for prime minister, Ehud Barak's Labour Party came nowhere near to achieving an overall Knesset majority. Barak's sweeping twelve-point lead in the race for prime minister did not carry over to his Knesset slate, which, with a bare third of the votes cast for its leader, gained only 23 seats in the 120-member legislature. That the 1999 poll did not represent a major shift of popular opinion is reflected further in the fact that the parties of Netanyahu's defeated coalition won a total of 60 seats. The swing to Barak can therefore be no more than a rejection of Netanyahu and his slippery style of government rather than renunciation of the right-wing ideology he represents. Moreover, despite the personal victory of Barak, the power and purpose of Jewish fundamentalists and other influential supporters of Greater Israel cannot be ignored. Justifying war to gain the 'other parts of Eretz-Yisrael', and targeting the Muslim holy shrines in Jerusalem, are set to continue. Over half-a-dozen Temple Mount-related groups, many financed by wealthy American Jews, are openly seeking to replace al-Aqsa Mosque and the Dome of the Rock with a rebuilt Temple. The Jewish fundamentalists will continue the appeals to use Joshua's destruction and subjugation of the ancient Canaanites or Amalekites as a model for solving the contemporary 'Arab problem'. The organised focus of the Jewish fundamentalist movement, the Gush Emunin settlers (armed and with influential sympathisers in the secular right-wing parties, in the army and even, inside the current Cabinet, the National Religious Party) has evolved into a powerful force within Israeli politics; they will continue to be a major obstacle to meaningful negotiations towards a comprehensive and just solution of the Israel–Palestine conflict.

For the main supporters of Greater Israel, the area between the Mediterranean and Jordan River is the irreducible minimum for fulfilling the purpose of Zionism, that is, an area to be settled with Jews. Jewish ultra-nationalists and fundamentalists believe that the aspirations to extend Jewish rule over Sinai, parts of Lebanon and much of the East Bank of Jordan should not be forgotten, and may some day become politically relevant. But in the meantime, direct actions to achieve these objectives may be postponed in the effort to consolidate Jewish rule west of the Jordan, in the West Bank.[5] Many fundamentalists and ultra-nationalists believe that Jews faithful to Eretz-Yisrael have the right to resist and even overthrow the elected government of Israel if it agrees to relinquish portions of the 'Land of Israel' to Arab rule.[6] Closely related with this expansionist perspective is the view that peace with the Palestinians and the Arab world is impossible. Israel must prepare for war; the necessity of war, no matter how moderate Palestinian negotiating positions may appear to be, flows from the incompleteness of Zionism's mission.

Since Jewish restoration of the 'completeness of the Land of Israel' is essential, territorial compromise as a price of peace, is nonsensical. Jews are commanded to conquer the whole Land of Israel, even at a high price. Any attempt to find a compromise solution of the Palestinian problem is futile. Israel must prepare to fight wars for the foreseeable future.

During and after the signing of the Oslo agreements, Israel, under both Labour and Likud, continued to expropriate Palestinian property, 'de-Palestinise' occupied East Jerusalem and expand Jewish settlements in and around the city. Under the cover of the 'peace process', Israel has been able to maintain and even strengthen its structure of domination over the Palestinians. The Oslo agreements themselves have reaffirmed the dispossession and exile of the Palestinian refugees, and the fragmentation of the Palestinian people as a whole. The cutting edge of Israel's post-Oslo policies has been shown most sharply in the settlement and Judaisation policies in and around Arab Jerusalem. The Israeli human rights organisation B'Tselem has recently issued a report stating that since 1967 Israel has confiscated nearly 25,000 dunums of Arab land in East Jerusalem and has established 40,000 residential units on this land for the exclusive use of the Jewish population.[7] In recent years, Israel has been seeking speedier ways to expand Jerusalem's parameters and to thin out its Arab population. After the June 1967 occupation and annexation of East Jerusalem, the Arab population of the city was not given Israeli nationality. Arab Jerusalemites were considered as 'permanent residents' and were allowed to carry 'Israeli ID cards of East Jerusalem', but they were not eligible for obtaining Israeli passports nor for voting for the Knesset. Apparently, there are about 200,000 Arabs today who hold Israeli ID cards of East Jerusalem. One-third of these do not live in the city, but reside in the West Bank. In recent years, thousands of families have lost the right to remain in Jerusalem because, Israel claims, they have chosen to live outside the city's boundaries. Moreover, Palestinian women and men from Jerusalem married to foreign nationals have been told their residence rights in Jerusalem have been cancelled.[8] Israel has continued to tighten its grip on the Arab sector of Jerusalem, strictly forbidding entry to the residents of the West Bank. Israeli practices of denying Palestinians building permits and levying high municipality taxes are also driving thousands of Palestinians out of the city in search of a more affordable place to live.

One of the victims of Israel's 'ethnic cleansing' policy in East Jerusalem has been Professor Musa Budayri, a political scientist at Al-Quds University, in Jerusalem, and a resident in East Jerusalem. A native of Jerusalem, his family has lived there for centuries. He was recently given a tourist visa, valid for several weeks, and told that he would have to leave the city by 22 August 1999. Budayri is one of thousands of other Palestinians in a similar situation who do not share his academic or international connections. They are all subject to the threat of being turned into 'tourists' in their birthplace. According to the Israeli Ministry of the Interior, 2,200 Jerusalem ID cards of Arab families (roughly 8,800 Palestinians) were confiscated between 1996 and May 1999. The Orient House Centre for Civil and Social Rights (CCSR) in East Jerusalem is handling the cases of 10,287 Palestinians who were deprived of their Jerusalem ID cards between early 1994 and the end of May 1999. According to CCSR, some 1,260 Arab Jerusalemites were deprived of the Jerusalem ID cards in the first half of 1999.[9] The Ministry of the Interior uses the following pretexts for the confiscation: 'a prolonged absence from Jerusalem', and 'the holding of foreign nationality'. Yet many Israeli Jewish citizens residing in Jerusalem hold dual nationality without ever running the risk of being expelled from their homes. The measures of the Ministry of Interior cannot but be seen as part of a general strategy to free Jerusalem from its Arab population. They talk about 'ethnic cleansing' in Jerusalem, the well-known Israeli journalist, Danny Rubinstein, commented recently in *Haaretz*, and B'Tselem has described the strategy as 'quiet transfer'.[10]

The combination of an unjust 'peace process', the continuing expansion of Israeli settlements and repeated closures of the West Bank and Gaza have continued to take their toll on the Palestinian economy. Throughout the post-Oslo years, from 1993 to 1999, Palestinian life has got progressively worse. GNP per capita fell from $500 in 1992 to $390 in 1995.[11] There were more Jewish settlers moving into the West Bank, more land seizures to build bypass roads for Jewish settlements, a Palestinian Authority responding to Israeli demands with more human rights violations, and repeated closures of the occupied territories that have brought 40 to 70 per cent unemployment and left socioeconomic devastation in their wake.[12] Moreover, access to water remains the greatest obstacle to Palestinian agricultural development. Israel is pumping more water from West Bank aquifers than nature can replace, even as it limits Palestinian water usage to barely 20 per cent more than they used in 1967 – this water is allowed only for personal use, not for agricultural and economic development. Indeed, of the water produced by the West Bank aquifers, 56.6 per cent is earmarked for Israeli citizens, 23.8 per cent for the 170,000 settlers in the West Bank, and 19.6 per cent for the 1.2 million Palestinians. The summer of 1998 saw both Israel and the occupied territories in the midst of a water emergency. Due to the unusually dry summer of 1998, Palestinian wells in the Hebron area ran dry in mid-July, and Hebron residents began strict rationing, with each house receiving water once every one to two weeks. In mid-August, despite the continuing heat, Israel further reduced the water supply to the Palestinian areas to meet increasing demands of Jews in Israel and the settlements in the West Bank, where watering lawns and washing cars was still permitted.

The political composition of the current Israeli Cabinet reflects a broad balance between hawks (such National Religious Party ministers, the official mentor party of the Gush Emunim settlers) and doves (such as Meretz ministers), defenders of religious status and champions of secular and liberal Zionism respectively. Women and the Palestinian citizens of Israel appeared disenchanted by the lack of representation in Barak's Cabinet. Of the 32 ministers and deputy ministers nominated by mid-July, 31 are males; the only woman Cabinet member, Dalia Itzik, holds the relatively marginal environment portfolio. Barak's treatment of Israel's Palestinian constituency was no better. Having received 95 per cent of the vote in Israel's Palestinian communities, he barely went through the motions of consulting the Arab parties.

In his election victory speech of 18 May 1999, Barak said that he would observe four 'security red lines' concerning the peace process with the Palestinians: Jerusalem remaining under Israeli 'eternal sovereignty', no return to the 1967 borders under any circumstances, most of the West Bank settlers staying in settlement blocs under Israeli sovereignty, and no 'foreign armies' west of the Jordan River. Barak also promised a referendum on the outcome of the final status talks. The head of the Palestinian Authority, Yasir 'Arafat, has since referred to Prime Minister Barak as 'my dear friend and partner' and both sides have since played variations on the theme of a 'new dawn'. Yet the basic thinking with regard to the territorial issue behind the negotiation strategy of Ehud Barak is 'the Allon Plan Plus' of assuring the maximum land and the minimum number of Arabs – or an overwhelmingly Jewish state from the demographic point of view[13] – this remains essentially the fundamental position of the

Labour Party. It was the relatively moderate former President of Israel and leading Labour politician Yitzhak Navon who declared during the 1984 general election campaign: 'The very point of Labour's Zionist programme is to have as much land as possible and as few Arabs as possible!'[14]

The current Labour coalition is against Israel's total withdrawal to the pre-1967 borders, against the Palestinian 'right of return', for the unilateral annexation of Arab Jerusalem, and for the preservation of most Jewish settlements in the occupied territories. Indeed after the Oslo agreements were signed, the then Labour government of Yitzhak Rabin did its utmost to strengthen most Jewish settlements in the West Bank. In 1995, the Rabin government allocated $330 million for the completion of bypass roads connecting Jewish settlements to each other and to Israel proper. Moreover, in September 1994, Rabin had given the go-ahead for the construction of about seven hundred new homes at Giva'at Tal, part of Alfei Menashe settlement, situated three kilometres inside the West Bank.[15] In the spring of 1995 the same government approved the construction of eight thousand new housing units in the settlement of Ma'ale Adumim, located at the centre of the West Bank and half way between Jerusalem and Jericho. A year later, in June 1996, the four thousand members of the Jahaleen Bedouin tribe lost their legal battle in the Israeli High Court to keep land on which they had pitched their tents for decades. They were forced by the Labour government and the Israeli court to make way for 20,000 Jewish settlers who wanted to expand their Ma'ale Adumim settlement by confiscating Arab property.[16] Moreover, the Jerusalem weekly *Kol Ha'ir* revealed on 13 October 1995 that Prime Minister Rabin had instructed the Ministry of Housing to expropriate Arab land in order to expand the city limits of Jerusalem to the east, to unite it with Ma'ale Adumim.[17] According to Rabin's plans, various fragments of the West Bank and most of Gaza, which is already administered by the Palestinian Authority, eventually should be linked to Jordan, forming a Jordan-Palestine state. This was basically the Labour scenario: to partition the West Bank between Israel and Jordan-Palestine, a scenario derived from the traditional Labour formula (or axiom): 'maximum land and minimum Arabs'.

For the pragmatists of Labour Zionism, responsive to the constraints exercised by the Western powers on Israel's territorial expansion, and sensitive to Western public opinion, the possibility of more land for Israel was also bound to come up against the hard reality of Palestinian demographics and Palestinian resistance. To incorporate Palestinian population centres would alter the very fundamentals of the Zionist enterprise. To incorporate millions of disaffected Palestinians into some kind of 'Greater Israel' would eventually transform the Jewish state into a bi-national state of Israel/Palestine. What was required was strict physical and political separation of Jews and Palestinians, the latter policed by the Palestinian Authority, while at the same time keeping the structures of domination and inequalities intact. Indeed for the Palestinians, under Ehud Barak the current Labour strategy of peace negotiations has little changed the facts on the ground. Redeployment and withdrawal of troops in parts of the West Bank have only strengthened the long-standing Labour policy of seeking maximum lands for Jewish settlers, while leaving Palestinian population centres outside Jewish control.

Over the years, Israeli Jews became more realistic in their attitudes towards the Palestinians in the occupied territories. The Zionist liberal camp sees the 'peace process' helping to maintain Israel as a Jewish state, territorially limited, secure within the framework of peace agreements with its neighbours. Six years into the 'Oslo process', many Israelis – according to recent opinion polls – believe there will be a Palestinian state in the West Bank and Gaza. However, judging by the continuous and relentless expansion of Jewish settlement throughout the West Bank and in Greater Jerusalem and the enormous power asymmetry between Israel and the Palestinians, the most likely outcome of this process would be the transformation of Israel's direct military occupation of the West Bank and Gaza into some kind of 'informal empire'. For Labour, the post-Oslo agreements do not preclude the annexation of over one-third of the West Bank and Greater Jerusalem. This outcome is unlikely to result in bringing an end to the occupation and of decolonising the West Bank and Gaza; it will not solve the Palestinian refugee problem or provide some sense of justice for the Palestinians. A mini-Palestinian state, created in two-thirds of the West Bank and Gaza, and controlled by and dependent on Israel, could not absorb the Palestinian refugees of the occupied territories along with refugees from Lebanon and Jordan and elsewhere. The Oslo final-status talks are supposed to deal with the core issues of refugees, Jerusalem, settlements and the borders of a future Palestinian entity. Israel's settlement expansion is part of an attempt to determine the final-status borders. But both the Palestinians and the Israelis are aware that among the toughest core issues of the final-status negotiations will be the territorial issue, especially as the most the new Israeli government appears ready to give falls well short of the least the Palestinian leadership could accept.

Notes

NOTES TO INTRODUCTION

1. See David Sharrock, in the *Guardian*, 3 June 1999, p. 16.
2. Hugh Harcourt, 'In Search of the Emperor's New Clothes', in Tomis Kapitan (ed.), *Philosophical Perspectives on the Israeli-Palestinian Conflict* (New York: M.E. Sharpe, 1997), p. 289; Thomas Thompson, *The Early History of the Israelite People* (Leiden, Netherlands: E.J. Brill, 1992).
3. Michael Prior, 'Zionism and the Bible', in Naim Ateek and Michael Prior (eds), *Holy Land Hollow Jubilee: God, Justice and the Palestinians* (London: Melisende, 1999), p. 70.
4. David Ben-Gurion, *The Rebirth and Destiny of Israel* (New York: The Philosophical Library, 1954), p. 100.
5. Keith W. Whitelam, *The Invention of Ancient Israel: The Silencing of Palestinian History* (London: Routledge, 1996), p. 40.
6. For a collection of Israeli-Zionist views, see articles in Adam Doron (ed.), *The State of Israel and the Land of Israel* (Tel Aviv: Beit Berl College, 1988). (in Hebrew).
7. Benedict Anderson, *Imagined Communities: Reflections on the Origins and Spread of Nationalism* (London: Verso, 1991).
8. Whitelam, *The Invention of Ancient Israel*, pp. 40–45.
9. For excerpts of Shamir's address, see *Journal of Palestine Studies* 21, No. 2 (Winter 1992), pp. 128–31.
10. Ibid.; Binyamin Netanyahu, *A Place Among the Nations* (London: Bantam Press, 1993), pp. 39–40.
11. Whitelam, *The Invention of Ancient Israel*, pp. 40–45.
12. Barnet Litvinoff (ed.), *The Letters and Papers of Chaim Weizmann*, Vol. I, Series B (Jerusalem: Israel University Press, 1983), pp. 256–57.
13. Amos Perlmutter, *Israel: The Partitioned State* (New York: Charles Scribner's Son, 1985), p. 9
14. 'Eretz Yisrael', in Susan Hattis Rolef (ed.), *Political Dictionary of the State of Israel* (New York: Macmillan Publishing Company, 1993), p. 101.
15. Perlmutter, *Israel: The Partitioned State*, p. 9.
16. Benny Morris, *The Birth of the Palestinian Refugee Problem, 1947–1949* (Cambridge: Cambridge University Press, 1987), p. 5.
17. Protocol of the Jewish Agency Executive meeting of 7 June 1938, in Jerusalem, confidential, Vol. 28, No. 51, Central Zionist Archives (CZA). See also Morris, *The Birth of the Palestinian Refugee Problem*, p. 24.
18. Ben-Gurion's memorandum dated 17 December 1938, S25/7627, CZA.
19. Simha Flapan, *The Birth of Israel: Myths and Realities* (New York: Pantheon Books, 1987), p. 37.
20. Tom Segev, *1949: The First Israelis* (New York: The Free Press, 1986), p. 19.

21. Benny Morris, *Israel's Border Wars, 1949–1956* (Oxford: Clarendon Press, 1993), p. 11.
22. Quoted in M. Medzini, 'Reflection on Israel's Asian Policy', in M. Curtis and S.A. Gitelson (eds), *Israel and the Third World* (New Brunswick, NJ: Transaction Books, 1976), p. 75.
23. A. Schweitzer, 'Moshe Dayan: Between Leadership and Loneliness', *Haaretz*, 12 December 1958, p. 3.
24. Samuel Roberts, *Survival or Hegemony? The Foundation of Israeli Foreign Policy* (Baltimore: Johns Hopkins University Press, 1973), p. 107.
25. Quoted in Morris, *Israel's Border Wars*, pp. 11–12, quoting Israel State Archives, Foreign Ministry, 2463/2.
26. Cited in ibid., p. 12.
27. Ibid.
28. Cited in the *New York Times*, 11 November 1956.
29. Ibid., 28 November 1956.
30. Motti Golani, *Israel in Search of a War: The Sinai Campaign, 1955–1956* (Brighton: Sussex Academic Press, 1998).
31. See Benjamin Beit-Hallahmi, *The Israeli Connection* (London: I.B. Tauris, 1988), pp. 6–7.
32. Avi Shlaim, 'Israel, the Great Powers, and the Middle East Crisis of 1958', *Journal of Imperial and Commonwealth History* 27, No. 2 (May 1999), p. 178.
33. Moshe Dayan, *Avnie Derekh: Otobiyografyah* [Milestones: An Autobiography] (Jerusalem and Tel Aviv: 'Edanim and Dvir, 1976), p. 255.
34. Michael Bar-Zohar, *Mool Hamarah Haakhzarit: Yisrael Berega'a Haemet* [Facing a Cruel Mirror: Israel's Moment of Truth] (Tel Aviv: Yedi'ot Aharonot Books, 1990), p. 27; Mordechai Bar-On, *Itgar Vetigrah: Haderekh Lemivtza'a Kadesh* [Challenge and Quarrel: The Road to Sinai 1956] (Beersheba: The University of Ben-Gurion, 1991), pp. 252–53; *Yedi'ot Aharonot*, 3 April 1986.
35. Shlaim, 'Israel, the Great Powers and the Middle East Crisis of 1958', p. 179.
36. Ibid., pp. 179 and 182.
37. Moshe Sharett, *Yoman Ishi* [Personal Diary], Vol. 2, (Tel Aviv: Sifriyat Ma'ariv, 1978), p. 377.
38. Shlaim, 'Israel, the Great Powers and the Middle East Crisis of 1958', p. 185.
39. Cited in ibid.
40. Cited in Ehud Maltz and Michal Sela', in *Kol Ha'ir*, 31 August 1984.
41. Nur Masalha, 'The 1967 Palestinian Exodus', in Ghada Karmi and Eugene Cotran (eds), *The Palestinian Exodus, 1948–1998* (Reading: Ithaca Press, 1999), pp. 87–89.
42. Amos Elon, *A Blood-Dimmed Tide* (New York: Columbia University Press, 1997), p. 40.
43. Quoted in Howard M. Sachar, *A History of Israel: From the Rise of Zionism to Our Time* (New York: Alfred A. Knopf, 1976), p. 673. See also Ehud Sprinzak, *The Ascendance of Israel's Radical Right* (Oxford and New York: Oxford University Press, 1991), p. 40.

44. Moshe Dayan, *Mapah Hadashah, Yehasim Aherim* [A New Map, Other Relationships] (Tel Aviv: Ma'ariv, 1969), p. 173.
45. Elon, *A Blood-Dimmed Tide*, p. 46.
46. Ibid., p. 45.
47. Ibid.
48. Yoram Peri, *Between Battles and Ballots: Israeli Military in Politics* (Cambridge: Cambridge University Press, 1983).
49. Elon, *A Blood-Dimmed Tide*, p. 45.
50. Zeev Sternhell, *The Founding Myths of Israel: Nationalism, Socialism and the Making of the Jewish State* (Princeton, NJ: Princeton University Press, 1998).
51. Segev, *1949: The First Israelis*, p. 19.
52. Sprinzak, *The Ascendance of Israel's Radical Right*, p. 113.
53. Cited in Nabeel Abraham, 'Making Israel's Plans Disappear', *Lies of Our Times* (New York), 1, No. 11 (November 1990), p. 20.
54. Nur Masalha, *Expulsion of the Palestinians: The Concept of "Transfer" in Zionist Political Thought, 1882–1948* (Washington, DC: Institute for Palestine Studies, 1992), pp. 93–141.
55. Nur Masalha, *A Land Without a People* (London: Faber and Faber, 1997), pp. 100–130.
56. Sprinzak, *The Ascendance of Israel's Radical Right*, p. 176.
57. Sammy Smooha, *Arabs and Jews in Israel*, Vol. 2 (Boulder, CO, and San Francisco, CA: Westview Press, 1992), p. 92.
58. See article by Gide'on Biger, in *Haaretz*, 15 November 1988.

NOTES TO CHAPTER ONE

1. The political influence of the movement on Israeli policies is variously assessed. Professor Michael Brecher, for instance, estimated in 1972 that the movement was a 'variable of some influence in Israel's policy on territorial and related issues': Michael Brecher, *The Foreign Policy System of Israel* (London, 1972), p. 156.
2. Ofira Seliktar, *New Zionism and the Foreign Policy System of Israel* (London: Croom Helm, 1986), p. 92
3. 'Manifesto of the Land of Israel Movement, August 1967', translated in Rael Jean Isaac, *Israel Divided: Ideological Politics in the Jewish State* (Baltimore, MD: Johns Hopkins University Press, 1976), p. 171; Ehud Sprinzak, *The Ascendance of Israel's Radical Right* (New York and Oxford: Oxford University Press, 1991), p. 38.
4. Sprinzak, *The Ascendance of Israel's Radical Right*, p. 35.
5. See interview with the late Simha Flapan, the former editor of the Israeli monthly *New Outlook*, *Journal of Palestine Studies*, 14, No. 1 (Fall 1984), p. 47.
6. For an example of Tabenkin's writings, see 'The Danger of Destruction and the Chances for Jewish Activism', in Aharon Ben-'Ami (ed.), *Sefer Eretz-Yisrael Hashlemah* [The Book of the Whole Land of Israel Movement] (Tel Aviv: Friedman Press, 1977), pp. 159–68. See also Yosef

Tabenkin (son of Yitzhak Tabenkin), 'Between the Wilderness and the Sea: The Land is One', *Artzi*, Vol. 2 (1982), pp. 51–52. (in Hebrew).

7. Sprinzak, *The Ascendance of Israel's Radical Right*, p. 39.
8. Nur Masalha, *Expulsion of the Palestinians: The Concept of 'Transfer' in Zionist Political Thought, 1882–1948* (Washington, DC: Institute for Palestine Studies, 1992).
9. Sprinzak, *The Ascendance of Israel's Radical Right*, p. 39.
10. Ian Lustick, *For the Land and the Lord: Jewish Fundamentalism in Israel* (New York: Council on Foreign Relations, 1988), p. 43.
11. Sprinzak, *The Ascendance of Israel's Radical Right*, p. 57.
12. Yair Kotler, *Heil Kahane* (New York: Adama Books, 1986), p. 89.
13. Nur Masalha, *A Land Without a People* (London: Faber and Faber, 1997), p. 44.
14. Cited in Tzvi Shiloah, *Ashmat Yerushalayim* [The Guilt of Jerusalem] (Tel Aviv: Karni Press, 1989), p. 45.
15. Ibid.
16. Sprinzak, *The Ascendance of Israel's Radical Right*, p. 300.
17. Aharon Ben-'Ami (ed.), *Hakol*, [Everything], (Tel Aviv: Madaf Publishing House, 1967).
18. See Uri Orbach, 'One Bank to the Jordan', *Nekudah*, No. 95, 21 January 1986, pp. 16–18.
19. Rahel Saborai, 'The Wholeness of the Country', *Hakol*, pp. 172–73. This article was first published in the Mapam daily *'Al-Hamishmar* on 23 June 1967.
20. The proposal for Zionist colonisation at Wadi El Arish in Sinai was first put forward by Theodor Herzl in 1902. However nothing came out of the scheme. See Raphael Patai (ed.), *Encyclopedia of Zionism* (New York: Herzl Press, 1971), Vol. 1, p. 284.
21. Ben-'Ami, *Hakol*, p. 180.
22. Ibid., pp. 85–90. Don's article was first published in *Haaretz*, 28 June 1967, p. 8.
23. Ibid., pp. 144–46 (Tzvi Shiloah), pp. 44–49 and pp. 231–35 (Eli'ezer Livneh), p. 34 (Yuval Neeman), pp. 163–64 ('Azaryah Allon).
24. Shiloah, *Ashmat Yerushalayim*, p. 59.
25. See, for instance, Avraham Heller, 'Hashed Dademografi' [The Demographic Demon], *Haumah*, No. 1 (January 1970), pp. 99–100; Avraham Heller, in *Haumah*, No. 3–4 (September 1976), p. 346. Dr Heller is the editor of *Haumah*, the most important periodical of the Herut (later Likud) Party.
26. See Dr Zeev von Weizel in *Haumah*, No. 3 (April 1973), pp. 294–95.
27. Ben-'Ami, *Sefer Eretz-Yisrael Hashlemah*.
28. Ibid., pp. 20–21.
29. Ibid.
30. Cited by Ephraim Urbach (then a professor of Talmud and Midrash at the Hebrew University), in *Midstream* (a Monthly Jewish Review), (April 1968), p. 15. Urbach thought that 'this sort of thing is very harmful and not at all edifying'.
31. Ben-'Ami, *Sefer Eretz-Yisrael Hashlemah*, p. 26,
32. Ibid., p. 101.

33. Ibid., pp. 312–13.
34. Ibid., pp. 349–50.
35. *Haumah*, No. 88 (Autumn 1987), pp. 20–26.
36. Ibid., p. 26. See also a response to Yosefi's articles in *Haumah*, No. 90 (Spring 1988), pp. 362–63. In the same issue of *Haumah* (pp. 275–76), K. Katznelson, a widely-known journalist in Israel and a supporter of Greater Israel, wrote that: 'Arab-Jewish co-existence in Israel is an absolute illusion. Israel could only exist as a Jewish society, with a very limited percentage of foreigners [that is, Arabs].' Katznelson believed that Israel should redefine its policies towards the Arabs on both sides of the Green Line: 'Zionism's achievements have always been the product of unilateral aggressive action.'
37. See Tzvi Shiloah in *Moledet*, No. 17 (March 1990), p. 14.
38. Moshe Shamir and Dov Yesefi, two leading member of the Whole Land of Israel Movement, were former members of Mapam. In his recent book *The Guilt of Jerusalem*, which dwells on the justification of Arab expulsion, Tzvi Shiloah explains that Moshe Shamir had read the manuscript of the book and has made significant contribution to it (p. 8).
39. Quoted in Ben-'Ami, *Sefer Eretz-Yisrael Hashlemah*, p. 192. See also an interview with General Aharon Davidi, ibid., pp. 199–203.
40. Ibid., p. 186.
41. Shlaim, 'Israel, the Great Powers, and the Middle East Crisis of 1958', pp. 183–84.
42. Kirsten Schulze, *Israel's Covert Diplomacy in Lebanon* (London: Macmillan Press, 1998).
43. Ibid., p. 2.
44. Ben-'Ami, *Sefer Eretz-Yisrael Hashlemah*, pp. 207–209.
45. Ibid., pp. 227–40.
46. *Zot Haaretz*, 6 November 1976, quoted in ibid., p. 33.
47. Schulze, *Israel's Covert Diplomacy in Lebanon*, p. 85.
48. Ben-'Ami, *Sefer Eretz-Yisrael Hashlemah*, p. 350.
49. Sprinzak, *The Ascendance of Israel's Radical Right*, p. 59.
50. See *Moznayim*, July 1967.
51. See for instance, Shim'on Ballas, in *Hamuah*, No. 2 (November 1967), p. 217.
52. Lustick, *For the Land and the Lord, p.* 104.
53. Israel Eldad, *The Jewish Revolution: Jewish Statehood* (New York: Shengold Publishers, 1971), pp. 134–35.
54. Yisrael Eldad, *Dagesh Hazak* [Strong Emphasis] (Tel Aviv: Schocken, 1989), pp. 69–71.
55. See 'Akiva Eldar and Amnon Barzalai in *Haaretz*, 7 September 1983, citing research carried out by Dr Amitzur Ilan on the affair of the assassination of Bernadotte; Amitzur Ilan, *Bernadotte in Palestine, 1948* (London: Macmillan, 1989), pp. 211–22.
56. Sprinzak, *The Ascendance of Israel's Radical Right*, p. 41.
57. See 'Eldad', in Susan Hattis Rolef (ed.), *Political Dictionary of the State of Israel*, 2nd edn, (New York: Macmillan, 1993), p. 90.
58. Sprinzak, *The Ascendance of Israel's Radical Right*, p. 41.

59. *Haumah*, No. 2 (November 1967), p. 217.
60. *Moledet*, Nos 22–23 (August–September 1990), p. 21.
61. David Hirst, *The Gun and the Olive Branch* (London: Faber and Faber, 1984), p. 378; Yisrael Eldad, 'The Transfer as a Zionist Solution', *Haaretz*, 9 July 1987; *Haumah*, No. 88 (Autumn 1987), pp. 11–13; Eldad, *Dagesh Hazak*, pp. 169–72.
62. Avraham Stern was the founder of Lehi (or the Stern Gang), which in the 1940s began a campaign of terrorism throughout Palestine.
63. Published in *De'ot* [Opinions], No. 35 (Winter 1968), quoted in Uri Davis and Norton Mezvinsky (eds), *Documents from Israel 1967–1973* (London: Ithaca Press, 1975), p. 187. *De'ot* is the organ of the religious academic professionals in Israel. See also Eldad, *The Jewish Revolution*.
64. *Haaretz*, 9 July 1987; *Yedi'ot Aharonot*, 26 February 1988, p. 15.
65. *Moledet*, No. 4 (January 1989), p. 3; *Moledet*, Nos 22–23 (August–September 1990), p. 21.
66. Excerpts from the interview were published in *Moledet*, No. 8 (June 1989), p. 6.
67. *Sunday Times* (London), 15 June 1969; John K. Cooley, *Green March, Black September* (London: Frank Cass, 1973), pp. 196–97.
68. Balata refugee camp exists within the municipal boundaries of Nablus. The Dehayshe camp is in the Hebron area.
69. Two well-known refugee camps within the municipal boundaries of Beirut.
70. *Moledet*, No. 8 (June 1989), p. 6. On 26 August 1982, after Israel invaded Lebanon, Eldad wrote an article entitled 'Arab Repatriation', in which he called for forcibly 'dispersing' half a million Palestinian refugees to 'at least eight Arab countries': see Eldad, *Dagesh Hazak*, pp. 167–68.
71. In 1968, the editor of *Zot Haaretz* was Yisrael Harel who later became the editor of *Nekudah*, the most important organ of the Gush Emunim settlers.
72. See Tzvi Shiloah in *Davar*, 3 July 1967, p. 4.
73. Shiloah, *Ashmat Yerushalayim*, p. 24.
74. Ibid., p. 13.
75. Tzvi Shiloah, *Eretz Gdolah Le'am Gadol* [A Great Land for a Great People], (Tel Aviv: Otpaz, 1970), pp. 33–34.
76. Ibid.
77. Ibid. Some of Schwadron's articles were published in his book *Mishne 'Ivre Hasha'ah* (1946).
78. Shiloah, *Eretz Gdolah Le'am Gadol*, ibid.
79. Ibid., pp. 115–16 and 129.
80. Tzvi Shiloah, 'The Destiny of Greater Israel in its Ancient Land', in Ben-'Ami, *Sefer Eretz-Yisrael Hashlemah*, pp. 213–40.
81. Shiloah, *Eretz Gdolah Le'am Gadol*, p. 107.
82. Ibid., p. 108.
83. Names of two adjoining settlements in the Esdraelon valley.
84. The inhabitants of the Arab village Fuleh were uprooted to make way for Merhavyah.
85. A kibbutz in the Esdraelon valley, established in 1926 and affiliated with Hashomer Hatza'ir movement.

86. Shiloah, *Eretz Gdolah Le'am Gadol*, p. 102.
87. Ibid., p. 104; Shiloah, *Ashmat Yerushalayim*, p. 8.
88. Shiloah, *Eretz Gdolah Le'am Gadol*, p. 105.
89. Shiloah, *Ashmat Yerushalayim*, p. 196.
90. Tzvi Shiloah, *Zot Haaretz*, No. 202, 16 April 1976.
91. All these are biblical names for places situated in the modern state of Jordan.
92. Shiloah, *Eretz Gdolah Le'am Gadol*, p. 115.
93. See Joshua Brilliant in the *Jerusalem Post*, 23 February 1988.
94. Shiloah, *Ashmat Yerushalayim*, pp. 264–65.
95. See *Moledet*, No. 12 (October 1989), p. 11.
96. Shiloah, *Ashmat Yerushalayim*, p. 266.
97. *Moledet*, No. 12 (October 1989), pp. 10–11.
98. *Moledet*, No. 8 (June 1989), p. 12.
99. Amnon Rubinstein, *The Zionist Dream Revisited: From Herzl to Gush Emunim and Back* (New York: Schocken Books, 1984), pp. 99–100.

NOTES TO CHAPTER TWO

1. The full name of the Revisionist party was 'Union of Zionists-Revisionists – HaTzohar'.
2. Bernard Wasserstein, 'The British Mandate in Palestine: Myths and Realities', *Middle Eastern Lectures* (Tel Aviv: Moshe Dayan Centre, 1995), pp. 31–32.
3. Mordechai Nisan, 'The Middle East between History and Reality', *Middle East Focus* 8, No. 6 (1986), p. 20; Paul Riebenfeld, 'The Integrity of Palestine', *Midstream* 21, No. 7 (1975), p. 8; William Ziff, *The Rape of Palestine* (New York: Longmans Green, 1938), pp. 98–9; Joan Peters, *From Time Immemorial* (New York: Harper and Row, 1984), p. 239.
4. Quoted in Lenni Brenner, *The Iron Wall: Zionist Revisionism from Jabotinsky to Shamir* (London: Zed Books, 1984), pp. 74–75.
5. Simha Flapan, *The Birth of Israel: Myths and Realities* (New York: Pantheon Books, 1987), pp. 36–37.
6. For further discussion of Jabotinsky's strategy, see Joseph Schechtman, *The Jabotinsky Story: Fighter and Prophet* (New York: Thomas Yoseloff, 1956), p. 324. See also *The Israel Shahak Papers*, No. 31, 'Collection on Jabotinsky: His Life and Excerpts from his Writings', p. 16.
7. Cited in Yossi Melman and Dan Raviv, 'Expelling Palestinians', *Washington Post*, Outlook section, 7 February 1988.
8. Ya'acov Shavit, *Jabotinsky and the Revisionist Movement 1925–1948* (London: Frank Cass, 1988), p. 264.
9. Cited in Ya'acov Shavit, 'The Attitude of Zionist Revisionism towards the Arabs', in *Zionism and the Arab Question* (in Hebrew), (Jerusalem: Zalman Shazar Centre, 1979), p. 74.
10. See Joseph Schechtman, *Rebel and Statesman: The Vladimir Jabotinsky Story, The Early Years* (New York: Thomas Yoseloff, 1956), p. 54.
11. Colin Shindler, *Israel, Likud and the Zionist Dream* (London: I.B. Tauris, 1995) p. 15.

12. Ibid., p. 177.
13. Brenner, *The Iron Wall*, pp. 194–199.
14. Cited in Amos Perlmutter, *The Life and Times of Menachem Begin* (New York: Doubleday and Company, 1987), p. 212.
15. Cited in Yosef Heller, 'Between Messianism and Realpolitik – Lehi and the Arab Question, 1940–1947', in Israel Gutman (ed.), *Yahdut Zemanenu* [Contemporary Jewry], A Research Annual, Vol. 1, 1984, p. 225.
16. Shindler, *Israel, Likud and the Zionist Dream*, p. xviii.
17. Quoted in ibid., p. 176.
18. Quoted in Emmanuel Katz, *Lechi: Fighters for the Freedom of Israel* (Tel Aviv: Lechi Memorial Committee and Yair Publishers, 1987), pp. 18–19.
19. Lohamei Herut Yisrael (Lehi), *Ketavim* [Writings], Vol. 2 (Tel Aviv, 1960), p. 581; *Ketavim*, Vol. 1 (Tel Aviv, 1959), pp. 27–28; Heller, 'Between Messianism and Realpolitik', pp. 204–207 and 237–39.
20. Quoted in Shavit, *Jabotinsky and the Revisionist Movement*, p. 267.
21. Samuel Katz, *Days of Fire* (London: W.H. Allen, 1968), pp. 31–37.
22. Benny Morris, *The Birth of the Palestinian Refugee Problem, 1947–1949* (Cambridge: Cambridge University Press, 1987), pp. 113–115.
23. Quoted in Joseph Heller, *The Stern Gang: Ideology, Politics and Terror, 1940–1949* (London: Frank Cass, 1995), p. 209.
24. Published in New York by W.W. Norton & Company, 1943.
25. Masalha, *Expulsion of the Palestinians: The Concept of 'Transfer' in Zionist Political Thought, 1882–1948* (Washington, DC: Institute for Palestine Studies, 1992), pp. 162–64.
26. Eliahu Ben-Horin, *The Middle East: Crossroads of History* (New York: W.W. Norton & Company, 1943), pp. 230–31.
27. Ibid., pp. 232–34.
28. Ibid.
29. Ben-Horin's file, A 300/54, CZA.
30. Ibid.
31. I first came across the manuscript of Schechtman's 'study' in Weitz's Papers, at the Institute for Settlement Studies, Rehovot, in 1989. In 1993 I saw a copy of the same manuscript in Weitz's Papers, in the Central Zionist Archives in Jerusalem.
32. Joseph Schechtman, 'The Case for Arab–Jewish Exchange of Population', manuscript in Weitz's Papers, Institute for Settlement Study, Rehovot, pp. 75–6.
33. Ibid., p. 103.
34. For further discussion of Ben-Horin's plan of transfer to Iraq, 1943–48, see Masalha, *Expulsion of the Palestinians*, pp. 161–65; Ben-Horin, *Crossroads of History*, pp. 224–37.
35. Masalha, *Expulsion of the Palestinians*, pp. 162–64.
36. Schechtman, 'The Case for Arab–Jewish Exchange of Population', p. 156.
37. Joseph Schechtman, New York, to Eliyahu Epstein, Washington DC, letter dated 20 May 1948, in Jabotinsky Institute, Schechtman's Papers, F. 2/10/227.

38. Ibid., pp. 103–104.
39. Ibid., p. 158.
40. Ibid., pp. 160–61.
41. Ibid., p. 163.
42. From Arthur Lourie, Consulate General of Israel, New York, to Moshe Shertok (Sharett), Foreign Minister, letter dated 15 October 1948, in Israel State Archives (ISA), Foreign Ministry, 2402/15.
43. From Joseph B. Schechtman to 'Ezra Danin, Israeli Ministry of Foreign Affairs, letter dated 7 December 1948, in Jabotinsky Institute, Schechtman's Papers, file F. 2/10/227.
44. Moshe Shertok, Paris, to Dr Schechtman, New York, letter dated 17 December 1948, Foreign Ministry, 2402/15.
45. For further discussion of Norman's plan, see Masalha, *Expulsion of the Palestinians*, pp. 141–55; Moshe Shertok, Paris, to Edward Norman, letter dated 17 December 1948, Foreign Ministry, 2402/15.
46. Ibid., p. 164.
47. Epstein to Schechtman, letter dated 18 May 1948, in Jabotinsky Institute, Schechtman's Papers, F. 1/10/227.
48. Edward Norman, to Foreign Minister Moshe Shertok, letter dated 24 December 1948, Foreign Ministry, 2402/15.
49. Joseph B. Schechtman, *Population Transfers in Asia* (New York: Hallsby Press, 1949), pp. 84–145.
50. Joseph B. Schechtman, *The Arab Refugee Problem* (New York: Philosophical Library, 1952).
51. Schechtman's letter to Hoover, dated 9 April 1949, in Jabotinsky Institute, Schechtman's Papers, File F. 1/11/227.
52. Perlmutter, *The Life and Times of Menachem Begin*, p. 24.
53. Eric Silver, *Begin: A Biography* (London: Weidenfeld and Nicolson, 1984), p. 12.
54. *Divrie Haknesset* [Knesset Debates], Vol. 1, p. 65, 3 August 1949.
55. Ibid., p. 107, 3 September 1949.
56. *Divrei Haknesset*, 3 May 1950.
57. *Herut*, 2 April 1954; Sasson Sofer, *Begin: An Anatomy of Leadership* (Oxford: Basil Blackwell, 1988), p.225.
58. *Jewish Herald* (Johannesburg), 26 April 1957.
59. Quoted in Shindler, *Israel, Likud and the Zionist Dream*, p. 57.
60. Silver, *Begin*, p. 138.
61. See Moshe Dotan 'Rov 'Ivri Ketzad?' [A Hebrew Majority How?], *Haumah*, No. 2 (November 1967), pp. 242–49.
62. Ibid., p. 244.
63. Ibid., p. 243.
64. Ibid., pp. 245–46.
65. Ibid., pp. 246–47.
66. Ibid., pp. 246 and 248.
67. Ibid., pp. 248, 249 and 242.
68. Moshe Dotan, 'Ye'odenu Haleumi Bazmam Hahadsh', [Our National Mission in the Contemporary Time], *Haumah*, No. 1 (May 1981), p. 39.
69. Shindler, *Israel, Likud and the Zionist Dream*, p. xvii.

70. Jimmy Carter, *The Blood of Abraham* (Boston: Houghton Mifflin Company, 1985), p. 42.
71. Silver, *Begin*, p. 160.
72. Ian Lustick, *For the Land and the Lord: Jewish Fundamentalism in Israel* (New York: Council on Foreign Relations, 1988), p. 47.
73. Ibid., p. 40.
74. David Neuman, *Population, Settlement and Conflict: Israel and the West Bank* (Cambridge: Cambridge University Press, 1991), pp. 21 and 34.
75. See 'Settlement Monitor', *Journal of Palestine Studies*, 91 (Spring 1994), p. 127.
76. See 'Excerpts from Israel Foreign Minister's Speech', in *New York Times*, 6 October 1981, p. 10. See also Yitzhak Shamir, 'Israel's Role in a Changing Middle East', *Foreign Affairs* 60 (Spring 1982), p. 791.
77. Shindler, *Israel, Likud and the Zionist Dream*, p. 221.
78. Ibid., p. 187.
79. Ibid., p. xviii.
80. Yitzhak Rabin wrote a hard-line article in *Yedi'ot Aharonot* on 28 February 1992 stating that he would keep at least half of the occupied territories under Israel's control, and would step up the settlement drive in the Golan Heights. However, he added that he would oppose 'politically motivated' settlements in the West Bank. Cited by Haim Baram, in *Middle East International*, No. 420, 6 March 1992, p. 6.
81. David Hirst, *The Gun and the Olive Branch* (London: Faber and Faber, 2nd edn, 1984), p. 398.
82. Cited in Elfi Pallis, 'The Likud Party: A Primer', *Journal of Palestine Studies* 21, No. 2 (Winter 1992), pp. 42–43.
83. Ibid., p. 43.
84. Quoted in Ian Lustick, 'The Fetish of Jerusalem: A Hegemonic Analysis', in Michael Barnett (ed.), *Israel in Comparative Perspective* (New York: State University of New York Press, 1996), p. 144.
85. See Danny Rubinstein in *Davar*, 26 January 1979, p. 17; Noam Chomsky, *Fateful Triangle* (London: Pluto Press, 1983), pp. 48–49.
86. See Yossi Melman and Dan Raviv, 'Expelling Palestinians', *Washington Post*, Outlook section, 7 February 1988.
87. Cited in Tzvi Shiloah, *Ashmat Yerushalayim* [The Guilt of Jerusalem] (Tel Aviv: Karni Press, 1989), p. 188.
88. Moshe Yegar, 'Hatziyonut, Medinat Yisrael Vehashelah Ha'arvit', [Zionism, the State of Israel and the Arab Question], *Haumah*, No. 2, May 1979, pp. 177–85.
89. Ibid., pp. 184–85. On 14 October 1983, the writer Moshe Shamir (a co-founder of the Whole Land of Israel movement) wrote in praise of Schwadron's maximalist views and advocacy of Arab transfer. See Moshe Shamir, *Hamakom Hayarok* [The Green Place] (Tel Aviv: Dvir Publishing House, 1991), pp. 95–99.
90. Holger H. Herwig, 'Geopolitik: Haushofer, Hitler and Lebensraum', *Journal of Strategic Studies* 22, Nos 2/3 (June/September 1999), pp. 218–41.
91. Samuel Katz, *Battleground: Fact and Fantasy in Palestine* (London: W.H. Allen, 1973), p. 205; Michael Palumbo, *Imperial Israel* (London:

Bloomsbury, 1990), p. 130; Herwig, 'Geopolitik: Haushofer, Hitler and Lebensraum', pp. 218–41.

92. Katz, *Battleground*, p. 224.
93. *Haumah*, Summer 1989, cited in *Moledet*, No. 11, September 1989, p. 11.
94. See Shiloah, *Ashmat Yerushalayim*, p. 8.
95. Shlomo Lev-'Ami, *Haim Hatziyonut Nikhshelah* [Did Zionism Fail?], (Tel Aviv: 'Ami Press, 1988).
96. Ibid., p. 298.
97. Ibid., pp. 298–99.
98. Robert Friedman, 'Hagai Lev – Revisionist', *Present Tense*, Autumn 1982, p. 20, quoted in Brenner, *The Iron Wall*, p. 176.
99. Shindler, *Israel, Likud and the Zionist Dream*, p. xviii.
100. Cited in Ilan Peleg, *Begin's Foreign Policy* (New York: Greenwood Press, 1987), p. 173.
101. Amos Perlmutter, 'Begin's Rhetoric and Sharon's Tactics', *Foreign Affairs*, Fall 1982.
102. Amos Perlmutter, *New York Times*, 17 May 1982.
103. Reported in the Hebrew press on 18 July 1988, quoted in Israel Shahak, 'A History of the Concept of Transfer in Zionism', *Journal of Palestine Studies* 18, No. 3 (Spring 1989), p. 32.
104. Harold H. Saunders, 'An Israeli–Palestinian Peace', *Foreign Affairs*, Fall 1982.
105. See, for instance, Meron Benvenisti, *The West Bank Data Project: A survey of Israel's Policies* (Washington, DC: American Enterprise Institute, 1984). Already in 1982 Benvenisti had argued that Israel's policies of settlement, land seizure and resource control had laid the basis for a virtual annexation of the West Bank, which may well be irreversible. See David Richardson in *The Jerusalem Post*, 10 September 1982.
106. Mattityahu Peled in *Middle East International*, 14 August 1981.
107. *The Jerusalem Post*, 10 September 1982.
108. *Ma'ariv*, cited in *International Herald Tribune*, 26 January 1981.
109. Cited in *Haaretz*, 23 May 1980, p. 5.
110. Arieh Ya'ari, 'Irreversible Annexation?', *New Outlook* 27, No. 5 (May 1984), p. 18.
111. Avishai, *The Tragedy of Zionism* (New York: Farrar, Straus & Giroux, 1985), p. 298. See also Yossi Melman and Dan Raviv, 'A Final solution to the Palestinian Problem', *Guardian Weekly*, 21 February 1988.
112. *'Al-Hamishmar*, 16 April 1982.
113. See Amos Wollin in *Middle East International*, 23 April 1982, pp. 3–4.
114. BBC: ME/6025/A2.
115. See Yossi Melman and Dan Raviv, 'Expelling Palestinians', *Washington Post*, Outlook section, 7 February 1988.
116. Quoted after Ian Lustick, *Arabs in the Jewish State* (Austin: University of Texas Press, 1980), p. 258.
117. David Bernstein (reporting from Jerusalem), 'Forcible removal of Arabs gaining support in Israel', *The Times* (London), 24 August 1988, p. 7.

118. Melman and Raviv, 'Expelling Palestinians', *Jerusalem Post*, 25 December 1987, p. 6 and 23 February 1988.
119. *Ma'ariv*, 23 June 1989.
120. *Ma'ariv*, 18 September 1979, pp. 1 and 15.
121. Cited in Meir Kahane, *Lesikim Be'enekhem* [They Shall be Strings in Your Eyes] (Jerusalem: Hamakhon Lara'ayon Hayehudi, 1980/1981), p. 230.
122. See Yosef Harif in *Ma'ariv*, 8 December 1976.
122. *Divrei Haknesset*, 19 May 1976, p. 2677.
123. David Shipler, *New York Times*, 4 April 1983, citing Meir Cohen-Avidov's remarks; also Nisan, *Hamedinah Hayehudit Vehabe'ayah Ha'arvit* [The Jewish State and the Arab Problem] (Tel Aviv: Hadar, 1986), p. 119.
124. Cited in *Jewish Post and Opinion*, 30 March 1983.
125. Cited by Eliakim Ha'etzni, a Tehiya Party MK, in Yair Kotler, *Heil Kahane* (New York: Adama Books, 1986), p. 173.
126. See Zeev Schiff and Ehud Ya'ari, *Intifada: The Palestinian Uprising – Israel's Third Front* (New York: Simon and Schuster, 1989), p. 95; Benny Morris, *Jerusalem Post International*, 3 October 1987; Arie Haskel (reporting from Jerusalem), *Observer* (London), 12 June 1988, p. 22; David Bernstein (reporting from Jerusalem), 'Forcible removal of Arabs gaining support in Israel', *The Times* (London), 24 August 1988, p. 7.
127. See Yair Kotler in *Ma'ariv*, 8 October 1982, p. 19.
128. See Dan Leon in *New Outlook*, December 1990–January 1991, p. 46.
129. See Melman and Raviv, 'Expelling Palestinians'.
130. *Ma'ariv*, 23 June 1989.
131. Netanyahu was also quoted by the weekend paper *Hotam* as saying: 'Israel should have exploited the repression of the demonstrations in China, when world attention focused on that country, to carry out mass expulsions amongst the Arabs of the territories. Regrettably, there was not support for this policy, which I put forward then and still recommend.' Cited in Elfi Pallis, 'The Likud Party: A Primer', in *Journal of Palestine Studies* 21, No. 2 (Winter 1992), p. 57. Interestingly, Netanyahu's father used to edit the right-wing daily *Yarden*, which in recent years carried a number of articles in favour of transfer.
132. See Joshua Brilliant, *Jerusalem Post*, 23 February 1988.
133. Kotler, *Heil Kahane*, pp. 88–89.
134. Ibid., p. 89. Kotler adds: 'This was later confirmed for me by one of Mrs Meir's spokesmen from that period.' Both *Haaretz* and *Yedi'ot Aharonot* reported on 25 October 1972 that Golda Meir once said that she could not sleep at night and was kept awake by the thought of all the Arab babies who were being born at that time.
135. See *Yedi'ot Aharonot*, 3 February 1991. Subsequently, Pappo published several articles in *Yedi'ot Aharonot* calling for the imposition of collective punishment on the Palestinians and the expulsion of their leaders. See *Yedi'ot Aharonot*, 22 April 1990 and 17 June 1990. Other Likud activists, such as Shim'on Gur, a member of the Herut Centre, and Eli Lopaz, the secretary of the Likud branch in the town of Holon, voiced openly their support for the 'transfer' solution of Moledet. See *Moledet*, No. 30, April 1991, pp. 13–14. *Yedi'ot Aharonot* also published

on 15 February 1991 another article in support of transfer written by Eliahu 'Amikam, a well-known journalist, former member of Lehi and supporter of Greater Israel.

136. Quoted in Nabeel Abraham, 'Making Israel's War Plans Disappear', *Lies of our Times* (New York), Vol. 1, No. 2 (November 1990), p. 20.

137. See Ian Black in the *Guardian*, 2 February 1991.

138. Shindler, *Israel, Likud and the Zionist Dream*, p. 262.

139. 'Oded Yinon, 'A Strategy for Israel in the 1980s', *Kivunim*, (Jerusalem), No. 8 (February 1982), pp. 53–58 (in Hebrew).

140. Yehoshafat Harkabi, *Hakhra'ot Goraliyot* [Fateful Decisions] (Tel Aviv: 'Am 'Oved, 1986), pp. 74–75.

141. Quoted in Vince Beiser, 'Fear of a New 1948: Palestinian Reactions to Soviet Jewish Immigration', *New Outlook* (December 1990/January 1991), pp. 18–19. The large-scale immigration of Soviet Jews raises the question whether this immigration will alter radically the demographic make-up of Israel and the occupied territories. Professor Sergio Della Pergola, a specialist in Jewish demography at Hebrew University, wrote in early 1991 that every group of 100,000 new (net) Jewish immigrants may result in a postponement of one year in the expected date when Arabs and Jews in Israel and the occupied territories reach a numerical balance of 50 per cent each. With half a million immigrants, this date might be in 2020; with one million, in 2025; and with one and a half in 2030. Sergio Della Pergola, 'Demography in Perspective', *New Outlook* (December 1990/ January 1991), p. 27.

142. Reserve General Aharon Yariv, a former Chief of Army Intelligence and now head of the Institute for Strategic Studies in Tel Aviv, is a typical 'demographic dove'. See interview with Yariv in *Ma'ariv*, 13 February 1987.

143. Quoted in Palumbo, *Imperial Israel*, p. 303.

144. Ibid., p. 304.

145. Cited in Julian Borger, 'Frontier spirit thrives in little Russia', the *Guardian*, 7 April 1998, p. 11

146. Ibid.

147. Cited in the *Guardian*, 7 April 1998, p. 11.

148. Ibid.

149. Shindler, *Israel, Likud and the Zionist Dream*, pp. 221–22.

150. Ibid., p. 223.

151. Ibid., p. 288.

152. Ibid., p. 284.

153. Ibid., pp. 285 and 288.

154. Quoted in Shyam Bhatia, 'Israel to squeeze Arabs from holy city', *The Observer*, 9 June 1996, p. 19.

NOTES TO CHAPTER THREE

1. Ian Lustick, *For the Land and the Lord: Jewish Fundamentalism in Israel* (New York: Council on Foreign Relations, 1988), pp. ix, 12–16, 153.

2. Ian Lustick, 'Israel's Dangerous Fundamentalists', *Foreign Policy*, Fall 1987, pp. 118–39.
3. Ibid., p. 127.
4. Yosef Gorny, *The State of Israel in Jewish Public Thought* (London: Macmillan, 1994), p. 150.
5. Ehud Sprinzak, *The Ascendance of Israel's Radical Right* (Oxford and New York: Oxford University Press, 1991), p. 113.
6. Lustick, *For the Land and the Lord*, p. 107.
7. David Shaham, *Yedi'ot Aharonot* supplement, 13 April 1979, cited in Donald S. Will, 'Zionist Settlement Policy', *Journal of Palestine Studies* 11, No. 3 (Summer 1979), p. 40.
8. Yehuda Elitzur, 'The Borders of Eretz Israel in the Jewish Tradition', in Avner Tomaschoff (ed.), *Whose Homeland* (Jerusalem: The World Zionist Organization, 1978), pp. 42–53.
9. Shindler, Colin, *Israel, Likud and the Zionist Dream* (London: I.B. Tauris, 1995), p. 155.
10. Yehuda Elitzur, 'Is Lebanon also the Land of Israel?', *Nekudah*, No. 48 (no date), pp. 10–13, cited in Lustick, *For the Land and the Lord*, p. 107.
11. *Ma'ariv*, 3 October 1982.
12. *Ma'ariv*, 18 March 1983.
13. *Nekudah*, 12 November 1982, p. 23, quoted in Lustick, *For the Land and the Lord*, pp. 107–108.
14. Shindler, *Israel, Likud and the Zionist Dream*, p. 155.
15. Ibid., p. 156.
16. Ibid., p. 193.
17. Lustick, *For the Land and the Lord*, p. 61.
18. *Koteret Rashit*, 14 November 1984, p. 23.
19. Lustick, *For the Land and the Lord*, p. 107.
20. Tzvi Yehuda Kook, 'Between the People and its Land', *Artzi*, Vol. 2 (1982), p. 19.
21. Lustick, *For the Land and the Lord*, p. 106.
22. *Nekudah*, No. 43, 12 May 1982, p. 17.
23. Lustick, *For the Land and the Lord*, pp. 8, 12–15; David Schnall, 'An Impact Assessment', in David Newman (ed.), *The Impact of Gush Emunim* (London: Croom Helm, 1985), p. 15.
24. Sprinzak, *The Ascendance of Israel's Radical Right*, p. 107.
25. Lustick, *For the Land and the Lord*, pp. 8–9.
26. D. Newman, 'Gush Emunim', in *New Encyclopedia of Zionism and Israel* (London and Toronto: Associated University Presses, 1994), Vol. 1, p. 533.
27. Cited in Masalha, *A Land Without a People: Israel, Transfer and the Palestinians, 1949–1996* (London: Faber and Faber, 1997), p. 143; Said Zeedani, 'Democratic Citizenship and the Arabs in Israel', in Nur Masalha (ed.), *The Palestinians in Israel* (Nazareth: Galilee Centre for Social Research, 1993), p. 72; Sa'id Zeedani, 'The Argument of Minister Hammer', *Al-Midan* (Nazareth), 23 March 1990.
28. Cited in Sprinzak, *The Ascendance of Israel's Radical Right*, p. 346, note 20.

29. For details of the survey, which was conducted by the Tzomet Institute, see 'The Rabbis of Judea, Samaria, and Gaza: Encourage the Emigration of the Arabs', *Nekudah*, November 1987, p. 37.

30. Cited in Clive Jones, 'Ideo-Theology and the Jewish State: From Conflict to Conciliation?' *British Journal of Middle Eastern Studies* 26, No. 1 (May 1999), p. 19.

31. Ibid.

32. See Eti Ronel, 'Inside Israel: The Battle over Temple Mount', *New Outlook*, February 1984, p. 12.

33. Jones, 'Ideo-Theology and the Jewish State', pp. 11–14; Michael Prior, 'Settling for God', *Middle East International*, No. 565, 19 December 1997, pp. 20–21.

34. Jones, 'Ideo-Theology and the Jewish State', p. 12.

35. Quoted in David Schnall, *Beyond the Green Line* (New York: Praeger & Co., 1984), p. 19.

36. Shaham, *Yedi'ot Aharonot* supplement, 13 April 1979.

37. See Kook's article in *Hatzofeh*, 23 June 1967. The article was also printed in a collection entitled *Hakol* [Everything], edited by Aharon Ben-'Ami.

38. Quoted in Rabbi Pichnik (ed.), *Shanah Beshanah, 5728* [Year by Year] (in Hebrew) (Jerusalem: Hekhal Shlomo Publication, 1968), pp. 108–109.

39. Shlomo Aviner, 'Haumah Veartzah', [The People and its Land], *Artzi* [My Country] (Jerusalem, 1982), p. 11.

40. Quoted in *'Al-Hamishmar*, 8 February 1980.

41. Shlomo Aviner, 'Yerushat Haaretz Vehabe'ayah Hamuosarit' [The Inheritance of the Land and the Moral Problem] *Artzi* [My Country] (Jerusalem, 1983), p. 10.

42. Tzvi Yehuda Kook, 'Bein 'Am Veartzo' [Between People and Its Land], *Artzi* [My Country], p. 10.

43. Cited in *Journal of Palestine Studies* 10, No. 1 (Autumn 1980), p. 150; Danny Rubinstein, *Mi La-H' Elai: Gush Emunim* [On the Lord's Side: Gush Emunim] (Tel Aviv: Hakibbutz Hameuhad Publishing House, 1982), p. 91. The settlers' statements were also published in the Gush Emunim journal *Nekudah*. See Yehuda Litani in *Haaretz*, 15 May 1984, p. 15. Another settler of 'Ofra, echoing the widely publicised aphorism of the late Prime Minister Golda Meir, said in June 1980: 'After all there are no Palestinian people. We invented them, but they don't exist (see *Jerusalem Post International*, 8–14 June 1980).

44. David Grossman, *The Yellow Wind* (London: Jonathan Cape, 1988), p. 207.

45. Quoted in *Jerusalem Post International*, 30 January 1988.

46. In recent years a very large number of settlers in the West Bank have written in support of Arab expulsion. For examples, see Tzvi Samorai, a member of the Ariel council, in *Moledet*, Nos 28–29 (February–March 1991), p. 31; Tuvia Simhon of Ariel in *Moledet*, Nos 31–32 (May 1991), p. 27; Eli'ezer Betinski of Ariel, in *Moledet*, No. 6 (March–April 1989), p. 14; No'ami Brokhi of Efrat in *Moledet*, No. 17 (March 1990), p. 28; Bo'az Schwartz of Kokhav Yair in *Moledet*, Nos 22–23 (August–September 1990), p. 26; Rabbi Eli'ezer Rabinovitch of Ma'ale

Adomim in *Moledet*, Nos 31–32 (May 1991), p. 10; Shoshana Helkiyahu of Kiryat Arba'a in *Moledet*, Nos 35–36 (August–September 1991), p. 26.
47. See Meron Benvenisti (with Ziad Abu-Zayed and Danny Rubinstein), *The West Bank Handbook* (Jerusalem: Jerusalem Post, 1986), p. 160.
48. See Yisrael Rosen in *Nekudah*, November 1987.
49. Rubinstein, *Mi La-H' Elai*, pp. 90–93 and 151.
50. Geoffrey Aronson, *Israel, Palestinians and the Intifada* (London: Kegan Paul, 1990), p. 289.
51. Amnon Kapeliouk in *'Al-Hamishmar*, 8 February 1980.
52. Cited in Amnon Kapeliouk in *Le Monde Diplomatique*, June 1980.
53. David Forman in *Jerusalem Post*, 22 June 1990.
54. Sprinzak, *The Ascendance of Israel's Radical Right*, p. 107.
55. Amnon Kapeliouk in *Le Monde Diplomatique*, June 1980; *Le Monde*, 19 June 1980.
56. Rubinstein, *Mi La-H' Elai*, pp. 157–59.
57. Sprinzak, *The Ascendance of Israel's Radical Right*, p. 130; Newman, 'Gush Emunim', p. 533.
58. Ibid.
59. Lawrence Joffe, *Keesing's Guide to the Mid-East Peace Process* (London: Cartermill Publishing, 1996), p. 153.
60. Lustick, *For the Land and the Lord*, p. 10.
61. Newman, 'Gush Emunim', p. 533.
62. Lawrence, *Keesing's Guide to Mid-East Peace Process*, p. 153.
63. See Dedi Zucker, *Report on Human Rights in the Occupied Territories, 1979–83*, International Centre for Peace in the Middle East (Tel Aviv, 1983), pp. 51–52; Lustick, *For the Land and the Lord*, p. 66.
64. Ibid.; Jan Demarest Abu Shakra, *Israeli Settler Violence in the Occupied Territories: 1980–1984* (Chicago: Palestine Human Rights Campaign, 1985), p. 15.
65. Quoted in Elfi Pallis in *Middle East International*, 24 April 1981, p. 12.
66. Joffe, *Keesing's Guide to the Mid-East Peace Process*, p. 153; Lustick, *For the Land and the Lord*, p. 67.
67. Cited in Rubinstein, *Mi La-H' Elai*, p. 91.
68. Joffe, *Keesing's Guide to the Mid-East Peace Process*, p. 153.
69. Husam Suwaylim in *Al-Hayat* (London), 29 December 1999, p. 14.
70. Lustick, *For the Land and the Lord*, pp. 68–69.
71. Ibid., p. 69.
72. Benvenisti, *The West Bank Handbook*, p. 135.
73. Ibid.
74. *New York Times*, 4 June 1980.
75. *Newsweek*, 16 June 1980; Rubinstein, *Mi La-H' Elai*, p. 94.
76. Quoted in Friedman, *Zealots for Zion: Inside Israel's West Bank Settlement Movement* (New York: Random House, 1992), p. 80. Haggai publishes a regular column in the Hebrew daily *Hadashot*. Friedman added: 'Many settlers told me that the worse they can make life for the Arabs, the easier it will be to drive them across the Jordan River.' Friedman also observed that the sentiment for transfer is particularly strong in the town of Ariel. Ibid., pp. 80–81.
77. Newman, 'Gush Emunim', p. 533.

78. Shindler, *Israel, Likud and the Zionist Dream*, pp. 200 and 204.
79. See Israel Shahak, 'Israeli apartheid and the intifada', *Race & Class* 3, No. 1 (1988), p. 3.
80. See Pinchas Inbari, 'Underground: Political background and psychological atmosphere', *New Outlook* (June–July 1984), pp. 10–11.
81. Shindler, *Israel, Likud and the Zionist Dream*, p. 200.
82. Lustick, *For the Land and the Lord*, pp. 11–12.
83. Joffe, *Keesing's Guide to the Mid-East Peace Process*, p. 153.
84. See *Haaretz*, 25 September 1984, p. 9, and 30 May 1985.
85. See Yehoshafat Harkabi's letter in *Haaretz*, 11 May 1984, p. 22.
86. See Avi Shlaim, 'The last testament of Yehoshafat Harkabi', *Middle East International*, 5 January 1996, p. 18.
87. Jones, 'Ideo-Theology and the Jewish State', p. 14.
88. Yisrael Ariel, 'Dvarim Kehavayatam' [Things As They Are], *Tzippiyah* (Jerusalem, 1980).
89. Quoted in Amnon Rubinstein, *Mehertzel 'Ad Gush Emunim Uvehazarah* [From Herzl to Gush Emunim and Back Again] (Tel Aviv: Schocken Press, 1980), p. 123. Amnon Rubinstein's reference is *Haaretz*, 9 May 1976.
90. Shlomo Dov Wolpo (ed.), *Da'at Torah Be'inyanei Hamatzav Beeretz Hakodesh* [The Opinion of Torah Regarding the Situation in the Holy Land] (Kiryat Gat, 1979), p. 146, note no. 4.
91. Ibid. p. 145.
92. 'Amos Ben-Vered in *Haaretz*, 23 October 1979, p. 8.
93. *Ma'ariv*, 14 June 1985.
94. *Ma'ariv*, 5 July 1985, p. 19.
95. Tzvi Yehuda Kook, 'Between A People and its Land', *Artzi*, Vol. 2 (Spring 1982), p. 19.
96. *Bat Kol*, 26 February 1980. In fact the association of the Palestinians with the ancient Amalekites was made in a book written in 1974 by Rabbi Moshe Ben-Tzion Ishbezari, the Rabbi of Ramat Gan. See *Yedi'ot Aharonot*, 20 December 1974.
97. *Bat Kol*, 26 February 1980; 1 Samuel, 15:3.
98. Ibid.
99. Rubinstein, *Mehertzel 'Ad Gush Emunim*, p. 125.
100. Ibid., p. 179.
101. See for instance *Torah Ve'avodah* [Torah and Work], No. 6 (Jerusalem, 1984).
102. Uriel Tal in *Haaretz*, 26 September 1984, p. 27; Hanna Kim, 'To Annihilate Amalek', *'Al-Hamishmar*, 12 March 1984; Yoram Peri, 'Expulsion is not the Final Stage', *Davar*, 3 August 1984; Yehoshu'a Rash, 'Uriel Tal's Legacy', *Gesher* (Summer 1986), No. 114, p. 77.
103. The article was also quoted in *Israeli Press Brief*, No. 28.
104. Ariel, 'Dvarim Kehavayatam'.
105. Rubinstein, *Mehertzel 'Ad Gush Emunim*, p. 124.
106. Ibid.
107. Mordechai Nisan, *Hamedinah Hayehudit Vehabe'ayah Ha'arvit* [The Jewish State and the Arab Problem] (Tel Aviv: Hadar, 1986), and second edition (Jerusalem: Rubin Mass, 1987).

108. In fact the emphasis on separation and the rejection of coexistence between Israeli Jews and the Palestinians is deeply rooted in Labour Zionism: the novelist A.B. Yehoshu'a, who is in favour of giving up the occupied territories writes: 'The most important thing is separation between us and the Palestinians, the partitioning of the country between the two peoples, this is the supreme task ...' A.B. Yehoshu'a, *Hakir Vehahar* [The Wall and the Mountain] (Tel Aviv: Zmora-Beitan, 1989), p. 188. Yehoshu'a also explained that he did not ask the Israeli Arab novelist Anton Shammas 'to go to Kuwait, Saudi Arabia or Transjordan', implying that if Shammas does not accept Israel as a Zionist state he should leave the Galilee and go to the Palestinian state to be set up in the West Bank.
109. Nisan, *Hamedinah Hayehudit*, pp. 117–19, 200.
110. Ibid., pp. 119, 200.
111. Ibid.
112. Ibid.
113. Ibid., p. 108.
114. Ibid.
115. See Shem-Ur, *Te'ud Politi*, pp. 182–83.
116. Mordechai Nisan, 'Judaism and Politics', *Jerusalem Post*, 13 January 1983, quoted in Chomsky, *Fateful Triangle: The United States, Israel and the Palestinians* (Boston: South End Press, 1983), p. 444.
117. *Haumah*, No. 102 (Winter 1990/91), pp. 139–141.
118. Mordechai Nisan, 'Arab Hostages', *Modelet*, Nos 28–29 (February–March 1991), p. 21.
119. Paul Eidelberg, 'Netrul Ptzatzat Hazman Ha'arvit: Habe'ayah Hademografit', [Neutralisation of the Arab Time-bomb: The Demographic Problem], *Haumah*, No. 90 (Spring 1988), pp. 238–48. Eidelberg is also the author of *Jerusalem vs. Athens: In Quest of a General Theory of Existence* (Lanham, New York: University Press of America, 1983). In this book, p. 366, Note 14, Eidelberg explains the difference between Ishmael and Isaac. Ishmael was born of Hagar, an Egyptian slave, and before Abraham's circumcision. Concerning Ishmael: His hand will be against everyone, and everyone's hand will be against him (Gen. 16:12). This is exactly descriptive of Ishmael's highly sensual descendants, the bellicose Muslim world whose Koran is a gospel of war. In contrast, Isaac, born of Sarah, was a man of peace, as have ever been his descendants.
120. Eidelberg, 'Netrul Ptzatzat Hazman Ha'arvit', p. 241.
121. Ibid., p. 242.
122. Ibid., pp. 243–44.
123. Ibid., p. 243.
124. Ibid., pp. 245–47.
125. Ibid., pp. 247–48.
126. Ibid., p. 248.
127. Chaim Simons, *Chelm or Israel?* (Australia: Jewish Commentary Publication, undated, apparently 1989). The author explains that Chelm is 'a small village in Lithuania where the inhabitants had a reputation for simple-mindedness'.

128. Simons, *Chelm or Israel?* pp. 3–4; the article was written in December 1987.
129. Simons, *Chelm or Israel?*, p. iii.
130. Joffe, *Keesing's Guide to the Mid-East Peace Process*, p. 151.
131. Meir Kahane, *Lesikim Be'eneikhim* [They Shall be Strings in Your Eyes] (Jerusalem: Hamakhom Lara'ayon Hayehudi, 1980/1981), p. 229.
132. Ibid.; Kotler, *Heil Kahane*, pp. 83–84.
133. Kotler, ibid., pp. 83, 88, 89; Kahane, *Lesikim Be'eneikhim*, p. 229. According to Kotler, Khouri apparently used Kahane to obtain money, and eventually left for Australia because of 'threats on his life'.
134. Quoted in Kotler, *Heil Kahane*, p. 84.
135. Masalha, *A Land Without a People*, pp. 90–100.
136. Statement made in an interview quoted in Raphael Mergui and Philippe Simonnot, *Israel's Ayatollahs* (London: Saqi Books, 1987), p. 48.
137. Kotler, *Heil Kahane*, pp. 85–86.
138. Ibid., p. 86.
139. Ibid., p. 88.
140. Kahane, *Lesikim Be'eneikhim*, p. 223.
141. Kotler, *Heil Kahane*, pp. 84–85.
142. Ibid., p. 87.
143. Ibid., p. 91.
144. Rabbi Meir Kahane, *They Must Go* (New York: Grosset & Dunlap, 1981), p. 57.
145. This letter was written in reply to an article by Philip Gillon in the *Jerusalem Post*, 19 June 1980, p. 8.
146. Quoted in Kotler, *Heil Kahane*, p. 86.
147. Cited in Mark Tessler, 'The Political Right in Israel: Its Origins, Growth and Prospects', *Journal of Palestine Studies* 15, No. 2 (Winter 1986), p. 31.
148. Mergui and Simonnot, *Israel's Ayatollahs*, pp. 49 and 85.
149. Kahane, *Lesikim Be'eniekhim*, p. 236.
150. See Urit Shohat in *Haaretz*, 13 May 1985, supplement.
151. Kahane, *Lesikim Be'eneikhim*, pp. 244–45.
152. The statement is found in Kotler, *Heil Kahane*, pp. 195–97.
153. Mergui and Simonnot, *Israel's Ayatollahs*, p. 86.
154. See *Haaretz*, supplement, 31 May 1985, p. 4.
155. Robert I. Friedman, *Zealots for Zion* (New York: Random House, 1992), pp. 116–17.
156. Kahane, *They Must Go*, pp. 263–64.
157. In 1980, Kahane and his colleague Andy Green plotted to blow up the Dome of the Rock Mosque in Jerusalem. But the Israeli Shin Bet discovered the plan. On 12 May 1980 the then Defence Minister 'Ezer Weizman ordered Kahane and Green be detained for six months under the 1945 Defence (Emergency) Regulations powers. In prison Kahane wrote his anti-Arab racist tract, *They Must Go*. See Robert I. Friedman, *The False Prophet* (London: Faber and Faber, 1990), pp. 242–43.
158. Quoted in an article by Haim Shivi, *Yedi'ot Aharonot*, 8 February 1980, p. 9.
159. Lustick, *For the Land and the Lord*, p. 67.

160. Kotler, *Heil Kahane*, p. 102.
161. See David Adams, 'Prospects for Peace in the Occupied Territories', *Journal of Palestine Studies* 14, No. 4 (Summer 1985), p. 68. In 1980, Adams worked for eight months as a volunteer in the occupied territories.
162. Quoted in Ahmad Khalifah, 'Terror in Israel', *al-Yawn al-Sabi'i* (Paris), 21 May 1984.
163. Cited in Tessler, 'The Political Right in Israel', p. 31; *Christian Science Monitor*, 5 June 1980.
164. Kotler, *Heil Kahane*, p. 102.
165. Ibid., p. 103.
166. Ibid., p. 120.
167. Joffe, *Keesing's Guide to the Mid-East Peace Process*, p. 151.
168. Kotler, *Heil Kahane*, p. 105.
169. Ibid., p. 109.
170. Cited in ibid., p. 121. See also Harkabi, *Hakhra'ot Goraliyot* [Fateful Decisions] (Tel Aviv: 'Am 'Oved, 1986), p. 230; Yossi Melman and Dan Raviv, 'Expelling Palestinians', *The Washington Post*, Outlook section, 7 February 1988.
171. Ran Kislev in *Ha'aretz*, 11 November 1990.
172. Kotler, *Heil Kahane*, pp. 105 and 108; *Ma'ariv*, 27 June 1985, p. 18.
173. Kotler, *Heil Kahane*, p. 110.
174. This proposed law is found in Kotler, *Heil Kahane*, pp. 203–207. In his article 'Jewish values', in *Haaretz*, 15 August 1983, Rabbi Kahane wrote: 'A Gentile who wants to live in the Land of Israel can only reach ... the status of 'resident alien'. Citizenship, political status ... the right to vote and to be elected to office, all these are reserved exclusively for Jews.'
175. Cited in Kotler, *Heil Kahane*, pp. 205–206.
176. Kahane, *Lesikim Be'eneikhim*, p. 234.
177. This draft bill is found in Kotler, *Heil Kahane*, pp. 198–201.
178. Cited in Kotler, *Heil Kahane*, p. 192.
179. Ibid., pp. 198 and 203; Harkabi, *Hakhra'ot Goraliyot*, pp. 220–21.
180. Cited in Kotler, *Heil Kahane*, pp. 123–27.
181. Ibid., pp. 142–45.
182. Ibid., p. 143.
183. Ibid., pp. 120 and 122.
184. Cited in an article by Dan Miron in *Yedi'ot Aharonot*, 3 February 1984.
185. See Heda Boshes in *Haaretz*, 12 December 1983, p. 12.
186. Kotler, *Heil Kahane*, pp. 115–16.
187. See Gad Leor in *Yedi'ot Aharonot*, 25 December 1983; Yehoshu'a Sobol in *'Al-Hamishmar*, 27 December 1983.
188. Avraham Cohen of MENA stated: 'the aim is to obtain a pure Jewish town'. The statement is similar to the Nazi slogan 'Judenrein', ('pure of Jews'). The term 'Arabrein' was also used by the *Haaretz* daily television commentator (12 December 1983), after viewing a television screening of a meeting attended by MENA's activists.
189. Aharon Bakhar in *Yedi'ot Aharonot*, 27 December 1983.
190. Yehoshu'a Sobol in *'Al-Hamishmar*, 27 December 1983, p. 3.

191. Cited in H.J. Skutel's review of Kahane's *They Must Go*, in *Journal of Palestine Studies* 12, No. 2 (Winter 1983), p. 83.
192. See Dan Miron in *Yedi'ot Aharonot*, 3 February 1984, pp. 10 and 19.
193. Also cited in an article by Yisrael Eilat, 'The Cancer of the State', *Davar*, 10 November 1983, p. 5.
194. *Yedi'ot Aharonot*, 3 February 1984. The extent to which racist notions and a demonic perception of Arabs had become rooted in the minds of Israeli youngsters was revealed in a study by Dr Adir Cohen and Dr Miriam Roth, both of Haifa University. The study, based on a poll of 260 boys and girls in fourth through sixth grades, showed that the Arab is perceived as a 'child kidnapper, criminal, murderer and terrorist'. See a report on the survey in *Haaretz*, 30 January 1985.
195. Mi'ari was interviewed for the *Journal of Palestine Studies* after his election to the Eleventh Knesset in July 1984. See *Journal of Palestine Studies* 14, No. 1 (Fall 1984), p. 44.
196. See Joanna Yehiel in *Jerusalem Post International*, 12 October 1985.
197. Kotler, *Heil Kahane*, p. 109.
198. On the comparison, see Kotler, *Heil Kahane*, pp. 209–12.
199. See Tova Tzimuki in *Davar*, 1 December 1987, p. 1.
200. According to Israeli law, any of the following disqualify a party from taking part in Knesset elections: (a) The rejection of the existence of the State of Israel as the state of the Jewish people (b) The rejection of the democratic character of the state (c) Incitement to racism.
201. The Progressive List for Peace succeeded in overturning the disqualification by persuading the Supreme Court that it did not reject the existence of the State of Israel.
202. Cited in Haim Bara'am, *Kol Ha'ir*, 9 November 1990.
203. Ibid.
204. Ibid.
205. Dan Leon in *New Outlook* (December 1990/January 1991), p. 46.
206. *Haaretz*, 11 June 1992; *Guardian*, 12 and 17 June 1992. The *Guardian* reported on 25 March 1991 that the Kach movement had appointed a successor to Meir Kahane, the 32-year-old Rabbi Avraham Toledano, who stated that his movement would continue its campaign for the expulsion of all Palestinians from Israel and the occupied territories.
207. David McDowall, *The Palestinians: The Road to Nationhood* (London: Minority Rights Publications, 1994), p. 123.
208. Joffe, *Keesing's Guide to the Mid-East Peace Process*, p. 151.
209. Ibid., pp. 151–52.
210. Ibid., p. 151.

NOTES TO CHAPTER FOUR

1. Shindler, *Israel, Likud and the Zionist Dream*, pp. 176, 187 and 191.
2. Ibid., p. 192.
3. Sprinzak, *The Ascendance of Israel's Radical Right*, p. 14.
4. Ibid., p. 176.
5. Lustick, *For the Land and the Lord*, p. 11.

6. Geula Cohen was born in Tel Aviv in 1925. In her youth she joined Betar, the youth movement of Revisionist Zionism and was recruited to the Irgun, which in the 1940s was commanded by Menahem Begin. However, in 1943 she left the Irgun to join Lehi and became its radio broadcaster. In the 1950s, she was on the editorial board of *Solam*, a monthly edited by Israel Eldad, advocating the establishment of the kingdom of Israel from the Nile to the Euphrates. In 1970, she joined the Begin-led Herut Party and in 1973 she was elected to the 8th Knesset. Between 1977 and 1981 she was the head of the influential Knesset Immigration and Absorption Committee.
7. See an article by Geula Cohen in *Yedi'ot Aharonot*, 26 December 1997, reproduced in *Middle East International*, 16 January 1998, p. 25.
8. Ibid.
9. Yuval Neeman, 'National Goals', in Alouph Hareven (ed.), *Haomnam Kasheh Lihyot Yisraeli?* [Is it Difficult Being an Israeli?] (Jerusalem: Van Leer Foundation, 1983), p. 268.
10. The Tehiya political platform for the 1988 elections.
11. *New Outlook* (February 1984), p. 12.
12. See Mark Tessler, 'The Political Right in Israel: Its Origins, Growth and Prospects', *Journal of Palestine Studies* 15, No. 2 (Winter 1986), p. 30.
13. See 'Tehiyah', in Susan H. Rolef (ed.), *Political Dictionary of the State of Israel* (New York: Macmillan Publishing Company, 1993), p. 296.
14. For further discussion on Neeman and the maximalist approach see Meron Benvenisti, *The West Bank Handbook*, pp. 42–45.
15. Amnon Kapeliouk in *Le Monde Diplomatique* (August 1981).
16. *Ma'ariv*, 18 June 1967, p. 9.
17. As we have seen, the idea reiterated by the supporters of Greater Israel that the Palestinians should be treated as 'resident aliens' is clearly linked with the advocacy of expulsion. In his book *Palestinians Between Israel and Jordan – Squaring the Triangle* (New York: Praeger, 1991), Dr Raphael Israeli, of the Hebrew University's Harry Truman Research Institute, writes: 'Regardless of the exact border between the two states [Israel and Jordan], the demographic threat against Israel will be neutralized if Palestinians are resident aliens, holding Palestinian passports. As aliens, they will have every interest in respecting the local law, lest they be expelled to their country [Jordan] in case of violence, misconduct, or subversive acts against the state'; (p.182).
   Israeli also writes: 'The West Bankers are Jordanian nationals, and their emigration could be legally considered as more of a repatriation than expatriation ... when the gap between the majority and the minority becomes too wide, especially when national conflicts are involved, then the majority may take steps to estrange the "aliens" from its midst, to the point of "transferring" them elsewhere. This is all the more so when the minority ... is large enough to pose an imminent danger to the hegemony of the majority and its different set of values'. (pp. 158–59).
   Israeli cites the biblical rationale for expelling the non-Jews from the Land of Israel: 'If you do not drive out the inhabitants of the land as you advance, any with whom you live will become like a barbed hook

in your eye and a thorn in your side. They shall continually dispute your possession of the land, and what I meant to do to them I will do to you.' (Numbers 33: 55–56, quoted on p. 171). He concludes: 'The hardcore believers in transfer cannot resist the logic, the relevance and the foresight of these words today.'

18. Yuval Neeman, *Mediniyut Hareeyah Hamefukahat* [The Policy of Sober Vision], (Ramat Gan: Revivim, 1984), pp. 168–69.
19. See *News from Within*, 15 April 1986; Nisan, *Hamedinah Heyehudit*, p. 119.
20. Cited in *News from Within*, 15 April 1986.
21. Ibid. However in order to counter the claim put forward by dovish Israelis that the 'demographic problem' can only be solved by giving up most of the territories, the Tehiya leaders convened an 'emergency' conference on demography in 1987, at which the transfer issue was reportedly not discussed. The conference seemingly relied on statistics purporting to show that the relative size of the Arab and Jewish populations in the 'western Land of Israel had not changed since June 1967'. See *Jerusalem Post*, 15 December 1987.
22. The Tehiya political platform for the 1988 elections.
23. Amnon Kapeliouk in *Le Monde Diplomatique* (August 1981).
24. See *Moledet*, Nos. 28–29 (February–March 1991), p. 15.
25. The Tehiya political platform for the 1988 election.
26. *Ma'ariv*, 30 March 1989, Part 1, p. 6.
27. *Hadashot*, supplement, 29 January 1989, p. 8.
28. Ibid.
29. Ibid.
30. Kotler, *Heil Kahane*, pp. 105, 108 and 165.
31. Quoted in ibid., pp. 166–67.
32. Ibid., p. 176.
33. Cited in Nabeel Abraham, 'Making Israel's War Plans Disappear', *Lies of Our Times* (New York), Vol. 1, No. 11 (November 1990), p. 20.
34. Ibid., citing *Kol Ha'ir*, 31 August 1990.
35. Cited in Michael Palumbo, *Imperial Israel* (London: Bloomsbury, updated edn, 1992), p. 303.
36. *Nekudah*, 31 August 1984, No. 77, pp. 34–5.
37. Joffe, *Keesing's Guide to the Mid-East Peace Process*, pp. 149–50.
38. Ibid., pp. 149 and 156.
39. Lustick, *For the Land and the Lord*, p. 64.
40. Joffe, *Keesing's Guide to the Mid-East Peace Process*, p. 150.
41. See Tzomet's political platform for the 1988 election, Pamphlet No. 2.
42. *Haaretz*, 7 April 1988.
43. Yoram Peri, *Between Battles and Ballots* (Cambridge: Cambridge University Press, 1983), p. 264.
44. Bernard Avishai, *The Tragedy of Zionism* (New York: Farrar Straus Giroux, 1985), p. 294.
45. Ibid., p. 310.
46. See Hagai Segal, *Ahim Yekarim: Korot Hamahteret Hayedudit* [Added title: Dear Brothers] (Jerusalem: Keter, 1987), p. 229.
47. *Haaretz*, 29 February 1988, pp. 1 and 8.

48. Quoted in Azmy Bishara, 'The Uprising's Impact on Israel', in Zachary Lockman and Joel Beinin (eds), *Intifada* (London: I.B. Tauris, 1990), p. 221.
49. *Haaretz*, 29 February 1988, pp. 1, 8.
50. See *Davar*, 21 February 1988, p. 7.
51. Quoted in *Ma'ariv*, 23 June 1989, part 2, p. 4.
52. See Tzomet's political platform for the 1988 election, Pamphlet No. 2.
53. Ibid.
54. Ibid.
55. Joffe, *Keesing's Guide to the Mid-East Peace Process*, pp. 150–51.
56. See *Haaretz*, 23 February 1988, p. 2.
57. Joshua Brilliant in the *Jerusalem Post*, 23 February 1988, pp. 1 and 4.
58. Cited in *Ma'ariv*, 23 February 1988, p. 12.
59. The *Jerusalem Post*, 23 February 1988, p. 4; *Ma'ariv*, 23 February 1988, p. 12.
60. The *Jerusalem Post*, 23 February 1988, p. 4; *Haaretz*, 23 February 1988, p. 2.
61. Meaning that the supporters of transfer in Israel say that Israel cannot give up the territories and should annex them, but at the same time it cannot and should not absorb the Arab inhabitants of the territories into Greater Israel. Consequently the only solution is transfer.
62. *Davar*, 5 July 1987.
63. See Rehava'am Zeevi in *Yedi'ot Aharonot*, 16 July 1988.
64. See *Koteret Rashit*, 16 November 1988.
65. Zeevi has also been suspected for years of having links with organised crime in Israel. See Gide'on Samit in *Haaretz*, 11 November 1988.
66. See Don Peretz and Sammy Smooha, 'Israel's Twelfth Knesset Election: An All-Loser Game', *Middle East Journal* 43, No. 3 (Summer 1989), p. 392. Because Kahane became outcast, the leader of Moledet was forced to distinguish himself from the Kach movement by saying that his position on the need to adopt a transfer policy did not apply to Israel's Arab minority, but only to the Palestinians of the West Bank and Gaza: *Devrei Haknesset* [Knesset Debates], 7 November 1990, p. 473; Shmuel Meiri and Yossi Bar-Muha, 'The Walls of Acre were not Toppled by Transfer', *Kolbo*, 9 August 1991 (in Hebrew).
67. See the result of a survey carried out by the Modi'in Izrahi research institute for Dr Yoav Peled of Tel Aviv University in *Ma'ariv*, 5 August 1988.
68. See Gide'on Biger in *Haaretz*, 15 November 1988.
69. See interview with Professor Shaul Gutmann, a Moledet leader, in *'Al-Hamishmar*, 5 January 1993, p. 10.
70. See *Mabat*, 25 August 1989.
71. See *Mabat Lekalkalah Velahevrah*, 13 November 1990, cited in *Moledet*, No. 27 (January 1991), p. 11; *Mabat Lekalkalah Velahevrah*, 21 December 1990, cited in *Moledet*, Nos 28–29 (February–March 1991), p. 9; *Nativ*, 2, No. 19 (March 1991).
72. 27.3 per cent would vote for Likud; 15.6 per cent for Tehiya; 15.6 per cent for Tzomet, 3.9 per cent for Kach, and only 2.6 per cent for Labour. See *Moledet*, No. 21 (July 1990), p. 12.

73. See *Yerushalayim*, 29 June 1990.
74. See Ian Black in the *Guardian*, 25 June 1992.
75. Cited in *Moledet*, No. 4 (January 1989), p. 2.
76. Cited in *Moledet*, No. 5 (February 1989), p. 3.
77. Cited in *Moledet*, No. 6 (March–April 1989), p. 5.
78. Cited in *Moledet*, No. 8 (June 1989), p. 11; *Moledet*, No. 7 (May 1989), p. 2.
79. Cited in *Moledet*, No. 5 (February 1989), p. 6.
80. For instance see Zeevi's statement in the debate of 5 April 1989, in *Moledet*, No. 7 (May 1989), p. 7, and Sprintzak's statement, in *Moledet*, No. 11 (September 1989), p. 5; *Moledet*, Nos 31–32 (May 1991), p. 2.
81. Cited in *Moledet*, No. 11 (September 1989), p. 5. See also Sprintzak's statement in a debate on 28 January 1991, in *Moledet*, Nos 28–29 (February–March 1991), p. 14.
82. Cited in *Moledet*, Nos 31–32 (May 1991), p. 2.
83. Cited in *Moledet*, Nos 28–29 (February–March 1991), p. 15.
84. Cited in *Moledet*, No. 7 (May 1989), p. 2.
85. See *Ha'ir*, 17 March 1989, pp. 1, 25–27.
86. Dr Moskowitz is a board member of Americans for Secure Israel, an extreme right-wing group that advocates annexing the occupied territories to Israel. Moskowitz is also a Miami-based physician and 'Ateret Cohanim' board member who has donated millions of dollars to its activities and projects in the Old City of Jerusalem, including the takeover of the St. John's Hospice of the Old City. In 1984, Moskowitz was among those who set up the American Friends of 'Ateret Cohanim', registered in New York State as a charitable foundation. According to the foundation's statement, 'Ateret Cohanim' was formed to publish and distribute material concerning 'the priesthood [and] functions of the [Jewish] Temple' and 'acquire in any manner whatsoever and especially by grant, gift lease of purchase – land, rooms or houses [in Arab East Jerusalem]'. See Friedman, *Zealots for Zion*, p. 113.
87. See Masalha, *A Land Without a People*, p. 229.
88. *Moledet*, No. 16 (February 1990), p. 24.
89. *Moledet*, No. 24 (October 1990), p. 3
90. *Moledet*, Nos 28–29 (February–March 1991), p. 4.
91. Ibid., p. 3.
92. Meir Lifschitz in *Ha'olam Hazeh*, 22 August 1990, reprinted in *Moledet*, No. 24 (October 1990), p. 18.
93. Joffe, *Keesing's Guide to the Mid-East Peace Process*, p. 392.
94. Ibid.
95. See Haim Baram in *Middle East International*, No. 565, 19 December 1997, p. 8.
96. Ora Shem-Ur, *Yisrael Rabati* [Greater Israel] (Tel Aviv: Nogah Press, 1985), p. 16. See also Ora Shem-Ur, *Yisrael: Medinah 'Al Tnai* [Israel: A Conditional State] (Tel Aviv: Nogah Press, 1978), pp. 110–12.
97. Shem-Ur, *Yisrael Rabati*, p. 17.
98. Ibid., p. 18.
99. See *Kol Ha'ir*, 26 March 1986.

100. Ora Shem-Ur, *The Challenges of Israel* (New York: Shengold Publishers, 1980), pp. 58–79.
101. Ora Shem-Ur, *Te'ud Politi: Hamefarkim* [The Liquidators: A Political Documentation] (Tel Aviv: Nogah Press, 1989), p. 10.
102. Shem-Ur, *Yisrael: Mendinah 'Al Tnai*.
103. See *Kol Ha'ir*, 26 March 1986.
104. Shem-Ur, *Te'ud Politi*, p. 30.
105. Ibid., p. 128.
106. Ibid., pp. 54–55, 64, 112.
107. See Danny Rubinstein in *Davar*, 26 January 1979, p. 17.
108. Shem-Ur, *Te'ud Politi*, p. 49.
109. See Eldad's sympathetic review of the English version of the book *The Challenges of Israel*, in *Yedi'ot Aharonot*, 19 June 1981.
110. Professor Moshe Atar himself wrote an article in *Haumah*, No. 76 (Autumn 1984), pp. 189–97, advocating the annexation of the occupied territories and implicitly the transfer of the Arabs 'either through agreement and peaceful means or in the storm of war and compulsion'.
111. Shem-Ur, *Te'ud Politi*, pp. 48–49.
112. Ibid., pp. 74–75.
113. Ibid., p. 204.
114. Shem-Ur, *Yisrael Rabati*, pp. 51, 52, 64–65.
115. Shem-Ur, *Te'ud Politi*, p. 101.
116. Shem-Ur, *Yisrael Rabati*, p. 58.
117. Ibid., p. 62.
118. Ibid., p. 65.
119. Ibid., pp. 63–64.
120. Ibid., p. 66.
121. See *Hadashot*, 30 July 1987.
122. Shem-Ur, *Te'ud Politi*, p. 202.
123. Shem-Ur, *Yisrael Rabati*, pp. 67 and 94.
124. Ibid., pp. 67–68.
125. Ibid.
126. Shem-Ur, *Te'ud Politi*, p. 93.
127. Shem-Ur, *Yisrael Rabati*, p. 68.
128. Ibid.
129. Ibid., pp. 68–70.
130. Ibid., pp. 89 and 91.
131. Yaron London in *Ha'ir*, 2 November 1985. See also Uri Sela' in *Yedi'ot Aharonot*, 1 November 1985. Sympathetic reviews of the book were written in *Ma'ariv* by Amnon Abramovitch on 24 January 1986 and by Tzvi Shiloah on 16 December 1985, and in *Kolbotek* by Tzvi Tal on 22 November 1985. See also *Laeshah*, 25 November 1985.
132. Shem-Ur, *Te'ud Politi*, p. 93.
133. Ibid., p. 91.
134. It is very unlikely that Dan Meridor shares Shem-Ur's views on mass expulsion, as he has already declared publicly his opposition to transfer.
135. Shem-Ur, *Te'ud Politi*, p. 96.

136. Ibid., p. 100.
137. See *Kol Ha'ir*, 26 March 1986.
138. The *Jerusalem Post*, 22 February 1977.
139. Shem-Ur, *Te'ud Politi*, pp. 116–17. See *Hadashot*, 30 July 1987, 6 October 1987 and 1 March 1988.
140. Shem-Ur, *Te'ud Politi*, pp. 119–20.
141. Ibid.
142. See *Laeshah*, 27 January 1986.
143. Shem-Ur, *Te'ud Politi*, pp. 127 and 133.
144. *Davar*, 21 January 1986; *'Al-Hamishmar*, 28 January 1986.
145. Shem-Ur, *Te'ud Politi*, p. 206.
146. See *Ha'ir*, 19 September 1986.
147. Shem-Ur, *Te'ud Politi*, p. 146.
148. See the *Jerusaelm Post*, 9 September 1986.
149. Shem-Ur, *Te'ud Politi*, p. 168.
150. Ibid., p. 148.
151. The *Jerusalem Post*, 9 September 1986. See also *Haaretz*, 9 September 1986.
152. Shem-Ur, *Te'ud Politi*, p. 178.

NOTES TO CHAPTER FIVE

1. Gad Barzilai and Efraim Inbar, 'The Use of Force: Israeli Public Opinion and Military Options', *Armed Forces & Society* 23, No. 1 (Fall 1996), p. 50.
2. Nadim Rouhana, *Palestinian Citizens in an Ethnic Jewish State* (New Haven and London: Yale University Press, 1997), pp. 153–54, and note 1, p. 268.
3. Ibid, p. 154.
4. Barzilai and Inbar, 'The Use of Force', p. 49.
5. Barzilai and Inbar, 'The Use of Force'; Giora Goldberg, Gad Barzilai and Efraim Enbar, 'The Impact of the Intercommunal Conflict: The Intifada and the Israeli Public Opinion', *Policy Studies*, No. 43 (Jerusalem: The Leonard Davis Institute of International Relations, February 1991).
6. *Hadashot*, 19 July 1987.
7. Lustick, *For the Land and the Lord: Jewish Fundamentalism in Israel* (New York: Council on Foreign Relations, 1988), p. 179.
8. Cited in Elia Zureik, 'Crime, Justice, and Underdevelopment: The Palestinians Under Israeli Control', *International Journal of Middle East Studies* 20 (1988), p. 414.
9. Cited by David Pedahtzur in *Davar*, 18 December 1992.
10. Cited in David McDowall, *Palestine and Israel: The Uprising and Beyond* (London: I.B. Tauris, 1989), p. 197.
11. Cited in Zureik, 'Crime, Justice, and Underdevelopment', p. 414.
12. Cited in Alouph Hareven (ed.), *Every Sixth Israeli* (Jerusalem: The Van Leer Foundation, 1983), pp. 6–9.

13. Sammy Smooha, *The Orientation and Politicization of the Arab Minority in Israel* (Haifa: University of Haifa, 1984), p. 78. See also Zureik, 'Crime, Justice, and Underdevelopment', p. 414 and p. 439, note 14.
14. In a speech at the session of the Knesset on 28 October 1982 Shim'on Peres, the leader of the Labour Party, stated: 'The Arab birthrate, between the Jordan and the Sea, numbers up to 76,000 children a year today, some of them Israeli citizens in every way, compared with 70,000 Jewish children. A majority of 6,000 children ... Mr Menachem Begin claims that the battle is over Eretz-Yisrael. I claim that the battle is over the State of Israel ... the State of Israel will not be a Jewish state unless a clear Jewish majority is ensured. Against your claim that we are ready to give up territory, we claim that you are ready to give up the certainty that Israel will remain a Jewish state', speech transcribed in *Foreign Broadcast Information Service, Middle East and Africa Daily Report* (FBIS), 28 October 1982.
15. Cited in *Ma'ariv*, 8 October 1982, p. 19.
16. Ora Shem-Ur, *Te'ud Politi: Hamefarkim* [The Liquidators: A Political Documentation] (Tel Aviv: Nogah Press, 1989), p. 100; and Ora Shem-Ur, *Yisrael Rabati* [Greater Israel] (Tel Aviv: Nogah Press, 1985).
17. Binyamin Netanyahu, *A Place Among the Nations* (London: Bantam Press, 1993), p. 303.
18. Benjamin Beit-Hallahmi, *Original Sins* (London: Pluto Press, 1992), p. 94.
19. Nur Masalha, *A Land Without a People: Israel, Transfer and the Palestinians, 1949–1996* (London: Faber and Faber, 1997), p. 150.
20. 'Uzi Benziman and 'Atallah Mansour, *Dayarei Mishne* [Subtenants] (Jerusalem: Keter Publishing House, 1992), p. 98.
21. The survey carried out by Dahaf research institute was part of a research project based at the Center for Middle East Peace and Development at the City University of New York. Cited in Rouhana, *Palestinian Citizens in an Ethnic Jewish State*, pp. 156 and 233.
22. See *Yedi'ot Aharonot*, 28 June 1985.
23. Bernard Avishai, *The Tragedy of Zionism* (New York: Farrar, Straus & Giroux, 1985), pp. 298 and 371, note 1.
24. The results were summarised in *New Outlook* 31, No. 2 (February 1988), p. 22.
25. See *Jerusalem Post International*, 11 October 1986 and the *Jerusalem Post*, 11 October 1986.
26. For a summary of this debate, see Avishai Ehrlich, 'Is Transfer an Option?', *Israeli Democracy* 1, No. 4 (Winter 1987), pp. 36–38.
27. Rouhana, *Palestinian Citizens in an Ethnic Jewish State*, p. 207.
28. Lustick, *For the Land and the Lord*, p. 15.
29. On the Tel Aviv University poll, see Arie Haskel, in the *Observer* (London), 12 June 1988, p. 22.
30. *Hadashot*, 19 July 1987.
31. Cited in the *Jerusalem Post*, 25 December 1987, pp. 1 and 17.
32. Quoted in David Bernstein, 'Forcible removal of Arabs gaining support in Israel', *The Times* (London), 7 September 1988.
33. See also Hanokh Bartov in *Ma'ariv*, 8 June 1990.

34. Cited in *Yedi'ot Aharonot*, 7 June 1991.
35. Barzilai and Inbar, 'The Use of Force', pp. 55 and 68.
36. See article by Professor Dan Meron in *Yedi'ot Aharonot*, 3 February 1984.
37. Yael Yishai, *Land or Peace: Whither Israel?* (Stanford, CA: Hoover Institution Press, 1987), pp. 177–78.
38. Ibid., p. 193.
39. Sammy Smooha's recent books are: *Arabs and Jews in Israel*, Vol. 1: *Conflicting and Shared Attitudes in a Divided Society* (Boulder, CO and San Francisco, CA: Westview Press, 1989); and *Arabs and Jews in Israel*, Vol. 2: *Change and Continuity in Mutual Intolerance* (Boulder, CO and San Francisco, CA: Westview Press, 1992).
40. See Smooha, *Arabs and Jews in Israel*, Vol. 1, pp. 64–66.
41. Ibid., pp. 77, 141–42.
42. Ibid., pp. 140–41.
43. Ibid., p. 220.
44. See Smooha, *Arabs and Jews in Israel*, Vol. 2, p. 153.
45. Smooha, *Orientation and Politicization of the Arab Minority in Israel*, p. 37.
46. Smooha's data from these two polls were reported in Smooha, *Arabs and Jews in Israel*, vol.2. About the same number of Arabs were interviewed in both surveys; however, the findings in this regard are outside the scope of our discussion.
47. See ibid., p. 60.
48. See ibid., pp. 60, 63, 68, 70–71, 74.
49. Ibid., p. 70.
50. Ibid., p. 112.
51. Ibid., pp. 111–15.
52. Ibid., pp. 150–52.
53. Ibid., p. 152.
54. Ibid., pp. 152–53.
55. Ibid., p. 153.
56. Ibid., p. 152.
57. Ibid.
58. Benjamin Beit-Hallahmi, *Original Sins: Reflections on the History of Zionism and Israel* (London: Pluto Press, 1992), p. 91.
59. For further discussion see Masalha, *A Land Without a People*, pp. 138–44.
60. Smooha, *Arabs and Jews in Israel*, Vol. 2, pp. 157–58.
61. Ibid., pp. 154–55, 238–40.
62. See Yigal Kotzer in *Hadashot*, 5 June 1990, p. 7; Israel Shahak, 'Why Shamir rules Israel: the deeper reasons', *Middle East International*, No. 379, 6 July 1990, p. 15.
63. Smooha, *Arabs and Jews in Israel*, Vol. 2, p. 153.
64. Cited by Yigal Kotzer in *Hadashot*, 5 June 1990, p. 7.
65. Ibid.
66. Rouhana, *Palestinian Citizens in an Ethnic Jewish State*, pp. 170 and 234; Mina Tzemah, *The Attitudes of the Jewish Majority Towards the Arab Minority* (Jerusalem: Van Leer Institute, 1980) (in Hebrew); Hareven, *Every Sixth Israeli*, pp. 6–9.

67. See *Yedi'ot Aharonot*, 18 December 1992; *'Al-Hamishmar*, 18 December 1992.
68. See Peretz Kidron in *Middle East International*, No. 440, 18 December 1992, p. 4.
69. See David Pedahtzur in *Davar*, 18 December 1992.
70. Cited in the *Guardian*, 15 May 1993, p. 16.
71. Derek Brown in the *Guardian*, 27 May 1993, p. 14.
72. David McDowall, *The Palestinians: The Road to Nationhood* (London: Minority Rights Publications, 1994), p. 158.
73. Cited in *al-Sharq al-Awsat* (London), 20 January 1998.
74. See, for example, Haim Baram, in *Middle East International*, 16 January 1998, p. 7; Rouhana, *Palestinian Citizens in an Ethnic Jewish State*, p. 162.
75. Rouhana, *Palestinian Citizens in an Ethnic Jewish State*, p. 208.

NOTES TO EPILOGUE

1. David Hirst, 'South Lebanon: The War That Never Ends?', *Journal of Palestine Studies*, Vol. XXVIII, No. 3 (Spring 1999), pp. 6–7.
2. See Avi Shlaim in the *Guardian*, 22 June 1992, p. 27.
3. See *Wall Street Journal*, National Edition, 6 July 1997, p. 5A.
4. Cited in *Summary of World Broadcasts*, Part 4, The Middle East, 20 January 1998, (Caversham Park, Reading: BBC Monitoring), p. 1.
5. Lustick, *For the Land and the Lord: Jewish Fundamentalism in Israel* (New York: Council on Foreign Relations, 1988), p. 109.
6. See, for instance, Eliyakim Ha'etzni, *The Shock of Withdrawal from the Land of Israel* (Jerusalem: Elisha, 1986) (in Hebrew); Baruch Leor, in *Nekudah*, 5 April 1985, pp. 11–12.
7. Cited in *Shaml* newsletter (Ramallah), No. 17 (July 1999), p. 6.
8. See Shyam Bhatia in the *Guardian*, 11 December 1996.
9. Cited in *Shaml* newsletter (July 1999), p. 7
10. http://www.geocities.com/Athens/Aegean/4773/cve-h.html
11. Cited in Toby Ash, *Guardian*, 3 July 1996, p. 16.
12. Phyllis Bennis in *Third World Emergence*, No. 71 (July 1996), p. 35; Nur Masalha, 'A different peace', *Index on Censorship*, No. 3, (May–June 1996), pp. 18–21; 'Special Report: The Palestinians', the *Guardian*, 3 July 1996, p. 16.
13. Cited from Yeruham Cohen, *Tochnit Allon* [The Allon Plan] (Tel Aviv: Hakibbutz Hameuhad Press, 1973), p. 13.
14. Bernard Avishai, *The Tragedy of Zionism* (New York: Farrar, Straus & Giroux, 1985), p. 340.
15. See *Meed* (London), 7 October 1994, p. 16.
16. See Shyam Bhatia in the *Observer*, 9 June 1996, p. 19.
17. See Haim Baram in *Middle East International*, 23 June 1995, p. 4. See also Sarah Helm, 'West Bank to be snared in a net of highways', the *Independent*, 12 December 1994.

Select Bibliography

ARCHIVAL SOURCES

Central Zionist Archives (CZA), Jerusalem, Jewish Agency Executives minutes;
E. Ben-Horin's file.
Israel State Archives, Jerusalem, Foreign Ministry files.
Jabotinsky Archives, Tel Aviv, Joseph Schechtman's files.

PRIMARY SOURCES

Ariel, Yisrael, 'Dvarim Kehavayatam', [Things As They Are], *Tzippiyah*
(Jerusalem, 1980).
Aviner, Shlomo, 'The Wholeness of the Land of Israel', *Artzi*, Vol. 1 (1982),
pp. 26–27.
——, 'Messianic Realism', in Avner Tomaschoff (ed.), *Whose Homeland*
(Jerusalem: World Zionist Organization, 1978).
——, 'Yerushat Haaretz Vehabe'ayah Hamusarit', [The Inheritance of the
Land and the Moral Problem], *Arzti* [My Country] (Jerusalem, 1983).
Ben-'Ami, Aharon (ed.), *Hakol* [Everything] (Tel Aviv: Madaf Publishing
House, 1967).
——, (ed.), *Sefer Eretz-Yisrael Hashlemah* [The Book of the Whole Land of
Israel] (Tel Aviv: Friedman Press, 1977).
Dayan, Moshe, *Mapah Hadashah, Yehasim Aherim* [A New Map, Other Rela-
tionships] (Tel Aviv: Ma'ariv, 1969).
——, *Avnie Derekh: Otobiyografyah* [Milestones: An Autobiography] (Jerusalem
and Tel Aviv: 'Edanim and Dvir, 1976).
Devrei Haknesset [Knesset Debates] (Jerusalem).
Dotan, Moshe, 'Rov 'Ivri Ketzad?' [A Hebrew Majority, How?], *Haumah*, No. 2
(November 1967), pp. 242–49.
Eidelberg, Paul, 'Netrul Ptzatzat Hazman Ha'arvit: Habe'ayah Hademografit',
[Neutralisation of the Arab Time-bomb: The Demographic Problem],
Haumah, No. 90 (Spring 1988).
Eldad, Israel, *The Jewish Revolution: Jewish Statehood* (New York: Shengold
Publishers, 1971)
——, 'The Transfer as a Zionist Solution', *Haumah*, No. 88 (Autumn 1987),
pp. 11–13 (in Hebrew).
Elitzur, Yehuda, 'The Borders of Eretz Israel in Jewish Tradition', in Avner
Tomaschoff (ed.), *Whose Homeland* (Jerusalem: World Zionist
Organization, 1978), pp. 42–53.
Elitzur, Yoel, 'Is Lebanon also the Land of Israel?: Northern Borders of the
Land of Israel in the Sources and According to the Halacha', *Nekudah*, No.
48, no date, pp. 10–13.

Ha'etzni, Elyakim, *The Shock of Withdrawal from the Land of Israel* (Jerusalem: Elisha, 1986) (in Hebrew).

Heller, Avraham, 'Hashed Hademografi' [The Demographic Demon], *Haumah*, No. 1 (January 1970), pp. 99–100.

——, 'The Golan Law and the Hypocritical Witch Hunt at Home and Abroad', *Haumah*, (December 1981), pp. 319–23 (in Hebrew).

Hess, Yisrael, 'Mitzvat Hagenocide Batorah', [The Genocide Commandment in the Torah], *Bat Kol*, Bar Ilan University, 26 February 1980.

Kahane, Meir, *Our Challenge: The Chosen Land* (Radnor, PA: Chilton Book Company, 1974).

——, *Lesikim Be'ineikhem* [They Shall be Strings in Your Eyes] (Jerusalem: Hamakhon Lara'ayon Hayehudi, 1980/81).

——, *They Must Go* (New York: Grosset and Dunlap, 1981).

Kook, Tzvi Yehuda, 'Bein 'Am Veartzo' [Between A People and its Land], *Artzi*, Vol. 2 (Spring 1982).

——, 'On the Genuine Significance of the State of Israel', *Artzi*, Vol. 1 (1982).

——, 'Zionism and Biblical Prophecy', in Yosef Tirosh (ed.), *Religious Zionism: An Anthology* (Jerusalem: World Zionist Organization, 1985).

Lev-'Ami, Shlomo, *Haim Hatziyonut Nikhshelah* [Did Zionism Fail?] (Tel Aviv: 'Ami Press, 1988).

Livneh, Eli'ezer, *Israel and the Crisis of Western Civilization* (Tel Aviv: Schocken Books, 1972) (in Hebrew).

Lohamei Herut Yisrael (Lehi), *Ketavim* [Writings] Vols 1–2 (Tel Aviv, 1959–1960).

Moskowitz, Irving, in *Moledet*, No. 16 (February 1990).

Neeman, Yuval, *Mediniyut Hareeyah Hamefukahat* [The Policy of the Sober Vision] (Ramat Gan: Revivim, 1984).

Nisan, Mordechai, *Hamedinah Hayehudit Vehabe'ayah Ha'arvit* [The Jewish State and the Arab Problem] (Tel Aviv: Hadar, 1986).

——, *Toward a New Israel: The Jewish State and the Arab Question* (New York: AMS Press, 1992).

Porat, Hanan, 'Policies towards the Arabs of the Land of Israel', *Artzi*, Vol. 4 (Spring 1986) (in Hebrew).

Segal, Haggai, *Ahim Yekarim* [Dear Brothers] (Jerusalem: Keter Publishing House, 1987).

Sharett, Moshe, *Yoman Ishi* [Personal Diary], 8 vols (Tel Aviv: Sifriyat Ma'ariv, 1978).

Shem-Ur, Ora, *Yisrael: Medinah 'Al Tnai* [Israel: A Conditional State] (Tel Aviv: Nogah Press, 1978).

——, *Yisrael Rabati* [Greater Israel] (Tel Aviv: Nogah Press, 1985).

——, *Te'ud Politi: Hamefarkim* [The Liquidators: A Political Documentation] (Tel Aviv: Nogah Press, 1989).

Shiloah, Tzvi, *Eretz Gdolah Le'am Gadol* [A Great Land for a Great People] (Tel Aviv: Otpaz, 1970).

——, *Ashmat Yerushalayim* [The Guilt of Jerusalem] (Tel Aviv: Karni Press, 1989).

Simons, Chaim, *Chelm or Israel?* (Australia: Jewish Commentary Publication, 1989[?]).

Tzuriya, Haim, 'The Right to Hate', *Nekudah*, No. 15, 29 August 1980 (in Hebrew).

Weitz, Yosef, *Yomani Veigrotai Lebanim* [My Diary and Letters to the Children], Vols 3–6, (Tel Aviv: Massada, 1965).

——, (ed.), *Yosef Nahmani: Ish Hagalil* [Yosef Nahmani: Man of the Galilee] (Ramat Gan: Massada, 1969).

Wolpo, Shlomo Dov (ed.), *Da'at Torah Be'inyanei Hamatzav Beeretz Hakodesh* [The Opinion of the Torah Regarding the Situation in the Holy Land] (Kiryat Gat, 1979).

Yosefi, Dov, 'A Humane Solution to the Demographic Problem', *Haumah*, No. 88 (Autumn 1987), pp. 20–26 (in Hebrew).

SECONDARY SOURCES

Abu Lughod, Ibrahim (ed.), *The Transformation of Palestine* (Evanston, IL: Northwestern University Press, 1971).

Abu Shakra and Jan Demarest, *Israeli Settler Violence in the Occupied Territories: 1980–1984* (Chicago: Palestine Human Rights Campaign, 1985).

Anderson, Benedict, *Imagined Communities: Reflections on the Origins and Spread of Nationalism* (London: Verso, 1991).

Aran, Gide'on, *The Land of Israel Between Politics and Religion: The Movement to Stop the Withdrawal from Sinai* (Jerusalem: The Jerusalem Institute for Israeli Studies, 1985) (in Hebrew).

Aronson, Geoffrey, *Israel, Palestinians and the Intifada* (London: Kegan Paul International, 1990).

Aruri, Naseer, *The Obstruction of Peace: The United States, Israel, and the Palestinians* (Monroe, ME: Common Courage Press, 1995).

Aviad, Janet, 'The Contemporary Israeli Pursuit of the Millennium', *Religion* 14, No. 3 (July 1984), pp. 199–222.

Avishai, Bernard, *The Tragedy of Zionism* (New York: Farrar, Straus & Giroux, 1985).

The Beirut Massacre: The Complete Kahan Commission Report (Princeton and New York: Karz-Cohl, 1983).

Begin, Menachem, *The Revolt*, rev. edn (New York: Nash, 1977).

Begin, Ze'ev B., 'The Likud Vision for Israel at Peace', *Foreign Affairs*, Fall 1991, pp. 21–35.

Beit-Hallahmi, Benjamin, *The Israeli Connection: Whom Israel Arms and Why* (London: I.B. Tauris, 1988).

——, 'Israel and South Africa 1977–1982: Business as Usual – And More', *New Outlook*, March 1983, pp. 31–5.

——, *Original Sins: Reflections on the History of Zionism and Israel* (London: Pluto Press, 1992).

Bell, J. Boyer, *Terror Out of Zion: Irgun Zvai Leumi, Lehi, and the Palestine Underground, 1929–1949* (New York: St. Martin's, 1977).

Benvenisti, Meron, *The West Bank Data Project: A Survey of Israel's Policies* (Washington, DC: American Enterprise Institute, 1984).

——, *1986 Report: Demographic, Economic, Legal, Social, and Political Developments in the West Bank* (Jerusalem: The West Bank Data Base Project, 1986).

——, *The West Bank Handbook* (Jerusalem: *Jerusalem Post*, 1986).

Benziman, Uzi, *Sharon: An Israeli Caesar* (London: Robson Books, 1987).

Bernstein, David, 'Forcible removal of Arabs gaining support in Israel', *The Times* (London), 24 August 1988.

Blum, Yehuda Zvi, 'The Missing Revisioner: Reflections on the State of Judea and Samaria', *Israel Law Review*, 3 (1968), pp. 279–301.

Brenner, Lenni, *The Iron Wall: Zionist Revisionism from Jabotinsky to Shamir* (London: Zed Books, 1984).

Caspi, D., Diskin, A. and Guttman, E. (eds), *The Roots of Begin's Success* (London: Croom Helm, 1984).

Chomsky, Noam, *Fateful Triangle: The United States, Israel and the Palestinians* (Boston: South End Press, 1983).

Cohen, Yeruham, *Tochnit Allon* [The Allon Plan] (Tel Aviv: Hakibbutz Hameuhad Press, 1972).

Davis, Uri and Norton Mezvinsky (eds), *Documents from Israel 1967–1973* (London: Ithaca Press, 1975).

Dayan, Arie, 'The Debate over Zionism and Racism: An Israeli View', *Journal of Palestine Studies* 22, No. 3 (Spring 1993).

Don-Yehiya, Eliezer, 'Jewish Messianism, Religious Zionism and Israeli Politics: The Impact and Origins of Gush Emunim', *Middle Eastern Studies* 23, No. 2 (April 1987).

Doron, Adam (ed.), *Medinat Yisrael Veeretz Yisrael* [The State of Israel and the Land of Israel (Beit Berl: Beit Berl College, 1988).

'Evron, Bo'az, *Hahishbon Haleumi* [A National Reckoning] (Tel Aviv: Dvir, 1988).

Flapan, Simha, *Zionism and the Palestinians 1917–1947* (London: Croom Helm, 1979).

——, *The Birth of Israel: Myths and Realities* (London: Croom Helm, 1987).

Friedman, I. Robert, *The False Prophet, Rabbi Meir Kahane: From FBI Informant to Knesset Member* (London: Faber and Faber, 1990).

——, *Zealots for Zion: Inside Israel's West Bank Settlement Movement* (New York: Random House, 1992).

Golani, Motti, *Israel in Search of a War: The Sinai Campaign, 1955–1956* (Brighton: Sussex Academic Press, 1998).

Goldberg, Giora and Ben-Zadok, Efraim, 'Gush Emunim in the West Bank', *Middle Eastern Studies* 22, No. 1 (January 1986).

Grossman, David, *Sleeping on a Wire* (London: Jonathan Cape, 1993).

Harkabi, Yehoshafat, *Hakhra'ot Goraliyot* [Fateful Decisions] (Tel Aviv: 'Am 'Oved, 1986).

Hecht, Richard D., 'The Political Culture of Israel's Radical Right: Commentary on Ehud Sprinzak's *The Ascendance of Israel's Radical Right*', *Terrorism and Political Violence*, Vol. 5, No. 1 (Spring 1993).

Heller, Joseph, *The Stern Gang: Ideology, Politics and Terror, 1940–1949* (London: Frank Cass, 1995).

Hirst, David, *The Gun and the Olive Branch* (London: Faber and Faber, 1984).

Israeli, Raphael, *Palestinians between Israel and Jordan – Squaring the Triangle* (New York: Praeger, 1991).

Jiryis, Sabri, *The Arabs in Israel* (New York: Monthly Review Press, 1976).

Kapeliouk, Amnon, *Israel: la fin des mythes* (Paris: Albin Michel, 1975).

Katz, Shmuel, *No Solution to the Arab-Palestinian Problem* (Montreal: Dawn Publishing, 1985).

Kim, Hanna, 'To Annihilate Amalek', *'Al-Hamishmar*, 12 March 1984 (in Hebrew).

Kimmerling, Baruch, *Zionism and Territory: The Socio-Territorial Dimensions of Zionist Politics* (Berkeley: University of California, Institute of International Studies, 1983).

Kotler, Yair, *Heil Kahane* (New York: Adama Books, 1986).

Litani, Yehuda, 'The Fanatic Right in Israel: Linking Nationalism and Fundamentalist Religion', *Dissent*, Summer 1985.

Lockman, Zachary and Joel Beinin (eds), *Intifada* (London: I.B. Tauris, 1990).

Lorch, Natanel (ed.), *Major Knesset Debates, 1948–1981* (London: University Press of America, 1993).

Lustick, Ian, 'Israeli State-Building in the West Bank and the Gaza Strip: Theory and Practice', *International Organization*, Vol. 41, No. 1 (Winter 1987), pp. 151–71.

——, 'Israel's Dangerous Fundamentalists', *Foreign Policy*, Fall 1987.

——, 'Israel and the West Bank after Elon Moreh: The Mechanics of De Facto Annexation', *Middle East Journal*, Vol. 35, No. 4 (Autumn 1980), pp. 557–77.

——, *For the Land and the Lord: Jewish Fundamentalism in Israel* (New York: Council on Foreign Relations, 1988).

Masalha, Nur, 'On Recent Hebrew and Israeli Sources for the Palestinian Exodus 1948–49', *Journal of Palestine Studies*, Vol. 18, No. 1 (Autumn 1988), pp. 121–37.

——, and F. Vivekananda, 'Israeli Revisionist Historiography of the Birth of Israel and its Palestinian Exodus of 1948', *Scandinavian Journal of Development Alternatives*, Vol. 9, No. 1 (March 1990), pp. 71–79.

——, 'Al-Tasawwur al-Suhyuni Le al-Transfer: Nazrah Tarikhiyyah 'Amah' [The Zionist Concept of Transfer: An Historical Overview], *Majalat al-Dirasat al-Filastiniyyah*, (Beirut), No. 7 (Summer 1991), pp. 19–45.

——, 'Debate on the 1948 Exodus', *Journal of Palestine Studies*, Vol. 21, No. 1 (Autumn 1991) pp. 90–97.

——, *Expulsion of the Palestinians: The Concept of 'Transfer' in Zionist Political Thought 1882–1948* (Washington, DC: Institute for Palestine Studies, 1992).

——, *Tard al-Filastinyyin: Mafhum al 'Transfer' Fi al-Fikr wa al-Takhtit al-Suhyuniyyan* [Expulsion of the Palestinians: The Concept of Transfer in Zionist Thinking and Planning 1882–1948], (Beirut: Institute for Palestine Studies, 1992) (in Arabic).

——, (ed.), *The Palestinians in Israel* (Nazareth: The Galilee Centre for Social Research, 1993).

——, 'A different peace', *Index on Censorship*, No. 3 (May–June 1996), pp. 18–21.

——, *Yosef Weitz and Operation Yohanan, 1949–1953*, Occasional Papers Series (Durham: Centre for Middle Eastern and Islamic Studies, University of Durham, 1996).

——, *Akthar Ard wa-Aqal 'Arab* [More Land and Less Arabs] (Beirut: Institute for Palestine Studies, 1997) (in Arabic).

——, *A Land Without a People: Israel, Transfer and the Palestinians, 1949–1996* (London: Faber and Faber, 1997).

——, 'The 1967 Palestinian Exodus', in Ghada Karmi and Eugene Cotran (eds), *The Palestinian Exodus, 1948–1998* (Reading: Ithaca Press, 1999).

——, 'A Critique on Benny Morris', in Ilan Pappe (ed.), *The Israel/Palestine Question* (London: Routledge, 1999).

——, 'A Galilee Without Christians?', in Anthony O'Mahony (ed.), *Palestinian Christians: Religion, Politics and Society in the Holy Land* (London: Melisende, 1999), pp. 190–222.

McDowall, David, *Palestine and Israel* (London: I.B. Tauris, 1989).

——, *The Palestinians: The Road to Nationhood* (London: Minority Rights Publications, 1994).

Melman, Yossi, and Raviv, Dan, 'Expelling Palestinians', The *Washington Post*, 7 February 1988.

——, 'A Final Solution to the Palestinian Problem', *Davar*, 19 February 1988 (in Hebrew).

Mergui, Raphael and Simonnot, Philippe, *Israel's Ayatollahs: Meir Kahane and the Far Right in Israel* (London: Saqi Books, 1987).

Morris, Benny, *The Birth of the Palestinian Refugee Problem 1947–1949* (Cambridge: Cambridge University Press, 1987).

Nedava, Yosef, 'Tochniyot Helufie Ochlosin Lepetron Be'ayat Eretz-Yisrael' [Population Exchange Plans for the Solution of the Problem of the Land of Israel], *Gesher*, Vol. 24, Nos. 1–2 (Spring–Summer 1978).

——, 'British Plans for the Resettlement of Palestinian Arabs', *Haumah*, No. 89 (Winter 1987/88) (in Hebrew).

Netanyahu, Binyamin, *A Place Among Nations* (London: Bantam Press, 1993).

Newman, David (ed.), *The Impact of Gush Emunim* (London: Croom Helm, 1985).

——, 'Gush Emunim Between Fundamentalism and Pragmatism', *Jerusalem Quarterly*, No. 39 (1986), pp. 33–43.

Oz, Amos, 'The Meaning of Homeland', *New Outlook*, Vol. 31, No. 1 (January 1988).

Palumbo, Michael, *Imperial Israel* (London: Bloomsbury, rev. edn, 1992).

Peleg, Ilan, *Begin's Foreign Policy, 1977–1983* (New York: Greenwood Press, 1987).

Peri, Yoram, *Between Battles and Ballots: Israeli Military in Politics* (Cambridge: Cambridge University Press, 1983).

——, 'Expulsion is not the Final Stage', *Davar*, 3 August 1984 (in Hebrew).

Perlmutter, Amos, *The Life and Times of Menachem Begin* (New York: Doubleday, 1987).

Ra'anan, Tzvi, *Gush Emunim* (Tel Aviv: Sifriyat Po'alim, 1980) (in Hebrew).

Rash, Yehoshu'a, 'Uriel Tal's Legacy', *Gesher*, No. 114 (Summer 1986) (in Hebrew).

Ravitzky, Aviezer, 'Roots of Kahanism: Consciousness and Political Reality', *The Jerusalem Quarterly*, No. 39 (1986), pp. 90–108.

Rolef, Susan Hattis (ed.), *Political Dictionary of the State of Israel*, 2nd edn (New York: Macmillan Publishing Company, 1993).

Roman, Michael, *Jewish Kiryat Arba vs Arab Hebron* (Jerusalem: The Jerusalem Post Press, 1986).

Rubinstein, Amnon, *The Zionist Dream Revisited: From Herzl to Gush Emunim and Back* (New York: Schocken Books, 1984).

Rubinstein, Danny, *On the Lord's Side: Gush Emunim* (Tel Aviv: Hakibbutz Hameuhad Publishing House, 1982) (in Hebrew).

Said, Edward, *The Politics of Dispossession* (London: Chatto & Windus, 1994)
——, *Peace and its Discontents: Gaza–Jericho 1993–1995* (London: Vintage, 1995).

Said, Edward, and Christopher Hitchins (eds), *Blaming the Victims* (London: Verso, 1988).

Sayigh, Rosemary, *Palestinians: From Peasants to Revolutionaries* (London: Zed Books, 1979).

Schiff, Zeev, 'The Spectre of Civil War in Israel', *The Middle East Journal*, Vol. 39, No. 2 (January 1985).

Schiff, Zeev and Ehud Ya'ari, *Intifada: The Palestinian Uprising – Israel's Third Front* (New York: Simon and Schuster, 1989).

Schnall, David, *Beyond the Green Line* (New York: Praeger & Co., 1984).

Schölch, Alexander (ed.), *Palestinians Over the Green Line* (London: Ithaca Press, 1983).

Schweid, Eliezer, *The Land of Israel: National Home or Land of Destiny* (Rutherford, NJ: Herzl Press, 1985).

Seliktar, Ofira, 'The New Zionism', *Foreign Policy*, 51 (1983), pp. 118–38.
——, *New Zionism and the Foreign Policy System of Israel* (London: Croom Helm, 1986).'

Sella, Amnon, 'Custodians and Redeemers: Israeli Leaders' Perception of Peace, 1967–1979', *Middle Eastern Studies*, Vol. 22, No. 2 (April 1986), pp. 236–51.

Shafir, Gershon, 'Changing Nationalism and Israel's "Open Frontier" on the West Bank', *Theory and Practice*, Vol. 13, No. 6 (November 1984), pp. 818–19.

Shahak, Israel, 'Is Israel on the Road to Nazism?', *Freedomways*, Vol. 23, No. 3, 1983.
——, 'A History of the Concept of Transfer in Zionism', *Journal of Palestine Studies*, Vol. 17, No. 3 (Spring 1989), pp. 22–37.
——, *Jewish History, Jewish Religion: The Weight of Three Thousand Years* (London: Pluto Press, 1994).
——, 'The Religious Settlers: An Instrument of Israeli Domination', *Middle East Policy*, Vol. 3, No. 1 (1994).
——, *Open Secrets: Israeli Nuclear and Foreign Policies* (London: Pluto Press, 1997).

Shamir, Moshe, *Natan Alterman: Hameshorer Kemanhig* [Natan Alterman: The Poet as a Leader] (Tel Aviv: Dvir, 1988).

Sharon, Ariel, *Warrior: An Autobiography* (New York: Simon and Schuster, 1989).

Shavit, Yaacov, *Jabotinsky and the Revisionist Movement 1925–1948* (London: Frank Cass, 1988).

Shindler, Colin, *Israel, Likud and the Zionist Dream* (London: I.B.Tauris, 1995).

Shlaim, Avi, 'Israel, the Great Powers, and the Middle East Crisis of 1958', *Journal of Imperial and Commonwealth History*, Vol. 27, No. 2 (May 1999).

Silberstein, Laurence J. (ed.), *Jewish Fundamentalism in Comparative Perspective* (New York: New York University Press, 1993).

Simons, Chaim, *International Proposals to Transfer Arabs from Palestine 1895–1947* (New Jersey: Ktav Publishing House, 1988).

Smooha, Sammy, *Arabs and Jews in Israel*, Vol. 2: *Change and Continuity in Mutual Intolerance* (Boulder, CO: Westview Press, 1992).

Sofer, Sasson, *Begin: An Anatomy of Leadership* (Oxford: Basil Blackwell, 1988).

Sprinzak, Ehud, 'Extreme Politics in Israel', *Jerusalem Quarterly*, No. 15 (Fall 1977).

——, 'Gush Emunim: The Tip of the Iceberg', *Jerusalem Quarterly*, No. 21 (Fall 1981).

——, *Gush Emunim: The Politics of Zionist Fundamentalism in Israel* (New York: The American Jewish Committee, 1986).

——, 'Kach and Rabbi Meir Kahane: The Emergence of Jewish Quasi-Fascism in Israel', in Asher Arian and Michael Shamir (eds), *The Elections in Israel 1984* (Tel Aviv: Ramot, 1986) (in Hebrew).

——, 'From Messianic Pioneering to Vigilante Terrorism: The Case of Gush Emunim Underground', Occasional Paper (Washington, DC: Woodrow Wilson International Center for Scholars, 1987).

——, *The Ascendance of Israel's Radical Right* (New York: Oxford University Press, 1991).

Sternhell, Zeev, *The Founding Myths of Israel: Nationalism, Socialism and the Making of the Jewish State* (Princeton: Princeton University Press, 1998)

Tal, Uriel, 'The Foundations of a Political Messianic Trend in Israel', *Jerusalem Quarterly*, No. 35 (Spring 1985).

Wasserstein, Bernard, 'The British Mandate in Palestine: Myths and Realities', *Middle Eastern Lectures* (Tel Aviv: Moshe Dayan Centre, 1995).

Weissbrod, Lilly, 'Gush Emunim Ideology – From Religious Doctrine to Political Action', *Middle Eastern Studies*, Vol. 18, No. 3 (July 1982).

Whitelam, Keith W., *The Invention of Ancient Israel: The Silencing of Palestinian History* (London: Routledge, 1996).

Yegar, Moshe, 'Hatziyonut, Medinat Yisrael Vehashelah Ha'arvit', [Zionism, the State of Israel and the Arab Question], *Haumah*, Vol. 2, No. 57 (May 1979), pp. 175–85.

——, *Hatziyonut Haintegralit: I'un Bemishnato Shel Avraham Sharon* [Integral Zionism: Examining Avraham Sharon's Thought] (Tel Aviv: Hadar, 1983).

Yellin-Mor, Nathan, *Lohamei Herut Yisrael* [The Fighters for the Freedom of Israel], (Jerusalem: Shekmona, 1974).

Yiftachel, Oren, *Planning a Mixed Region in Israel* (Aldershot, England: Avebury, 1992).

Yinon, 'Oded, 'A Strategy for Israel in the 1980s', *Kivunim* (Jerusalem), No. 8 (February 1982) (in Hebrew).

Yishai, Yael, 'Israel's Right-Wing Jewish Proletariat', *Jewish Journal of Sociology*, December 1982.

——, 'The Jewish Terror Organization: Past or Future Danger?', *Conflict*, Vol. 6, No. 4 (1986).

——, *Land or Peace: Whither Israel* (Stanford, CA: Hoover Institution Press, 1987).

Zucker, Dedi, *Report on Human Rights in the Occupied Territories* (Tel Aviv: International Center for Peace in the Middle East, 1983).

NEWSPAPERS AND PERIODICALS

Hebrew

Bat Kol
Davar
Gesher
Haaretz
Hadashot
Ha'ir
'Al-Hamishmar
Haumah
Herut
'Al-Ittihad
Kolbotek
Kol Ha'ir
Koteret Rashit
Lamerhav
Ma'ariv
Mahanayim
Moledet
Nekudah
Politikah
Torah Ve'avodah
Yedi'ot Aharonot
Zot Haaretz

English and French

Christian Science Monitor (Boston)
Foreign Broadcast Information Service,
    Middle East and Africa Daily Report
    (FBIS)
Forum (Jerusalem)
Guardian (London)
Jerusalem Post
Jerusalem Quarterly
Middle East International (London)
Midstream (New York)
Le Monde
Le Monde Diplomatique
New Outlook
Observer (London)
Summary of World Broadcast (SWB),
    Part 4: The Middle East and Africa
    (Reading, BBC)
The Times (London)
Washington Post

Arabic

Al-Fajr (Jerusalem)
Kol al-'Arab (Haifa)
Majlat al-Dirasat al-Filastiniyyah
    (Beirut)
Al-Midan (Nazareth)
Shaml (Ramallah)
Al-Sinnarah (Nazareth)

Index